A DSM-III-R Casebook
of Treatment Selection

A DSM-III-R Casebook
of Treatment Selection

by
Samuel Perry, M.D.
Allen Frances, M.D.
John Clarkin, Ph.D.

Brunner/Mazel, *Publishers* • **New York**

The historical cases on pp. 311, 214, 155, 95, 225, 199, and 53, are reprinted with permission as follows:

Hervey Cleckley, *The Mask of Sanity,* 5th Ed., C. V. Mosby Co., St. Louis, 1976, pp. 64–70.

Sigmund Freud, *The Collected Papers of Sigmund Freud,* vol. 3, edited by Ernest Jones, M.D., authorized translation by Alix and James Strachey. Published by Basic Books, New York, 1959, by arrangement with The Hogarth Press, Ltd. and the Institute for Psychoanalysis, London. From "A Case of Obsessional Neurosis," pp. 296–297, 299, 303–306.

Emil Kraepelin, *Lectures on Clinical Psychiatry,* translated by Thomas P. Johnstone, New York, Hafner Publishing Co., 1968. "Music Student," p. 74; "Widow," p. 157; "Suffering Lady," p. 252; and "Schoolmaster," p. 262.

Wilkins, R. H., & Brody, I. A. Alzheimer's disease. *Archives of Neurology,* July 1969, 21:109–110, American Medical Association, Chicago, 1969.

Library of Congress Cataloging-in-Publication Data
Perry, Samuel.
    A DSM-III-R casebook of treatment selection / by Samuel Perry,
Allen Frances, John Clarkin. — 2nd ed.
        p.   cm.
    Rev. ed. of: A DSM-III casebook of differential therapeutics.
© 1985.
    Includes bibliographical references.
    ISBN 0-87630-572-9
    1. Psychiatry—Differential therapeutics—Case studies.
I. Frances, Allen. II. Clarkin, John F. III. Perry,
Samuel. DSM-III casebook of differential therapeutics.
IV. Title.
    RC480.52.P47   1990   90-1317
    616.89—dc20   CIP

Published by
BRUNNER/MAZEL, INC.
19 Union Square West
New York, New York 10003

Manufactured in the United States of America
10 9 8 7 6 5 4 3

To Vera, whose grace and strength
are an inspiration and a delight.

Contents

vii

Foreword

As the science of psychiatry progresses at such a rapid pace, it is apparent that its art must advance just as quickly. With every development, the selection of the most appropriate treatment becomes more complex, but also more critical.

The growth of therapeutic modalities, whether biological, psychosocial, or psychotherapeutic, has proceeded as it always does in science—fitfully, nonsequentially, and unpredictably. The introduction of family care preceded other alternatives to mental hospital treatment by over six centuries; psychoanalysis preceded cognitive therapy by almost 100 years; group therapy preceded family therapy by over 50 years; and electrotherapy preceded modern psychotropic medications by 20 years. We are currently in either the fortunate or perplexing situation, depending upon your viewpoint, of having a plethora of therapeutic interventions, each of whose advocates, adherents, and practitioners claim primacy for their form of treatment for a variety of psychiatric illnesses. The trick now, as it is for the rest of medicine, is to define clearly what works best for whom and in what setting.

The authors of this current work blazed the first trail in this uncharted wilderness in 1984 with the publication of their landmark book, *Differential Therapeutics in Psychiatry*. For the first time, they provided guidelines for answering the question of what treatments should be given to which patient, as well as specific recommendations concerning setting, format, orientation, duration, intensity, and use of medication.

Now, with the publication of this *Casebook*, the authors have refined their technique, supplying real life case examples to illustrate their new field. The cases conform to selected categories from DSM-III-R, which the authors helped develop, and the authors provide a mixture of case presentations from their own experience, as well as classics from the literature, accompanied by discussions written either by themselves or guest experts. The cases are rich, comprehensive, and complex, as are all real clinical examples, and the authors really make their material come alive. The reader expecting a "cookbook" approach to treatment for any specific diagnosis will be thoroughly disappointed. Real life problems, even though paraphrased and disguised, do not lend themselves to such simplistic solutions.

The authors recognize that much work remains to be done in the field of research on differential therapeutics. But again, they are in a similar situation with those in the rest of medicine who are evaluating treatment efficacy. All must carefully attempt to assess scientifically which treatment (whether angioplasty versus coronary bypass, or cognitive therapy versus antidepressants) has the best outcome for which persons.

Too often, patients receive the treatment known best to, or practiced primarily by, the first person they consult rather than that from which they might best benefit. Since we now know that the majority of professionals that patients contact first are not psychiatrists, and the majority of psychiatric treatment is provided by nonpsychiatric physicians, such information on differential therapeutics must eventually become available to a wide community of practitioners and patients.

This current work represents a giant step forward in presenting such material about the field of differential therapeutics clearly, interestingly, and nonsimplistically. Like all good teaching, it is fun along with being informative. I look forward with eagerness to their next effort.

JOHN A. TALBOTT, M.D.
Professor and Chairman,
Department of Psychiatry,
University of Maryland,
School of Medicine,
Baltimore, Maryland;
Past President,
American Psychiatric Association

Preface

As a clinician, you will recognize many of the people and treatment problems presented in this book—a homeless schizophrenic in the emergency room telling bizarre tales; an alcoholic on a surgical ward intent upon leaving against medical advice; an acutely psychotic mother unable to accept the sudden death of her son; an obsessive graduate student about to flunk out because of crippling compulsive rituals; a suburban housewife depressed after discovering her husband's extramarital affairs; an elderly woman in a general hospital who has become agitated and combative with the staff; a cocaine abuser who requests a psychiatric evaluation to sidestep a court hearing; and so on.

The patients we have selected come from our private practices and from our experiences as supervisors in various settings at Cornell University Medical Center. With so many possibilities, we needed some general guidelines regarding which cases to include. We used five:

First, we chose at least one prototypic patient to represent the most common DSM-III-R adult diagnoses.

Second, recognizing that treatment selection is rarely based on diagnosis alone, we included only those situations in which we had enough information (past history, lifestyle, current situation, interaction with the consultant) so that the discussion of treatment selection would always be individually tailored to the specific patient and never based only on the diagnosis.

Third, we chose cases that could be summarized within a few pages and yet would remain sufficiently interesting and complex.

Fourth, we included only those cases that could be modified to protect confidentiality and yet would retain their uniqueness.

And *fifth*, mainly for fun, but also to remind us how the presentation of major psychopathological disorders has remained relatively constant over the years, we have selected a few famous cases from the past—Freud's, Kraepelin's, Alzheimer's, Cleckley's—to discuss how those patients might be treated today. Long after the DSM-III-R has been replaced and the choice of psychiatric treatments has been unrecognizably modified, the basic problems confronting the clinician will be little changed.

Because these inclusion criteria are rather loose, we are aware that our selection of cases has no doubt been influenced by our own clinical experiences and interests. Of greater importance, we are also aware that our discussion of possible treatments for those cases reflects our particular training, experience, location, personalities, and prejudices. We have tried to compensate for this bias in three ways:

First, intermittently throughout the text we have included cases that are presented and discussed by guest experts from around the country. Their names, professional affiliations, and areas of expertise precede these case discussions, which were originally published in *Hospital and Community Psychiatry* in the section on differential therapeutics.

Second, we have listed after each case a few suggested readings which relate to the issues of treatment selection raised by that particular case. The recommended books and articles either support our decision or present a view different from ours.

And *third*, we have tried to buffer our own biases by beginning this casebook with a conceptual guide to treatment selection. This introductory chapter summarizes the background and rationale of the different components of psychiatric treatment, including some therapies that were omitted in the case discussions because of our unfamiliarity with them. This introduction provides the structure for many of the discussions of treatment selection and defines terms used throughout the text. We suggest you read it before the individual cases and refer to the accompanying tables in the Appendix when looking for case examples of the various treatment options.

Though we have taken the above measures to guard against—or at least to admit—our own biases, paradoxically we suspect that a major value of this casebook will be exposing the way our individual preferences have influenced our treatment selections. In our first book, *Differential Therapeutics in Psychiatry: The Art and Science of Treatment Selection*

(Brunner/Mazel, 1984), we described systematically the advantages, disadvantages, and outcome research regarding available psychotherapeutic techniques, drugs, settings, formats, and time frames; but throughout that text we acknowledged that, at present, the choice of treatment ultimately depends more on the informed judgment of the consultant than on any well-established selection criteria. This sequel is a more personal statement—the consensus judgment of three clinicians who, considering the possible range of psychotherapeutic knowledge and skills, are probably more alike than different. As you think through the cases along with us, our hope is that, even when you believe our opinions to be clearly wrong or at least doubtful, the resulting dialectic will spur further thoughts and investigation into this interesting area of treatment selection in psychiatry.

■ ABOUT THE REVISED EDITION

We are of course delighted that our previous edition, *A DSM-III Casebook of Differential Therapeutics: A Clinical Guide to Treatment Selection*, was so well received and reviewed. In this second edition, we have made three basic changes: 1) modifying the diagnostic categories so they adhere to DSM-III-R; 2) updating the discussion of treatments for the various disorders so they consider more recent research; and 3) making the introductory chapter less pedantic and more practical so that it fits with the overall tone of the book.

In traveling around the country lecturing about differential therapeutics and, closer to home, teaching our psychiatry residents, especially those preparing for Part II of their Boards, we have had lots of fun discussing the cases, hearing alternative points of view, and most of all, seeing how the discussion of treatment selection for actual patients can stir up an audience and get clinicians debating and learning from each other. Similarly, in addition to stimulating debate and learning, this book was intended from the start to be fun. In this regard, we hope you will find that this second edition is unchanged.

Acknowledgments

Clinical practice is a great privilege and a great joy. It provides an opportunity to know an individual in a way that has no true parallel in any other kind of relationship. Our first acknowledgment must therefore be to our patients. They have been our best teachers. Not only have they taught us about psychiatry, but they have also taught us about ourselves and helped us to see the world more richly. We apologize to them for using the words "case" and "casebook." Even if they are familiar and serviceable, these words suggest an impersonal and formal relationship. None of our patients has ever been just a case, and some of our most important personal experiences have occurred in the consulting room.

We are grateful to our colleagues and trainees who, over the years, have shared thousands of evaluations and treatment experiences with us. This sharing has broadened our clinical base and revealed the many options available in every clinical situation.

We also thank John Talbott, our longstanding friend and mentor, who has somehow managed to stay young while becoming one of the grand old men of American psychiatry.

And, finally, we thank our wives and children for the time we borrowed and never returned.

A DSM-III-R Casebook
of Treatment Selection

I

A Conceptual Guide
for Treatment Selection

The evaluation of a new patient is one of the most challenging encounters in clinical practice. The excitement of the task is matched only by its difficulty. After a brief period of time, the consultant and a relative stranger must collaborate together and decide what treatment, if any, has the best chance of helping at this time. Of course, the decision is not necessarily final. The consultant's recommendations may change after further negotiation with the patient and perhaps be modified as treatment proceeds. Yet there is no doubt that the initial treatment selection may have a profound and, in some cases, irreversible impact on the patient's therapy—and life.

Treatment selection is a difficult endeavor in all specialties of medicine, but for a number of reasons it is especially difficult in psychiatry. The treatments themselves come from such varied sources—some derive from meticulous animal experiments and pharmacological research, others are innovations introduced by creative clinicians and charismatic personalities. Additionally, the acceptable options are so numerous. Attempts simply to list the more "conventional" psychosocial treatments, not including the somatic therapies, have ranged from 130[1] to well over 200[2] contenders, and alternative approaches continue to proliferate.

In reaction to this array of possibilities (and in the absence of compelling scientific data that document the efficacy of one treatment over another), therapists have assumed different clinical positions. A minority[3,4]—the "nihilists"—have asserted that neurotic patients treated in psychotherapy do not improve any more than those who receive no treatment. Aggregate reviews[1,5,6] have convincingly disproved this pro-

3

vocative claim and have shown that the average treated patient does better than 80% of nontreated controls. However, the research literature provides only scant evidence that a specific psychosocial treatment is unquestionably indicated for a specific kind of mental disorder.

This situation has spawned other clinical positions. The "specialists" concentrate on a particular kind of treatment (e.g., psychoanalysis, sexual therapy, pharmacotherapy, psychodrama) and exclude techniques and patients who do not fit the mold. The "eclectics" use a variety of overlapping methods, often without being sure what specific technique is the most helpful for a particular patient. Finally, there are the "skeptics," who doubt that the benefits of therapy can ever be attributed to any specific intervention and maintain that expectations and a good relationship with the patient—based on "nonspecific factors"[7,8]—will always be more crucial than the choice of one treatment over another.

In this introductory chapter we will not argue for any one of these different positions, nor will we intentionally favor any particular school of psychotherapy. Instead, our intention is to provide a way of conceptualizing the choices a consultant must make when recommending psychiatric treatment.

As we conceive it, all psychiatric treatments, no matter how divergent in theory or style, have five inherent axes that must be considered in treatment selection:

1) *Setting*—private office, psychiatric hospital, halfway house, medical ward, etc.;
2) *Format*—individual, group, family, marital, etc.;
3) *Time*—length and frequency of sessions and duration of treatment;
4) *Approach*—different techniques and shared objectives; and
5) *Somatic*—need for medication or electroconvulsive therapy (ECT).

The consultant also has a metadecision that overrides the consideration of these five components, namely, should *any treatment* be recommended or is *no treatment* the prescription of choice?

In this introductory chapter, first we briefly describe the background and rationale regarding the many choices within each of these components, then we conclude with a review of how biases, both the clinician's and the patient's, influence the process of treatment selection. This summary serves as a scaffold to support our discussion of the cases that follow. In the last chapter, we make some generalizations based on our case method, on our first book *Differential Therapeutics in Psychiatry*, and on subsequent publications by ourselves and others.

We recognize that the reader may come to somewhat different conclusions—an inevitable problem in differential therapeutics, but also one of its attractions. At the end of the book, we have appended five tables to indicate which cases illustrate which treatment decisions. A sixth table indicates the secondary psychiatric diagnoses of the presented cases; for as clinicians know all too well, patients commonly present with more than one emotional problem. Referring to this table, the reader will find that the major DSM-III-R diagnoses are represented by more than the one or two cases indicated in the table of contents.

Setting

Setting is *where* the treatment occurs. The choice of setting depends primarily on the therapeutic goal. If the main goal is to resolve an urgent problem so that the patient can quickly return to a previous level of functioning, then one of the acute settings is chosen: intensive care psychiatric hospitalization; intensive care partial (day/night) hospitalization; or an outpatient crisis intervention or home care facility. If the main goal is to help the patient function at a higher level than was previously obtained, then the treatment will be administered at a longer-term reconstructive hospital, a longer-term day/night hospital, or the traditional office setting of outpatient psychotherapy. And if the goal is primarily to maintain the chronically impaired patient and thereby prevent acute exacerbations and further insidious decline, the treatment will most likely occur in a chronic care psychiatric hospital, a chronic care partial hospital, or an outpatient maintenance program. In clinical practice, these goals—acute care, rehabilitation, maintenance—cannot always be sharply demarcated; they overlap considerably and change as treatment proceeds.

The selection criteria for the different therapeutic settings have been described by us[9] and by others.[10-12] Our aim here is not to raise the advantages and disadvantages of each, but to correct two common misconceptions. First, the choice of setting does not necessarily depend on the severity of the patient's illness. Many patients who are severely disturbed can be and should be treated on an outpatient basis, whereas inpatient care may be necessary for those who are less severely ill but refractory to outpatient interventions. Second, although the choice of setting will inevitably influence the other four components of treatment, the setting does not automatically exclude or preclude their consideration. For example, in recommending inpatient care, the consultant must still consider whether a family or marital format is indicated, whether the treatment should be time-oriented or open-ended, whether exploratory or directive approaches would be more helpful, and whether medication or ECT should be prescribed.

Format

Format indicates who participates in the treatment. In the minds of most laymen and some clinicians, psychiatric treatment is automatically viewed as occurring within an individual format, i.e., a therapist and a patient. Despite the impact of alternative formats (marital, family, group), many still hold to this traditional view. For thousands of years man has sought advice by consulting individually a designated authority—an oracle, shaman, village elder, witch doctor, priest, rabbi, or physician. The contemporary relationship between psychotherapist and patient maintains these same elements of delegated expertise and confidentiality. Because the individual format is familiar, private, relatively flexible, and built on the basic trust inherent in a dyadic relationship, [13,14] it remains the most prevalent format for psychiatric treatment.

With these advantages of the individual format come certain disadvantages. The data from an individual patient are incomplete and distorted, and the isolation from the "real" world can foster a protective, even magical air to the therapeutic situation. This, in turn, can encourage a regression that leads to unwarranted dependency and infantilization.

Over the past 40 years, partly because the limitations of an individual format have been more appreciated and partly because of a subtle shift towards theoretical models that emphasize interpersonal rather than intrapsychic dynamics, clinicians have increasingly used family and marital formats to administer psychiatric treatments. [15] The underlying premise that family members contribute to emotional problems is, of course, not new; Confucius described how one spouse can inflict anguish upon another, and Greek mythology often traced the struggle of an individual to the dynamics within the "House." What is new is the growing acceptance that certain kinds of interventions (e.g., interpretation of scapegoating, demarcating boundaries, behavioral treatment of sexual dysfunction) are most effective if given within a family or marital format. [16] As the benefits of these alternative formats have gained wider appreciation, clinicians have become less defined and segregated by the formats they prefer. They are less often stereotyped as "group therapists" or "family counselors."

Like family and marital formats, heterogeneous groups stemmed from an increasing emphasis on interpersonal rather than intrapsychic dynamics; but unlike family and marital formats, group therapy has not been a natural extension of individual psychotherapy. On the contrary, the small group format was introduced by individuals who came from radically different backgrounds: psychoanalysts,[17,18] social scientists,[19,20] and clinical innovators.[21,22] Partly because the theoretical and clinical contributions have derived from such varied fields, different group therapists base their interventions on very different assumptions, methods, and goals; nevertheless, some common themes can be found.

Groups are labeled "heterogeneous" when their members do not share any one particular symptom or situation and differ in their ages, sex, backgrounds, strengths, and personality traits.[23] In spite of these differences, a feeling of commonality develops; the patient realizes he or she is not alone. Gradually feeling more accepted, accepting, and acceptable, the patient is more capable of taking interpersonal risks within and outside the group. The interactions offer group members a chance to correct distortions about others and themselves and to alter maladaptive responses, with less chance of becoming locked into a regressive transferential-countertransferential involvement with the therapist. Despite the many advantages of heterogeneous groups (including cost-effectiveness), some patients have urgent problems that demand more immediate, intense, and individualized treatment than a group format can reasonably provide. In addition, some patients have such a dread of groups that they cannot be inducted into the format or, alternatively, seek group therapy to avoid intimacy and to conceal deeper problems, which might more likely be uncovered in an intensive individual treatment.

As opposed to heterogeneous groups, "homogeneous" groups are targeted at a condition or situation that is shared by all their members.[23] Although the range of interactions tends to be more restricted, there is no doubt that these "self-help" groups, both within and outside the psychiatric profession, can provide a structured social network for those who previously felt they must suffer their problems in isolation (e.g., alcoholism, obesity, gambling, homosexuality, substance abuse, medical illness, anorexia nervosa). In one way or another, homogeneous group members are usually given specified procedures, responsibilities, rights, and expectations. This role definition in itself relieves the tension of uncertainty and alienation and enhances a loyalty to the group and fellow sufferers. Some homogeneous groups even provide a program for promotion and eventual leadership. Although homogeneous groups tend to be accepting and acceptable to new members, the format may enable individuals to avoid obtaining help for other emotional problems that require more extensive and personally tailored treatment.

Time (Duration and Frequency)

The above summary about different settings and formats reminds us that no treatment can be defined by a single component. Terms such as "psychiatric hospitalization" or "group therapy" are not in themselves sufficient to describe a therapeutic process. Unless qualified, these terms can foster the misconception that a given setting or a chosen format defines a particular psychiatric treatment and automatically excludes others. The same argument is true of the third treatment component: time. How long the treatment will last (duration), how often the patient will be seen (frequency), and even how much time is allotted for a given appointment (length of session), all influence the therapeutic process; but they do not in themselves preclude the use of diverse settings, formats, or techniques. Terms such as "brief therapy" or "marathon session" or "long-term treatment" suggest but do not adequately indicate the type of treatment used.

Although the other four components are often modified as treatment evolves, the component of time is even less predetermined and fixed. In the course of most treatments, psychotherapist and patient inevitably reconsider whether sessions should be more or less frequent and whether termination is in sight. Because the issue of time is relatively more fluid and is interwoven into other aspects of treatment, it is often not seen as a specific and discernible component. In recent years, therapists have become more cognizant of this oversight and have described how the length, frequency, and duration of sessions have their own therapeutic valence.

LENGTH OF SESSIONS

The reasoning and research supporting the controversial 50-minute hour are not very convincing. Freud saw his analytic patients on the hour with a short time between patients for a breather and note-taking. Those whose practice is not psychoanalytic have been influenced by this precedent, although for convenience and financial reasons, many have reduced the length to 45 minutes. This tradition is being challenged. Some[24] have suggested that a "20-minute hour" is more cost-effective and comfortable for certain patients in supportive psychotherapy. At the other extreme, some[25] have suggested sessions of several hours or more to wear down defenses and thereby to compress years of treatment into a relatively short period of time. Others[26] have even provocatively asserted that the length of sessions should never be predetermined, but be based on the patient's receptiveness on a given day. Since the most efficient and effective length of an individual session awaits systematic investigation, the point to be made here is that current conventions about optimal length of sessions should not be followed slavishly. Allowances can be made for the individual needs of the patient and the availability of therapeutic resources.

FREQUENCY OF SESSIONS

Patients often mistakenly assume that the frequency of appointments reflects the seriousness of the problem. Actually, frequency is more related to the technical requirements and goals of the treatment than to the severity of the illness. Highly functional patients may be seen almost daily in psychoanalysis; in contrast, sessions for severely ill patients may be scheduled weeks apart if the goals are to monitor medications and to prevent relapses or deterioration. As the case discussions will illustrate, the frequency of sessions (such as once or twice a week) cannot be prescribed routinely. Frequently scheduled sessions are more likely to produce dependency, regression, and transferential distortions, whereas infrequent sessions may not provide the necessary support and intensity to mobilize change.

DURATION OF TREATMENT

Unlike the length and frequency of sessions, the issue of treatment duration has received far more discussion and research, stimulated in part by third-party payers and by "consumers" understandably seeking quicker cures. At one pole are advocates of the brief therapies (e.g., focal therapy), in which therapist and patient engage quickly, focus attention more or less on one event or symptom or conflict, and agree that decisions will need to be made with incomplete data and that the goals of treatment will be limited.[13,27-30] At the other pole are advocates of those extended, even lifelong treatments that come closest to the valued relationship offered by priest or family physician who are sought over the years to lend an ear and give advice as the situation requires.[31,32]

Duration is strongly influenced by other treatment variables. For instance, behavioral techniques or family formats are more often associated with briefer treatments; psychoanalytic techniques or heterogeneous groups are associated with treatments that generally take longer. This association does not mean, however, that duration of treatment is simply a consequence of other factors and does not have a therapeutic impact of its own. Psychoanalysis is intentionally open-ended, so that a fixed, premature termination will not be used to avoid exploring especially difficult conflicts. Time-oriented treatments[29] intentionally establish a date of termination at the beginning phase of treatment to highlight issues of separation and autonomy.

Approach: A. Different Techniques

Whereas therapists might politely disagree about which setting or format or medication or time frame is chosen for a given patient, the choice of psychotherapeutic approach is often contested more fervently. Technique—what a clinician actually does with a patient—most closely reflects the personal view of the human condition and the causes and cures of disordered mental life. We will, therefore, discuss this component at somewhat greater length.

Not only is therapeutic approach the most controversial component, but it is also the most difficult to describe and categorize. Of the various attempts, no method has been entirely satisfactory. One review of outcome research[1] clustered 29 specific therapies into two larger classes: behavioral therapies (e.g., systematic desensitization) and verbal therapies (e.g., psychodynamic techniques). Another research review[6] compared behavior therapy versus psychotherapy and client-centered therapy versus traditional therapy. Another system[33] was designed as a way of conceptualizing different techniques and not for retrospective research reviews. It suggested three categories: psychodynamic, behavioral, and experiential.

We have made our own attempt at trying to categorize different therapeutic techniques (see table on p. 12). "Exploratory" is a term we use for those treatments primarily aimed to increase the patient's understanding of his or her problems. We prefer the term "exploratory" to "psychodynamic" because some treatments in this category (e.g., interpersonal therapy, rational-emotive therapy) are not predominantly based on a psychodynamic-psychoanalytic model and do not examine unconscious processes, yet are based on exploring the patient's motives, thoughts, and feelings. "Directive" is a term we use for those treatments primarily designed to modify maladaptive behavior and thoughts by explicitly directing the patient. We prefer the term "directive" to "cognitive-behavioral" because some therapies in this category (e.g., strategic or problem-solving) are not based on behavioral-learning models. We are aware that all clinicians (including psychoanalysts) explicitly or implicitly direct the patient on what to say, think, and feel, but for those treatments in the "directive" category, the therapists' directions are considered the primary therapeutic maneuver and are more overt. "Experiential" is the term we use for the third category. Included here are those treatments primarily intended to allow patients to discuss and share feelings. This intimate interpersonal experience with the therapist is viewed as the main therapeutic ingredient.

Like other attempts, our categorization has many shortcomings. Psychoanalysts or behavioral therapists would rightfully be offended by any implication that only experiential therapists use emotional sharing as part of their therapeutic repertoire. The distinctions that we are suggesting must be considered a matter of degree and not absolute. They are made in full awareness that any one function of the mind (cognition, behavior, emotion) inevitably affects and is affected by any other function, and that therapists may address one function with one set of techniques at one point in treatment and then another function with different techniques later on—perhaps even later in the same session. We are also aware that our method of categorizing approaches is strongly influenced by the historical development of different theoretical schools of psychotherapy: psychoanalytic, behavioral, and existential. But in treatment planning, clinicians often go beyond the traditional confines of these schools and use interventions that cut across different theoretical orientations.

Categorizing approaches has an additional limitation: it fails to acknowledge that most techniques share common objectives that provide the bedrock of psychotherapy whatever its theoretical orientation. Therefore, after summarizing the background and rationale for exploratory, directive and experiential approaches, we outline their shared objectives and common strategies used to achieve them.

EXPLORATORY APPROACHES

Psychoanalytic pioneers developed the techniques used today in most exploratory therapies. Prior to this development, psychopathology was primarily regarded as idiopathic, constitutional, or inherited. Freud hypothesized that neurotic-like symptoms were linked with unconscious wishes, memories, and fantasies which the mind actively prevented from reaching full awareness or expression. Because Freud at first believed that psychoneurotic symptoms could be cured simply by overcoming this repression, he initially used hypnosis, suggestion, and encouragement to help the unconscious become conscious. When he

PSYCHOTHERAPEUTIC APPROACH

Different Techniques	Shared Objectives

Exploratory
  e.g., psychoanalysis
    interpersonal therapy
    psychodynamic life
      narrative
	Establishing therapeutic
	  relationship
	
	Providing support
	
	Educating

Directive
  e.g., systematic desensitization
    cognitive-behavioral
    problem solving
	Reducing painful affects
	
	Decreasing maladaptive behaviors

Experiential
  e.g., client centered
    Gestalt
    psychodrama
	Modifying misperceptions
	
	Expanding awareness
	
	Enhancing interpersonal behavior

found that the resistances and defenses mounted by patients were often too strong, he discovered the technique of simply instructing patients to say whatever came into their minds, i.e., to "free associate." Given time, patients could gradually overcome their censoring and understand— "psychoanalyze"—how dreams, memories, perceptions, and everyday behavior were influenced by internal wishes and fantasies. "Clarifications" helped organize various associations and make them explicit, and "interpretations" made inferences about material that had not reached the patient's consciousness but, on the basis of accumulative trends, could no longer be denied.

While these techniques (free association, clarification and interpretation) were being used to produce and analyze previously repressed material, many patients developed an intense relationship with the analyst that was reminiscent of earlier real or imagined relationships with parents and significant others. The need to reexperience these past relationships—to "transfer" them onto the analyst—also provided crucial data for understanding unconscious processes.

To enhance this transference neurosis, Freud suggested additional exploratory techniques:

> 1) that the analyst remain a relatively unknown figure ("anonymity") so that the patient's view of the analyst would be pre-

dominantly a product of the patient's regressive fantasies and not represent the reality of the situation;

2) that the patient's desire for approval, support, love, and reassurance not be gratified by the analyst ("abstinence") because the resulting frustration would intensify the underlying needs and thereby make them more obvious;

3) that the analyst not take sides with any of the forces involved in a given conflict ("neutrality"), so that all aspects of the conflict— the wishes, fears, guilt, defenses, and reality of the situation—could come into view and be analyzed; and

4) that the patient lie on a couch with the analyst out of view, in order to facilitate the regressive process of freely associating without distraction and to make abstinence, anonymity, and neutrality more feasible.

From the wealth of data obtained by these innovative exploratory techniques, Freud and other psychoanalysts constructed many theories about human behavior which have been extensively elaborated and revised over the years. With these revisions, the focus of interest has changed from "libido theory" to "ego psychology" and more recently to "object relations theory" and "self psychology."

Because psychoanalytic theory has had a pervasive influence on understanding all of human behavior, an unfortunate confusion has developed between psychoanalytic theory, psychoanalytic treatment, and psychoanalytic techniques. Although they grew up together, they are not the same. In any clinical situation, psychoanalytic theory can be useful in providing a dynamic understanding of the patient. In contrast, only a small number of patients are recommended for a psychoanalysis, that is, four or five sessions per week for an indefinite period of time during which the main therapeutic strategy is the working-through of a well-established transference neurosis.

Psychoanalytic techniques are the mainstay of most exploratory treatments. Psychoanalytically oriented psychotherapy[34] is a case in point. Although not as precisely defined as psychoanalysis, the patient generally comes one or two times per week, faces the therapist, and is encouraged to speak freely without dwelling on any preselected area. Because a full transference neurosis is considered neither necessary nor desirable, the therapist interprets transference phenomena whenever they serve as resistances or are related to the person's problems. The therapist is not concerned that these interpretations might inhibit the development of the more regressive transference experience. Similarly, because the goal is not a complete character analysis, the therapist may choose to influence the patient by offering some structure, suggestions, education, and support as indicated.

Advocates of the psychodynamic psychotherapies[35] believe that the rigid selection criteria for a traditional psychoanalysis exclude many patients who might benefit from a sustained psychodynamic therapy. They also contend that equivalent benefits may be obtained by a psychodynamic treatment that is not as costly, intensive, or prolonged as psychoanalysis. They point out that regression may be detrimental for some patients and that many patients lack the time, money, motivation, and necessity for understanding more subtle aspects of their character styles. They argue, as well, that because psychodynamic psychotherapy can be tailored to the needs of the individual patient, it can have a wider applicability than psychoanalysis and can be more efficient.

DIRECTIVE APPROACHES

Unlike exploratory techniques, directive techniques did not evolve primarily from one school of thought. They emerged from many different kinds of experiments, philosophies, professions, and clinical studies. Although the behavioral school had not obtained wide acceptance until recent decades, directive techniques—such as encouragement, instruction, discipline, punishment, reward, and simply giving advice—are not new. Throughout history they have been used in child-rearing, social conditioning, and education. What is new is the realization that those with mental illness are not refractory to these techniques; the task is to find the right directive given in the most effective way for a particular problem. We will here summarize those directive treatments that are frequently considered in the case discussions.

Systematic Desensitization. In the tradition of classical (Pavlovian) conditioning theory, Joseph Wolpe[36] first made cats fearful of a cage in which they had received electric shocks; he then "systematically desensitized" the cats by bringing them gradually closer to the cage in a series of discrete steps and feeding them at each step. He reasoned that feeding the hungry cats psychophysiologically inhibited their acquired fearfulness ("reciprocal inhibition").

Wolpe applied this experiment to the clinical situation by first performing a careful behavioral analysis and determining the discrete situations that made a patient increasingly anxious. He then constructed a hierarchy of anxiety-provoking scenes ("antecedent stimuli"). Instead of using food to inhibit this anxiety, he would use progressive relaxation of muscle groups. Others since Wolpe have used hypnosis, biofeedback, and drugs (such as a benzodiazepine or a rapidly acting intravenous barbiturate). Wolpe would begin by having the patient imagine the first frightening scene in the hierarchy and deconditioning that anxiety by pairing it with the relaxation response. When a sufficient number of repetitions had been performed to minimize the anxiety, he would systematically proceed to the next graded step until even the most terrifying situation had become tolerable.

Modifications of Wolpe's original methods have been developed in recent years. Although they do not precisely parallel Wolpe's laboratory model, their advantages have been convincingly demonstrated. With graded exposure,[37] instead of just imagining the frightening situation, the patient actually approaches the stimuli through a series of small steps. No specific relaxation training is involved; the patient eventually "extinguishes" the anxiety in the first situation and then is encouraged to go on to the next step. An even more rapid procedure for the treatment of phobic anxiety is flooding.[37] The patient is instructed to place him/herself in the most terrifying situation and withstand the anxiety at its full intensity for an increasingly prolonged period of time. As with children repeatedly riding a roller coaster, the fear is eventually overcome. This clinical finding, though used intuitively for years, is supported by animal experiments: A conditioning response will gradually be extinguished if it is not reinforced by avoidance or escape. Although graded exposure and flooding are very effective treatments for phobias and compulsions, sometimes they are not feasible, because the patient simply refuses to risk the anxiety involved or because the patient has a physical condition (such as a heart problem) that would contraindicate a severe psychophysiological response to the stress.

Positive Reinforcement. Animal experiments have shown that if a behavioral response is consistently followed by a reward, such as food, stroking, praise, or absence of pain, then that "positively reinforced" behavior will occur more vigorously and more frequently. On the other hand, if a piece of behavior is followed either by punishment (an "aversive stimulant'") or by no stimulus at all ("extinction"), then the response tends to occur weakly and less frequently under similar conditions in the future. Complex behavior can also be shaped by a combination of subtle responses in the environment; for example, B. F. Skinner[38] arranged an elaborate system of positive reinforcements and extinction to make pigeons perform colorful and outlandish feats. Skinner was the pioneer of operant conditioning, in which behavior is determined by its environmental consequences (as opposed to classical conditioning, discussed above, in which behavior is determined by the environmental cues).

Because operant conditioning requires arranging the environment to respond to behavior in a particular way, its clinical use was first reserved primarily for patients in institutions where positive reinforcement and extinction could be programmed systematically into the setting. The token economy[39] was used for institutionalized patients who received a token for responsible behavior (e.g., bathing or making beds) and who lost tokens for obstreperous or assaultive behavior. Tokens could be used to buy special treats or privileges (e.g., additional TV time). In the past few years, positive reinforcement has been advocated in the treatment of those who are outpatients and who are less severely ill.[40] Instead of the institutional staff arranging the environmental consequences, the therapist and patient collaborate to find an adequate reinforcer and to establish a contract. A more complicated "contingency contracting" includes a significant person in the patient's life (such as a parent or spouse) who is "trained" to ignore maladaptive behavior and consistently and systematically reinforce more adaptive behavior. As the case discussions suggest, positive and negative reinforcement no doubt play a role in most treatments, but the techniques are not always applied systematically and explicitly.

Cognitive Techniques. When conditioning therapies were first applied to clinical situations, the focus was more on what the patient did and less on what the patient felt or thought. The goal of treatment was for the patient to *act* differently. Of course, therapists recognized that patients who changed maladaptive behavior had a more positive regard for themselves and a less distorted view about frightening situations, but these intangibles were first considered merely "secondary reinforcers." In the past few years, behavior has become even more broadly defined and includes both psychophysiological activities emanating from the "black box" and mental activities within the black box as well. Although "peripheralists" have been opposed to examining mental processes that must be inferred and are not easily measurable, some behaviorists have argued that because cognitive functions have such an important influence on behavior, these "covert behaviors" cannot be ignored.[41,42] The impetus for cognitive therapy arose partly out of this school's persuasive argument.

Cognitive therapy also borrows heavily from the psychoanalytic belief that changing ideas can alter behavior (though some cognitive therapists would not regard Freud as part of their intellectual heritage). Because cognitive therapy can trace its roots to several different academic traditions, it cannot tidily be placed with other behavioral techniques. We have placed it in this section because the methods of cognitive therapy are predominantly directive, that is, the therapist actively teaches the patient what tasks to perform and when and how to do them.

Though many have contributed to the development of cognitive therapy, Beck[43] has been most influential in popularizing this treatment, refining it, and testing its effectiveness. Borrowing from the behaviorists' clear description of methods and empirical verification, Beck devised a strategy to modify a depressed person's mode of thinking. Though psychoanalytically trained, he concluded from his clinical work that patients are depressed not because of some deep unconscious conflict, but because they have acquired ("learned") misconceptions about themselves and about the way the world is. This negative view of themselves, of the world, and of the future ("the cognitive triad") has inherent internal and external reinforcements that perpetuate the depression.

Since Beck considered neurotic depression to be primarily cognitive in origin, he believed treatment should aim at correcting cognitive distortions rather than exploring their ideological roots. Moreover, he believed that the most efficient method of changing the misconceptions of depressed patients was by using the well-documented directive techniques of behavioral therapy. He designed a precise blueprint delineating each therapeutic maneuver, and he carefully documented the effectiveness of each step as well as the overall therapeutic outcome. The results have been quite promising, but there are certain limitations in Beck's approach. Not all depressions are primarily based on cognitive misconceptions and depressed patients often refuse to withstand the frontal assault against self-derogating attitudes. They may also be unable to take an active role in suddenly changing lifelong trends of passivity.

Some techniques used in cognitive therapy have been an implicit part of the therapeutic armamentarium since the beginning of psychotherapy. Therapists have often confronted patients on the irrationality of their beliefs and then have suggested ways to change, but these tactics have not always been applied in a consistent and systematic way. Furthermore, psychoanalytically oriented therapists at times may have not been aware (or at least not acknowledged) that they were actually directing patients to change their distorted beliefs. Beck explicitly describes some of the common components of directive treatments: (a) assuming an authoritative stance; (b) clearly defining the target symptoms; and (c) designing a specific program to be followed in order to "reframe" dysfunctional thoughts.

Other Directive Techniques. Many different kinds of therapists have developed innovative ways of directing behavior. Haley[44,45] and Erickson[46] are renowned for their imaginative and often controversial approaches; but even traditional psychoanalysts, such as Bibring[47], have appreciated that "suggestion" and "manipulation" subtly direct the patient to feel and act adaptively. Some directive techniques are straightforward, such as advice or homework assignments, whereas others are more theoretically and technically complex, such as actually prescribing a symptom to an oppositional patient (paradoxical injunction). Many cases in this book confirm the clinical impression that the choice of directive techniques innovatively tailored to the particular needs of a patient is usually based more on art than science—and that this choice may be the determining factor in whether or not a treatment is effective.

EXPERIENTIAL APPROACHES

In contrast to those directive techniques which developed from experimentation and from a belief that problems could be outmaneuvered, experiential techniques developed as a reaction against this view. Proponents of the experiential school maintain that our alienation, meaninglessness, and boredom arise because we are being subordinated to a depersonalized and dehumanized existence. Accordingly, any therapy which imposes directive and mechanistic methods only contributes to the basic problem rather than solves it. In fact, one type of experiential treatment was originally called "nondirective psychotherapy."[48]

Experientialists distrust intellectual solutions and place greater emphasis on spontaneously experiencing events to acquire a sense of personal authenticity. This emphasis on expressing feelings is not new. Aristotle discussed the cathartic value of drama, and an important aspect of all psychotherapies through the ages has been to provide a situation for those who are troubled in which they can "get things off their minds." Along with others, Mesner, Janet, Breuer, and Freud recognized the value of ventilating feelings that had not been given direct and full expression. Abreaction continues to be a recommended therapy for traumatic neuroses, adjustment disorders, and delayed grief responses; it is also the essential ingredient of funeral rituals that facilitate the mourning process.

But at their most extreme, some schools of experiential psychotherapy advocate more than empathic understanding and abreaction. They view all psychopathology as the result of dampened feelings. Emotional problems are not caused by one's inheritance, constitution, biological inflictions, or developmental trauma; they are caused by not realizing (not "actualizing") one's potential. Anxiety is conceptualized as the tension between what one is and what one can become. Those with emotional distress are therefore no different than the rest of us and should not be labeled as "sick"; they should not be "diagnosed." Since the goal is to reach a universal consciousness, anyone can benefit from a therapeutic experience, and there are no limits to how much can be accomplished by such an encounter. This spiritual orientation of psychotherapy can be traced to oriental religions and to western existential philosophies.

These existential ideas have been logically applied to therapeutic techniques and have affected the stance, maneuvers, and goals set by existential therapists.[9,48-51] In the process of rejecting the medical model of classifying psychiatric diseases, the experiential schools have also rejected the authoritative and patronizing stance inherent in the doctor-patient relationship. Patients are clients, not helpless children, and should be treated as equals rather than infantilized. The psychoanalytic position of anonymity, abstinence, and neutrality is rejected as well. The therapeutic relationship should not be obscure, abstract, or asymmetrical, but rather a real encounter between two persons that will change and actualize both of them. The therapist should be genuine, have unconditional positive regard for the client, and, rather than withholding gratification, should provide the support, affection, and praise that would naturally emanate from a personal friendship.

Because many experiential schools have disdain for the therapeutic importance of understanding the past or, at the very least, view it as irrelevant, their representative therapies do not dwell on a developmental family and personal history as is characteristic of exploratory methods, nor do they perform a behavioral analysis of symptoms and their contexts as is done with more directive treatments. Instead, experiential therapists prefer to approach the client with no preconceived notions based on the "there and then," while treasuring the potential worth of the "here and now"; and since intellectual understanding is not emphasized, the therapists do not strive to have clients articulate their insights. Therapeutic change is the result of the emotional experience itself; putting that experience into words is not a goal. To heighten the emotional experience and to break through and to break down defenses, the therapist may use confrontation, sensory motor tasks, encounters, and even physical and emotional exhaustion. Since social and parental pressure to achieve are seen as contributing to unwarranted anxiety, every effort is made to deemphasize achievement. The goals of treatment are therefore left unspecified; the client should only strive to experience the therapeutic encounter as fully as possible. By not struggling but by simply allowing it to happen, the client takes another step towards self-awareness, cohesiveness, and actualization.

For purposes of contrast and exposition, we have presented above the more extreme experiential view. In fact, psychoanalysts have described the therapeutic value of a "corrective emotional experience,"[52] or a "holding environment,"[53] or the healing process of the "real" relationship with patients;[7,8] and after reading the presented cases, you will be impressed with how often the outcome was greatly influenced by experiential factors.

Experiential therapies tend to be defined less sharply than the interventions used for either exploratory or directive therapies. Some proponents of the experiential method would oppose any definition of techniques, fearing that a description might be regarded as a rule that would limit the necessary flexibility required to be as open and receptive and unbiased as possible when interacting with the client. Nevertheless, some experiential therapies have been articulated and, as we have done in discussing exploratory and directive techniques, we will now present some representative therapies to illustrate their development, methods, and rationale. Even when not labeled as such, elements of these techniques appear in the case reports.

Client-Centered Psychotherapy. The central hypothesis of this treatment is that the person has vast internal resources for change and that these resources can be realized in the process of a nonjudgmental and nondirective relationship that, unlike the medical model, is not hierarchal, manipulative, or demeaning.[54] The encounter is not designed for "treatment" but for "growth." Therapeutic maneuvers are seen as potentially destructive; the emphasis is, therefore, on therapeutic attitudes— empathic understanding, unlimited positive regard, and genuineness. Unlike many other experiential approaches, client-centered psychotherapy has attempted to trace its theoretical roots, to describe its specific methods, to delineate the stages of change, and to document its results with outcome research.[55]

Gestalt Therapy. This approach is based on the theory that the best adaptation requires a full awareness of physiological and psychological needs.[56] Maladaptive behavior will inevitably arise when those needs are repressed by the forces of society. Treatment thereby attempts to bring the various parts of oneself into total awareness. This holistic view—the gestalt—will give meaning to one's different ideas and feelings and experiences. The techniques are designed to overcome those experiences that prevent an individual from being totally aware of his or her needs. Both psychological and sensory motor exercises are used. The results of Gestalt therapy are quite impressive when related at workshops, but, as with other techniques, more systematic study is needed.

Psychodrama. This approach attempts to provide greater self-awareness by having the patient actually enact those situations where conflicts are likely to arise.[57] The role-playing is designed to have the individual experience the problem; the goal is for the individual to understand the problem as well. Interpretations are used for this purpose. In this sense, psychodrama is also related to the exploratory approaches. The techniques are derived from impromptu theater. For example, one patient might be instructed to enact an anxiety-laden situation, while another patient serves as an auxiliary ego and comments "offstage" what the first patient might self-consciously be thinking. Meanwhile, the director (the therapist) constructs the scene with other "actors" to elicit the patient's worst fears and thereby make these problems more accessible to consciousness and understanding. Though rarely so explicit, elements of psychodrama can be seen in many.

Approach: B. Shared Objectives

The above description of psychodrama is a good example of how difficult it is to place a designated method of psychotherapy into one specific school or category. Although psychodrama uses emotional experiences as a primary therapeutic mode, it certainly uses exploratory and directive techniques in addition to experiential techniques. As many of the following cases will illustrate, clinicians often use strategies that represent an admixture of the three schools of technique we have described. This finding is consistent with an observation made by Goldfried:[87]

> In picking up the textbook of the future, we should see in the Table of Contents not a listing of School A, School B, and so on—perhaps ending with the author's attempt at integration—but an outline of the various agreed-upon intervention principles, a specification of varying techniques for implementing each principle, and an indication of the relative effectiveness of each of these techniques together with their interaction with varying presenting problems and individual differences among patients/clients and therapists. (pp. 997–998)

Although the mental health profession is far from reaching "agreed-upon intervention principles," we do have a wealth of clinical experience and research data to begin to itemize shared objectives and common strategies used by therapists in actual practice and for the patients presented in this book:

1) ESTABLISHING AND MAINTAINING A THERAPEUTIC RELATIONSHIP

There is no doubt that the relationship between therapist and patient is instrumental in engaging the patient, instilling hope and ultimately catalyzing therapeutic change. Luborsky and colleagues,[6] for example, have documented that an early positive alliance between therapist and patient correlates significantly with positive outcome. The problem is being able to isolate those specific factors that establish and maintain this alliance.

As mentioned at the beginning of this chapter, some have acknowledged the crucial importance of the relationship but, rather than dissecting its specific ingredients, have chosen to refer to them as "nonspecific factors."[7,8] Others have attempted to describe the specific strategies and attitudes that strengthen this enigmatic therapeutic bond which psychoanalysts have variously labeled as "the working alliance,"[14] "the therapeutic alliance,"[58] "the analyst's presence,"[59] "the facilitating environment,"[53] "the effective transference,"[60] "the rational transference,"[61] and "the mature transference."[62] Carl Rogers,[54] though approaching the issue from a different theoretical orientation, has described three essential therapeutic attitudes that closely resemble what analysts have proposed: 1) genuineness; 2) nonjudgmental caring; and 3) communicated empathic understanding. Behavioral therapists, even if not discussing the elements of the therapeutic relationship so explicitly, certainly have recognized its importance.[37,39,41-43]

Our intention here is not to review the many interpersonal skills required to develop a therapeutic relationship, but rather to suggest that, when assessing the cases in this book, the reader note how the induction into treatment (including its negotiation[63]) and the final outcome often depend on the establishment of the therapeutic relationship more than on other interventions.

2) PROVIDING SUPPORT

The provision of support is commonly devalued and seen as "something less" than other therapeutic strategies, yet clinical experience as well as some research studies[64] indicate that supportive psychotherapy often requires the greatest skill and expertise. This devaluation of support stems in part from a confusion over what is meant by the term. Support actually has several dictionary meanings,[65] each with its own distinct therapeutic implications:

(a) *To carry or bear the weight of, keep from falling, slipping, or sinking; hold up.* In this sense of support, the therapist provides from the outside what the patient lacks internally; in Kernberg's phrase, the therapist serves as an "auxiliary ego."[66] This may involve orienting the confused patient, correcting misperceptions in those whose testing of reality is impaired, and offering suggestions or advice to those less capable of deciding upon the best course of action. The arranging of scheduled sessions, as well as the informed phrasing of questions and responses within a given session, can also provide an external organizing structure.

(b) *To give courage, faith, or confidence to.* In this sense of support, the therapist conveys a belief in the patient's capacity to master the problem. The patient thereby feels hopeful that change is possible and also encouraged to confront the distress associated with various therapeutic tasks, such as recalling painful memories, approaching a phobic situation, or changing a familiar way of interacting with others.

(c) *To give approval to or be in favor of; subscribe to; uphold.* In this sense of support, the therapist acknowledges, accepts, and even reinforces the parts of the patient that do not need changing and may in fact be useful assets. The therapist thereby increases self-esteem because the patient does not hold the global view that all functioning is impaired, but rather that many, perhaps most, mental capacities are not seriously disturbed. In addition, the therapist uses (i.e., supports) the patient's adaptive coping and defense mechanisms to help change those areas that are maladaptive. For example, the intellectual defenses of a male obsessive patient may be used when offering insight about the causes and effects of his passive-aggressive behavior; or the sensitivity of a hysterical female patient may be used when suggesting how her awareness of the feelings of others can give her a measuring stick to see how her over-dramatic responses affect others; or the self-directedness of the paranoid patient may be used when recommending a job that requires limited interpersonal involvement; or the immutable persistence of a schizophrenic patient may be used when assigning him or her to the rote tasks in a structured workshop.

By extension, this form of support is closely linked to the procedure of positive reinforcement in that the therapist (often intuitively and maybe unsystematically) offers praise for adaptive feelings, ideas, and behavior, while withholding praise or perhaps being critical when less acceptable attributes are presented by the patient (negative reinforcement).

(d) *To maintain or provide with money or subsistence.* In this sense of support, the therapist combines a knowledge of the patient's available resources with the knowledge of the patient's specific psychopathology and needs. At its extreme, this intervention may involve arranging for foster care or public assistance or, more subtly, may involve directing relatives or staff members on how to meet the patient's specific requirements without assuming too much responsibility and thereby infantilizing the patient.

(e) *To show or tend to show to be true; help prove, indicate or corroborate.* In this sense of support, the therapist decreases the patient's alienation and self-doubt by confirming certain feelings, thoughts, perceptions, and actions that appear reasonable and well-founded.

(f) *To bear; endure; submit to; tolerate.* In this sense of support, perhaps the most important, the therapist provides the sustained presence of another. This presence, based on both a knowledge of psychopathology and on a dynamic understanding of the patient, reduces the isolation and loneliness often accompanying emotional disorders. This presence is not, however, simply "hand-holding," that is, a kindly and stereotypic responsiveness. In fact, with certain kinds of patients an overly sympathetic "pseudohumanitarian"[67] approach may be the *least* supportive: It may be experienced by paranoid patients as intrusive; by hysterical patients as seductive; by obsessive patients as demeaning; by depressed patients as unworthy; and by dependent or phobic patients as a sanction for further regression or avoidance. For this reason, the therapist's presence or stance must be tailored to the patient's individual style and needs.

This feature of support also connotes the therapist's capacity to tolerate distressing affects. This tolerance indicates to the patient that powerful feelings are not in themselves harmful, that they can be safely abreacted and understood, and that partly through identification with the therapist and a "corrective emotional experience,"[68] these feelings can be mastered. When feelings themselves become less frightening, the patient's emotional repertoire is expanded. This tolerance for distressing affects in the therapist is based on not only a personal understanding of oneself, but also an appreciation of intense positive and negative transferences and the purposes they magically serve for the patient.

3) EDUCATING

Clinicians have traditionally been reluctant to inform psychiatric patients about the nature of their illness, especially its diagnosis and prognosis. The rationale behind this reluctance has been the belief that this kind of information might, at the least, lead to rationalization and intellectualization and, at worst, lead to demoralization and hopelessness. This view has been increasingly contested by both consumers and legal advocates outside the profession, as well as by individuals within the profession. After studying the psychoeducational approach to schizophrenic patients, Anderson[69] reported that when such patients and their families were armed with information about the illness, they could mutually establish reasonable expectations, make appropriate plans for the future that would reduce stress, and diminish those emotional interactions they now knew were destructive. Others[70] have reported the value of psychoeducation in limiting the unrealistic expectations of neurotic and borderline patients. Throughout this casebook we often suggest that psychoeducation is a crucial aspect of the negotiation phase in treatment planning, much the way a physician would outline different possible approaches to a specified medical problem.

4) REDUCING PAINFUL AFFECTS

The common strategies used to reduce painful affects—especially anxiety, but also depression and anger—include: (a) abreaction; (b) determining the unrealistic preconscious or unconscious meaning or consequences of the feeling; (c) restructuring the environmental precipitants; or (d) designing tasks that provide eventual mastery over the overwhelming affect (graded exposure, flooding, symbolic desensitization, covert modeling, reinforced practice, and relaxation techniques).

5) DECREASING SPECIFIC MALADAPTIVE BEHAVIORS

Strategies aimed at treating specific maladaptive behaviors (e.g., phobias, compulsive rituals, premature ejaculation, vaginismus, social avoidance, professional timidity) are often indistinguishable from supportive and anxiety-reducing interventions, except that the emphasis is more on action than on affect. For example, hierarchal assignments, sensitivity exercises, and assertiveness training may focus primarily on performing step-by-step tasks and only secondarily on the associated discomfort. Similarly, positive and negative reinforcement (e.g., token economy, contingency contracting, social skills training) establish a reward-punishment system that focuses more on behavior than on feelings.

6) MODIFYING SPECIFIC MISPERCEPTIONS

As discussed above, cognitive restructuring has been most systematically described and studied by Beck with regard to modifying depressed patients' misperceptions about themselves, the world, and the future (the cognitive triad). The strategies include: eliciting automatic thoughts; identifying maladaptive assumptions behind such thoughts; analyzing the validity of these maladaptive assumptions; and then challenging these assumptions and offering structured tasks to correct them. In a less systematic manner, many clinicians from different theoretical orientations use similar strategies to change maladaptive beliefs.

7) UNCOVERING AND CONVEYING PSYCHODYNAMIC EXPLANATIONS

The use of clarification, interpretation, and free association have been summarized above in the discussion of exploratory techniques. But even patients not strictly participating in a psychodynamically oriented treatment may acquire a reassuring sense of being understood when their particular problems are placed meaningfully and insightfully in the context of their own personal development and of their internal life— their aspirations, dreams, fantasies, conflicts, memories, and fears. To present this psychodynamic understanding in a convincing manner, the therapist must sometimes also use confrontation, not in the sense of opposing the patient but, more neutrally, in the sense of presenting for examination certain feelings or behaviors that are not being openly identified or expressed by the patient.[71]

8) EXPANDING EMOTIONAL AWARENESS

Although many of the strategies listed above secondarily increase emotional awareness, some interventions have this as the primary goal and are therefore listed here separately. The sensorimotor tasks used in Gestalt therapy, meditation-yoga exercises, and the confrontational-abreactive methods of primal scream therapy are examples of such strategies.

9) ENHANCING INTERPERSONAL BEHAVIOR

Strategies used to improve interpersonal behavior, especially between spouses and family members, include: communication training; problem-solving; assigned interpersonal tasks; contingency contracting;

relabeling; changing interpersonal expectations; reenacting dysfunctional interpersonal transactions; establishing boundaries; unbalancing techniques; paradoxical interventions; social skills training; and the various techniques for sex therapy.

This list of nine common strategies used in psychotherapy is not intended to be complete or to go unchallenged. Its primary purpose is to convey that what clinicians actually do in psychotherapy often cuts across various philosophical and theoretical orientations. Its secondary purpose is to provide a convenient method for itemizing on the reference tables (pp. 378–381) the interventions used for the cases presented in this book.

Somatic Approaches

Regarding somatic therapies (psychotropic medication and ECT), the consultant has two major questions to answer: Is a somatic treatment indicated and, if so, how should it be prescribed—which one in which dosage at which frequency and for how long? The answer to the first major question is quite easy when the patient clearly has a severe impairment amenable to a somatic intervention. Other times, however, the decision is much more uncertain. Every patient is more or less anxious or depressed or has "ups and downs." Because research has not yet determined precisely when a somatic treatment should be introduced in conjunction with a psychosocial treatment, this decision will be greatly influenced by the individual preferences of clinician and patient.

To date, psychopharmacological research has been more systematic in answering the second major question confronting the consultant. Once a decision is made to use a somatic treatment, many studies are available to guide the consultant in the choice, dosage, frequency, and duration of the drug. A number of excellent texts have consolidated this information for the clinician.[72-74] As with the other components of psychiatric treatments, here we will only categorize the various options and briefly present the background and rationale for each. The interesting issues of placebo response, target symptoms, polypharmacy, and combining psychopharmacotherapy with psychotherapy will not be discussed in this chapter, but will directly or indirectly be addressed in many of the cases.

ANTIPSYCHOTIC AGENTS

Chlorpromazine was initially introduced in 1951 as a preanesthetic sedative for surgery. A dramatic psychobiological revolution was sparked when a few years later this drug was tried as an antipsychotic with astounding success. Over the past 30 years a large variety of substances have been derived from phenothiazine, butyrophenone, thioxanthene, dibenzoxazepine, and indolone groups. Though the offsprings from these families are different in their basic structure, they share many common characteristics. They are not addictive, are remarkably non-lethal even in large overdosages, demonstrate no tolerance for their beneficial antipsychotic effect, and yet do have tolerance for their anticholinergic side effects. Their exact mechanism of action remains unclear; because they all tend to be powerful dopamine antagonists, their antipsychotic effect presumably derives from their ability to block dopamine neurotransmission in the limbic forebrain. Their parkinsonian side effects possibly result from dopamine blockade in the basal ganglia.

Despite these many shared characteristics, antipsychotic drugs vary in two important ways: their potency and their side effects. The high potency antipsychotics tend to be less sedating and have fewer anticholinergic and cardiovascular side effects, but they are much more likely to affect the extrapyramidal motor system and to cause acute dystonia, akathisia, and parkinsonism. The skill of prescribing antipsychotic medication and enhancing compliance involves matching the side effect profiles with the particular patient. Unfortunately, the most distressing complication of the antipsychotic medications, tardive dyskinesia, is likely to occur with the same degree of risk from all the compounds under discussion.

TRICYCLIC ANTIDEPRESSANTS

In the mid-1950s, in response to the dramatic discovery that chlorpromazine had antipsychotic properties, many other phenothiazines were synthesized. It was noted, almost in passing, that some of these drugs, like imipramine, were rather ineffective as antipsychotic drugs but they did induce mood elevation. With this observation, a larger litter of tricyclic antidepressants was born. As it has since turned out, these drugs are probably misnamed in that they are effective for many conditions besides classical depression including panic disorder, enuresis, and possibly eating, sleep, and obsessive compulsive disorders.

Like antipsychotic drugs, the mechanism of therapeutic action is not known. It is known that tricyclics block the reuptake of neurotransmitters at the presynaptic nerve endings. Some tricyclics block the reuptake of norepinephrine, while others operate more on the serotonin system. This difference may explain why some tricyclics are more effective with certain patients.

Also like the antipsychotics, the selection of one tricyclic from the many others is based mostly on matching the most or least desirable side effect. For example, amitriptyline is the most sedating and may be especially indicated for patients who are agitated or have severe insomnia; but this drug is also the most anticholinergic and may not be the best drug if constipation, urinary retention, visual blurring, sweating, dry mouth, or drowsiness will interfere with concomitant medical problems, general functioning, or compliance. Two additional problems in the use of antidepressant medications are: 1) These drugs can be lethal when ingested in even small overdoses (one week's supply); and 2) they require two or more weeks to obtain therapeutic effectiveness and therefore cannot be relied upon alone to treat a seriously suicidal patient. A structured, protective setting may be necessary until a sufficient therapeutic effect has been achieved.

NEWER ANTIDEPRESSANT MEDICATIONS

In the last few years a new generation of antidepressants has been marketed (e.g., trazodone, amoxapine, metrotoline, fluoxetine). Though the chemical structure of these drugs is appreciably different from the tricyclics, their mode of action, effectiveness, and range of indications are similar to the tricyclics and newer heterocyclics except that they may produce a faster onset of action and have fewer side effects (particularly cardiovascular).

MONOAMINE OXIDASE INHIBITORS (MAOIs)

These drugs were used to treat depression after it was serendipitously noted that one MAOI (isoniazid) caused euphoria as a side effect when given to patients for tuberculosis. They presumably work by inhibiting the enzyme monoamine oxidase, thereby increasing the synaptic availability of norepinephrine and serotonin; but since some potent inhibitors of monoamine oxidase are not good antidepressants, the precise method of therapeutic action remains to be elucidated.

Since these drugs were introduced to treat depression 35 years ago they have been in and out of favor (mostly out), because they were considered more dangerous than tricyclic antidepressants and also less effective. As it has turned out, neither concern may be true. MAOIs do occasionally cause hypertensive crises in response to the ingestion of foods containing large amounts of tyramine or other aromatic amines (aged cheeses, chocolates, nuts, beans, citrus fruits, chopped liver, beer, wine, etc.); but there are some preliminary indications that certain

MAOIs may not produce this tyramine effect. As for the question of their efficacy, it now appears that the early pessimism may have been a result of inadequate dosage. Until the dangerousness and efficacy of these drugs are more systematically documented, the indications for their use will remain controversial. Clinical lore would prescribe MAOIs preferentially for a patient whose depression is associated with prominent phobias or anxiety or with reverse "atypical" vegetative symptoms (i.e., increased rather than decreased sleep or appetite) or with a poor response to an adequate trial of tricyclics, heterocyclics or newer antidepressants.

ELECTROCONVULSIVE THERAPY (ECT)

Over 50 years ago, based on the belief (later disproved) that epileptics had a lower incidence of schizophrenia, seizures were electrically induced in mental patients. Though the results were less than satisfactory for the majority of mental disorders, the results for those with either mania or depression were miraculous. These well-documented benefits have been exceeded only by the mystery or controversy surrounding the procedure. Like so many treatments in medicine, including psychotropic drugs, no one knows exactly how the procedure works (although it has been shown that ECT acts on brain neurotransmitters, receptors, and electrolytes). Despite the harsh connotation of "shock treatment," the procedure is actually at least as safe and effective as antidepressant medication, if not more so, especially in patients with a delusional depression, serious suicidal ideation and life-threatening agitation, insomnia, retardation, or weight loss. The only absolute contraindication is increased intracranial pressure. With modern anesthetic techniques and neuromuscular blockade, even those with severe osteoporosis or fractures can receive the treatment. The major limitations of ECT when compared to antidepressants are cost, transient memory loss, social stigma, and inconvenience (e.g., hospitalization). If relapses occur after a course of ECT, the patient may require maintenance ECT or maintenance antidepressants.

LITHIUM

This unassuming salt has been used for generations in the treatment of gout. During the late 1940s Cade was investigating how lithium affected the metabolism of uric acid and noted that the salt had a sedating effect on his experimental animals. Cade then tried lithium with manic patients; the dramatic results heralded the psychopharmacological era. How lithium works is not clearly understood but probably involves its most characteristic action on intracellular-extracellular neuronal electrolyte concentrations, on the workings of the sodium pump, and on receptor activity. Whatever its therapeutic mechanisms, lithium is remarkably effective in the treatment of acute manic episodes, in prophylaxis against bipolar cycling, and possibly in the treatment of the depressive phase of bipolar disorder. Its acute and prophylactic effects in unipolar depression, in activated schizophrenic and violent patients, and in those with cyclothymic and emotionally unstable personality disorders remain more controversial. Because the salt can be potentially quite toxic if not prescribed and monitored carefully, it must be given cautiously to patients who are suicidal, psychotic, suffering from poor judgment, likely to have medical complications, or subject to fluid and electrolyte imbalance (e.g., gastroenteritis or marathon running). Because of these precautions and because acutely manic and hypomanic patients are notoriously poor compliers, hospitalization is often required to begin treatment.

BENZODIAZEPINES

Anxiety is a ubiquitous, unavoidable, and unpleasant aspect of the human experience. The quest for its relief probably began even before Dionysus was made a demi-God for his patronage of wine. The quest has continued through recent centuries with the use of bromide salts, synthetic opioids (heroin), paraldehyde, chloral hydrate, barbiturates, and propanolols (meprobamate). At present, the benzodiazepines (chlordiazepoxide, diazepam) are the leading contenders. All of these various antianxiety agents cause degrees of CNS depression that are roughly proportional to dosage, but the benzodiazepines are superior to their predecessors in that they induce less sedation for a given antianxiety effect, produce less tendency towards abuse, and have lower lethality on overdosage. Their wide popularity, fulfilling the grandest dreams of the pharmaceutical industry, is proof of their effectiveness; yet even these modern antianxiety agents are burdened by the undesirable characteristics of tolerance and withdrawal and a tendency to induce physiological and psychological dependence. Their main indications in psychiatric practice for withdrawal syndromes, for assistance in emergency coping, for transient insomnia, and as a temporary means of encouraging patients to attempt activities they might otherwise avoid because of expectant anxiety.

OTHER PSYCHOTROPIC MEDICATIONS

Psychopharmacotherapists may wince over the above superficial description of psychotropic medications, no doubt mirroring the reactions of psychotherapists who have devoted their clinical lives to mastering a technique mentioned only in passing. But our intention in this chapter is only to outline the components of the decision tree in treatment selection and to summarize their background and rationale. The discussion of the case themselves will address the art and science of psychotherapy and pharmacotherapy, including both the management of resistances to therapeutic approaches and the use of other medications (endaural, verapamil, busipirone, carbamazepine, etc.) when first-line drugs are ineffective, not indicated, or poorly tolerated.

NO TREATMENT AS RECOMMENDATION OF CHOICE

We have so far categorized the kinds of choices the consultant must make if treatment is indicated. We must remember, however, that psychiatric treatment is not necessary or effective for all those who seek it, and in some cases may be contraindicated. The clinician must therefore always consider whether the recommendation of no treatment is the best choice. This decision is frequently deferred or avoided or left in the hands of the patient. We have discussed this option elsewhere at greater length[75,76] and mention it here so that this possible recommendation will not be overlooked.

To summarize, there are four main reasons for recommending no treatment. First, some patients have a negative response to psychiatric treatment. These include certain borderline patients with a history of treatment failures; certain masochistic, narcissistic, or oppositional patients who are prone to severe negative reactions; and patients who are in a treatment primarily to support a lawsuit or to justify a claim for compensation or disability.

Second, there is a group of patients who may not get worse in treatment but are very unlikely to respond. These include those with refractory antisocial or criminal behavior; patients with malingering or factitious illness; and poorly motivated patients without incapacitating symptoms who often seek treatment under the coercion of others.

Third, there is a group of patients who are likely to improve spontaneously without treatment. These include individuals who are in crisis and who have available sufficient internal or external means of support; or individuals whose minor chronic problems do not warrant the effort and expense of extended psychiatric care.

Finally, no treatment may be the recommendation of choice as a therapeutic intervention; for example, some oppositional patients may paradoxically enter treatment to "defy" such a recommendation; and some patients, wary of being infantilized, may find the recommendation of no treatment as reassuring and supportive of their adaptive pseudo-independent defenses. The several case discussions in this book that consider the recommendation of no treatment will clarify the indications for this option.

The Process of Treatment Selection

Given the various components of psychiatric treatment, how does the clinician go about deciding which patient gets what? There are several possibilities. The simplest follows the medical model: The clinician makes the diagnosis and prescribes the accepted treatment for that disorder. But this model not only oversimplifies what occurs in medical practice, it also presumes that psychiatric diagnosis is closely linked with a specific psychiatric treatment. Such is rarely the case. Although establishing a diagnosis is an important first step, it is not a clarion call for one particular approach and, as many studies have documented,[77] diagnosis alone has only a slight correlation with what treatments are chosen and what outcomes are achieved. To emphasize this point, we purposefully have included more than one case of some diagnostic categories, each of which has different treatment requirements.

A preferable method in the process of treatment selection is to consider other aspects of the patient in addition to diagnosis (e.g., presenting problem, character traits, premorbid adjustment, motivation, psychological-mindedness, socioeconomic and familial situation, ego strengths). These many variables are then matched to the enabling factors, indications, and contraindications of all available psychiatric treatments. This process is, of course, far more complex and is attempted with varying degrees of success in our discussion of some cases. Yet despite its complexity, this method of treatment selection is advocated in the clinical literature representing many different theoretical orientations.[33,78-80]

We cannot ignore, however, that this complex process of treatment selection has been found to be the exception rather than the rule. Clinicians are not knowledgeable about all the different possibilities, nor are all treatments available from which any one consultant can choose. Furthermore, inevitable biases take their toll. As suggested by Newman,[81] one problem is that therapists are rewarded for automatically selecting their favorite form of psychotherapy without considering alternatives. The problem begins with the method of referral: A physician, a friend, another clinician, a pastor, or rabbi makes a preliminary assessment and on the basis of this prejudgment (prejudice) recommends a particular therapist, who then proceeds to apply his or her usual type of therapy. If the results are positive, the therapist's approach is positively reinforced; and if therapy proceeds with no effect, the patient (and too rarely the therapist or the choice of therapy) is seen as the problem. In such cases, the patient is usually referred for other treatments only after all become fed up. This method of treatment selection leads to a happy ending when, largely by chance, the preliminary incomplete assessment by the referral source is fortuitously linked with the treatment routinely performed by the therapist.

Newman's description of the effect of bias in treatment selection would not surprise many clinicians and is, in fact, supported by other kinds of studies. For example, regarding the possible role of sex bias, one study[82] found that although the gender of the therapist or patient did not significantly affect the number of sessions, it did affect how the severity of emotional problems was viewed: Both male and female therapists rated the problems of female patients more severely than similar problems in males. Another study[82] examined how theoretical orientation biases the therapist. Psychodynamic, behavioral, family, and eclectic therapists were presented with a hypothetical patient with 70 information elements. They were asked to rate which elements they would use in designing a treatment plan and which elements they would pursue during the course of therapy. Psychodynamic therapists placed greater emphasis on personal, family, marital, and sexual history. In yet another study[83] psychodynamic therapists, when compared with behavioral or eclectic therapists, judged three sample patients with moderate depression as being more disturbed and therefore requiring more intensive treatment.

The documented existence of bias is not in itself surprising or disturbing. A more disheartening fact is that bias is so difficult to reduce. Informing therapists of their biases does not have much impact.[83,84] They simply provide support for their choices, avoid arguments that present an opposing view, and even falsely "recall" events which were not present but which support their biased assessments.[85]

On a more encouraging note, some studies have indicated that bias can be reduced if clinicians are forced to delay diagnostic judgment and closure until they have completely assessed the range of problems and been asked to predict positive and negative consequences of treatment.[86] Partially for this reason, we have recommended[76] that a consultation period precede any decision about treatment selection. Patients themselves typically do not make this distinction. They present themselves, explain their problems, and expect the therapist to select the best treatment and then perform it. In fact, they often believe that the evaluation period is part of the treatment itself and do not realize that a decision has not yet been made regarding what treatment, if any, would be best suited for their problems and what therapist would be the best person to perform it. Throughout this book (and in our clinical practice), we attempt to make clear this distinction between the evaluation and treatment phase; for example, we refer to the clinician performing the initial assessment as the "consultant" and the individual conducting the actual treatment as the "therapist."

A particular value of making this distinction between consultation and therapy is that neither the therapist nor the patient will be inclined to avoid an important aspect of any evaluation, namely, the negotiation phase. During this phase, the consultant structures the nature of the problem and explains what treatment options are available and what are their relative advantages and disadvantages in this situation and for this patient. The patient actively participates as well, for, as interviews with outpatients have indicated,[63] psychiatric patients often have very specific ideas about what they need and want. Lazare and Eisenthal[63] have emphasized the importance of considering the patient's perspective and of negotiating a treatment plan to increase compliance. When one considers the astounding degree of noncompliance (even patients with serious medical illnesses comply with their prescribed medication regimen only about 50% of the time), the importance of this negotiation phase cannot be overemphasized.

The reader will note in the cases that follow that often, especially when one treatment is not definitely superior to another, the patient's taste and proclivity are given high priority and the results are quite favorable. The reader will also note cases in which the treatment failed because the negotiation phase was poorly handled or ignored altogether, or because the patient's psychopathology and personality problems precluded the consultant and patient arriving at an acceptable plan.

Summary

This chapter has provided a conceptual scheme for the consultant confronted with the difficult task of selecting a psychiatric treatment for a given patient. In all clinical situations, the consultant and the patient must choose a setting, a format, a time frame, and an approach, and will also need to decide if a somatic therapy is indicated, if various components of treatment should be combined, and if no treatment might be the recommendation of choice. As the following cases will illustrate, the process of selecting and negotiating a treatment plan will be affected by many confounding variables, including the biases of clinician and patient.

REFERENCES

1. Smith, M. L., Glass, G. V., & Miller T. I. *The Benefits of Psychotherapy.* Baltimore: Johns Hopkins University Press, 1980.
2. Parloff, M. B. Psychotherapy and research: An anaclitic depression. Frieda Fromm-Reichman Memorial Lecture, Washington School of Psychiatry, April 1980.
3. Eysenck, H. J. *The Effects of Psychotherapy.* New York: International Science Press, 1966.
4. Rachman, S. *The Effects of Psychotherapy.* Oxford: Pergamon Press, 1971.
5. Meltzoff, J., & Kornreich, M. *Research in Psychotherapy.* Chicago: Aldine, 1970.
6. Luborsky, L., Singer, B., & Luborsky, L. Comparative studies of psychotherapy. Is it true that "everyone has won and all must have prizes"? *Archives of General Psychiatry,* 32:995, 1975.
7. Rozenzweig, S. Some implicit common factors in diverse methods of psychotherapy. *American Journal of Orthopsychiatry,* 6:412, 1936.
8. Frank, J. D. *Persuasion and Healing.* New York: Schocken Books, 1973.
9. Klar, H., Frances, A., & Clarkin, J. Selection criteria for partial hospitalization. *Hospital & Community Psychiatry,* 33:929, 1982.
10. Herz, M., Endicott, J., Spitzer, R., & Mesnikoff, A. Day versus inpatient hospitalization: A controlled study. *American Journal of Psychiatry,* 127:1371, 1971.
11. Washburn, S., Vannicelli, M., Longabaugh, R., & Scheff, B. J. A controlled comparison of psychiatric day treatment and inpatient hospitalization. *Journal of Consulting and Clinical Psychology,* 44:665, 1976.
12. Fenton, F., Tessier, L., & Struening, E. A comparative trial of home and hospital care. *Archives of General Psychiatry,* 36:1073, 1979.
13. Perry, S., Frances, A., Klar, H., & Clarkin, J. Selection criteria for individual dynamic psychotherapies. *Psychiatric Quarterly,* 55(1):3–16, 1983.
14. Greenson, R. R. *The Technique and Practice of Psychoanalysis.* New York: International Universities Press, 1967.
15. Clarkin, J. F., & Glick, I. Recent developments in family therapy: A review. *Hospital & Community Psychiatry,* 33:550, 1982.
16. Gurman, A. S., & Kniskern, D. B. Research on marital and family therapy: Progress, perspective, and prospect. In S. Garfield & A. Bergin (Eds.), *Handbook of Psychotherapy and Behavior Change* (2nd ed.). New York: Wiley, 1978.
17. Schilder, P. The analysis of ideologies as a psychotherapeutic method especially in group treatment. *American Journal of Psychiatry,* 93:601, 1936.
18. Wolf, A. The psychoanalysis of groups. *American Journal of Psychotherapy,* 3:525, 1949.

19. Burrow, T. *The Social Basis of Consciousness.* New York: Harcourt, Brace & World, 1927.
20. Anthony, E. F. The history of group psychotherapy. In H. I. Kaplan & B. J. Sadock (Eds.), *Comprehensive Group Psychotherapy.* Baltimore: Williams & Wilkins, 1971.
21. Slavson, S. *A Textbook on Analytic Group Psychotherapy.* New York: International Universities Press, 1964.
22. Bion, W. R. *Experiences in Groups.* London: Tavistock Publications, 1961.
23. Frances, A., Clarkin, J. F., & Marachi, J. P. Selection criteria for outpatient group psychotherapy. *Hospital & Community Psychiatry,* 31:245, 1980.
24. Castelnuovo-Tedesco, P. *The Twenty-Minute Hour.* Boston: Little-Brown, 1965.
25. Stoller, F. H. Accelerated interaction. *International Journal of Group Psychotherapy,* 18:244, 1968.
26. Lacan, J. *The Four Fundamental Concepts of Psychoanalysis.* New York: Norton, 1978.
27. Malan, D. H. *A Study of Brief Psychotherapy.* New York: Plenum, 1963.
28. Sifneos, P. *Short-term Psychotherapy and Emotional Crisis.* Cambridge, MA: Harvard University Press, 1972.
29. Mann, J. *Time-limited Psychotherapy.* Cambridge, MA: Harvard University Press, 1973.
30. Frances, A., & Perry, S. Transference interpretations in focal therapy. *American Journal of Psychiatry,* 140:405, 1983.
31. Levy, J. Relationship therapy. *American Journal of Orthopsychiatry,* 8:64, 1938.
32. Caplan, G., & Killilea, M. *Support Systems and Mutual Help: Multidisciplinary Explorations.* New York: Grune & Stratton, 1976.
33. Karasu, T. B. Psychotherapies: An overview. *American Journal of Psychiatry,* 134:851, 1977.
34. Langs, R. *The Technique of Psychoanalytic Psychotherapy, Vol. 1, 2.* New York: Jason Aronson, 1973.
35. Blanck, G., & Blanck, R. *Ego Psychology Theory and Practice.* New York: Columbia University Press, 1974.
36. Wolpe, J. *Psychotherapy by Reciprocal Inhibition.* Stanford: Stanford University Press, 1958.
37. Wolpe, J. *The Practice of Behavior Therapy.* New York: Pergamon, 1973.
38. Skinner, B. F. *Science and Human Behavior.* New York: Free Press, 1953.
39. Hunt, H. F. Behavior therapy for adults. In S. Arieti (Ed.), *American Handbook of Psychiatry* (2nd ed.). New York: Basic Books, 1975.
40. Kazdin, A. Chronic psychiatric patients: Ward-wide reinforcement programs. In M. Hersen & A. S. Bellack (Eds.), *Behavior Therapy in the Psychiatric Setting.* Baltimore: Williams & Wilkins, 1978.
41. Bandura, A. *Principles of Behavior Modification.* New York: Holt, Rinehart & Winston, 1969.
42. Goldfried, N. R., & Davison, G. C. *Clinical Behavior Therapy.* New York: Holt, Rinehart & Winston, 1976.
43. Beck, A. T. *Cognitive Therapy and the Emotional Disorders.* New York: International Universities Press, 1976.
44. Haley, J. *Strategies of Psychotherapy.* New York: Grune & Stratton, 1963.
45. Haley, J. *Problem-solving Therapy.* New York: Harper, 1976.
46. Haley, J. *Uncommon Therapy: The Psychiatric Techniques of Milton H. Erickson, M.D.* New York: Norton, 1973.

47. Bibring, E. Contribution to the symposium on the theory of the thera-peutic results of psychoanalysis. *International Journal of Psychoanalysis*, 18:170, 1937.
48. Rogers, C. R. *Counseling and Psychotherapy.* Boston: Houghton Mifflin, 1942.
49. Ofman, W. A. *Primer of Humanistic Existentialist Counseling and Therapy.* Los Angeles: Psychological Affiliates Press, 1974.
50. Bugental, J. *The Search for Authenticity.* New York: Holt, Rinehart and Winston, 1965.
51. Rogers, C. R. *On Personal Power.* New York: Delacorte, 1977.
52. Alexander, F., & French, J. *Psychoanalytic Therapy.* New York: Ronald Press, 1946.
53. Winnicott, D. W. *The Maturational Processes and the Facilitating Environment.* New York: International Universities Press, 1965.
54. Rogers, C. R. *Client-centered Therapy.* Boston: Houghton Mifflin, 1951.
55. Truax, C. B., & Mitchell, K. M. Research on certain therapist interpersonal skills in relation to process and outcome. In A. E. Bergin & S. L. Garfield (Eds.), *Handbook of Psychotherapy and Behavior Change* (1st ed.). New York: Wiley, 1971.
56. Perls, F. S., Hefferline, R. F., & Goodman, P. *Gestalt Therapy.* New York: Julian Press, 1951.
57. Moreno, J. L. *Psychodrama.* New York: Beacon House, 1946.
58. Zetzel, E. R. Current concepts of transference. *International Journal of Psycho-analysis*, 37:369–376, 1956.
59. Nacht, S. Variations in technique. *International Journal of Psycho-analysis*, 39:235–237, 1958.
60. Freud, S. (1913). On beginning the treatment. *Standard Edition*, 12:121–144. London: Hogarth Press, 1958.
61. Fenichel, O. *Problems of Psychoanalytic Technique.* Albany, N.Y.: 1941. The Psychoanalytic Quarterly.
62. Stone, L. *The Psychoanalytic Situation.* New York: International Universities Press, 1961.
63. Lazare, A., & Eisenthal, S. A negotiated approach to the clinical encounter. In A. Lazare (Ed.), *Outpatient Psychiatry: Diagnosis and Treatment.* Baltimore: Williams & Wilkins, 1979.
64. Kernberg, O. F., Bernstein, C. S., Coyne, R., et al. Psychotherapy and psychoanalysis: Final report of the Menninger Foundation's psychotherapy research project. *Bulletin of the Menninger Clinic*, 36:1–276, 1972.
65. Guralnik, D. B. (Ed.). *Webster's New World Dictionary.* New York: Simon & Schuster, 1970.
66. Kernberg, O. F. *Borderline Conditions and Pathological Narcissism.* New York: Jason Aronson, 1975.
67. Perry, S., & Viederman, M. Adaptation of residents to consultation-liaison psychiatry. *General Hospital Psychiatry*, 3:141–156, 1981.
68. Alexander, F., & French, T. *Psychoanalytic Therapy.* New York: Ronald Press, 1946.
69. Anderson, C. M., Hogarty, G. E., & Reiss, D. J. Family treatment of adult schizophrenic patients: A psycho-educational approach. *Schizophrenia Bulletin*, 6:490–505, 1980.
70. Bennett, M. I., & Bennett, M. B. Use of hopelessness. *American Journal of Psychiatry*, 141:559–562, 1984.

71. Kernberg, O. F. *Severe Personality Disorders: Psychotherapeutic Strategies.* New Haven: Yale University Press, 1984.
72. Usdin, E., Davis, J. M., Glassman, A., Greenblatt, D., Perel, J. M., & Shader, R. (Eds.). *Clinical Pharmacology in Psychiatry.* New York: Elsevier, 1981.
73. Kalinowsky, L. B., Hippins, H., & Klein, H. E. *Biological Treatments in Psychiatry.* New York: Grune & Stratton, 1982.
74. Reid, W. H. *Treatment of DSM-III Psychiatric Disorders.* New York: Brunner/Mazel, 1983.
75. Frances, A., & Clarkin, J. No treatment as prescription of choice. *Archives of General Psychiatry,* 38:542, 1981.
76. Frances, A., Clarkin, J., & Perry, S. *Differential Therapeutics in Psychiatry: The Art and Science of Treatment Selection.* New York: Brunner/Mazel, 1984.
77. Longabaugh, R., Fowler, D., Stout, R., & Kriebel, G., Jr. Validation of a problem-focused nomenclature. *Archives of General Psychiatry,* 40:453–461, 1983.
78. Offenkrantz, W., Altschul, S., Cooper, A., Frances, A., Michels, R., Rosenblatt, A., Schimel, J., Tobin, A., & Zaphiropoulos, M. Treatment planning and psychodynamic psychiatry. In J. M. Lewis & G. Usdin (Eds.), *Treatment Planning in Psychiatry.* Washington, D.C.: American Psychiatric Association, 1982, pp. 1–41.
79. Barr Taylor, C., Liberman, R. P., Agras, W. S., Barlow, D. H., Bigelow, G. E., Gelfand, D. M., Rush, A. J., Sobell, L. C., & Sobell, M. B. Treatment evaluation and behavior therapy. In J. M. Lewis & G. Usdin (Eds.), *Treatment Planning in Psychiatry.* Washington, D.C.: American Psychiatric Association, 1982, pp. 151–224.
80. Wynne, L. C. The family and marital therapies. In J. M. Lewis & G. Usdin (Eds.), *Treatment Planning in Psychiatry.* Washington, D.C.: American Psychiatric Association, 1982, pp. 225–285.
81. Newman, F. L. Therapist's evaluation of psychotherapy. In M. Lambert, E. Christensen, & S. Dejulio (Eds.), *The Assessment of Psychotherapy Outcome.* New York: Wiley, 1983, pp. 498–536.
82. Giladi, D. Differences among therapeutic approaches in the use of patient information. Paper presented at the Society for Psychotherapy Research meeting, Aspen, Colorado, June 1981.
83. Kopta, S., Newman, F., McGovern, M., & Sandrock, D. Psychotherapeutic orientations: A comparison of conceptualizations, interventions, and recommendations for treatment planning. Paper presented at the 15th annual meeting of the Society for Psychotherapy Research, Lake Louise, Canada, June 1984.
84. Arkes, H. R. Impediments to accurate clinical judgment and possible ways to minimize their impact. *Journal of Consulting and Clinical Psychology,* 49:323–330, 1981.
85. Arkes, H. R., & Harkness, A. R. Effects of making a diagnosis on subsequent recognition of symptoms. *Journal of Experimental Psychology: Human Learning and Memory,* 6:568–575, 1980.
86. Elstein, A. S., Shulman, L. S., & Sprafka, S. A. *Medical Problem Solving: An Analysis of Clinical Reasoning.* Cambridge, MA: Harvard University Press, 1978.
87. Goldfried, M. R. Toward the delineation of therapeutic change principles. *American Psychologist,* 35:991–999, 1980.

II
Organic Mental
Disorders

■ DELIRIUM

1. The Case of the Disruptive Lady

A psychiatry resident was awakened at 2:00 in the morning by a phone call from a medical intern requesting an emergency consultation for a 74-year-old woman who was screaming up and down a hospital ward and demanding her clothes so that she could go home. The intern explained that the patient was calm and cooperative when admitted three days ago to evaluate a mass in her right lung, but unexpectedly this evening she "flipped out" and began shouting something about doctors cutting out holes in her chest.

When the psychiatric consultant arrived on the ward 15 minutes later, the situation had deteriorated. The patient had run onto the elevator in her night clothes and had bitten the head nurse when she tried to prevent the patient from leaving. Security guards had been called to help strap the patient in bed. She had then been given 100 mg amobarbital by intramuscular injection.

The consultant went with the intern to see the patient. A disheveled and drowsy woman lying restrained in bed, she fluctuated between screaming and thrashing or staring bewilderedly at the ceiling and rambling on about "pulling out the plug" or "getting dressed for the hairdresser." When the psychiatrist introduced himself, the patient responded for an instant, looked at who was speaking and gave an automatic, yet slurred "nice to know you," but she then abruptly turned away and spoke to the wall about "tall men dropping by unannounced."

After speaking with the patient for only a few minutes, the consultant had sufficient evidence to support the diagnosis of delirium: clouding of consciousness; diminished alertness with moment-to-moment fluctuations; limited attention span with distractability; disorientation to time and place; inability to organize and comprehend surroundings; impaired memory (particularly recent); concrete preoccupation with immediate stimuli (e.g., constantly ruminating about the consultant's name); loss of capacity to reflect and conceptualize; apparent visual illusions or hallucinations (e.g., talking to the blank wall); mislabeling of percepts (e.g., viewing the doctor as a gentleman caller); and bizarre thoughts without an internally consistent theme (e.g., ideas about the hairdresser and pulling the plug).

Although the nursing staff was still quite upset from the disruptive events during the previous half hour, the psychiatrist concluded after his brief assessment of the patient that the immediate crisis was essentially over and that nothing drastic was likely to happen medically or psychiatrically within the next half hour. He therefore stepped out into the hall with the intern to get more history. Apparently, the patient was a fairly intact widow who had been followed for years by one of the attending physicians because of her mild hypertension and congestive heart failure, both of which were made worse by her heavy cigarette smoking. A week before admission she complained to her doctor about a persistent cough; a mass in the upper right lobe was found on X ray and she was admitted for evaluation. A bronchoscopy was supposed to be done promptly upon her hospitalization, but because of various scheduling problems, the procedure had been delayed for three days. While waiting around in the hospital, in the intern's words, "tonight out of the blue the old lady simply went bananas."

Additional information was then obtained from the head nurse, who explained that the patient seemed a pleasant and spry "with it" woman when she arrived at the hospital with one of her three daughters and a son-in-law. Because she was a little anxious about the "lump" in her lung and because she slept restlessly the first night, she was started the next morning on diazepam 5 mg by mouth four times a day. She was so calm the next evening that she was napping when the daughter came to visit, and she slept off and on throughout the following day as well. In fact, the patient was so sleepy when visitors came that they had left a note rather than awakening her. The nurse wondered aloud whether the patient might have become upset when she awakened and read the note, but otherwise had no explanation for the disruptive incident.

The consultant obtained further information from a review of the chart. According to the nurse's notes, the patient gave a coherent and detailed history upon admission, but during the middle of the second night of hospitalization, she momentarily lost her way to the bathroom and had to be escorted back to bed. The medication sheet was also revealing: The patient had been continued on digoxin and chlorothiazide for her congestive heart failure and mild hypertension, but during the hospitalization, in addition to the diazepam she had also received ethyl turpin hydrin with codeine every three hours as necessary for her cough, Percodan every four hours for chest pain, and Benadryl 50 mg at night for difficulty sleeping.

Having the data from the intern, head nurse, medical chart and interview with the patient, the consultant decided on a treatment plan, while the staff waited eagerly for something to be done and while the elderly restrained patient continued to scream from her room.

DSM-III-R DIAGNOSIS

Axis I: Delirium
Axis II: None known
Axis III: Congestive heart failure, hypertension, possible pulmonary carcinoma
Axis IV: Stress—severe (hospitalization, pending surgical procedure)
Axis V: Highest level of functioning past year—unknown, but apparently managed her own personal affairs while living alone

TREATMENT PROBLEM

Disruptive behavior on a medical ward in a delirious elderly woman.

DISCUSSION OF TREATMENT SELECTION

Setting. This kind of disruptive behavior in a general hospital often leads to controversy concerning the best treatment setting. The staff on the medical unit may urge for the prompt and appropriate transfer of the patient to a psychiatric ward in the belief that the patient's behavior is unmanageable in a general hospital. If at all possible, such a transfer should be prevented because generally this kind of patient's medical care and evaluation are logistically much more difficult on a psychiatric ward. Furthermore, the patient's delirium has not yet been treated and may rapidly improve on the ward without traumatizing the patient and requiring her to acclimate to yet another strange setting.

Format. The patient's family and the nursing staff should be actively involved in applying the recommended psychological interventions. Many assume that talking with the delirious patient will be futile and frustrating and that only drugs can be effective. The opposite is more often true: These patients require an engaging relationship with another to become oriented and organized, whereas medication is more often the cause and not the cure for the confusion. To convince the staff and relatives that a direct psychological approach can be effective, the psychiatrist will need to involve them in the patient's treatment and have them witness how the delirious patient can be oriented and calmed down in the same way one reassures a child who awakens from a night terror (e.g., simple, declarative, and orienting sentences; correcting misperceptions the moment they occur; describing simply what is happening and what is about to happen in the near future).

Duration and Frequency. Ideally the duration of the staff's reassurance should be constant since delirious patients will quickly become confused if left alone. This time requirement is usually more than any one staff member has available and for this reason extended visiting privileges should be granted to suitable relatives. As the patient's sensorium begins to clear, the persistent vigil will be less necessary and frequent, brief contact will suffice.

Approach. The primary intervention during the acute delirious phase will be directive (telling the patient who she is, why she is hospitalized, what is planned, what is expected of her, etc.). As the delirium clears, exploratory techniques may be helpful in understanding the specific nature of the patient's fears, and experiential techniques may be helpful in offering the patient an opportunity to share these fears and receive an empathic response.

Somatic Treatment. Haloperidol is efficacious for acute confusion and agitation in the elderly. The limited postural hypotension and anticholinergic side effects are valuable features of this drug, whereas amobarbital, diazepam, Percodan and codeine (all of which this patient received during the hospitalization) may actually cause the kind of delirious disruption seen in this case. The therapeutic endpoint when administering the haloperidol should not be a completely clear sensorium, but rather, a sufficient diminution in the patient's agitation and confusion to make her manageable in the general hospital. If the haloperidol is given repeatedly in the expectation that the patient's confusion will completely resolve, too much of it is likely to be administered and this will result in oversedation. With this patient, if any psychotropic medication is required at all, 1 mg oral or parenteral haloperidol given every two to four hours for extreme agitation and unmanageable behavior would probably be sufficient. Antiparkinsonian drugs should not be administered prophylactically because severe dystonic reactions occur in less than 20% of patients and because these drugs can cause or worsen confusion.

Liaison Interventions. The treatment in this particular consultation will need to involve not only the patient but also the staff. Liaison interventions might include a clear documentation that the disruptive behavior is on an organic basis so that the enraged and frustrated doctors and nurses are not left with the impression that the patient has more control over her behavior than is in fact the case. Other suggestions to the staff would be to make the patient's unfamiliar surroundings more familiar (e.g., having relatives bring items off the dresser or bedside table at home, such as family pictures, a clock, a calendar; reading the patient a newspaper; keeping the television tuned to regularly watched programs; bringing in home cooking; avoiding keeping the patient off the ward for delayed procedures). Similarly, because delirious patients often become more confused and agitated if given too little or too much stimuli, the staff can be shown how to increase the stimuli when necessary (extending visiting hours throughout the day; moving the patient's room nearer to the nurses' station; arranging for the patient to have a suitable roommate; having a close friend or relative telephone around nine or 10 o'clock at night; leaving a quiet radio on; maintaining a night light that is placed so that it does not make upsetting moving shadows). Conversely, the staff can be shown ways to decrease stimuli (arranging for a private room; limiting visitors to those who are actually familiar to the patient; keeping visiting periods brief and cheerful; regulating the patient's sleeping patterns).

A most important liaison function for this particular patient would be to make sure that the staff searches for an etiology to the patient's delirium and does not simply attribute the evident organic problem to the patient's age or to the stress of hospitalization.

CHOICE AND OUTCOME

The consultant indicated both in his note and directly to the head nurse and intern that he believed the patient's acute organic mental syndrome (delirium) was causing her panic, agitation, belligerence, and visual hallucinations. He indicated that although the etiology of the delirium was unknown, one very likely possibility was that the various medications had led to drowsiness, confusion, and a change in her sleep pattern; this, in turn, had made her less able to cope with the stresses of hospitalization, the impending test, and the threat of cancer. He recommended that the patient's nonessential medications be discontinued, and that an effort be made to titrate the patient's stimuli, to adjust her sleep patterns by having her ambulate during the day instead of letting her nap, and to have reliable relatives come and stay with her for the purpose of orientation and support. He further recommended that the patient be given 2 mg oral haloperidol that night and then 1 mg every two to three hours up to a total of 8 mg, if she remained unmanageable and combative.

When the psychiatry resident paged the intern the following morning to find out how the patient was doing, he reported that the situation had improved, the patient no longer required restraints, and her daughter was spending the day with her. When the consultant came by to see the patient later that afternoon, he discovered that her sensorium had cleared remarkably. Off all nonessential medications, she still felt "hung over," but was conversing coherently and animatedly with her daughter and was somewhat embarrassed about her behavior when told what she had done.

Because the surgery had been postponed over the weekend, she was given a day pass and accompanied by her daughter. The pass helped reestablish the patient's confidence; it also implicitly conveyed that the staff did not view her as "crazy," but rather as someone who had become confused in the hospital because of a sensitivity to the medications she had received. When she returned from the day out, her fears about the biopsy were talked over with the psychiatrist in the presence of two daughters, who also had a chance to talk about their fears of the mother's illness.

The patient tolerated the rest of the hospitalization well, but her fears proved to be true: An inoperable lesion was found throughout her lungs. After four months of living first alone in her apartment and then with a daughter, she was readmitted later that year and died after a few days of hospitalization.

SUGGESTED READING

1. Hackett, T. D., & Cassem, N. H. (Eds.). *Massachusetts General Hospital Handbook of General Hospital Psychiatry.* St. Louis: Mosby, 1978. (A practical guide for management of psychiatric problems in the physically ill.)

2. Drugs that cause psychiatric symptoms. *Medical Letters* (No. 576), 23:9–12, 1981. (A handy reference.)
3. Lishman, W. A. *Organic Psychiatry: The Psychological Consequences of Cerebral Disorder.* Philadelphia: Lippincott, 1978. (Encyclopedic in scope, yet readable and clinically-oriented.)
4. Perry, S., & Viederman, M. Management of emotional reactions to acute medical illness. In L. Sherman & H. Kolodny (Eds.), *Medical Clinics of North America,* 65:3–4, 1981. (Approach for physically ill patients who deny illness, do not comply with treatment, become disorganized, regress inappropriately, etc.)
5. Salzman, D., Green, A. I., Rodriguez-Villa, F., et al. Benzodiazepines combined with neuroleptics for acute and severe disruptive behavior. *Psychosomatics,* 27:S17–21, 1986. (Alternative pharmacological approach used for this patient.)

2. The Case of the Elderly Dysphoric

(Guest Expert: Paul Teusink, M.D.)

Authors' Note:
Dr. Teusink is Associate Director of Adult Services at Four Winds Hospital, Katonah, New York. He presents the case of a confused elderly woman and discusses the important differential diagnosis between a psychogenic depression versus a disorder due to either side effects of medication or an underlying medical problem. The case also demonstrates the important role of psychotherapy in the treatment of the elderly.

Mrs. T is a 79-year-old wife and retired schoolteacher who was in good emotional health until her husband was hospitalized for 10 days for relatively minor surgery. About a month after her husband returned home, he and two married daughters, who do not live at home, reported a noticeable change in Mrs. T's mental status. She became somewhat hyperactive and seemed to have excessive energy, was irritable and agitated at times, had difficulty getting to sleep at night, and became preoccupied with concerns that she was going to die. She began to prepare for death and wanted to visit relatives in the Midwest in order to see them for the last time.

Mrs. T was taken to see a psychiatrist, who made a diagnosis of depression and started her on imipramine. Shortly after, Mrs. T's agitation decreased slightly, but she began to have difficulty remembering recent events and at times was confused and disoriented. The daughters thought, in retrospect, that she may have had some mild memory impairment for the previous six months. Her confusion and disorientation continued, and after about six weeks she called the police one day, telling them she was being poisoned by pills she was being given.

At this point she was admitted to a psychiatric hospital, where she was diagnosed as having an acute hypomanic reaction. Her antidepressants were discontinued, and she was treated first with haloperidol and then with a phenothiazine, showing some improvement. Psychological testing showed what appeared to be a decrease in intelligence, as well as markedly impaired learning and recent memory. There was no indication of functional psychosis, and the origin of her difficulties was felt to be organic.

The patient was discharged, and after being home about two weeks, she developed parkinsonian symptoms with severe rigidity. Her neuroleptics were discontinued, and desipramine was begun. Mrs. T's condition then deteriorated again, the desipramine was stopped, and she was started on thioridazine. She became disoriented to time and place, markedly confused, and incontinent, and began wandering away from home. When she encountered anyone, she became abusive and assaultive both verbally and physically.

After about two weeks Mrs. T was admitted to another psychiatric hospital. Her mental status examination on admission showed her to be disoriented to time and place, agitated, and confused, with both verbal and visual hallucinations and assaultive behavior. The initial diagnostic impression was of a psychotic depression superimposed on a dementing illness. Amitriptyline was added to her thioridazine, and her condition deteriorated further. She had no peripheral signs of excessive anticholinergic effects except for dry mouth.

All medications were discontinued, and Mrs. T's condition rapidly improved. Her agitation and confusion cleared over a few days, as did her psychotic thinking and assaultiveness. Mild cognitive deficits, particularly poor learning and recent memory, persisted for several months but gradually improved. Mrs. T remained depressed, with little energy. She was socially withdrawn and preoccupied with fears about the future, particularly focused on financial issues, and fears that her husband could not provide adequately for her. She showed no evidence of psychotic thinking, however.

Mrs. T was born in the Midwest, where her father, who was a good provider, suddenly died when she was eight years old. It was a profound loss for her and threw her family into poverty, since they lost both businesses that the father had owned. She attended college, however, working to support herself, and married at age 24. Her husband, who was a college graduate, was somewhat of a romantic who wanted to be a writer. He turned out to be a poor provider, and at times the patient had to teach school to support him and her two daughters.

During her mid-thirties the patient became increasingly dysphoric, particularly for a few weeks each year around the time of her father's death. Because of these symptoms, she underwent psychoanalysis for several years. Although she found it helpful, she continued to become dysphoric annually around the date of her father's death. However, she suffered no major depressions, and had no history of any other psychiatric disorder until her husband's hospitalization. There also was no history of psychiatric illness in any relatives.

DSM-III-R DIAGNOSIS

Axis I: Dysthymia; Anticholinergic delirium
Axis II: No diagnosis
Axis III: Osteoporosis
Axis IV: Stress—moderate (hospitalization of husband)
Axis V: Highest level of functioning past year—very good

DISCUSSION OF TREATMENT SELECTION

This case illustrates many of the difficulties that arise in both the diagnosis and the treatment of depressive illness in the elderly. Mrs. T was most likely suffering a relatively mild reactive depression after her husband's hospitalization for minor surgery, which also occurred at the time of her yearly dysthymic reaction to her father's death.

Her husband's hospitalization also seemed to reawaken fears that she would be abandoned and left destitute, in part a reactivation of the trauma of her father's death, which had never been entirely worked through in her previous psychoanalysis. When the patient received antidepressants for her dysphoria, she developed an acute organic brain syndrome secondary to the drugs' anticholinergic effects. The syndrome was misidentified as a dementia until her second hospitalization.

The early signs of memory loss recalled by her daughters may have simply been normal difficulties with recall, which the elderly tend to develop. Mrs. T also did not show the fluctuating course typical of most acute deliriums; rather, her symptoms presented as a florid organic psychosis. Although she initially appeared severely demented, this pseudodementia should have been distinguished from true dementia by its fairly clear and rapid onset, her dysphoric mood, her sudden loss of social skills, both recent and remote memory loss, and her variable performance on psychological testing.

The presence of prominent anticholinergic side effects is a frequent and often difficult complication of treating elderly patients with psychotropic drugs. Peripheral anticholinergic effects such as decreased sweating, dry mouth, and constipation are commonly seen in young and old patients alike. In the elderly these effects are frequently more troublesome, and even reduced doses of drugs can cause more profound peripheral effects, such as dilation of the pupils, increased heart rate, and urinary retention. This case demonstrates that the central anticholinergic syndrome can occasionally occur without much evidence of peripheral anticholinergic effects.

Symptoms of central anticholinergic syndrome include excitement, agitation, confusion, paranoid delusions, hallucinations, suicidal intentions, stupor, ataxia, and dysarthria. All these symptoms rapidly disappear when the drug is withdrawn. Granacher and Baldessarini[1] recommend treating such reactions with physostigmine, a parenteral anticholinesterase, which promptly reverses the effect of the drug. This procedure is not without complications in the elderly, however; I do not recommend it since simply discontinuing the medications should lead to rapid clearing of the acute organic brain syndrome.

The differentiation of pseudodementia from true dementias is often difficult. Pseudodementia is usually characterized by a relatively clear onset, some degree of awareness of the memory problems, complaints about memory loss, a relatively rapid progression of symptoms, a depressed mood, variable performance on cognitive testing, and a loss or decrease in both recent and remote memory, with free recall impaired but recognition memory intact. Cognitive functioning also tends to worsen at night.

True dementias usually have a more vague onset, and a denial of the memory problems tends to be more prominent. The course is usually slower, and rarely is there a history of previous psychiatric symptoms or disorders, as is usually present in pseudodementia. In dementia, mood tends to be blunted or labile rather than depressed, social skills may be relatively well retained, early memory loss is usually for recent events, and both free recall and recognition memory are impaired. True dementias also often worsen at night.

In practice, 10%–20% of dementias are misdiagnosed and turn out to be pseudodementias. Although guidelines are helpful in differentiating the two disorders, they are by no means foolproof. When there is any

question about the diagnosis, and when there are no medical contraindications, a course of antidepressant therapy should probably be given.

CHOICE AND OUTCOME

In Mrs. T's case, once the medications were discontinued, there was
no longer a question about dementia. She was clearly depressed but not
psychotically so. Because of her exquisite sensitivity to the anticholinergic effects of psychotropics, psychotherapy and marital counseling
became the treatments of choice.

Clearly the husband's hospitalization had reawakened fears of abandonment that had been a theme throughout this woman's life. The task
for psychotherapy, therefore, became one of examining whether her
fears were legitimate—and if they were legitimate, to determine what
could be done to lessen them, and if they were not, what the unconscious sources were. Mrs. T expressed anxiety not only about her husband's health but also about his ability to continue to provide for them
financially. Actually he had recovered nicely from his surgery and was in
excellent physical health. As she had become more dependent in recent
years, he had become more responsible in providing for her. In fact,
since her retirement he was working steadily for the first time in his life.

Initially, the patient was seen weekly in individual psychotherapy.
Joint sessions were held occasionally to help reinforce the patient's perceptions that indeed her husband was in good health and was providing
well for her. During these sessions he would review their financial situation and confront her misperceptions.

In her individual sessions Mrs. T was able to review the profound
losses she experienced with the death of her father and the subsequent
financial losses to the family. She was able to see how the resulting
anxieties had influenced and still influenced her perception of her financial and emotional security. She began to realize that her own anxieties
and her need to control the financial situation may have played a role in
her husband's apparent irresponsibility early in their marriage. This acknowledgment led to a temporary recurrence of depressive mood, which
gradually improved as she realized how much influence she had always
had within this relationship. As her treatment progressed, Mrs. T was
able to take a less dependent stance, and the joint sessions allowed her
to confront her husband's somewhat insensitive way of relating to her.

In conjunction with the psychotherapy, the patient was strongly
encouraged to pursue her own interests in socializing and enjoying the
arts. She had done nothing without her husband for years, but again

began to attend group activities at her church and cultural events with friends. These activities helped her reestablish a sense of being able to provide for herself.

After these initial gains were accomplished, psychotherapy was gradually decreased from one session a week to approximately one every two months. The positive transferential aspects of the relationship with the therapist were preserved by not terminating the relationship. Mrs. T has continued to function well now for three years, and has been able to maintain these gains through her husband's subsequent rehospitalization and through her own hospitalization when she fell and broke her hip.

Pfeiffer[2] has suggested that significant modifications in techniques used in psychotherapy must be made to accommodate the special needs and limitations of older people. These modifications include greater activity by the therapist, symbolic giving within the therapeutic relationship, specific or limited goals in therapy, increased awareness of the differences in transference and countertransference phenomena, and empathic understanding of elderly patients. In my experience, psychotherapy with the elderly can be an effective means of treatment in carefully selected cases.

REFERENCES

1. Granacher, R. P., & Baldessarini, R. J. Physostigmine: Its use in acute anticholinergic syndrome with antidepressant and antiparkinson drugs. *Archives of General Psychiatry*, 32:375–380, 1975. (Indications and drug administration clearly presented.)
2. Pfeiffer, E. Psychotherapy with elderly patients. In L. Bellak & T. Karasu (Eds.), *Geriatric Psychiatry*. New York: Grune & Stratton, 1976. (Surprisingly, more similarities than differences in treating older populations.)
3. Perry, S. Substance-induced organic mental disorders. In R. Hales & S. Yudofsky (Eds.), *Textbook of Neuropsychiatry*. Washington, DC: American Psychiatric Press, Inc., 1987. (Focuses on substances commonly used and abused by psychiatric patients.)

■ PRIMARY DEGENERATIVE DEMENTIA, PRESENILE ONSET, WITH DELUSION

3. The Case of the Perplexed Woman

(Historical Case: Alois Alzheimer)

Authors' Note:
In 1907 Alzheimer described the clinical and pathological findings of a middle-aged woman who developed a severe "senile" dementia. In recognition of this contribution, Kraepelin subsequently termed this presenile dementia "Alzheimer's disease." Although there remains some controversy about the exact relation of this condition to the common idiopathic dementia that occurs in the elderly, Alzheimer's precise description of the disorder has stood the test of time.

A woman, 51 years old, showed jealousy towards her husband as the first noticeable sign of the disease. Soon a rapidly increasing loss of memory could be noticed. She could not find her way around in her own apartment. She carried objects back and forth and hid them. At times she would think that someone wanted to kill her and would begin shrieking loudly.

In the institution her entire behavior bore the stamp of utter perplexity. She was totally disoriented to time and place. Occasionally she stated that she could not understand and did not know her way around. At times she greeted the doctor like a visitor, and excused herself for not having finished her work; at times she shrieked loudly that he wanted to cut her, or she repulsed him with indignation, saying that she feared from him something against her chastity. Periodically she was totally delirious, dragged her bedding around, called her husband and her daughter, and seemed to have auditory hallucinations. Frequently, she shrieked with a dreadful voice for many hours.

Because of her inability to comprehend the situation, she always cried out loudly as soon as someone tried to examine her. Only through repeated attempts was it possible finally to ascertain anything.

Her ability to remember was severely disturbed. If one pointed to objects, she named most of them correctly, but immediately afterwards she would forget everything again. When reading, she went from one line into another, reading the letters or reading with a senseless emphasis. When writing, she repeated individual syllables several times, left out others, and quickly became stranded. When talking, she frequently used perplexing phrases and some paraphrastic expressions (mild-pourer instead of cup). Sometimes one noticed her getting stuck. Some questions she obviously did not comprehend. She seemed no longer to understand the use of some objects. Her gait was not impaired. She could use both hands equally well. Her patellar reflexes were present. Her pupils reacted. Somewhat rigid radial arteries; no enlargement of cardiac dullness; no albumin.

During her subsequent course, the phenomena that were interpreted as focal symptoms were at times more noticeable and at times less noticeable. But always they were only slight. The generalized dementia progressed however. After four-and-a-half years of the disease, death occurred. At the end, the patient was completely stuporous; she lay in her bed with her legs drawn up under her, and in spite of all precautions she acquired decubitus ulcers.

ALZHEIMER'S DIAGNOSIS

A peculiar disease of the cerebral cortex

DSM-III-R DIAGNOSIS

Axis I: Primary degenerative dementia, presenile onset, with delusions

TREATMENT PROBLEM

A woman approaching her mid-fifties with a deteriorating dementia, which began insidiously at age 51 with delusional jealousy and which now is characterized by persecutory delusions, auditory hallucinations, disorientation to time, place, and person, markedly impaired immediate and recent memory, aphasia, agnosia, apraxia, echolalia, perseveration, and agitated, disruptive behavior.

DISCUSSION OF TREATMENT SELECTION

Even if this middle-aged woman described by Alzheimer were 30 years older, the first step in her treatment should be an extensive evaluation. Despite the time, effort, and expense involved, a thorough diagnostic assessment has a 15%–20% chance of detecting a reversible dementia (e.g., benign tumors, depression, normal pressure hydrocephalus, pernicious anemia, hypothyroidism, subdural hematoma, drug toxicity, or epilepsy), and another 20%–25% chance of finding a disease that can be improved if not cured by effective medical management (e.g., hypertensive encephalopathy, alcoholic dementia). In those cases in which a reversible or at least treatable cause is not found, the evaluation can nevertheless be helpful to reassure the patient and family that all available, potentially curative treatments have been considered. Appropriate guidance can then be given regarding the prognosis of the dementia, its suspected course, and the patient's possible requirements for supportive care.

The diagnostic assessment begins with obtaining a detailed history from a family member. Perhaps this patient's daughter and husband who first noticed the mental changes could correlate the onset with medical problems or the use of drugs. A waxing and waning course would be more suggestive of a vascular etiology, whereas a steady decline, such as occurred in this patient, would indicate an Alzheimer's type of dementia.

In addition to a complete physical, neurological, mental status, and cerebral spinal fluid examination, the diagnostic workup would include an electrocardiogram, electroencephalogram (EEG), chest X ray, computerized axial tomography (CAT scan), drug screen, and laboratory test (complete blood count, urine analysis, serology, serum thyroxine, folate, B12, electrolytes, liver enzymes, urea nitrogen, creatinine, and perhaps ceruloplasm and uroporphyrins). A helpful mnemonic to organize these diagnostic considerations is DEMENTIA:

D—drug intoxication;

E—emotional disturbances (e.g., depression);

M—metabolic/endocrine (e.g., diabetes, hyperthyroidism);

E—eyes and ears (insidiously producing a pseudodementia);

N—nutritional (e.g., iron, thiamine, or folate deficiency);

T—tumor and trauma (e.g., menigioma, subdural hematoma);

I—infection (e.g., brain abscess, fungal infection);

A—arteriosclerotic (e.g., coronary artery disease, carotid artery obstruction, autoimmune vasculitis).

We know that this particular patient did not have any of the more treatable diagnostic possibilities for, coincidentally, she represented the first case to reveal the characteristic histopathological changes of what has become known as Alzheimer's disease. We would therefore assume that her EEG probably would have showed diffuse slowing, that her CAT scan would have revealed cortical atrophy, and that her other laboratory data would have been generally normal. These findings would not, however, have precluded the necessity of selecting the best treatment plan for managing her illness.

Setting. In the early stages of the patient's illness, every reasonable effort should be made to keep this patient in a structured, monitored, and supportive home environment. Patients with even a mild dementia have difficulty adjusting to new environments. Despite the best care and facilities provided by nursing homes and institutions, this patient would probably receive more personally tailored attention in familiar surroundings where she does not have to interact with strangers. Auxiliary help from visiting nurses or homemakers could be arranged if necessary. If the patient became too disruptive or dangerous to manage at home, even with the help of medication, or if the relatives and ancillary help could no longer provide the necessary support and monitoring, then institutional care may be unavoidable.

Format and Approach. Family sessions can be used to educate both the patient and her relatives about the nature of the disease, the indications and side effects of prescribed medications, and the management of the patient's delusional ideas and disruptive behavior. For example, when the patient misperceives or becomes disoriented, the family can be instructed to correct the patient's distortions and help orient her to time, place, and person; and when the patient becomes disruptive—dragging her bedding around or shrieking with dreadful voice for many hours— the family will need guidance about how and when to administer the prescribed medications and how to set firm limits.

The therapist can also explain the value of maintaining a set schedule, having familiar people and objects in the patient's presence, limiting naps, encouraging ambulation, and titrating external stimuli so that the patient is neither alone in the dark without some light and some noise (e.g., a soft-playing radio) nor in situations in which the stimuli are overwhelming (crowds, loud noises, unfamiliar topics, etc.). Family sessions will also provide a format for members to discuss any feelings of resentment or guilt that might arise from being forced to tolerate the patient's strange behavior or from having to institutionalize the one they love. The therapist can honestly state that institutional care with an experienced staff can actually be more comforting and comfortable for those patients with a severe dementia whose capacities are so limited and who become overwhelmingly distressed by even the simplest demands of living at home.

Duration and Frequency. The deteriorating course of presenile dementia can be quite prolonged. This patient suffered from the disease for four-and-a-half years. Accordingly, the treatment plan should consider from the start the personal and financial resources that may be required. In terms of frequency, the patient should not be left without interpersonal contact during large segments of the day, but this contact should generally be cheerful and superficial in nature and sufficient to note the response, indications, and side effects of prescribed medication, as well as to orient the patient and correct misperceptions.

Somatic Treatment. After reports that choline acetyltransferase was markedly decreased in the cortices of patients with this disease, investigators have tried to reverse the specific cholinergic deficiency by administering choline, lecithin, arecoline, and cholinesterase inhibitors. The results have in general been disappointing and are still under investigation. At present, psychopharmacological management consists primarily of using neuroleptics to decrease the confusion, agitation, and misperceptions. In this patient, haloperidol 1 mg by mouth at night on a maintenance basis may be helpful in decreasing her disruptive behavior and reorganizing her sleep pattern. Depending on how this medication is tolerated, higher doses may be necessary. Hypnotics and sedatives in general should be avoided, because they can produce a paradoxical agitation, hyperactivity, and confusion.

SUGGESTED READING

1. Crook, T., & Gershon, S. (Eds.). *Strategies for the Development of an Effective Treatment for Senile Dementia.* New Canaan, CT: Mark Powley, 1981. (Emphasis on current and future pharmacologic treatments.)
2. Mace, N. L., & Rabins, P. V. *The 36-Hour Day.* Baltimore: Johns Hopkins University Press, 1981. (Written for the layperson, but also useful for professionals concerned with care of the elderly with or without dementia.)
3. Reisberg, B., Ferris, S. H., & Gershon, S. Overview of pharmacologic treatment of cognitive decline in the aged. *American Journal of Psychiatry,* 138:593–600, 1981. (Introduction to problem, with superb bibliography.)
4. Perry, S., Markowitz, J. Organic mental disorders. In J. A. Talbott, R. E. Hales, S. C. Yudofsky (Eds.), *Textbook of Psychiatry.* Washington, DC: American Psychiatric Press, Inc., 1988. (Summary of more recent advances in etiology and diagnosis.)

■ ORGANIC PERSONALITY DISORDER

4. The Case of the Wallowing Writer

Mr. F is a 28-year-old unpublished author referred for psychiatric consultation by his neurologist, who felt the patient was functioning far beneath his capacities and was probably depressed. The neurologist, a longtime friend of the family, had been following Mr. F for many years because of the patient's well-controlled temporal lobe epilepsy, which began when he was 12.

Mr. F, a burly and brusque-mannered man, started the consultation in an outspoken and somewhat argumentative fashion. He announced that he had taken a few psychology courses in college and had concluded that the entire specialty—as well as those who practiced it—were all "nuts"; but rather than offend his friendly neurologist and be viewed as a "wise guy" he had agreed to come for one visit. Furthermore, Mr. F stated from the start that he did not agree with the neurologist's diagnosis of depression. He was willing to concede that "conventional folks" might consider his life as something less than a total success, because he had dropped out of three different preparatory schools and four different colleges without obtaining a degree, and because he had written five novels and countless short stories, none of which had been published. However, he saw these "so-called problems" as no more than the plight of an artist whose "philosophy of life" differed from the masses in general and from his family in particular.

When asked to elaborate on his unique philosophy of life, Mr. F launched a verbose, platitudinal, and impossibly detailed lecture that was sprinkled with various ideas enunciated by Christ, Muhammad Ali, Norman Vincent Peale, Hemingway, and Confucius, but without any conceptual organization. When asked about more personal matters, such as his current relationships or his childhood, Mr. F maintained the same opinionated, cliché-filled style of relating and revealed only that his mother was nervous, his father was a successful physician, and his two older siblings were accomplished professionals. In contrast, Mr. F lived alone in a small apartment, socializing little and writing night and day.

By the end of the first session, the consultant had little more information than the paucity of facts presented above. The problem in obtaining a more thorough history was that Mr. F measured his words carefully, as though they were going to be carved in stone. Attempts to elicit a more spontaneous response repeatedly failed, as Mr. F slowly and deliberately appeared "stuck" on the previous idea and could only sluggishly move to the next thought. Because of this problem, a second consultation visit was scheduled and only towards the end of that second visit was the consultant able to obtain more specific information about Mr. F's seizure disorder and his feelings about this illness.

The seizures (generalized motor with an aura of nausea and irritability) began unpredictably at the onset of adolescence. Until that time, Mr. F had been regarded as a smart aleck in grade school and less capable academically than his siblings, but he had always been in good health. The cause of the seizures was not determined; however, the left-sided focus was easily found on EEG, and temporal lobe atrophy was found with axial tomography. In retrospect, the family and neurologist felt that Mr. F's argumentative manner and failure to complete a task, both in grade school and at home, may have been related all along to the underlying temporal lobe lesion. But Mr. F himself dismissed such "guesstimates" and believed he simply "danced to a different drummer." During the interview, he also dismissed the consultant's questions about his relationships with others and his financial arrangement with the family as "middle-class" questions that were not relevant to his unique interests. As far as Mr. F was concerned, because he had not had a seizure for years and had developed no serious side effects with the anticonvulsant medication, everything was fine—and yet, as the second session drew to a close, he asked the consultant matter-of-factly when the next appointment would be, volunteering that he found these discussions "interesting."

DSM-III-R DIAGNOSIS

Axis I: Organic personality disorder
Axis II: None
Axis III: Temporal lobe epilepsy
Axis IV: Stress—none apparent
Axis V: Highest level of functioning past year—fair (takes care of himself in his own apartment but has only intellectual discussions and superficial relationships, and continues to require financial support from his parents)

TREATMENT PROBLEM

A young man with a well-controlled temporal lobe seizure disorder. Both in his life and during the consultation, he appears "stuck" in his philosophical ruminations, while explaining his isolation, argumentativeness, and failures as an author as being attributes and testimonies to his uniqueness.

DISCUSSION OF TREATMENT SELECTION

Setting. This decision is easy: Outpatient treatment is the only reasonable choice.

Format. A family format might be helpful in reaching some preliminary goals, such as making Mr. F more financially responsible for his own affairs and less dependent on his parents, who may be inadvertently infantilizing him. After these goals are reached, a continuing family format might keep Mr. F too close to the nest and impede his establishing a more independent life.

A heterogeneous group might be an option to consider in the future to help Mr. F understand how his argumentative, philosophizing manner turns people away; however, without some preliminary work, Mr. F might simply reject the suggestion of a group and even if he did accept this suggestion, he no doubt would be attacked by outspoken group members. A therapeutic alliance would need to be well established to help buffer these blows. Another consideration in terms of a heterogeneous group is Mr. F's potential to elicit countertransferential problems. A heterogeneous group could diffuse a negative countertransferential response if and when it should develop. The therapist would need to be sure that the referral to a group was not made in hopes that members of the group would act out the therapist's hostile feelings towards Mr. F.

A homogeneous group consisting of other patients with similar problems might make sense, but would be difficult to form, except in conjunction with a large neurology clinic. Most likely, Mr. F's treatment will be predominantly within an individual format.

Duration and Frequency. Weekly hour-long sessions with an unstated date of termination will probably be the best way to start. Sessions that are more frequent might in the early phases be too threatening for Mr. F, who would prefer to view the sessions as "classes." Extending the customary 45-minute hour to one full hour will probably be necessary because of Mr. F's tendency to be "viscous" and sluggishly move from topic to topic. Once a closer relationship is established, sessions will probably need to be more frequent in order to generate sufficient intensity for Mr. F to make character and life changes. Dates of termination—or at least dates to accomplish certain goals—will need to be stated as a therapeutic maneuver to confront Mr. F's tendency to live day by day without any reasonable plans for the future. These measures might prevent treatment from becoming simply one more unpublished novel—endless ramblings that never come to the point.

Approach. At first glance, Mr. F appears refractory to whatever interventions might be tried. He dismisses any exploratory treatments as "theorizing"; he is not interested in any behavioral/cognitive approaches because he finds nothing in his emotional state, thoughts, or deeds that he would like to change; and he also admits to no desire for an empathic relationship that would be the foundation of an experiential approach. And yet Mr. F's protestations may be somewhat misleading: There are subtle indications that he wants help and would be willing to accept it. He has complied with his medical treatment and has established a close relationship with his neurologist; he accepted the recommendation for psychiatric consultation with minimal fuss; he kept his second consultation visit and implicitly asked for a third session with the consultant; and even his choosing psychology courses in college may be an indication that he is more interested in himself and emotional issues than he is comfortable admitting.

If these subtle clues are indeed indications that Mr. F is hurting and wants help, then the preferred initial approach would be an experiential one, that is, offering a face-saving kind of treatment that would not at first explore dynamic conflicts or push for behavioral change. Instead, for some time the therapist would leave unchallenged Mr. F's desire to have "philosophical discussions." After a comfortable relationship had been established, the therapist could gradually attempt to modify Mr. F's annoying behavioral traits, first by depersonalizing these traits and describing them as neurological characteristic features of the disease. The second step would be to design a behavioral program that would limit Mr. F's hypergraphia and establish less grand goals which he could complete.

Somatic Treatment. Given the remarkably good control of Mr. F's seizure disorder, no adjustments in his medication appear warranted at this time, nor are psychotropics likely to be effective in altering the personality characteristics associated with Mr. F's temporal lobe seizures.

CHOICE AND OUTCOME

Mr. F began the third consultation as though he had been in treatment for months, making himself comfortable in his usual chair and spontaneously beginning the hour by discussing a religious book he was reading and that he found particularly meaningful. The session was more than half over before the consultant could actually interrupt and discuss the main issue at hand, namely, whether Mr. F should have a psychiatric treatment at this time and, if so, what kind of treatment and with whom. With unanticipated candor, Mr. F said that he assumed the consultant would be the therapist, though the consultant had actually stated from the beginning that such might not be the case. As though anticipating the referral to another therapist, Mr. F acknowledged in a roundabout way that he enjoyed speaking with the consultant and would not like to face another "rejection," although he had never before mentioned any feelings of being rejected whatsoever.

The consultant accepted this statement by Mr. F as a request for help and, without explicitly stating what the goals and process of treatment would be, began meeting with Mr. F weekly in a supportive psychodynamically based therapy. Only after four months of treatment did Mr. F stop philosophizing and start discussing more personal concerns— his feelings of being less accomplished than his siblings, the repeated rejections from prospective publishers, and the sadness he felt when the therapist went on a month's vacation in the summer.

Using this sense of loneliness as an opening, the therapist then suggested that Mr. F enter a heterogeneous group to examine and work out the problems he had in interacting and establishing closeness with others. The turning point in treatment came when many of the group members, as predicted, confronted Mr. F and explained how his philosophical ruminations were boring preoccupations that drove people away. Though upset, Mr. F did not fall apart or go into a rage. Instead, he admitted quite openly that he was unaware of the effect that he had on others.

While Mr. F continued to attend the heterogeneous group, the therapist began videotaping individual sessions. Half the session was taped, then the second half was used to look at the videotape. The goal was to make Mr. F aware of his behavior and how, even with the therapist whom he respected and liked, Mr. F rambled on and on as though impervious to the other person in the room. With this awareness, Mr. F was more willing to accept some cognitive and behavioral programs that were designed to "teach" him to talk no more than one minute, then wait 30 seconds to receive the responses of others before proceeding. With difficulty, Mr. F was able to implement this rather mechanical method of altering his behavior.

A similar technique was used to modify his hypergraphia. He was instructed to condense each rambling paragraph to two or three declarative sentences that captured the central idea. Whether for psychological or organic reasons, Mr. F was never very successful in completing this task. Nevertheless, in the process of trying to complete it, Mr. F came to recognize, with understandable despair, that his writings were not artistic enterprises, but rather the same bland ruminations that had annoyed and bored the group members. With this painful recognition, Mr. F lowered his sights, no longer aspired to be the next great American novelist, and resigned himself to a computer technology school that offered the kinds of structure, both in the school and in the work, that Mr. F required.

After completing the computer courses, Mr. F took a job located 300 miles from the therapist. Over the next several years, he would call every few months to "touch base" and let the therapist know how he was doing, which, all things considered, was quite well. He was now financially self-sufficient, dated frequently, was being promoted at the usual pace through the company, and felt that he had come to terms with his limitations; however, even when speaking on the phone, his tendency to stay stuck on various themes and to ruminate philosophically without any sense of how he was affecting the listener was apparent. From time to time, either through these phone calls or through conversations with the neurologist who continued to follow Mr. F, the therapist would keep in touch, but in view of the chronic underlying neurological problem, he never was quite sure how much of Mr. F's difficulties would ever change.

SUGGESTED READING

1. Yalom, I. D. *The Theory and Practice of Group Psychotherapy* [third edition]. New York: Basic Books, 1985. (Remains the basic text regarding this format.)
2. Berger, M. M. (Ed.). *Videotape Techniques in Psychiatric Training and Treatment.* New York: Brunner/Mazel, 1978. (Modern technology as a didactic and therapeutic tool.)
3. Bear, D. M., Freeman, R., Greenberg, M. Behavioral alterations in patients with temporal lobe epilepsy. In D. Blumer (Ed.), *Psychiatric Aspects of Epilepsy.* Washington, DC: American Psychiatric Press, Inc., 1989. (Helpful in distinguishing peri-ictal and interictal phenomena and their treatment.)
4. Benson, D. F. Interictal behavior disorders in epilepsy. *Psychiatric Clinics of North America,* 9:283–291, 1986.

■ ORGANIC MOOD DISORDER

5. The Case of the Irate Quadriplegic

(Guest Experts: Marshall R. Thomas, M.D.,
and Troy L. Thompson, II, M.D.)

Authors' Note:
Thomas and Thompson discuss the treatment planning for a man with chronic crippling medical and psychiatric problems who developed an iatrogenic manic psychosis.

Mr. B is a 35-year-old single male who has been wheelchair-bound since a motorcycle accident that created a partial C-5 quadriplegia one year prior to this admission to the urology service for obstructive uropathy. Subsequent to the accident he developed spasticity, a neurogenic bowel syndrome, and a neurogenic bladder with recurrent urinary tract infections, bilateral nephrocalcinosis, and acute renal failure. In addition, he reportedly had "psychiatric problems" that made it difficult for him to get along with doctors and nurses.

Mr. B had an unhappy childhood. He twice fell out of a second-story window and, at age six, was hit by an automobile driven by his mother. His father was allegedly quite strict. As an adolescent, the patient became quite rebellious and involved with illicit drugs, gang activities, and auto theft. The three months that he spent in reform school during adolescence were considered by him as the happiest times of his life.

He has been married five times with two children by his first marriage, but their whereabouts are unknown. He has had numerous impulsive and self-damaging fights due to his temper and drug abuse. He has not held a steady job since being discharged 10 years previously from the Marine Corps. Prior to the accident, his primary social activity was as a member of a motorcycle gang.

During this hospitalization, his urinary output decreased, despite antibiotics and nephrostomy tubes. When surgery was recommended, he became increasingly uncooperative, argued for more pain medications, and refused both blood drawing and care for his sacral ulcers. Following supportive therapy with a psychiatric consultant, the patient agreed to surgery but then, in the operating room, refused to have an intravenous or to allow the procedure. Without notifying the consulting psychiatrist, the frustrated surgeons discharged Mr. B against medical advice that very day for refusing treatment.

The next day Mr. B returned to the hospital and agreed to the surgical procedure. After surgery he became even more demanding of pain medications, cigarettes, and a television in his room. He pushed the nursing call button several hundred times daily and would begin yelling and swearing if a nurse did not respond within one or two minutes. He threatened to have the staff fired, claimed that a staff member had assaulted him, and demanded to see the hospital administrator.

In response to Mr. B's repeated complaints relating to his spasticity (and perhaps in response to their own frustrations), the urologist more than doubled Mr. B's baclofen to 25 mg q4h. Over the next four weeks Mr. B became progressively more pleasant and euphoric. Although he slept and ate very little and left the ward in his wheelchair to "preach the word of God," several days passed before psychiatric consultation was again sought. The psychiatrist diagnosed an organic affective disorder, manic type, due to baclofen toxicity. The baclofen was tapered and low-dose haloperidol was begun. When Mr. B was no longer euphoric and his hostile personality returned, the nursing staff and urologist experienced partial dismay.

Following stabilization, Mr. B sabotaged five possible disposition plans for discharge. He was transferred to the psychiatry service and, because an underlying affective disorder was considered possible, he was given unsuccessful trials of antidepressants and lithium carbonate. Firm limits and strict behavior modification were the only approaches that proved useful in his management.

DSM-III-R DIAGNOSIS

Axis I: Organic mood disorder, manic type (baclofen toxicity); past history of mixed psychoactive substance abuse
Axis II: Borderline personality disorder
Axis III: Quadriplegia with spasticity, neurogenic bowel and bladder, recurrent urinary tract infections, bilateral nephrocalcinosis, and acute renal failure
Axis IV: Stress—severe (serious medical illness, no friends or social supports)
Axis V: Highest level of functioning past year—very poor

DISCUSSION OF TREATMENT SELECTION

Mr. B has characteristics of a borderline personality disorder, especially aggressive, impulsive, and self-destructive behaviors, probably dating back to childhood, and some antisocial personality characteristics as well. Falling out of a second story window twice as a child and reckless motorcycle riding in a gang as an adult seem to be characteristic of his numerous risk-taking behaviors. His recurrent accidents and fights are probably associated with a strong conscious or unconscious wish to be punished, seriously injured, or killed. Any successful treatment plan must attend to the recurrent manifestations of his need to undermine constructive treatment efforts.

His borderline personality characteristic not only played a major role in bringing about his accident, and contributed to his numerous subsequent medical problems by increasing his noncompliance, but also created repeated disruptions in his relationships with doctors, nurses, and others in his life who might be helpful. He has a strong but ambivalent wish for human contact and interactions, as evidenced by his long history of numerous intense but transient relationships (including five marriages) and by his repeatedly pushing the call button for the nurses, only to be verbally abusive to them when they respond.

A behavior modification program was implemented by the nursing staff in which cigarettes and television privileges were awarded for self-control. If he did not call the nurses for a specified period, then he was given an agreed-upon reward. Gradually the time was increased and these rewards were also negotiated for other constructive behaviors. This was partially successful. Confronting and interpreting Mr. B's psychodynamics and empathically talking with him did not influence his behaviors.

Not only was Mr. B hostile and provocative, but also his medical problems were very frustrating to the doctors and nurses. His infections could not be well controlled, and numerous surgical procedures failed to alleviate his condition. This contributed to the feeling of inadequacy and guilt on the part of his physicians and nurses. Although their guilt was initially unrealistic, they later acted out their annoyance with Mr. B through the increased baclofen dosage and ignoring his real needs. In doing so, they colluded with Mr. B to repeat the abuse that he had experienced in the past and provided themselves with a more realistic reason to feel guilty about his care.

Part of the surgeons' anger may have also been directed towards the psychiatrist who had failed to simply remove the difficult problem, as is ideally accomplished in a surgical procedure. A "failure" of this type should alert the consulting psychiatrist to reestablish a vigilant management plan and ensure that the primary physician remains closely involved in the treatment and followup of the patient. Part of the psychiatric consultation must be to indicate to the referring physician the realistic goals and limitations of the consultation.

Baclofen inhibits reflexes at the spinal level and is used to treat spasticity of spinal origin. The total daily dose should not exceed 80 mg (20 mg q.i.d.), and it is contraindicated at usual dosages in patients with impaired renal function. Increasing Mr. B's baclofen dosage to well above the daily recommended amount may have been an unconscious attempt to simultaneously treat and punish Mr. B for his deviant and seemingly defiant behaviors. In planning and monitoring the treatment of psychologically difficult patients, consultants must be alert for staff acting out their dislike for the patient. Neuropsychiatric side effects of baclofen are well known, sedation being the most common. Baclofen is structurally related to the inhibitory transmitter, gamma-aminobutyric acid (GABA). It also influences CNS dopamine metabolism. Manic psychosis is known to occur due to baclofen toxicity or during the withdrawal from baclofen.

In one sense the baclofen "treatment" of Mr. B was successful. He became somewhat manic and euphoric, and this was a definite change of his personality in a positive direction. This "improvement" undoubtedly led to a delay in recognizing and seeking psychiatric consultation regarding his mania, partially due to the fear that correction of the condition would lead to a return of his usual personality, which of course occurred. Other patients who are subjected to iatrogenic problems due to an acting-out of their physicians' or nurses' feelings may not be so fortunate. If an organic affective disorder of a severe depressive type or a delirium develops, the patient may hurt him/herself or others.

Due to his combination of severe medical and psychiatric disorders, a long-term institutional placement is being arranged for Mr. B. For a patient with a combination of severe psychiatric and medical disorders, longterm institutional care in a medium skill nursing home may provide the best chance for the longest, healthiest, and happiest life. A structured environment where limits are maintained seems best able to provide the external controls that are lacking internally in patients like Mr. B. This setting also enables regular monitoring of his medical conditions and may diminish self-damaging and noncompliant or other neglectful actions. The disposition being arranged for Mr. B is similar, in terms of firm structure and limits, to the reform school environment, which the patient described as the happiest time of his life. Further hospitalizations for his medical conditions are inevitable; therefore, it is very important that his hospital chart be "flagged" in some manner, so that an explanation of his psychiatric disorder and effective treatment strategies will be called to the attention of future physicians and nurses involved in his care.

SUGGESTED READING

1. Kirubakaran, V., Mayfield, D., & Rengachary, S. Dyskinesia and psychosis in a patient following baclofen withdrawal. *American Journal of Psychiatry,* 141:692–693, 1984.

2. Wolf, M. E., Almy, G., Toll, M., et al. Mania associated with the use of baclofen. *Biological Psychiatry,* 16:757–759, 1982.
3. Perry, S., & Viederman, M. Adaptation of residents to consultation-liaison psychiatry. Part I: Working with the physically ill; Part II: Working with the nonpsychiatric staff. *General Hospital Psychiatry,* 3:141–156, 1981. (The special requirements and suggested strategies for the psychiatric consultant in a general hospital.)
4. Ayllon, T., & Azrin, N. H. *The Token Economy: A Motivational System for Therapy and Rehabilitation.* New York: Appleton-Century-Crofts, 1968. (How to use this reinforcement procedure in an institutional setting.)

III

Psychoactive

Substance Use

Disorders

■ **ALCOHOL DEPENDENCE**

6. The Case of the Aging Attorney

Mr. W, a 68-year-old lawyer, is accompanied to the consultant's office by his devoted wife and their two married children. Although Mr. W is immaculately tailored and conveys an air of confidence in his manner, he has come for the appointment only at the insistence of the children, who are alarmed by their father's depression and thinly veiled hints of suicide.

The problem, at least as recognized by the family, began two years ago when Mrs. W returned earlier than planned from a visit with one of her children and discovered Mr. W in bed with a secretary half his age. Throughout their 38 years of marriage, Mrs. W had silently and stoically suffered many subtle and not so subtle abuses from her husband, who treated her more as a housemaid and mistress than as a loving partner. For reasons of her own, Mrs. W voiced no objections to this treatment and allowed her husband to dictate conversations, recreational activities, vacations, friends, the children's discipline and schooling, and even what every member of the family should wear, eat, and feel. Except for some minor defiant struggles during the children's adolescences, all the family members were willing to sacrifice their autonomy because if they disagreed and did not continually praise and thank Mr. W for all that he gave and accomplished, he would become scornful, bitter, critical, and enraged. The cost of disagreement was simply not worth the price.

The family's submission and fear were most notably apparent regarding Mr. W's alcoholism. Though he was a prominent member of the community and a highly regarded attorney, family members and friends were aware that for many years Mr. W would drink heavily on most nights, telling story after story in a manner he thought was most charming and entertaining. (His captured guests did not usually share this view.) Despite his drinking pattern, Mr. W developed none of the physical signs of alcoholism: He had no morning tremulousness, blackouts, or liver abnormalities. On the contrary, even with his additional problem of chain-smoking, he was far more vigorous than many of his professional and social associates. The toll taken by alcoholism was more emotional; for as the years went on, the drinking appeared to accentuate his worst personality traits, particularly his ruminative bitterness and his intolerance of all those who did not share his outspoken opinions.

Mrs. W had tolerated her husband's rigid, demeaning attitude and his excessive drinking out of a sense of obligation and, more deeply, because she believed that despite his contemptuous treatment, he cared about her. This view was shattered by the completely unsuspected discovery of the extramarital sexual affair. Mr. W dismissed the entire episode, explaining to his wife that the affair was the first ever and had been caused only by his loneliness and his smoldering depression about the changes in his law practice as he was becoming older and receiving fewer referrals. His wife accepted these explanations at first, but when she discovered that the sexual affair was continuing, the illusions that had enabled her to tolerate her husband's treatment were now shattered. With unprecedented resolve, she left her husband and, to his humiliation, took what he considered to be a menial job as a church secretary.

In response to this marital separation, to an age-related decreased tolerance for alcohol, and to a declining law practice, Mr. W's alcoholism and depression became more pronounced and public. In an attempt to blackmail his wife into returning, he would phone his two married children and threaten to kill himself or to disown the entire family if the children did not convince Mrs. W to return. The children, relatives, and friends all had various opinions as to who was at fault and what should be done, but no action was taken until Mr. W had a car accident while driving home intoxicated from his girlfriend's house. The car was totally wrecked but, miraculously, Mr. W escaped any severe injury. At this point, the children, though divided in other ways, agreed that psychiatric consultation was unavoidable despite their father's protests.

During the interview, as the above story was pieced together, Mr. W maintained that he was the wronged party—by a wife who left him after many years of marriage in his time of need, and by children who did not appreciate the inevitable despair that comes with growing old and seeing one's professional and social stature diminish. He agreed that at times his drinking was a bit excessive, but he did not see the drinking per se as much of a problem; it was only a way of self-treating a depression others had caused.

DSM-III-R DIAGNOSIS

Axis I: Alcohol dependence; possible major depressive episode without melancholia

Axis II: Mixed personality disorder with narcissistic, paranoid, and obsessive features

Axis III: Moderately elevated amylase on previous physical examinations; asymptomatic emphysema; productive bronchitis; cervical arthritis with occasional paresthesiae of the right hand

Axis IV: Stress—severe (separation from wife and decline of law practice)

Axis V: Highest level of functioning past year—good (despite nightly intoxification, has maintained his office practice, is still a competent attorney, and has kept up physical appearances)

TREATMENT PROBLEM

Accomplished 68-year-old lawyer with longstanding history of alcoholism and a more recent history of depression and general deterioration, including a poorly concealed extramarital affair, threats of suicide, and an automobile accident while intoxicated. He does not admit that he has a problem and needs help.

DISCUSSION OF TREATMENT SELECTION

Setting. Mr. W needs a thorough psychiatric and medical evaluation, alcohol detoxification, and protection from his self-destructive and suicidal impulses. Hospitalization would provide a supportive and structured setting to meet these needs and would also facilitate the implementation of prescribed treatments, such as an alcoholism program or antidepressant medication. The problem is that Mr. W, a proud man who for years has denied his emotional problems and alcoholism, continues to either rationalize his difficulties or attribute them to his wife's leaving. In his view, all the problems would be solved if his wife would simply return. If Mr. W refuses psychiatric hospitalization, the grounds for involuntary commitment are slim. Even if admission is forced upon him, the hopes of a therapeutic alliance may be lost in the process. Two alternatives would be either to facilitate the therapeutic alliance by starting with an outpatient treatment before prescribing hospitalization, or to recommend an inpatient evaluation in a general hospital, which would be viewed by him as less humiliating.

Format. Mr. W's relationship with his family is both his strength and his weakness. His wife and children have tolerated his many abuses and now are instrumental in his being brought for help; but along with being concerned, they are also bitter and intimidated, wishing to separate emotionally and geographically from his problems. Though they would probably agree to family sessions, the risk of such meetings at this time cannot be underestimated since their rage rather than love may be the prominent initial affect. An unleashing of their anger in family sessions at this time might confirm Mr. W's fears of rejection at the very moment that he needs support to help face his problems. On the other hand, a family format may be the only way of inducing Mr. W into any treatment. He has come for consultation only at the insistence of his wife and children and, at present, is motivated only by the hope of having his wife return.

As long as the therapist can contain the family's anger towards Mr. W and can avoid Mr. W's using family sessions simply to manipulate his wife's return, this format combined with individual and marital sessions appears the best option. Individual sessions will provide a format for Mr. W to be more candid about his extramarital affairs and more revealing about the extent of his alcoholism and severity of his depression. A homogeneous group, such as Alcoholics Anonymous, will be immensely helpful if and when Mr. W will make even a tentative admission that his use of alcohol is contributing to some problems in his life.

Duration and Frequency. Mr. W's alcoholism must be viewed as a chronic illness that will require some kind of monitoring for the duration of his life. By explicitly conveying to Mr. W from the beginning that help will be available all along the way, the therapist conveys a recognition not only that some remissions and exacerbations are likely, but also that "falling off the wagon" need not be construed as a failure that will inevitably lead to rejection. This kind of hope and commitment in terms of treatment duration is a powerful therapeutic component of many self-help groups for alcoholics.

Approach. Mr. W has a rigid "go-by-the-book" approach to life. He is not by nature psychologically-minded or reflective, and he has many biases against psychoanalytically oriented psychiatrists. For these reasons, a directive medical approach that straightforwardly describes the illnesses (alcoholism and depression) and prescribes specific solutions will be more effective. At the same time, because education and advice alone are not likely to be sufficient, Mr. W will probably also need an empathic and supportive relationship that nurtures his narcissistic needs. Great skill will be required to provide this support in an unobtrusive manner that Mr. W will not perceive as infantilizing, patronizing, or demeaning. In addition, his lack of insight, his need to control others, and his false pride are likely to evoke countertransference problems, especially when he does not comply with treatment, challenges its value, or resumes drinking.

Somatic Treatment. A major depression is difficult to diagnose and treat in the presence of severe alcohol abuse. If Mr. W's cooperation can be elicited, the best initial treatment would be a detoxification and withdrawal from alcohol. The indications for antidepressant medication will be clearer after the alcoholism itself is treated. A temptation is to start antidepressant medication in hopes that as Mr. W's mood lifts, his willingness to obtain treatment for his alcoholism will also increase. Unfortunately, given the chronicity of his drinking problem, it is unlikely that a stabilization of his mood will in itself enhance his motivation to receive treatment for his drinking problem. Moreover, while Mr. W is still drinking heavily, he might take the antidepressant medications unreliably and, intentionally or not, endanger his life.

CHOICE AND OUTCOME

By the end of the first session, although the consultant recognized the seriousness of Mr. W's problems, as well as the deterioration and self-destructiveness in recent weeks, she was also aware that any recommendations—psychiatric hospitalization or even medications—would probably be strenuously resisted by Mr. W until he was more willing to admit that he had a problem and was not simply going along with the consultation in an effort to coerce his wife into returning home. The consultant therefore recommended that the entire family return for another session the following week.

When they returned for the second session, a subtle change in attitude towards the consultant was immediately apparent. Mr. W was even more self-assured and felt somehow vindicated, repeatedly reminding his wife and children that he must not be the psychiatric cripple and drunk they portrayed or the consultant would have insisted upon medication and hospitalization. On the other hand, not only were the wife and children disappointed that more was not accomplished (after all the efforts they had made in arranging for the consultation and insisting Mr. W attend), but they were also angry at the consultant for not confronting Mr. W more directly about his alcoholism and characterological problems. In effect, they were hoping the consultant would "do the dirty work" by challenging Mr. W in the very way they had avoided all these years.

To establish a doctor-patient relationship on the medical model acceptable to Mr. W and his family, the consultant recommended that the patient be admitted by an internist to a general hospital. The consultant explained that the reason for this hospitalization would be to evaluate Mr. W's productive bronchitis, mild urinary retention and urgency, and paresthesiae, as well as to evaluate possible medical consequences from his drinking.

Mr. W was probably well aware that hospitalization on these grounds provided a face-saving alternative to psychiatric hospitalization or referral to an alcoholism treatment program, and he agreed to the recommendation. The family was relieved that finally some positive steps were being taken. The internist in charge of Mr. W's hospital care, at the recommendation of the consultant, did not prematurely confront Mr. W about his drinking problem and thereby avoided a potentially adversarial relationship. Instead, he informed Mr. W that relatively large doses of a benzodiazepine would be prescribed during the week of hospitalization to help relieve the anxiety and distress of alcohol abstinence. Again, Mr. W accepted this regime—and the issue about being labeled an alcoholic was side-stepped.

After six days of hospitalization, the various tests were completed and the benzodiazepines were tapered. The internist then approached Mr. W on a positive rather than a punitive note, stating that Mr. W was fortunate in having a resilient body but that certain signs of deterioration were evident in the abnormal pancreatic chemistries; however, with improved dietary habits, including alcohol abstinence, this physical problem could most likely be reversed. The internist further recommended that because alcohol was such a conditioned behavior in Mr. W's life, disulfiram (Antabuse) would be prescribed so that the decision about whether or not to drink would only need to be made once a day rather than the countless times the opportunity would arise. He added that Mr. W had shown an ability to go without alcohol in the hospital and, although his abstinence would be more difficult outside the hospital where alcohol was more easily available, he was sure that with support the job could be done. Without demanding these restrictions, the internist asked Mr. W to give the issue further thought—on the way out of the door, almost as a parenthetical remark, he mentioned that the Antabuse might be taken more reliably if Mrs. W would return home to remind him.

The following day, while still in the hospital, Mr. W told the internist that he understood the medical indications for not drinking (the illicit affair, the auto accident, and the social deterioration had still not been mentioned), and agreed that it would be helpful to have his wife remind him about the Antabuse. The internist then went to Mrs. W and explained that Mr. W was simply too proud to admit at this time that he was an alcoholic and was incapable of humbly seeking forgiveness for his transgressions, illicit affair, and need to control others; but inwardly he very much needed Mrs. W's support and would welcome her return and companionship in the coming years. The internist told Mrs. W that she must have needs of her own to play the subservient role, otherwise she would not have stayed with her husband through all these years of marriage. He then asked, quite frankly, if she wanted to change this pattern of caring for her husband. She replied that she could never forgive herself if she were to abandon him now that he needed her more than ever.

Finally, the internist explained that Mr. W would not at this time accept psychotherapy from a psychiatrist but would accept a medical followup, which the internist would provide so that Mrs. W and the children need not fear that they would be without professional support. The internist cautioned Mrs. W that she should neither expect nor demand any characterological changes, but indicated that an improvement in mood and behavior might occur if abstinence from alcohol was maintained.

For four years the internist followed Mr. W once a month for "medical checkups," and Mrs. W, having returned home, went through the daily ritual of giving her husband the Antabuse along with his daily vitamin. Only after all this time had transpired did Mr. W mention during one visit, as an aside, that he was grateful for the tactful manner in which the internist had handled his "drinking problem," and for helping him ease into retirement. Three years later, seven years after the initial consultation, when Mr. W was 73 years old, he discontinued Antabuse when his wife left for a brief period of time to care for a dying sister. He then resumed his drinking and went on a severe binge that lasted seven weeks. After another face-saving admission to a general hospital, he went back on the Antabuse and maintained abstinence until dying of lung cancer four years later.

SUGGESTED READING

1. Vogler, R. E., Compton, J. V., & Weissbach, T. A. Integrated behavior change techniques for alcoholics. *Journal of Consulting and Clinical Psychology,* 43:233–243, 1975. (Behavior therapy for alcoholism.)
2. Howard, J. H., Marshall, J., Rechnitzer, P. A., et al. Adapting to retirement. *Journal of Geriatric Society,* 30:488–500, 1982. (Combines research with insight to present a conceptual view of the topic.)
3. Birren, J. E., & Schaie, K. W. (Eds.). *Handbook for the psychology of aging.* New York: Van Nostrand Reinhold, 1977. (Encyclopedic and comprehensive. The other two volumes in this excellent series are on 1) aging and the social sciences, and 2) the biology of aging.)

7. The Case of the Businesswoman with Blackouts

(Guest Expert: Richard Frances, M.D.)

Authors' Note:
Frances discusses the difficulties in planning treatment for a patient whose alcohol dependence is compounded by depression, dependent personality traits, marital conflicts, and physical deterioration.

Mrs. C, a 40-year-old married businesswoman with four children, is drinking a quart of gin per day and, because of this, she is having frequent severe fights with her husband. Her heavy drinking began 10 years ago, soon after she discovered that he was having an affair. Since then, she has had great contempt for her husband, but also feels dependent on him to make decisions. She also feels unable to leave the marriage because they are business partners. In the past two years, she began drinking in the morning, has periods of loss of memory for recent events, and has been arrested for driving while intoxicated. She denies other substance use.

Though indispensable to the family business because of her high capabilities, she has become increasingly undependable, often missing work, making major errors in judgment, and creating scenes. Her daughter complained that her mother's behavior was an embarrassment to the entire family. One year ago, Mrs. C had a one-month stay in a freestanding alcohol treatment program, where she appeared to make rapid progress with alcohol counseling and involvement in Alcoholics Anonymous (AA). She had planned to stop drinking, to continue with AA, to reduce her involvement with the business, and to consider separating from her husband. Within two months, she resumed a full load of work, stopped AA meetings, battled with her husband, and resumed drinking. During the past 10 months, she has also experienced increasing hopelessness, inability to concentrate, weight gain, and early morning awakening. She expressed a wish to die; however, she feels she does not have the courage to commit suicide.

Mrs. C is the third of four children. She has a strong family history of alcoholism, including an alcoholic father who was violent with her mother. Throughout her childhood, she felt embarrassed and humiliated by her father whom she both loved and despised. At age 16, she eloped with her present husband and soon became pregnant. Though he was abusive and tyrannical, she felt trapped in her marriage and proceeded to have three more children.

Mrs. C has an unsteady gait, wears no makeup, and is dressed in a baggy business suit. Her speech is slightly slurred and her affect is depressed. Embarrassed at needing help, she has tried many times to stop drinking, both on her own and with her internist's help. She knows that at home she will surely drink, but is furious at her husband and children who insist on her seeking help. She is cognitively intact. On physical examination, she is tremulous, with rapid pulse, elevated blood pressure, enlarged liver, and she has elevated SGOT, SGPT, and LDH.

DSM-III-R DIAGNOSIS

Axis I: Alcohol dependence; alcohol withdrawal; major depression, single episode, with melancholia
Axis II: Dependent personality disorder with narcissistic traits (provisional)
Axis III: Fatty hepatosis; possible hypertension
Axis IV: Stress—severe (marital and occupational deterioration)
Axis V: Highest level of functioning past year—fair

DISCUSSION OF TREATMENT SELECTION

The complex interaction between alcoholism and other psychiatric disorders makes a psychiatric evaluation especially necessary. Abstinence is required during treatment, both for diagnostic and therapeutic reasons. Making the diagnosis of alcoholism early is difficult, because patients often deny problems until life situations have deteriorated. What the patient does not say is as important as what she does. Initially, the history-gathering and the evaluation of her mental status must be combined with confrontation of denial about alcoholism, both in the patient and her family, in order to help them acknowledge and accept the problem.

Since Mrs. C is being forced to see the therapist by her family, it will be essential that the therapist establish rapport with her. Motivation for treatment, though initially low in many patients with alcoholism, can be increased through a combination of confrontation, support, and education.

Mrs. C has also denied her intense dependency needs and the need for her to continue in treatment after she has stopped drinking. Confronting the patient with the dimensions of her problems may create a crisis as the patient acknowledges the full impact drinking has had on major areas of functioning. It is in this context that the physician and patient begin to work out a treatment contract. Use of medical evidence, such as laboratory results, liver scans, and support of other physicians known to the patient, may be very helpful. Outcome studies indicate that factors such as having a family, a stable job, and absence of sociopathy are better prognostic factors than whether or not someone sought out treatment or was pushed into it by job, family, or physician.

The first phase of treatment for Mrs. C is detoxification, preferably as an outpatient. Outpatient alcohol detoxification can be done in patients who are reliable, have good family and social support systems, and are highly motivated for treatment. The patient is started on chlordiazepoxide (Librium) 25–50 mg q.i.d. and multivitamins, with daily outpatient visits and gradually decreasing doses of chlordiazepoxide over three-to-five days. If the patient continues to drink or abuse medications, this warrants inpatient detoxification. Patients admitted to the hospital usually require slightly longer detoxifications. They are started on chlordiazepoxide 50–100 mg q.i.d., multivitamins, folic acid, thiamine 100 mg q.i.d., and are detoxified over a five-to-seven day period. Those with history of seizures are given magnesium sulphate 50% 2cc I.M. every eight hours for nine doses. Inpatient detoxification is required when: 1) there is severe concurrent medical and/or psychiatric illness; 2) detoxification cannot be done safely as an outpatient because of severe withdrawal symptoms or lack of a stable family; and 3) the patient is not able to stop using substances outside the hospital or has failed to respond to less intensive forms of treatment.

Mrs. C has not cooperated in previous outpatient detoxifications, is currently struggling with her husband, and is suffering from a major depression, all of which indicate a need for both detoxification and inpatient hospital rehabilitation. A hospital-based facility, psychiatrically staffed to evaluate and treat the patient's major affective illness, makes it possible to develop a tailored treatment plan that addresses issues not effectively dealt with in her previous treatment.

Involvement of the family is mandatory if the treatment is to have a chance of success. Alcoholics present behavioral problems which directly affect the family, and the family may also reinforce the patient's drinking. Awareness of the family's dynamics may aid in the treatment and prevent relapses. Mrs. C's children are also in need of evaluation and are at higher than usual risks for behavioral problems, attention deficit disorders, and abuse of substances. They have been victims of abuse and neglect, and may have had to take care of themselves and of Mrs. C. Including the family in treatment also increases the chance that the patient will be engaged in treatment.

Rehabilitation provides an environment that allows an extended period of sobriety, thus breaking the cycle of addiction and promoting increasing responsibility. A full schedule of activities includes group therapy, lectures on alcoholism, study groups, and AA meetings, in addition to individual psychotherapy, family therapy, and alcoholism counseling. Patients' families are involved in a weekly family group, a children's group, and are encouraged to attend Al-Anon. Mrs. C will continue in aftercare treatment with both individual and family therapy, and AA.

AA has been highly successful in helping patients like Mrs. C accept their illness and find a network of social support and provide auxiliary superego support and an alternative means of having dependency needs met. At AA, the patient discovers that being an alcoholic doesn't mean that she is an immoral outcast, but rather that this is an illness that afflicts many fine people from all walks of life.

Disulfuran (Antabuse) can be an important adjunct in treating alcoholism. The patient need only make the decision about drinking once every day when she takes her medication. This gives her time to cope with the urge to drink when it becomes very strong, eliminates the temptation, and thereby reduces craving. Because of her fatty hepatosis and depression, I would wait three weeks for her enzymes to return towards normal and then prescribe Antabuse 125 mg per day. Severe liver disease, heart disease, high suicide potential, and psychosis are all contraindications to Antabuse. In elderly patients or those with relative contraindications to Antabuse, I recommend half the usual dose of 250 mg.

Alcoholism can be the result of depression or can lead to depression, which may remit at various intervals after abstinence. Though 50%–80% of patients admitted to alcohol treatment programs score high on depression rating scales, only 5% have major affective illnesses likely to respond to somatic treatments. Mrs. C requires a traditional diagnostic workup with evaluation of mental status, course of symptomatology, a two-week drug free period, and medication trials with antidepressants, when indicated. Psychological screening test for organicity, depression, and personality disorders are useful. The dexamethasone suppression test is not likely to be useful for at least a month because of a high incidence of false positives in patients with alcoholism.

Mrs. C's individual therapy is likely to have as its major focus a tendency towards repeating self-defeating relationships with men. Her need to see herself as a victim of a powerful and yet dependent husband related to her experience with her violent alcoholic father. It will be difficult for her to develop closeness with her therapist, especially if her therapist is male. She should be encouraged to develop friendships, both in AA and through her considerable exposure to people in her business.

Much of the program for Mrs. C will be geared towards helping her achieve the experience of accepting herself as an alcoholic. She has used alcohol to ward off severe shame and guilt and, in giving up alcohol, will need to accept her own dependency needs and to admit to an illness. This change in identity can occur with a combination of psychotherapy, social pressure, identification with counselors as role models, and education. AA facilitates this process by providing normative social pressure, gratification of dependency needs, and a route for identification with an ego ideal of sobriety.

SUGGESTED READING

1. Bean, M. (Ed.). Alcoholics Anonymous, I, II. *Psychiatric Annals*, 5(2,3), (February, March), 1975. (Reviews the methods, rationale, and outcome studies of this well-established treatment.)
2. Stern, S. L., Rush, A. J., & Mendels, J. Toward a rational pharmacotherapy of depression. *American Journal of Psychiatry*, 137:545–552, 1980. (Describes how Mrs. C's alcoholism, personal history and style, psychological testing and liver disease would all be considered by the clinician when choosing the particular antidepressant drug and dosage.)
3. Frances, R. J., Franklin, J. E. Alcohol and other psychoactive substance use disorders. In J. A. Talbott, R. E. Hales, S. C. Yudofsy (Eds.), *Textbook of Psychiatry*. Washington DC: American Psychiatric Press, Inc., 1988. (Excellent overview with references to major studies.)

8. The Case of the Noncompliant Painter

Mr. V, a 54-year-old unemployed house painter, was admitted to a general hospital because of an acute gastrointestinal (GI) bleed, which required 22 units of blood and three weeks of intensive care before the crisis had passed and he was relatively stable. His course had been further complicated by the onset of seizures and delirium on the fourth hospital day, which were due to alcohol withdrawal. The staff was relieved that the patient had survived and now planned to investigate further the possible causes of the GI bleed; however, while waiting for these tests to be performed, Mr. V abruptly announced one evening after dinner that he was leaving the hospital. The intern refused to give the patient his belongings and called for an emergency psychiatric consultation.

In a half-hour interview, the psychiatrist learned from the patient that he had suffered from alcoholism for over 25 years, had not worked for the past five years, and had not heard from anyone in his family since three years ago, when he began living on the streets. He had no idea where any of his relatives were now living. Mr. V understood the possible consequences of refusing treatment and of continuing to drink, but he frankly admitted that he had not improved previously in three expensive alcoholism inpatient services nor had heroic efforts by sponsors at Alcoholics Anonymous been of any help.

Although he was a bit annoyed and argumentative at the beginning of the interview about not being given his clothes immediately so that he could leave, Mr. V gradually became more cooperative and conversational without any evidence of disordered thinking, delusions, or dementia. He showed no evidence of suicidal intent in the past or present—he simply wanted to return to the streets and drink because hospitals gave him "the creeps." Furthermore, he had had a similar severe GI bleed two years previously, had started drinking as soon as he left the hospital, and had had no recurrence until the present episode. He persuasively argued, "If I want to live the life of a drunk and die like one, what right do you have to stop me?"

DSM-III-R DIAGNOSIS

Axis I: Alcohol dependence
Axis II: Undetermined
Axis III: Gastrointestinal bleed and liver cirrhosis
Axis IV: Stress—severe (life-threatening medical illness)
Axis V: Highest level of functioning past year—poor (homeless and unemployed)

TREATMENT PROBLEM

Fifty-four-year-old homeless man who has a life-threatening dependence on alcohol and who refuses medical or psychiatric care.

DISCUSSION OF TREATMENT SELECTION

The therapeutic choices for this patient may be irrelevant. Because he is neither psychotically disorganized nor an immediate threat to himself or others, he cannot be involuntarily hospitalized ("committed"). In addition, because he understands the nature of his acts and their possible consequences, there is no indication that he would be judged incompetent in a court of law. Moreover, his medical condition is not now so immediately life-threatening that emergency measures could (in some states) be implemented without informed consent. In short, he is free to leave the hospital and is not required to sign anything ("sign out against medical advice"). Indeed, to force treatment upon him at this point might legally be considered an assault.

Although Mr. V has a legal right to leave the hospital, the consultant must guard against accepting the patient's own assessment of his refractoriness to treatment and his inevitable fatal prognosis. Many alcoholic patients have failed countless well-intended and well-administered treatment programs and then, finally, and for reasons that are not always clear, responded remarkably well to one more effort. The consultant must also be cautious about accepting the patient's version of previous treatments. Mr. V may be consciously or unconsciously distorting his prior therapeutic experiences, because he is determined to leave and wants to discourage the consultant from standing in his way.

The most pressing task for the consultant is to engage Mr. V in a way that will promptly implant some seed of hope. Since the patient has been willing to discuss his past life and is not adamantly insisting upon leaving the hospital at once, an effective method of engaging Mr. V might be to place the present crisis into the context of Mr. V's past and use this dynamic understanding to explain why he feels discouraged. For example, if these were the facts that emerged, he might be told the following:

"Having heard what you've been through in your life, I now understand why you're so eager to leave the hospital. All your life you feel people have been telling you what to do. When you were a kid, your drunken father was always screaming at you to do this or that, and when you took out your frustrations in school, the teachers would get on your case. Then, when you quit school because you had to get married, once again you felt trapped and that you were being ordered around by your wife and yelled at for not being a better father and provider. The same thing kept happening at work; it seems to you that your many bosses were always on your back about one thing or another. So over the years you found that the one thing that gave you peace of mind was a stiff drink. Drinking also gave you a feeling that *you* were boss and all those people giving orders could go screw themselves. So now, here in the hospital, once again you feel people are telling you what to do and they're getting on your nerves—and once again you feel that to get peace of mind and to get them off your back you should go back to drinking. Now I understand why you want to leave.

"I also understand why you feel so discouraged about getting help for your problems. Because treatment has failed so often in the past, you believe it must fail in the future. But that belief and feeling of hopelessness are very common among alcoholics. It's part of the disease and one of the things we know how to treat.

"I want you to understand one other thing. If you decide to stay in the hospital, it's your choice. The doctors and nurses are not like your father or teachers or wife or bosses. You may feel that the staff here is giving you orders and pushing you around, but this time in your life you have a choice about what you do. I hope you'll choose to get help so that even the bottle will no longer be your boss."

This psychodynamic life narrative might reverse Mr. V's current demoralization by making him feel less estranged and more acceptable. He might then be willing to stay in the hospital long enough to receive more adequate medical care and reconsider having a member from Alcoholics Anonymous or an equivalent program visit him in the hospital and begin rehabilitation. The abandonment by his family, the mounting loneliness, and the recurrent critical medical problems might make him now more receptive to a homogeneous group than he has been in the past.

CHOICE AND OUTCOME

Having worked so hard to save Mr. V's life, the staff was enraged over the prospect that he could simply leave, resume drinking, and "bleed to death." The doctors and nurses wanted the psychiatric consultant to talk the patient into staying, convince him that he must stop drinking, and, if these approaches failed, "to commit the son-of-a-bitch." They were feeling unappreciated.

The consultant did not handle the situation well. He resented the pressure from the staff and accepted Mr. V's pessimistic outlook at face value. Unfortunately, he failed to make any vigorous attempts to engage the patient and also assumed a rather patronizing attitude toward the staff. In an ad hoc conference in the nurses' station, as the staff watched the patient nonchalantly get dressed and cavalierly wave goodbye, the consultant explained Mr. V's legal rights and the feelings of frustration that some people can have when working with alcoholics.

As might have been predicted, the effect of the meeting was an escalating anger at the patient, and also at the psychiatrist for not being more assertive and effective in convincing Mr. V to stay and for his condescending manner. Efforts to interpret this "displacement" were met with skepticism and further derision. The consultation ended on this dyspeptic note. The patient was never seen again.

SUGGESTED READING

1. Wise, T. N. Psychiatric management of patients who threaten to sign out against medical advice. *International Journal of Psychiatry and Medicine,* 5:153–160, 1974. (Description of common causes for this overt and often life-threatening form of noncompliance, along with suggested interventions.)
2. Viederman, M., & Perry, S. Use of a psychodynamic life narrative in the treatment of depression in the physically ill. *General Hospital Psychiatry,* 3:177–185, September 1980. (How a succinct, supportive summary of the patient's past life and dynamic conflicts can convey a feeling of being understood, increase self-esteem, and decrease hopelessness.)
3. Wiseman, J. P. *Stations of the Host: The Treatment of Skid Row Alcoholics.* Chicago: University of Chicago Press, 1970. (Thorough documentation of the lifestyle and management problems of a skid-row population; enables the clinician to approach patients like Mr. V with understanding, if not optimism.)
4. Lamb, H. R. (Ed.). *The Homeless Mentally Ill.* Washington, DC: American Psychiatric Press, Inc., 1984. (Historical perspective of this increasing population.)

■ OPIOID DEPENDENCE

9. The Case of the Enraging Addict

Mr. K, a 24-year-old self-proclaimed pimp and heroin dealer, was readmitted to the medical service in a coma because of severe endocarditis. After five days of being in the intensive care unit and receiving intravenous antibiotics, he was considered medically stable, though still critically ill. Psychiatric consultation was requested by the intern and nursing staff. They hoped that, since the patient had come so close to dying, he might now be more motivated to change his ways and stop abusing drugs. Despite his obvious fatigue and wasted frame, Mr. K greeted the psychiatrist with the same admixture of charm and disdain that, according to the medical records, had characterized his response to the psychiatric consultations during his previous three admissions.

Mr. K made it clear from the start that he had no objections to chatting with anyone on the medical staff who happened to drop by, but he also had no intentions of being maintained on "soft dope" (methadone) or of "being wrapped around and hassled in one of those rehab houses." When he was ready to stop using dope, he would—and if he couldn't do it on his own, he would "knock on the door of some shrink." With the same glibness, he explained how he got started on drugs in the first place—broken home, poverty, peer pressure, social injustices, sadness over the death of an older brother (from an overdose of heroin)—but he acknowledged that whatever the reasons for getting started, his use of drugs now had a life of its own. His only real regret was that he had stupidly used the same "works" (needles and syringe) as "the fillies in my stable" (the call girls he managed). He was determined not to make that mistake again.

Unable to engage the patient and feeling frustrated, the consultant abruptly ended the interview and left the ward. When she returned the following day to complete her note, she again saw Mr. K and obtained a few more facts (e.g., mild withdrawal symptoms during two short imprisonments; currently living alone with many "contacts" but with no close family or friends). However, this second go-around was no more successful in motivating Mr. K to participate in a treatment plan. Just barely concealing her frustration, the consultant wrote a note in the chart that had the same tone of helpless resignation reflected in other notes during previous hospitalizations.

But the problem of Mr. K would not go away. Three days later the consultant was again called, this time because unused hospital syringes and needles were discovered hidden in his bedside table. The staff's feelings about Mr. K had changed from controlled anger to outright fury. They resented wasting their time on someone so self-destructive, when they could be giving attention to more deserving patients. They suspected Mr. K's visitors were sneaking in drugs, and they were convinced that he was the reason the bathroom reeked of marijuana. When the psychiatric consultant confronted Mr. K with these charges, he gave the flimsy excuse that he had no idea how the needles got in his bedside drawer. Although he did not deny that he used marijuana, Mr. K saw no reason for the staff to make a fuss since "everybody smokes the stuff and, after all, I am bored and upset about being in the hospital—why shouldn't I have something to calm my nerves?" It was just this attitude that was dividing the staff, half of whom were insisting that Mr. K be discharged at once, whereas the other half, realizing Mr. K's endocarditis could be fatal if left untreated, hoped the consultant could somehow convince Mr. K to change his behavior.

DSM-III-R DIAGNOSIS

> Axis I: Opioid dependence
> Axis II: Antisocial personality disorder
> Axis III: Status postinfectious hepatitus; tri-valvular endocarditis
> Axis IV: Stress—severe (life-threatening physical illness)
> Axis V: Highest level of functioning past year—poor (preoccupation with getting "high" dominates his day-to-day life and impairs his ability to run his illegal businesses)

TREATMENT PROBLEM

Twenty-four-year-old antisocial heroin abuser, whose provocative behavior in the hospital is enraging the staff and jeopardizing medical care for his severe endocarditis. He has no apparent motivation for treatment nor does he see a need for change in his behavior.

DISCUSSION OF TREATMENT SELECTION

Setting. When emotional problems are causing a situation that is difficult to manage, the medical staff commonly believes that transferring the patient to a psychiatric service is a reasonable solution. This belief is based not simply on a wish to dump the patient on someone else, but also on the naive view that the psychiatric staff will be immune to Mr. K's provocativeness or at least be able to manage him effectively.

In addition, the medical staff does not always realize that most psychiatric wards are ill-equipped, and the staff is not experienced in providing the kinds of medical care Mr. K will need. In some ways this comparison between the medical and psychiatric wards is academic; even if advisable, Mr. K would probably not accept a psychiatric hospitalization.

Another option for a therapeutic setting is outpatient treatment. Mr. K could be discharged and followed on oral or intramuscular antibiotics with daily clinic appointments. The problem is that the chances of Mr. K complying with this regime—both in taking his medication regularly and in keeping the appointments—are slim; furthermore, even if he did comply, this method of administering antibiotics would probably not be effective in treating his cardiac disease.

One other possibility would be to transfer Mr. K to another medical ward. Although this move might provide a fresh start and thereby temporarily relieve the current tension, such a transfer is generally not a good idea. It can foster a resentment between the staff members on the different wards, can suggest that one group is more capable of handling the problem than another, and can preclude the opportunity for the staff currently treating Mr. K from developing an expertise in managing the problems he presents.

Once his acute medical problems have been treated, Mr. K will probably need to reside in a highly structured drug rehabilitation program if he is ever going to become drug free. Such a setting provides strict limits, unremitting peer pressure, and an atmosphere of both support and confrontation. Unfortunately, Mr. K may lack the high motivation that is necessary before most patients are willing to commit themselves to this approach.

Format. At the present time, an individual treatment is the only possible option for Mr. K, especially since he explicitly refuses to accept a homogeneous group for drug rehabilitation. The hope would be, however, that once his motivation for treatment improves, he could be inducted into a drug rehabilitation program that would have as one of its components a self-help group. Recovering substance abusers are often the most skilled at simultaneously confronting and supporting new members who present with the kinds of problems the group members know only too well.

Duration and Frequency. Since Mr. K may leave or be discharged at any moment, the therapist will need to stay on top of the situation by seeing Mr. K at least once a day, as well as conferring daily with the staff. The sessions need not be long—10 or 15 minutes—because a reflective, uncovering inquiry will probably not change his hospital behavior and may only convey that the therapist has time to waste, a perception that will diminish Mr. K's regard for the therapist. If, after the first phase of treatment is over and the crisis in the hospital has passed, Mr. K should agree to a longer-term rehabilitation program, then the duration of the treatment will need to be open-ended and prolonged.

Approach. The challenge posed by Mr. K is to find a therapeutic approach that will provide him with some immediate reward. His style is to live moment to moment, seeking instant gratification and using whatever ways he can find to diminish physical or psychic pain. This tendency is exacerbated by the threat of physical illness and the necessity for hospitalization. Though one might expect Mr. K's current medical circumstances to inspire a desire for reform, actually he is now feeling overwhelmed, oblivious to long-term consequences, and even more inclined to live moment to moment. Although Mr. K did accept hospitalization for his physical illness, he waited until he was deathly ill before coming to the emergency room. Now that he is somewhat stronger, he is liable to leave the hospital impulsively with little provocation. It is possible that some of the enraged staff members might consciously or unconsciously provide this provocation by giving Mr. K an offer he will not, and probably cannot, accept.

With these considerations in mind, the most effective therapeutic approach would be to defer discussing any long-term rehabilitation and, instead, attempt to obtain Mr. K's respect and participation by designing a program that has the immediate goal of making Mr. K more comfortable. In many ways, the staff's attitude and the hospital situation are more changeable than Mr. K's character, so these would be the initial areas of attack. First, in order to depersonalize the current conflicts and to provide the staff with the objectivity of a medical model, the consultant can remind the staff that although Mr. K's attitude can be experienced as controlling, he is actually a man out of control and governed by his illness, i.e., substance abuse. The characteristic signs and symptoms of this psychiatric illness as manifested by Mr. K can then be described. Second, in order to diminish the staff's sense of helplessness and hopelessness, the consultant can emphasize that the crisis of physical illness is often a turning point for many abusers. A consistent and nonvindictive approach by the staff may hold some small but definite potential for Mr. K to reverse his self-destructive path.

Mr. K lacks motivation and an alliance with a therapist. For now, he will probably be more responsive to the same kind of psychoeducation recommended above for the staff. In a nonpunitive but frank manner, he should be told that although he tries to give the impression that he is a "cool guy" running the show, in fact he is being controlled by his illness—drug addiction—and is likely to die if he does not accept treatment for this disease.

The consultant must then indicate a knowledge of both substance abuse and its treatment, conveying hope that based on the consultant's prior experience with similar problems, an effective and tolerable therapy can be implemented. The temptation must be overcome to have Mr. K start "behaving" by only using threats: "If you keep abusing drugs, you'll kill yourself!" This approach, when not coupled by a specific treatment plan, often makes substance abusers more anxious and more inclined to seek immediate relief from illicit drugs. When describing the treatment plan, the consultant can point out, in passing, those behaviors of Mr. K that are most infuriating to staff members and that thereby jeopardize his medical care; but the consultant should place the greatest emphasis on the recommended pharmacological approach. This aspect of treatment will be the greatest concern for Mr. K, who will want to know what drugs he will get, how frequently, and in what dosages (see Somatic Treatment below).

Somatic Treatment. There are two decisions to make regarding the use of drugs for Mr. K. One decision is how vigorously the staff should attempt to stop his use of illicit drugs during hospitalization; the other decision is whether to prescribe licit drugs either for Mr. K's state-related anxiety or for his chronic substance abuse.

A good starting point for the first decision is the realization that the chances of totally preventing Mr. K from acquiring illicit drugs while in a general hospital are slim. Even if all visiting privileges were discontinued and even if his bedside were frequently searched and perhaps even if Mr. K were placed under constant observation, he is far more experienced in acquiring and hiding drugs than the medical staff is experienced in preventing this behavior. In addition, a constant surveillance would require an inordinate amount of the medical staff's time and effort.

With this realization, the consultant can inform both the staff and Mr. K that reasonable precautions will be taken during the medical hospitalization to limit the chances of Mr. K's taking illicit drugs—he will be observed during visits and his belongings will be searched on a regular basis—but the presence of illicit drugs, although these will of course be taken away to protect him (and other patients), will not indicate that he must now automatically be discharged. By taking away this threat, the staff might be able to outmaneuver Mr. K by diminishing his need to challenge the hospital system and prove that he has the upper hand.

However, the staff should be warned that Mr. K may need to test the system by sneaking in drugs and seeing if the stated plan will be followed.

Some staff members may find this compromise unacceptable, but they may be persuaded if informed that the current medical situation is life-threatening and that a vindictive approach runs too high a risk of Mr. K's leaving against medical advice. With both the staff and Mr. K, the consultant will need to emphasize that the compromise is the first phase of the overall treatment plan. When Mr. K is more medically stable, less threatened, and has established some working alliance, the second phase can begin, namely, induction into a drug detoxification and rehabilitation program.

The decision whether to prescribe drugs for Mr. K has two parts—immediate and long-term. Although Mr. K seems quite unaffected by the stress and fears of hospitalization, this appearance probably has more to do with his style than with his actual frame of mind. His provocative behavior might diminish if his underlying anxiety were reduced. The staff's reluctance to use dependency-producing anxiolytics is ill-founded. Prescribing a benzodiazepine during the hospitalization is not going to make Mr. K more of an addict than he already is. Even though he elicits certain negative reactions from the staff, he should not be deprived of those safe drugs that would commonly be prescribed for an anxious patient with a serious heart problem.

Another possibility, also controversial, is the prescription of methadone during the hospitalization both to reduce Mr. K's need for heroin and to treat whatever narcotic withdrawal symptoms he may be experiencing. When his fear of being "sick" from withdrawal is reduced, he may be more willing to discuss long-term rehabilitation. In addition to the methadone, adequate analgesia (including parenteral narcotics if necessary) should be prescribed. Any pain will be poorly tolerated by Mr. K and the use of narcotics for pain is not going to increase his addictive behavior.

A complicating and so far unanswerable question regarding Mr. K is whether he has been abusing and has become physically dependent on other drugs besides heroin. Though he denies anything more than the occasional use of alcohol or barbiturates, his word is suspect. He may have been self-treating withdrawal from these drugs by receiving them from his visitors and if this supply is diminished, a safe detoxification in the hospital will be necessary to prevent the serious consequences of a withdrawal from these depressant drugs in a man with a compromised cardiac status. Frequent blood and urine drug screening tests during the hospitalization will help the staff distinguish which signs and symptoms are due to the medical illness and which are possibly due to persistent abuse of illicit drugs.

CHOICE AND OUTCOME

The consultant, realizing that any recommendations would fail without the support of the ward nurses and physicians, arranged an ad hoc conference to discuss Mr. K. She began by identifying the frustration and anger this patient elicited and acknowledged that her own consultation note with its tone of helpless resignation had contributed to the problem. She then countered this feeling by pointing out that the staff actually did not have to be dictated by Mr. K's whims and could choose one of at least four options: discharge; transfer to a psychiatric service; transfer to another medical service; or a modification of the treatment plan on the present service.

The pros and cons of each option were hotly contested. All agreed that, at the present time, Mr. K would never consent to psychiatric hospitalization or a drug detoxification/rehabilitation program. Some argued that Mr. K deserved whatever he got and should be placed back on the streets. Others contended that he was no worse than the emphysematous patient who continued smoking or the duodenal ulcer patient who continued to be hard-driving and to be noncompliant with his dietary regime; in such cases the staff's job was to treat the illness and not decide who should or should not be treated on the basis of their personal problems. In the end, the consensus was that Mr. K should not be discharged and the staff should accept the challenge of keeping him on the present ward with the option of transfer or discharge if changes in the present management were not effective.

The next decision was what those changes in his management should be. Here again the staff was divided. Some wanted to set up a police-like security system to ensure that Mr. K had no visitors and could receive no illicit drugs; others saw this effort as a waste of time. A compromise was reached. The patient would be absolutely prevented from abusing any drugs in the presence of other patients—in his room, halls, or solarium—and his bedside belongings would be searched daily in his presence and disruptive visitors would be told to leave, but round-the-clock guards and other more stringent measures would not be employed.

The third decision was what drugs should be prescribed for Mr. K. As expected, this issue was also potentially divisive. Some of the staff resented "feeding his habit free of charge"; and at the other extreme, some wanted to keep Mr. K "snowed" until his medical condition improved and he could be safely discharged. The compromise was that Mr. K could receive moderate dosages of diazepam at his request unless heavy sedation or lowered blood pressure were noted. He would also be placed on methadone maintenance, using sedation and respiratory rate to titrate the dosage. The nursing staff would check Mr. K every 15 minutes to ensure that he had not overdosed from either the licit or illicit drugs. If and when he should start to complain of pain, the intern and psychiatric consultant would decide what analgesics and what dosages should be ordered.

As a result of this discussion, the staff members saw that the situation was not completely out of their control and some options were available. The consultant then invited Mr. K into the conference being held on the ward. In a nonvindictive and clear manner, she explained to him the staff's current treatment plan and the plan's rationale. She emphasized that the most crucial consideration at present was to ensure that Mr. K received adequate medical treatment for his life-threatening illness, after which long-term treatment for his other illness—substance abuse—could be negotiated. The consultant openly admitted that Mr. K would be able to beat the system and acquire illicit drugs if he so chose, but she suspected that the doses of methadone, benzodiazepines and pain medicines would be adequate for his current needs. Mr. K was clearly impressed by the consultant's expertise and frankness. He accepted the general treatment plan but negotiated for some minor changes—lorazepam in place of diazepam and the opportunity of being present when his bedside belongings were searched. These requests were granted.

During the next few days Mr. K appeared to be testing the staff as he frequently requested his anxiolytics, but either because he became convinced that the staff would concede to his wishes or because the methadone 20 mg twice a day was relieving the anxiety as well as the fears of withdrawal, he soon stopped requesting the lorazepam altogether. Because of complications in his medical course, including a pulmonary embolus, he returned to the intensive care unit and the hospitalization was extended for several weeks. He was given sufficient dosages of intravenous morphine to treat his pain during this critical period. During this time the psychiatrist got to know, and in some ways came to like, Mr. K. In addition to being compassionate during this medical crisis, she was also confrontational in a way that he could hear and respect.

Towards the end of Mr. K's hospitalization, when he was medically stable and far less anxious, the psychiatrist asked two recovering heroin addicts to visit Mr. K in the hospital. They were unsuccessful in convincing him to enter a drug-free rehabilitation program; but as a result of their up-front approach and the supportive encouragement of the psychiatrist, Mr. K agreed to enter a methadone maintenance outpatient program. Two years later he is still in that program and has had no recurrence of his endocarditis, although he is probably still abusing some drugs.

SUGGESTED READINGS

1. Woody, G. E., Luborsky, L., McLellan, A. T., O'Brien, C. P., & Beck, A. Psychotherapy for opiate addicts: Does it help? *Archives of General Psychiatry,* 40:639–645, 1983. (According to this careful outcome study, the answer is yes—if one chooses the right patient and the right approach.)
2. Dole, V. P., & Nyswander, M. A medical treatment for diacetylmorphine (heroin) addiction. *Journal of the American Medical Association,* 192:646–650, 1965. (A classic article, which introduced "methadone maintenance" *and* emphasized psychosocial support.)
3. Kreek, M. S. Medical management of methadone-maintained patients. In J. H. Lewinson & P. Ruiz (Eds.), *Substance Abuse: Clinical Problems and Perspectives.* Baltimore: Williams & Wilkins, 1981, pp. 660–673. (A useful guide when patients like Mr. K are on methadone, have a medical illness, and are receiving other drugs.)
4. *Confronting AIDS: Update 1988.* Washington, DC: National Academy Press, 1988. (Cited as a reminder—though one hardly is needed—that the AIDS epidemic would today further complicate the treatment of Mr. K.)

IV

Schizophrenia

■ SCHIZOPHRENIA, PARANOID

10. The Case of the Widow

(Historical Case: Emil Kraepelin)

Authors' Note:
Trained as a neuropathologist and heavily invested in Virchow's concept of disease, Kraepelin attempted to define clinical syndromes by systematically recording their symptoms, signs, course, and outcome. As illustrated here, he gave little consideration to familial, environmental or psychodynamic factors. Moreover, because he viewed dementia praecox as incurable, his descriptions of such patients have a fatalistic tone. Nevertheless, his methodical case reports not only remain classics from the past, but also are consistent with the contemporary move towards a more scientific psychiatry.

The widow, aged 35, whom I will now bring before you . . . gives full information about her life in answer to our questions, knows where she is, can tell the date and the year, and gives proof of satisfactory school knowledge. It is noteworthy that she does not look at her questioner, and speaks in a low and peculiar, sugary, affected tone. When you touch on her illness, she is reserved at first, and says that she is quite well, but she soon begins to express a number of remarkable *ideas of persecution*. For many years she has heard voices, which insult her and cast suspicion on her chastity. They mention a number of names she knows, and tell her she will be stripped and abused. The voices are very distinct, and, in her opinion, they must be carried by a telescope or a machine from her home. Her thoughts are dictated to her; she is obliged to think them, and hears them repeated after her. She is interrupted in her work, and has all kinds of uncomfortable sensations in her body, to which something is "done." In particular, her "mother parts" are turned inside out, and people send a pain through her back, lay ice-water on her heart, squeeze her neck, injure her spine, and violate her. There are also hallucinations of sight—black figures and the altered appearance of people—but these are far less frequent. She cannot exactly say who carries on all the influencing, or for what object it is done. Sometimes it is the people from her home, and sometimes the doctors of an asylum where she was before who have taken something out of her body.

The patient makes these extraordinary complaints without showing much emotion. She cries a little, but then describes her morbid experiences again with secret satisfaction and even with an erotic bias. She demands her discharge, but is easily consoled, and does not trouble at all about her position and her future. Her use of numerous strained and hardly intelligible phrases is very striking. She is ill-treated "flail-wise," "utterance-wise," "terror-wise"; she is "a picture of misery in angel's form," and "a defrauded mamma and housewife of sense of order." They have "altered her form of emotion." She is "persecuted by a secret insect from the District Office. . . . " Her former history shows that she has been ill for nearly 10 years. The disease developed gradually. About a year after the death of her husband, by whom she has two children, she became apprehensive, slept badly, heard loud talking in her room at night, and thought that she was being robbed of her means and persecuted by people from Frankfurt, where she had formerly lived. Four years ago she spent a year in an asylum. She thought she found the "Frankfurters" there, noticed poison in the food, heard voices, and felt influences. After her discharge, she brought accusations against the doctors of having mutilated her while she was there. She now thought them to be her persecutors, and openly abused the public authorities for failing to protect her, so she had to be admitted to this hospital two months ago. Here she made the same complaints day after day, without showing much excitement, and wrote long-winded letters full of senseless and unvarying abuse about the persecution from which she suffered, to her relations, the asylum doctors, and the authorities. She did not occupy herself in any way, held no intercourse with her fellow patients, and avoided every attempt to influence her.

KRAEPELIN'S DIAGNOSIS

Dementia praecox, paranoid

DSM-III-R DIAGNOSIS

Axis I: Schizophrenia, paranoid type, chronic

TREATMENT PROBLEM

Thirty-five-year-old widowed mother of two with a 10-year history of persecutory hallucinations and delusions. This present hospitalization began two months ago when she continually complained to public authorities that she had been molested by doctors during her one-year stay at another asylum.

DISCUSSION OF TREATMENT SELECTION

Setting. Kraepelin's description suggests that this patient is still too disorganized to function outside the structured hospital environment. Although she need not be kept in the hospital until she is no longer psychotic (this may never happen), she should not be discharged until there is reasonable chance that she can manage her affairs with assistance and can contain her delusional beliefs rather than immediately act upon them. A prompt readmission will be demoralizing to the patient and the staff. On the other hand, although a premature discharge followed by a "revolving door" readmission has its risks, a hospitalization that is too prolonged can also be harmful. Regression, loss of social skills, and loss of contact with her two children during their formative years could result while the staff awaits a full remission. The previous hospitalization lasted one year and the duration may have contributed to the patient's delusional overinvolvement with her doctors. For these reasons, once her more flagrant psychopathology subsides, a transition to either a partial hospital or to a halfway house would provide supervised contact with the children and steps towards vocational rehabilitation.

Format. Kraepelin does not tell us much about this patient's family, only that she has two children (who must now be in their early teens) and that she has "relations" to whom she writes long-winded letters. Family sessions, with and without the patient, would be helpful in educating the children and relatives about the nature of the patient's illness, the kinds of treatment that will be used, and the ways to reduce tension and respond to her accusations and delusional ideas. Family sessions would also be helpful to uncover the patient's strengths and capabilities before her husband died and she became ill.

Group therapy—or even community meetings on the ward—would not be advisable while the patient remains disruptively psychotic; but when her more florid symptoms subside, both a task-oriented homogeneous group (such as prevocational training programs for hospitalized psychiatric patients) and a heterogeneous group would be helpful to diffuse her persecutory preoccupations, to restore her social skills, and to reduce her isolation and avoidance behavior. An individual format, however, will likely remain the rudder to stabilize her through the storms and rough seas of her illness. This format can provide a focused attention on her symptoms and her response to medication and its side effects, and can titrate the level of interpersonal involvement the patient can tolerate at any given time.

Duration and Frequency. The patient's illness is chronic and will require continuing care. Even when her symptoms are in remission, she should be seen frequently enough to assess the need for medication, its dosage and side effects, and to intercept a psychotic decompensation before it becomes severe.

Approach. This patient is highly suspicious of others and should not be expected to form a trusting relationship. In fact, she may experience the therapist as too intrusive or even "mutilating" if, for some time, he does not maintain a concerned, but distant, therapeutic stance. Although the dynamic determinants of her sexual preoccupations are intriguing, the patient may experience any deep exploration of this problem as "a rape." Similarly, the patient will not at first be reassured by remarks by the therapist that are intended to be warm, consoling, and comforting. She is more likely to experience such premature statements as being condescending, demeaning or seductive. An initial approach that is direct, respectful, and honest is more likely to succeed. For example, the therapist can indicate that the patient's thinking at times becomes confused and that her imagination "plays tricks on her." The therapist must attempt to make these observations in an uncritical way and without the expectation that the patient will be simply talked out of her delusional beliefs. Rather, the intent is to address the healthier aspects of the patient and to indicate that the therapist will not accept or be influenced by ideas and accusations that he does not believe are true. In this way, the therapist conveys a solid sense of reality and of his own autonomy and the patient feels reassured that she will not destroy or merge with him.

Somatic Treatment. Neuroleptic medication is indicated for this widow's agitation, disorganized thinking, hallucinations, persecutory delusions, thought-broadcasting, and resulting social withdrawal. Because of her suspiciousness, particularly towards doctors, every effort must be made to explain to her the rationale for prescribing medication as well as the drug's name, dosage, and potential side effects. During the induction phase of psychopharmacotherapy, she should take the medication in the presence of the therapist who can then observe the patient's response to the drug, offer reassurance, and answer any additional questions she may have as she experiences the effect of the drug. Given her history and the nature of her persecutory ideas, she will no doubt be frightened of any substance that she perceives as "invading" her body and taking control. For this reason, she herself should be given as much control as is clinically reasonable, such as being encouraged to read articles about the drug, being permitted to take the medication by mouth rather than by injection, and being asked to become a participant in deciding at what time of day she finds the taking of medication most convenient and the least likely to cause annoying side effects.

Since the patient has no prior history of taking neuroleptics, choosing the best drug and proper dosage may require some experimentation. A less sedating neuroleptic may be less likely to make her feel "drugged" or "controlled." Although these less sedating neuroleptics have a greater risk of causing parkinsonian-like side effects on the motor system, these effects can be treated if and when they occur. Because the risk of significant dystonic reactions is less than 30%, prophylactic use of antiparkinsonian medication is not advised. In addition, these drugs have side effects on the central nervous system (sedation, confusion) that may complicate the clinical picture.

There is a suggestion from the history that this patient's paranoid schizophrenic illness has a strong affective component in that her decompensation began shortly after her husband's death. Depressive signs and symptoms may emerge after the patient is less psychotic, whereupon antidepressant medication may be indicated in conjunction with the neuroleptics. Whether or not this patient will require maintenance on antipsychotic medication is at present not clear. Recent studies indicate that after the florid and disturbing psychotic symptoms remit, some patients can be treated intermittently with medication in response to early signs of relapse.

SUGGESTED READING

1. Wallace, C. J., Nelson, C. J., Liberman, R. P., et al. A review and critique of social skills training with schizophrenic patients. *Schizophrenia Bulletin,* 6:42–64, 1980. (Description of specific behavioral techniques along with indications and methods for their implementation.)
2. May, P. R. A. *Treatment of Schizophrenia: A Cooperative Study of Five Treatment Methods.* New York: Science House, 1968. (Though a study of first-admission schizophrenics, its primary finding, the efficacy of antipsychotic drugs, is applicable to patients like the one Kraepelin describes in the above case.)
3. Davis, J. M. Overview: Maintenance therapy in psychiatry: I. Schizophrenia. *American Journal of Psychiatry,* 132:1237–1245, 1975. (Further evidence to support the efficacy of neuroleptic medication to prevent psychotic relapse and rehospitalization.)
4. Kerr, T. A., Snaith, R. P. (Eds.). *Contemporary Issues in Schizophrenia.* Washington, DC: American Psychiatric Press, Inc., 1986. (Good update.)

11.   The Case of the Relapsing Patient

(Guest Experts: Blaine Greenwald, M.D.,
Kirk Denicoff, M.D., Arthur T. Meyerson, M.D.)

Authors' Note:
This case is an edited version of a Grand Rounds held at Mount Sinai School of Medicine, New York City, in 1984. At the time, Dr. Greenwald was an Instructor, Dr. Denicoff was a psychiatry resident, and Dr. Meyerson was Vice-Chairman and Associate Professor of Psychiatry. Dr. Meyerson has been active in promoting the cause and increasing the understanding of chronic patients similar to the one presented here.

Mr. M is a 25-year-old single unemployed male with a six-year history of a psychotic illness. He is treated in an aftercare program of a university hospital, lives in a supervised apartment, and is supported by supplemental security income and medicaid. Staff frustration at limited gains, despite active psychopharmacologic and rehabilitative interventions, have prompted presentation for review and reassessment. He remains partially symptomatic and cannot function vocationally or in peer relationships; nevertheless, he and his parents sustain an expectation that he will become "normal" and work.

Mr. M's childhood history is remarkable for his peculiar, detached manner with consequent difficulty forming friendships. When he was 12, psychiatric consultation revealed a "personality problem." When he was 13, Mr. M's mother was diagnosed as having a malignant lesion and she died after a three-year debilitating course. During this period Mr. M began weekly treatment for five years. Despite declining school performance, Mr. M graduated high school at age 18. He matriculated at a private college but failed all first semester courses and returned home. During the next year Mr. M lived at home, was socially isolated, and was unemployed. When he was 19, a new psychiatrist made a diagnosis of "borderline schizophrenia." Psychological testing suggested "incipient psychosis" in a "passive-aggressive individual with high anxiety and marked passive-dependency needs."

Mr. M had his first overt psychotic episode and hospitalization at age 20, within one week of his father's remarriage. He had delusions of grandeur stating that he could fly, and he became sexually preoccupied and aggressive. Mental status on that hospital admission revealed a cooperative but agitated young man whose mood was fearful and suspicious, and whose affect was inappropriate and blunted. Thought processes were characterized by derailment and racing thoughts. Thought content included grandiose delusions that he was God, ideas of reference, paranoid ideation, and auditory hallucinations. He felt he could read minds and that sometimes his thoughts did not seem like his own. He had vague suicidal and homicidal ideation without intent.

The patient's symptoms improved somewhat on chlorpromazine (Thorazine) 400 mg/day, and he was discharged after three-and-a-half weeks. Diagnostic impression at that time was paranoid schizophrenia. Mr. M returned home to his family, began treatment with a new private psychiatrist, and entered a rehabilitative day hospital program with family therapy. Mr. M occupied a very sheltered, nondemanding role in a household characterized by parents who were overinvolved and whose attitude was protective and infantilizing. Both parents had also been critical of Mr. M, with strong denial about his degree of dysfunction.

Over the next two years, while in the day program, he was isolated, had trouble socializing, had poor concentration, and was anxious, with frequent displays of provocative, intrusive behavior. When he was 22, his stepmother gave birth to a son. He had an exacerbation of symptoms and his parents decided to have him placed in an out-of-state residential program. Soon thereafter, he had his second florid psychotic decompensation and was again hospitalized. His mental status was marked by agitation, pressured speech, flight of ideas, inappropriate affect, intrusiveness, hypersexuality, paranoid and grandiose delusions, auditory hallucinations and reduced sleep. He was treated with haloperidol (Haldol), averaging 40 mg/day, and improved slightly.

Because of the manic features, the diagnostic impression was changed to schizoaffective disorder. He was started on lithium and soon grew more subdued, better able to focus, and less inappropriate, hypersexual, and delusional, though decreased concentration and intermittent childish impulsivity persisted. Mr. M was discharged after two months on haloperidol 10 mg/day, trihexyphenidyl (Artane) 2 mg twice daily, and lithium 900 mg/day. His lithium level was stable at 1.0 mEq/L. He was placed in a supervised apartment program and continued in his day program. He also continued outpatient treatment with his inpatient resident physician, and over the next two years was maintained on low dose haloperidol (5–10 mg/day) and lithium (900 mg/day). Although he was periodically symptomatic, he was never overtly psychotic. Despite his participation in work rehabilitation programs, Mr. M's prevocational and social functioning stayed marginal. At age 23, he was referred to a new day program for ongoing social and vocational rehabilitation, while continuing in the hospital's outpatient clinic, an "alumni group," and a family group with his parents.

Several months later, Mr. M was assigned to a new, female resident psychiatrist. The patient showed a resurgence of paranoid symptoms and would often call home for reassurance. Because affective symptoms were not prominent, the new resident reformulated the diagnosis from schizoaffective disorder to chronic paranoid schizophrenia. Haloperidol was increased from 5 mg to 20 mg/day and lithium was discontinued, without evident change in symptoms.

Approximately five months later the patient's paranoid symptoms again exacerbated despite the higher haloperidol dosage. This convinced another new resident to attempt a trial of higher dose neuroleptics. Haloperidol was pushed to 50 mg/day. After two months there was minimal symptomatic improvement. Medications were switched from haloperidol to fluphenazine hydrochloride, which was rapidly increased to 50 mg with moderate improvement. Still another resident was assigned four months later.

Mr. M's symptoms were highlighted by mild psychomotor agitation, tangentiality and social inappropriateness, which was obvious during group therapy. For example, in one session, a patient was discussing a memory of childhood dreams of snakes. Mr. M stopped her and stated that snakes are phallic symbols and repeated this interpretation several times. He would often interject an inappropriate personal experience and seemed unable to follow the group process or focus on one topic at a time.

Within a month after being switched to fluphenazine, Mr. M reported "paranoid episodes" every two to three days, accompanied by intense anxiety, and his stepmother noted that calls home increased in frequency, and he would complain of fright at leaving his apartment and would express suicidal ideation. Because of this disturbing behavior, Mr. M's dose of fluphenazine was increased to 60 mg/day, with Artane 6 mg/day. This increase was briefly helpful, but previous symptoms soon recurred and were accompanied by overt akathisia. Fluphenazine was then tapered to 40 mg and Mr. M appeared less restless.

DSM-III-R DIAGNOSIS

AXIS I: Schizophrenia, paranoid type, chronic
AXIS II: Passive-aggressive and dependent personality traits (premorbid)
AXIS III: Childhood asthma, in remission
AXIS IV: Stress—moderate (changes in treatment; in past, death of mother and father's remarriage)
AXIS V: Highest level of functioning past year—poor

DISCUSSION OF TREATMENT SELECTION

Unlike DSM-III-R, the Research Diagnostic Criteria (RDC) allow for subtypes within the schizoaffective diagnosis. Mr. M's RDC diagnosis is chronic schizoaffective disorder, manic type, mainly schizophrenic. This diagnosis allows one to recognize the patient's clear schizophrenic diathesis, while acknowledging the existence of manic symptoms during acute episodes, leaving the door open for psychopharmacological approaches more typically aimed at affective symptoms.

Brown and Birley[1] demonstrated a significantly greater percentage of crises and life changes in the three-week period immediately preceding onset of an acute schizophrenic episode than at other times. Furthermore, patients with such a precipitating event were much more likely to be rated as coming from homes with a high tension level during the three months before onset. Brown and Birley concluded that environmental factors can precipitate a schizophrenic exacerbation. These data confirm the susceptibility to environmental stressors that this patient's history suggests. Three weeks prior to the first hospitalization, the father remarried. It seems reasonable to surmise the presence of high tension in the home. Similarly, the birth of the half-brother predated by four months the patient's second acute psychotic episode. Again, tension was high in the home and the patient's behavior was sufficiently disturbing so as to provoke the family to decide precipitously to place him in a residence. Later, after a period of relative stability, the assignment of a new physician was associated with an increase of symptoms sufficient enough to bring about both a discontinuation of a fairly successful two-year drug regimen and an increase of neuroleptic dosage (a trend which has continued until recently).

In light of Mr. M's increase in symptoms each time he changed psychiatrists and considering the relative stability of his course during the two-year period with one physician, the frequent rotation of psychiatrists should be minimized. At the least, Mr. M should be followed by one doctor for the tenure of that doctor's residency. Transitions should include frequent meetings with the outgoing and incoming therapists to arrange for a consistent treatment plan. One reason for the limited number of hospitalizations may be the continuity of medical treatment at one hospital. When he was transferred to an unaffiliated day program, the patient continued receiving medical and family treatment in the hospital outpatient department. That concept of maintaining stability in treatment services should continue.

Brown and Birley's finding that long-term tension in the home is often a precursor of schizophrenic onset laid the foundation for later work concerning the influence of family life on the course of schizophrenic illness. Schizophrenic patients coming from homes with a high index of expressed emotion had a marked and significantly greater relapse rate. Expressed emotion (EE) refers to critical comments made by relatives, hostility, overinvolvement, overconcern, and overprotectiveness. Results also suggested that patients living in high EE homes were less likely to relapse if they either received regular phenothiazine medication or managed to avoid close face-to-face contact with the family.

It appears that Mr. M's home had a high EE marked by criticism, overconcern, and overinvolvement. Hence, the decision to place Mr. M into a structured setting, regardless of motivation, was probably therapeutic. Controlled investigations have demonstrated that as an adjunct to medication both short-[2] and longer-term[3] family treatment of schizophrenic patients reduce relapse rates. Thus, the inclusion of family therapy in Mr. M's treatment is well supported. Attention needs to be given to modifying his parents' critical, overprotective attitude and to fostering both the recognition of Mr. M's limited vocational abilities and the acceptance of his current level of adjustment. This patient's frequent phone calls to his stepmother (for reassurance that he will not be shot) may represent a desperate appeal for such acceptance.

Major rehabilitative treatment goals for Mr. M have included improved social relations, vocational function, and independent living skills. Treatment interventions targeted at these areas have been termed *sociotherapy*, and its effectiveness with and without drug treatment has been examined in a series of controlled clinical trials.[4] These studies reaffirmed that drug treatment has a significantly prophylactic effect in forestalling relapse as compared to placebo. Sociotherapy also lowered relapse rates, but only in those patients surviving in the community for six months after discharge. Drug and sociotherapy together achieved maximum benefits in reducing relapse and improving community adjustment. However, the effect on adjustment also had a lag time of at least 18 months. These reports indicate that schizophrenic patients must be continued in treatment for well beyond a single year following hospital discharge. Again, these data support the multimodality treatment of Mr. M, as well as the continuity of psychosocial treatment he has received.

Major role therapy may not be suitable for every schizophrenic patient. Whereas asymptomatic patients benefited most from major role therapy, in patients with greater symptom severity major role therapy actually *hastened relapse*. The conclusions drawn were that symptomatic patients may be encouraged to perform beyond their capacity, resulting in social failure, a flight to a sick role, and psychotic exacerbation. Thus, Mr. M may be too disorganized to fully exploit these opportunities. Because gainful employment is a standard of achievement in society, perhaps the patient, his family, and his treatment team appear to be wed to the idea that unless he works, he is a failure. Rehabilitation goals for Mr. M have to generate alternative types of meaningful activity, while adjusting to a level of functioning that is realistically attainable. The appropriateness of Mr. M's participation in what appears to be an insight-oriented group is also questionable. Aftercare programs appear to help schizophrenic patients if they focus on specific reality factors related to everyday life, but *not* on psychologically oriented issues. In support of this view is the finding that those day treatment centers that reduced symptoms and relapse rates provided more occupational therapy and recreational activities, whereas day programs with *poor* outcome results had *more* professional counseling staff and more group therapy.[5]

Unequivocally, pharmacotherapy is the mainstay of aftercare treatment. Reasonable stability occurred when Mr. M was maintained on the combination of low-dose haloperidol (5–10 mg/day) and lithium for two-and-a-half years. At the end of this period, the patient was terminated with his therapist of over two years and assigned a new, female therapist. That is change enough. The decision to discontinue lithium because the patient had no affective symptoms seems misinformed and hasty, ignoring over two years of fairly successful treatment. Lithium appears at least partially responsible for his stability. Furthermore, it makes little sense to change so many variables at once in a patient so demonstrably sensitive to change. A more prudent course would be to maintain the medication then, during an acutely stressful transition period, increase the medication and number of sessions on an as-needed basis.

The patient has been on spiraling doses of neuroleptics—often precipitated by a change of therapists. Yet the clinical picture is not characterized by positive symptoms that are usually drug responsive, but rather by lack of drive, anxiety, and social inappropriateness. These symptoms are often less sensitive to drugs. As he had no clear-cut benefit from high doses of neuroleptics over one year and better success at lower doses combined with lithium, one should reinstitute the latter regimen. Furthermore, although Mr. M had demonstrated an obvious akathisia at 60 mg of fluphenazine, it is quite possible that a more subtle akathitic process has been ongoing at lower neuroleptic dosages. Akathisia is often misdiagnosed as anxiety, agitation, or psychotic exacerbation, and Mr. M's transient bursts of increasing anxiety (expressed as paranoia?) may correlate with increasing doses of neuroleptics.

REFERENCES

1. Brown, G. W., & Birley, J. L. T. Crisis and life changes and the onset of schizophrenia. *Journal of Health and Social Behavior,* 9:203–214, 1968.
2. Goldstein, M. J., Rodnick, E. H., Evans, J. R., et al. Drug and family therapy in the aftercare of acute schizophrenics. *Archives of General Psychiatry,* 35:1169–1177, 1978.
3. Falloon, I. R. H., Boyd, J. L., McGill, C. W., et al. Family management training in the community care of schizophrenia. In M. Goldstein (Ed.), *New Directions For Mental Health Sciences: New Developments in Interventions with Families of Schizophrenics.* San Francisco: Jossey-Bass, 1981.
4. Goldberg, S. C., Schooler, N. R., Hogarty, G. E., et al. Prediction of relapse in schizophrenic outpatients treated by drug and sociotherapy. *Archives of General Psychiatry,* 34:171–184, 1977.
5. Epstein, N. B., & Vlok, L. A. Research on the results of psychotherapy: A summary of evidence. *American Journal of Psychiatry,* 138:1027–1035, 1981.

12. The Case of the Delusional Dropout

(Guest Expert: William T. Carpenter, Jr., M.D.)

Authors' Note:
Dr. Carpenter is Professor of Psychiatry at the University of Maryland School of Medicine, and Director of the Maryland Psychiatric Research Center. He has done extensive research on the phenomenology, diagnosis, and treatment of schizophrenic patients, one of whom is presented here.

Mr. D is a 24-year-old single and unemployed college dropout, who was admitted to the hospital three weeks after he had painted everything in sight black and white, including his room, his furniture, his clothes, and finally even himself. He was responding to a persistent male voice indicating that this behavior would somehow solve the race problem in America and bring peace to his family.

Mr. D has been hospitalized on at least five previous occasions during the past five years, each time for four to six weeks, because of an exacerbation of his illness with some combination of hallucinations, strange behavior, and persecutory delusions. He has always responded fairly rapidly to treatment with phenothiazines, but hates to take the medication because it makes him feel "even deader than dead." Between hospitalizations, he is likely to take medication irregularly or not at all and to miss more outpatient appointments than he keeps.

Mr. D's functioning between episodes is poor and seems to be getting worse, with increasing social withdrawal, sloppy personal hygiene, and disordered thinking. When on medication, however, the patient makes a much better appearance and speaks more coherently.

Mr. D is the fourth of five children in an extremely close-knit, guilt-provoking, and argumentative family. His mother has been hospitalized twice for hallucinations and persecutory delusions, but now functions reasonably well without medication. She believes that she knows better than the doctors what is best for her son. Her other children have all left the family apartment, and Mrs. D has become increasingly attached to and dependent upon "the only kid I have left." Mr. D responds to his mother's ministrations with annoyance and avoidance but, when they are not forthcoming, becomes annoyed.

Mr. D spends most of his time in the apartment doing yoga and reading about Jungian archetypes and social oppression. He sleeps all day and stays up most of every night and, except when hospitalized, rarely talks to anyone outside his immediate family circle. He is afraid to go outside, especially during the day, because he believes that strangers on the street are talking to each other about him and are able to control his thoughts and actions. He is convinced that the transmission of these command thoughts requires solar energy and that he is safer at night. He also believes that a "right-wing, neo-Nazi" group is attempting to ruin his reputation by spreading rumors that he is one-eighth Jewish.

As usual, Mr. D has responded well to phenothiazine treatment during this hospitalization. He remains half-convinced of his delusions but in a low-key way, and can to some extent be argued out of them. He is also able to talk to staff with less suspicion and greater coherence than at the time he was admitted, and his behavior is no longer overtly bizarre. He seems ready for discharge.

Mr. D's mother has had his room repainted, and she is quite eager to have him back. His therapist has focused attention on Mr. D's resistance to medication and the detrimental impact that it has had on his treatment and on his life. Mr. D seems somewhat more insightful about this behavior than in the past. Efforts to enlist his mother's cooperation have not been conspicuously successful.

DSM-III-R DIAGNOSIS

AXIS I: Schizophrenia, paranoid, chronic
AXIS II: None
AXIS III: None
AXIS IV: Stress—none
AXIS V: Highest level of functioning past year—very poor

DISCUSSION OF TREATMENT SELECTION

Mr. D presents treatment dilemmas common to the longitudinal treatment of patients with chronic psychotic illness. An optimal clinical approach is based on an integration of therapeutic, rehabilitative, and social support strategies rather than on the simultaneous but independent application of various interventions. Fundamental to integrated treatment is the continuity of a clinical relationship; it serves as the basis for developing the information necessary for treatment decisions in each domain and provides the best opportunity for psychotic patients to sustain collaboration in treatment. Within that framework, the following comments address five specific issues in the treatment of Mr. D.

1) Mr. D conveys considerable information about his subjective experience through verbal communication and symbolic behavior (e.g., the painting). This allows the clinician to become increasingly informed about manifestations of illness in Mr. D and to develop an understanding of circumstances associated with improvement and deterioration.

Mr. D's participation in this information-gathering process with the clinician as a participant-observer may decrease his sense of isolation and bizarre uniqueness. Moreover, as the clinician gains understanding, he is able to articulate a view of illness that may also be understood and shared by Mr. D, reducing his confusion. This longitudinal approach enables the clinician to keep informed about the patient's many attributes that are germane to therapeutic decision-making.

2) Mr. D's illness is responsive to antipsychotic medication, but continuous use of drugs has not proven feasible and may not be desirable. Recognizing his noncompliance and the unpleasant subjective experiences associated with medication, I would recommend sustained periods without drugs and would attempt to elicit his participation in an early-intervention pharmacotherapeutic strategy.

This approach would require Mr. D and his clinician to agree on the early indicators of psychotic decompensation and to plan a rapid drug intervention at the first sign of relapse. Drugs could be discontinued once stability has been reestablished. Antipsychotic medication during acute exacerbation may not be dysphoric; hence, Mr. D may find such a pharmacotherapeutic approach more agreeable.[1]

3) Mr. D and his mother need to be involved in a conjoint evaluation, including a home visit. Her cooperation is crucial, since her assistance in detecting prodromal symptoms and encouraging treatment compliance is needed. Furthermore, there is no reason to believe that the home environment is unduly emotional and may have an untoward impact on the course of Mr. D's illness. His dependence, however, may preclude autonomous living, and his mother's mental health is likely to be an important consideration in planning psychosocial interventions and optimal living circumstances for Mr. D.

The evaluation process will also provide an opportunity to educate mother and patient about the illness and various therapeutic interventions. Finally, it will provide a basis for determining what family therapeutic strategy is advisable.

4) I am concerned about the extensive time that Mr. D spends alone and his involvement in inner-directed processes such as meditation. Work or alternative structured experiences outside the home might beneficially interfere with his autistic retreat, diminish the emotionality

in his relationship with his mother, and provide a social network that can improve his functioning over time.

5) I would further stress the importance of sharing information and concepts about the nature of schizophrenia with Mr. D and his mother. Of particular relevance is an explication of negative symptoms and the deficit syndrome, attributes of illness often not regarded as part of schizophrenia by patients and relatives. They are often the subject of family dissention and inadequate treatment planning.

The successful integration of multidimensional treatment requires that the clinician be conversant with the scientific models and data relevant to schizophrenia, and with the range of psychotropic and interpersonal therapeutic and rehabilitative approaches.[2] The work of multidimensional treatment is often shared by more than one mental health professional; it is essential that the psychiatrist and other clinicians establish an ongoing relationship with the patient and that the various aspects of treatment are carefully integrated. There is an intimate interplay among social, psychological, and biological factors in illness, and pharmacotherapeutic and interpersonal treatment strategies have ramifications at each level.[3]

Intelligent decision-making within each therapeutic domain requires that all members of the treatment team be aware of the full range of data generated by the various team members. It is unlikely that two treatment approaches will be mutually exclusive, but clinicians working in isolation can undermine each other's efforts and can be basing their own approach on incomplete information.

REFERENCES

1. Carpenter, W. T., Jr., Stephens, J. H., Rev, A. D., et al. Early intervention vs. continuous pharmacotherapy of schizophrenia. *Psychopharmacology Bulletin*, 18:21–23, 1982.
2. Strauss, J. S., & Carpenter, W. T., Jr. *Schizophrenia*. New York: Plenum, 1981.
3. Engel, G. L. The need for a new medical model: A challenge for biomedicine. *Science*, 196:129–136, 1977.

■ SCHIZOPHRENIA, UNDIFFERENTIATED

13. The Case of the Once-Contented Car Washer

Mr. J, a gaunt and wasted 48-year-old man, is brought to the emergency room by the police after he was reported by local residents wandering around an exclusive neighborhood dressed only in an oversized wool coat and thong sandals.

Mr. J has a long and most unfortunate psychiatric history. He was raised by a struggling immigrant family in which his emotional problems as a child went largely unnoticed. At age 17, his complete withdrawal could no longer be ignored. Whereas he had always been an average-to-good student, he quit high school at the end of his junior year for no apparent reason and spent his days aimlessly wandering the streets. During meals with the family, Mr. J began performing stereotypic rituals, such as tapping his earlobes to an imagined tune or wrapping the knives in napkins. These rituals became increasingly complex, were repeated at bedtime, and gradually progressed until they occupied most of the day.

The family remained surprisingly tolerant of Mr. J's various bizarre behaviors, even though they suspected (correctly) that he was following instructions from imaginary voices. By the time Mr. J was 19, however, his grimacing, wild stares, and explosive verbal outbursts became intolerable; Mr. J was taken by his father to a nearby municipal hospital where he was psychiatrically hospitalized.

After a three-month stay and a course of electroconvulsive therapy, he was discharged home with only minimal improvement. Unable to work, he spent the days pacing around his parents' apartment, mumbling and resuming his complex rituals. At age 20 and again at age 22, he had two more relatively brief hospitalizations, but, if anything, Mr. J only deteriorated further despite extremely high levels of neuroleptics. The medical staff finally resigned themselves to a treatment which both the family and Mr. J had advocated years before, namely, chronic care in a psychiatric hospital.

During the ensuing 17 years, from age 24 to 41, Mr. J resided in a state mental hospital. From time to time, as a result of changes in his ward location or in his assigned physician, changes would be made in therapeutic technique or in the dosage of various psychotropics. Despite these efforts, Mr. J's symptoms and behavior remained relatively unchanged. The absence of improvement was not in itself a great concern to Mr. J. Though one could not say that he enjoyed the hospitalization—joy was a stronger emotion than Mr. J ever showed—one could say that Mr. J preferred being a patient to being at home. The staff and other patients were far more accepting of his unusual rituals and, in general, found him a quiet and unobtrusive fixture on the ward.

Mr. J's one distinguishing quality was a passion for washing cars. Hospital employees—physicians, nurses, grounds keepers, engineers, ward attendants, whoever—would regularly sign up on a list to have Mr. J clean their cars. He would attack the job with a perseverance and fervor that would bring a shine to the most rundown vehicle. The small amount of extra money he earned was used for candy bars and cigarettes, as well as for new improved waxes and polishes.

Mr. J would no doubt have spent the rest of his years living reasonably contentedly within the confines of the state hospital but, seven years ago, a major effort was made to deinstitutionalize chronic patients and return them to the community. After several months of preparation, Mr. J was discharged on medication to a single-room-occupancy hotel (SRO) in his designated catchment area. Completely bewildered by this change, Mr. J spent the first three days locked in his room, paralyzed by fear and continuous rituals. He then began wandering the streets, soon lost his appointment for the aftercare clinic, and had no more medication. Three weeks later, unkempt and unfed, he was found sleeping in a parked car and was taken by the police to a municipal hospital emergency room.

Because he was no longer in the revised catchment area of his previous hospital, Mr. J was sent to another chronic facility and sedated with high dosages of phenothiazines in an attempt to stop the hallucinations and rituals; after a few months, he was discharged once again into the community with little improvement and with no greater motivation or ability to acclimate to the outside world. This cycle—discharge, disorganization, readmission—has been repeated several times with little variation for the past several years. His appearance now in the emergency room is merely another verse of the same sad song.

DSM-III-R DIAGNOSIS

Axis I: Schizophrenia, undifferentiated, chronic
Axis II: None
Axis III: Chronic bronchitis
Axis IV: Stress—moderate (adjustment to new environment)
Axis V: Highest level of functioning past year—very poor

TREATMENT PROBLEM

Disposition for psychotic man unable to live outside the hospital and (for administrative reasons) unable to remain in the hospital for maintenance care.

DISCUSSION OF TREATMENT SELECTION

Setting. Because Mr. J is too psychotically disorganized to care for himself and because he has no established support systems outside the hospital, inpatient care is the only available option at this time. In the long run, the most cost-efficient setting would be chronic care hospitalization which Mr. J himself views as a blessing rather than an anathema. The repeated cycles of discharge and readmissions not only are expensive and frustrating, but they no doubt accelerate Mr. J's deterioration as he becomes repeatedly stressed with changes in his physicians, medications, and surroundings.

Format. A homogeneous group of chronic hospitalized patients might be helpful if the group process is focused on highly structured tasks (e.g., cleaning the day room of the hospital) and if the goals of the group are kept limited (e.g., functioning at a specific job in the presence of others). Any group—heterogeneous or homogeneous—with goals that are too ambitious or with members who are either frightened or intolerant of Mr. J's bizarre rituals would be an unduly stressful format and might make Mr. J's symptoms even worse.

Duration and Frequency. Mr. J will require psychiatric care for the rest of his life; the duration of treatment, therefore, has been predetermined by the nature of his illness and is only a major consideration when the treatment does not take into account Mr. J's need to have continuous care that is not disrupted by administrative changes. In terms of frequency, Mr. J has repeatedly shown over the past few years that his symptoms worsen unless some therapeutic structure is provided on a day-to-day basis. Weekly scheduled appointments to an aftercare clinic are simply not sufficient.

Approach. Exploratory therapy is not indicated. Mr. J does not have the enabling factors for this approach and, at best, would find any uncovering of unconscious material only a means of increasing his autistic withdrawal and at worst would increase his confusion. Directive techniques could be useful if the goals are not overly ambitious and the instructions are simple, specific, and closely monitored. For example, Mr. J might respond to a carefully designed program of a token economy to improve his social skills, which would not involve his becoming conversational but, more modestly, involve limiting bizarre behavior in the presence of others. Mr. J's difficulty relating on any personal terms would most likely make him refractory to any experiential techniques.

Somatic Treatment. The actual benefits of psychotropic drugs for Mr. J are difficult to assess because Mr. J has been continuously stressed over the past few years with changes in his surroundings and therapeutic program. In a highly structured setting, he may require neuroleptics only when his symptoms become disorganizing or unacceptable to others. In the less structured settings, in which he has been placed over the past few years, high dosages of psychotropics may be necessary. A possible danger in choosing his somatic treatments is that the therapist, convinced that some drug somewhere somehow will help Mr. J, will continue to readjust his medication. In the end, these constant alterations will only make his therapeutic regimen more confusing. Without being unduly pessimistic, any therapist must recognize that the patient has not responded to extremely high doses of all kinds of psychotropic medications in the past and "a magic bullet" to destroy his chronic illness will not likely be found; moreover, the continuing search is likely to increase the risk of tardive dyskinesia.

CHOICE AND OUTCOME

Mr. J spent four hours in the emergency room while the psychiatry resident made several phone calls and was finally able to arrange hospitalization at the municipal psychiatric facility in Mr. J's catchment area. The patient was not seen again until, by coincidence, two years later the psychiatry resident, now in her final year of training, was assigned to administer a day hospital and discovered that one of the clients was Mr. J.

He was now physically more disabled, having developed rather severe tardive dyskinesia and chronic obstructive pulmonary disease; but mentally, he had improved. His record indicated that a major effort on the part of the day hospital staff had enabled Mr. J to live a marginal existence. He would come to the day hospital at 7:30 in the morning and would not leave until 9:30 at night, when he would return to his SRO around the corner from the hospital. On the ward, his days were spent chain-smoking in the corner or indifferently watching whatever program happened to be on television. On rare occasions he spoke nostalgically about the days past when he "worked" as a car washer at "a country place," but was relatively content living the life now arranged for him by others. The social worker, devoted to Mr. J, took pride in the fact that Mr. J was no longer wandering the streets or continually being brought to the emergency rooms by the police.

SUGGESTED READING

1. Paul, G. L., & Lentz, R. J. *Psychosocial Treatment of Chronic Mental Patients: Milieu Versus Social-Learning Programs.* Cambridge, MA: Harvard University Press, 1977. (Summarizes outcome studies and specific indications for non-pharmacological treatments of schizophrenic patients.)
2. Munetz, M. R., Roth, L. H. Informing patients about tardive dyskinesia. *Archives of General Psychiatry,* 42:866–871, 1985. (Practical *and* legal guidelines.)
3. Turner, J. C., & Ten Hoor, W. J. The NIMH community support program: Pilot approach to a needed social reform. *Schizophrenia Bulletin,* 4:319–348, 1978. (The 10 major components of such programs and their usefulness for patients like Mr. J.)

14. The Case of the Square-Dancing Spiritualist

Miss H is a 39-year-old woman with a long psychiatric history who arrives at the emergency room in the middle of the night seeking rehospitalization. She is no stranger to the hospital staff and is well-known for her cowgirl outfits and bizarre tales. During the past several years she has arrived every few months at the hospital with a new story of woe that often requires admission and always elicits sympathy.

The history is well documented in her lengthy chart. Miss H has had auditory hallucinations more or less continuously for 22 years. The voices are those of pleasant female companions, strangers who have died but now cannot make it to heaven. Miss H believes that God has chosen her to comfort these lost souls and also to convey their messages to those who are still on earth. From time to time she journeys to Times Square to fulfill this duty, but finds few listeners. Never discouraged, she takes consolation in the belief that her thoughts are being transmitted on television to reach those who are not yet receptive to a more personal message. She worries only that these transmissions might be intersected by powerful messengers representing a malevolent force. Unless she is extremely cautious, this "counterpower" could influence her thoughts and force her to behave strangely.

Miss H's family wants nothing to do with her, and she has spent long stretches of her life in custodial state hospitals. In recent years, she has spent increasingly longer periods of time out of the hospital while being maintained on low-dose phenothiazines. The medication helps her feel more relaxed but, even when pushed to extremely high doses, has not been helpful in reducing her hallucinations, delusions, or thought-broadcasting. For the past several months she has been living in a fostercare placement with two other former inpatients and has been spending her weekdays at a low-intensity day hospital, where she bakes cookies, crochets, and, to the delight (or at least tolerance) of all, leads the afternoon square-dancing. Normally, she finds this living arrangement quite satisfactory, although the weekends are boring—unless she makes her occasional sojourn into the streets to do God's work.

Miss H presents now in the emergency room in an agitated and disorganized state that is superimposed on her chronic difficulties. Her welfare check is missing and she assumes, for what appear to be far-fetched reasons, that the check has been stolen by one of her roommates. Convinced that her apartment is now not safe, she wants to return to the hospital where she doesn't have to worry about money.

DSM-III-R DIAGNOSIS

Axis I: Schizophrenia, undifferentiated, chronic
Axis II: None
Axis III: Tardive dyskinesia, mild
Axis IV: Stress—minimal (misplaced welfare check)
Axis V: Highest level of functioning past year—poor

TREATMENT PROBLEM

Disposition of woman who presents in the emergency room with severe agitation and disorganization superimposed on chronic psychotic process.

DISCUSSION OF TREATMENT SELECTION

The easiest arrangement for this chronically ill woman would be to grant her wish and to arrange for rehospitalization, but this disposition has high risks of its own and is an error unless circumstances make it absolutely unavoidable. Once in the hospital, she most likely will have great difficulty leaving it. Furthermore, although her current existence is at best marginal and at worst bizarre, there is no indication that one more hospitalization will alter the course of her disease.

The psychiatric consultant in the emergency room is also well advised to resist making any major changes in the other components of Miss H's treatment. When confronted with an agitated patient who is obviously psychotic, the consultant may be tempted to assume that hospitalization is necessary and also be tempted to change the format (e.g., ask the roommate to come to the emergency room for a joint session that would clarify what happened to the welfare check and how Miss H has been behaving recently); or to change the frequency of sessions (e.g., see Miss H briefly every day to usher her through the current crisis); or to change the technique (e.g., explore the relationship with her roommates to find the sources of her mistrust, or be more directive in advising Miss H how to modify her lifestyle, or be more empathically involved with Miss H's present and past difficulties).

Although some argument could be made for these and other changes, a much stronger argument could be made for resisting any such interventions at this time for fear that they are likely to disrupt a delicate balance. A wiser course would be to acknowledge Miss H's limited capacities and grant, as well, that other clinicians with more experience and knowledge regarding Miss H have no doubt attempted similar approaches along the way with little success. In short, the primary task of the consultant regarding treatment selection in this case is to resist altering a reasonably successful course that has been established by others. If changes in format, intensity, technique, or psychotropic regimen are made, they could be administered more effectively in a setting other than an emergency room where continuity of care is less certain.

CHOICE AND OUTCOME

Miss H was told that it was not a good idea for her to be hospitalized and that she would be helped through this crisis in her life without the need for such a major change. At first enraged and then sullen, she spent the remaining hours of the night in the emergency room. By dawn she was once again telling stories to the nurses aides about her days as a cowgirl in the South (except for an occasional bus trip, Miss H had probably never been out of the metropolitan area).

The patient's social worker at the day hospital was called in the morning and she agreed to look into the problem of Miss H's welfare check and to get emergency assistance, if necessary. The psychiatrist at the day hospital program was informed that Miss H's medication might need to be elevated to tide her over this period of symptomatic exacerbation and that close monitoring might be necessary because of possible noncompliance. He agreed and arranged for Miss H to be escorted from the emergency room back to the day hospital program.

The crisis passed. Miss H's life resumed its former pattern and for several months Miss H was not seen. Then, one night, the police brought her to the emergency room after a violent argument with a new roommate. At this time, the day hospital had closed for lack of funding. Inpatient acute care was the only choice.

SUGGESTED READING

1. Fairweather, G. W., Sander, S., Cressler, D. H., et al. *Community Life for the Mentally Ill: An Alternative to Institutional Care.* Chicago: Aldine, 1969. (A cogent, persuasive argument for community-based settings to treat patients like Miss H.)
2. Mosher, L. R., & Keith, S. J. Psychosocial treatment: Individual, group, family and community support approaches. *Schizophrenia Bulletin,* 6:10–41, 1980. (A review of controlled outcome studies that support the efficacy of psychosocial treatments for schizophrenia.)
3. Perry, S. Emergency management of functional psychosis. In W. Dubin, N. Hanke, & H. Dickens (Eds.), *Clinics in Emergency Medicine—Psychiatric Emergencies.* New York: Churchill Livingstone, 1984. (A step-by-step description of assessing and managing psychotic patients in the emergency room.)

V

Psychotic Disorders Not
Elsewhere Classified

■ **SCHIZOPHRENIFORM DISORDER**

15. The Case of the Confused Connoisseur

Mr. T, a 22-year-old self-proclaimed failure, was brought to the emergency room by his parents for psychiatric hospitalization. During the past few weeks, Mr. T's private psychotherapist had noted that the patient was becoming increasingly suspicious; Mr. T was now convinced that his coworkers in a secretarial pool were trying to have him imprisoned for "stealing their personal secrets." Alarmed by this deterioration, the therapist had contacted the parents and advised them to seek admission for their son at a nearby hospital. Mr. T had gone along with this recommendation and he sat in the emergency room, overwhelmed and dazed, while his parents provided most of the history.

Mr. T first sought psychiatric help four years previously at the age of 18 when he contacted a campus counselor while a sophomore at an Ivy League college. At that time his chief complaint was difficulty completing his term papers. He would come up with grand topics, such as the use of symbolism in Victorian literature, then get lost in the minutiae, while accumulating stacks of completed index cards. The first paragraph of the paper never got written and, too scared to discuss the problem with his instructors, Mr. T simply took a failure in the course.

Academic failure was an unprecedented event for Mr. T. He had done exceptionally well in high school, winning the science prize and a National Merit Scholarship. Socially, however, he had always been a flop. A delicate blonde and blue-eyed boy, he was ostracized by his peers for being effeminate, a "closet queen." To avoid their teasing, he remained aloof and, as a result, developed no friendships whatsoever. He was the only child of two college professors who took delight in their son's academic accomplishments, while regarding his social isolation as the price of genius. When the three of them were together, they would typically quiz each other on esoteric topics, thereby avoiding anything personal.

Like Mr. T's parents, the college counselor also did not discuss social and personal problems. Instead, in individual weekly sessions over a four-month period, the counselor focused on practical and concrete issues involving Mr. T's academic difficulties—but to no avail. Despite suggestions that Mr. T restrict the scope of his term papers and go over his progress regularly with professors and advisors, the patient buried himself more deeply into the library stacks. By the end of the sophomore year, he had flunked out. Through the next several months, he hung around his parents' home "emptying the garbage and cleaning the gutters" with no more luck planning his future than planning his term papers. His parents, at first consoling but eventually exasperated, insisted he either get a job or get psychiatric help. Mr. T chose the latter.

Mr. T was referred by his former pediatrician to an elderly internist who now, during his semi-retirement, had become interested in doing psychotherapy. According to Mr. T's parents, this "grandfatherly figure" believed Mr. T's basic problem was immaturity. During the first year of treatment, while Mr. T continued to hang around the house and to do nothing else, he would spend half-hour weekly sessions with this kindly therapist, chatting about this or that—about a teacher in grade school, a summer research project in a university lab, traumatic experiences at sleep-away camp, and so on.

After many months of treatment, the therapist, prodded by Mr. T's parents, began to encourage the patient to move out of the home and to look for even a menial job. Such a move, though presented only as a first step towards getting his life back on track, was laden with many fears. Mr. T spent session after session discussing some new fear about leaving home. Finally, after being coached each inch of the way, Mr. T rented a small furnished apartment and went to work in a secretarial pool, though still receiving some financial support from his parents. Following this move, many months of treatment were spent with Mr. T discussing every detail of his fears about work and living an isolated life.

Three months ago, Mr. T finally began to reveal in his treatment more private and upsetting experiences, especially his concern about being "an impotent fag." This concern had been on Mr. T's mind night and day since early adolescence, though he had actually experienced only one homosexual encounter. This had occurred at the beginning of his sophomore year, when an older man led Mr. T into a movie theater bathroom and tried to perform fellatio; Mr. T, overwhelmed and impotent, fled and spent the night tearfully walking the streets in a daze.

After several weeks of recovering from the shame of this "confession" to the therapist, Mr. T dared to reveal another personal matter. Ever since eighth grade, he had secretly been "investigating" standard supermarket food items, such as canned soups, boxed cereals, and frozen dinners. This research had started off being no more than a school science assignment, but then Mr. T began making elaborate charts of the containers' contents (caloric value per ounce, preservatives, additives, etc.). The project then grew into preparing various foods either on a hot plate in his bedroom or in the kitchen when his parents were not home. During these experiments, Mr T would rate the quality of the food and then prepare the data for eventual "feeding" into a computer.

In sharing this secret with the therapist, Mr. T was quite embarrassed, for he knew that the idea of being a "connoisseur of supermarket crap" was silly and strange. He was, therefore, surprised that the therapist appeared to be fascinated by the project, asked about each detail, and seemed eager to hear as much as Mr. T would dare confide. Apparently, this attitude was characteristic of the therapist who, over the course of treatment, had always found Mr. T a likeable young man and who had accepted the patient's idiosyncracies, without suspecting that a more malignant process was at work.

The therapist was, therefore, quite surprised when, four weeks after Mr. T had first described his secret project, the patient became increasingly suspicious about events at work; for example, Mr. T believed that he was able to decode typing assignments and determine that everyone in the office knew that he was homosexual. Furthermore, Mr. T believed that his male supervisors were making these accusations because they suspected that Mr. T had found out very personal matters about them (whereas actually Mr. T had only the most superficial relationship with every one of his coworkers).

The therapist, at a loss what to do, contacted Mr. T's parents following an especially alarming session and advised them to arrange for immediate hospitalization.

DSM-III-R DIAGNOSIS

Axis I: Schizophreniform disorder
Axis II: Mixed personality disorder with paranoid, avoidant, and
          schizotypal features
Axis III: Neurodermatitis

AXIS IV: Stress—moderate (divulging personal material to psycho-
           therapist, moving away from parents, starting first job)
AXIS V: Highest level of functioning past year—fair (able to work
           and manage own affairs, but socially isolated and achiev-
           ing far below his intellectual capacities)

TREATMENT PROBLEM

Timid young man who became psychotically disorganized after
moving away from home, starting his first job, and revealing private
concerns to his psychotherapist.

DISCUSSION OF TREATMENT SELECTION

Setting. The most comfortable option for all concerned is psychiatric
hospitalization. In that setting, Mr. T's therapist would feel relieved that
his patient was now being treated by a psychiatrist more experienced in
managing severe psychopathology. Similarly, Mr. T's parents, who have
always tended to avoid difficult emotional problems, would be relieved
to have their disturbed son "in good hands" (and not in theirs). Even Mr.
T, by his passive resignation, has indicated that he, too, would feel
reassured when no longer forced to deal with the outside world, especially his coworkers. In addition, since this is Mr. T's first known and
definite psychotic episode, there is little available information upon
which to base his risk of suicide, aggressiveness, and noncompliance
while in this suspicious state and, in addition, no knowledge of how he
will respond to psychosocial and somatic therapies. A psychiatric hospitalization is the safest choice and will allow the most complete diagnostic
evaluation, as well as the most structured setting.

Despite the therapeutic advantages of hospitalization and the reassurance it would offer to all parties, the hospital setting might not be the
best option in Mr. T's situation. He does not appear to pose an immediate risk to himself or others. Furthermore, since his delusional system
does not currently involve either the therapist or the consultant, he
probably would comply with outpatient treatment. Although hospitalization offers the advantage of decompressing the current situation and
of facilitating a thorough assessment with close observation, a psychiatric admission also has many disadvantages. These include most particularly some degree of social and personal humiliation, demoralization,
increased risk of repeated hospitalizations when future crises occur, financial cost, and the possibility of further regression in the hospital with
a delayed return to work and to living alone, accomplishments that have
taken Mr. T many months to achieve.

Format. At least some family involvement will clearly be a necessary ingredient in Mr. T's recovery. The parents will need to learn, as part of a systematic educational program, the kinds of support—financial and personal—they should provide during the ensuing months. A family format could be useful in teaching the parents to interact with their son in a somewhat less stilted and more emotionally available manner, so that he can eventually feel less intimidated by and alienated from them.

If only a family format is used, however, Mr. T might remain infantilized, without an opportunity to separate from his parents. A problem in the previous treatment may have been that the boundaries were not clearly demarcated between what material would or would not be shared between therapist and parents. An individual format that made these boundaries more clear would enable Mr. T to divulge his shame-ridden fantasies and peculiar habits without fearing that these secrets would be transmitted to others. Finally, a heterogeneous group might be helpful in overcoming Mr. T's avoidance of interpersonal relationships. Unless group therapy is part of an inpatient treatment, however, this format should be deferred until the acute psychotic disorganization improves. If placed in an outpatient group in his current state, Mr. T might suspiciously withdraw even further from "strangers" or be ostracized by them. Resentment or ridicule from other group members would only increase and confirm Mr. T's feelings of being strange and unwanted.

Frequency and Duration. Mr. T will need to be seen frequently for the next several days or even weeks, in or out of a hospital. Regularly scheduled appointments (every day or so) can provide a reorganizing structure and enable the therapist to monitor the evolution of the psychotic symptoms and their response to treatment. Although the scheduling of sessions should be frequent, the duration of individual sessions should be flexible. Lengthy sessions (over 30 minutes) might tax Mr. T's fragile ego boundaries and lead to the same kind of disorganization and projective defenses that apparently were a result of "confessing" to his previous therapist. The duration of treatment must also be kept flexible at this time, since it is not clear whether Mr. T's acute psychotic decompensation will be an isolated episode or will be the first psychotic break in what turns out to be a chronic psychiatric illness. He may require treatment only for the next few weeks, for several years, or for life.

Approach. A directive medical approach would now be the best choice. Despite his delusional system, Mr. T is not so distrustful of either the consultant or the therapist that he would be unable to accept their suggestions and advice, and in the past Mr. T has been willing to follow the therapist's "coaching" to overcome inordinate fears.

Experiential techniques would seem contraindicated at the present time. Although the kindly approach used by Mr. T's therapist was no doubt helpful in overcoming the patient's feelings of complete isolation, it appears, in retrospect, that Mr. T's sharing of feelings and "secrets" may have contributed to his recent decompensation. A cognitive and educational psychotherapeutic approach that reminds Mr. T of his difficulty in distinguishing fantasies and reality might be helpful. In Mr. T's current confused state, exploratory techniques will also not be advisable. He is having difficulty with his ego boundaries, i.e., separating his own thoughts and feelings from those around him. An uncovering therapy may be experienced as too intrusive and bewildering, since Mr. T experiences the therapist as getting "inside his head."

Somatic Treatment. The main indication for neuroleptics at this time would be to treat Mr. T's delusional system. It is conceivable that his acute psychosis might improve without medication if he is removed from the stressors (his job and perhaps his therapist) and if he is provided an organizing structure in or outside of the hospital; but neuroleptics are likely to enable a more rapid recovery that would prevent Mr. T from losing his job, his self-esteem, and his determination to live on his own. Furthermore, maintenance neuroleptics might be helpful prophylactically and also enable therapy to be more productive by reducing Mr. T's suspiciousness.

Change of Therapists. An additional consideration regarding Mr. T is whether or not the consultant should advise the patient to change therapists at this time. The current therapist hints that he wants to be off the case, at least temporarily. The temptation is to go along with this request for the sake of the therapist and the patient, both of whom seem eager to have a cooling-off period. The younger consultant in the emergency room might also be inclined to view the "grandfatherly" elder therapist as kindhearted but essentially unknowledgeable about the severity of Mr. T's psychopathology and about its appropriate somatic treatment. This attitude is common when a patient has clearly gotten worse during the course of treatment. But there is an alternative view. Perhaps Mr. T would have decompensated anyway, or even sooner, without the involvement with the therapist. Moreover, before advising the patient to change therapists, the consultant should learn more about the treatment and the participants' attitudes towards it and towards one another. In a liaison capacity, the consultant may be able to suggest to the present therapist certain modifications in his approach. An important consideration is that two years of treatment have been necessary for a trust to develop between the therapist and Mr. T. This relationship must be valued and not discarded lightly under the unproven presumption that another therapist would be more effective. In this sense, the most productive management might be to treat the acute disruption in the therapist-patient relationship.

CHOICE AND OUTCOME

While Mr. T and his parents waited in the emergency room, the consultant tried to phone the therapist. He learned from the housekeeper that the therapist had left for an extended vacation (it was later learned that the therapist had actually put off leaving town for the past few weeks because he was so concerned about Mr. T).

Still uncertain about whether or not Mr. T should be hospitalized, the consultant discussed with Mr. T and his parents the advantages and disadvantages of such a disposition. Hospitalization would offer structure and a close assessment of the problem but may be a more extreme intervention than Mr. T's current difficulties warrant. The consultant indicated that other approaches, including psychotropic medication and daily outpatient visits, might be sufficient to resolve the current crisis, without taking Mr. T too far off the path of living outside of home and of working.

In weighing the pros and cons of hospitalization versus outpatient care, Mr. T shrugged indifferently and said he would do whatever his parents and the consultant advised; but the parents, especially the rigid professorial father, insisted that inpatient care was the only choice. He wanted to assume no responsibility for "an area outside my expertise." Whatever was motivating the father to insist upon hospitalization, his mind was set. A further attempt to negotiate other possibilities would only have ended up with the consultant and the father locking horns, a situation that would have been more destructive for Mr. T. The patient was, therefore, admitted.

Within the first two days in the hospital, while still being evaluated and without resort to psychotropic medication, Mr. T's paranoid system disappeared completely. He was fully aware that he had "flipped out" and that his ideas about his male supervisors at work were "crazy." With the nursing staff and other patients, he remained characteristically aloof but cooperative; and with his assigned therapist (a woman) he related in a vague, shy, but coherent manner.

His psychological testing showed a "scattering" on the WAIS, a high intelligence quotient with a capacity for higher functioning when not impaired by anxiety, a paucity of responses on projective testing, but no confabulation or contamination. The psychologist's diagnostic impression was "avoidant personality disorder" along with the suggestion but not confirmation of an underlying thought disorder.

Because of the patient's unusually rapid remission and because his diagnosis and further treatment were unclear, he was presented at a clinical conference. The staff were divided in their diagnostic impressions and therapeutic recommendations. At one extreme, half the staff believed that Mr. T had a well-concealed chronic psychotic disorder, which would meet the DSM-III criteria for paranoid schizophrenia if he were not so guarded. This faction believed that Mr. T should be prescribed a neuroleptic and followed in a directive–supportive treatment with limited goals. The rest of the staff believed that Mr. T suffered a mixed personality disorder, with a brief and self-limited psychotic episode secondary to the stress of an overly friendly therapeutic relationship. Noting Mr. T's past intellectual accomplishments, his rapid improvement in the hospital, and his likeable though aloof manner, this faction advised against prescribing neuroleptic treatment. They suggested instead a long-term supportive but also uncovering psychotherapy on a trial basis in an outpatient setting, using a reconstructive inpatient hospital or a day hospital if Mr. T did not respond within a few weeks to outpatient care. These staff members judged that Mr. T would do better with a female therapist because the evolving intimate relationship would not be unconsciously associated with frightening homosexual wishes or with fears of retaliation by a competitive, fatherlike figure.

A compromise was reached: Medication would be deferred for two more weeks while the assigned therapist attempted to establish a working relationship with Mr. T and to obtain a clearer understanding of Mr. T's psychopathology and its severity. This trial period would also determine Mr. T's capacity to form a tolerable closeness and to undergo further exploration of his problems.

Three days after the conference, Mr. T abruptly submitted a "signout letter" in the middle of the night. He was persuaded to stay until the following morning, but then immediately contacted a mental aide attorney and his former therapist, who had just returned from vacation. At noon the following day, Mr. T left the hospital against advice, though never departing from his ingratiating and mild-mannered style.

Numerous phone calls to the patient's former therapist were not returned and for months nothing was ever heard from or about Mr. T. Almost a year later, a therapist at another psychiatric hospital contacted the female therapist who had taken care of Mr. T during his first admission. She learned that Mr. T's second hospitalization was involuntarily enforced after the FBI had traced to Mr. T threatening letters written to the Food and Drug Administration. She also learned that this second psychotic decompensation was more directly related to a developing transference psychosis with the original therapist; specifically, Mr. T now believed that this therapist was involved in a plot to contaminate the nation's milk and other dairy products.

During this second hospitalization, Mr. T was placed on small dosages of haloperidol, again quickly reorganized, and was discharged after 10 days, to be followed by the female therapist who had cared for Mr. T during his first admission. This therapist had now become Mr. T's choice. Despite the strong attachment and gratitude he felt towards the elder therapist, Mr. T had come to believe that their relationship was too fraught with risk to continue.

In a prolonged treatment lasting seven years, Mr. T was seen twice weekly in a directive and dynamic-supportive psychotherapy, while being prescribed small doses of neuroleptics during critical phases of his treatment. Though the treatment was lengthy and at times stormy, the results were gratifying. Mr. T completed college, maintained a responsible job as a laboratory scientist, experienced satisfactory relationships with homosexual lovers, and has not required psychotropic medication for three years. At the termination of treatment, he was still stilted in his manner and living alone but was able to function very well within the constricted confines of his life. He saw his parents once a week and they continued to play quiz games comparing their knowledge of esoterica. He regarded himself as reasonably happy.

SUGGESTED READING

1. Wynne, L. C. Current concepts about schizophrenics and family relationships. *Journal of Nervous and Mental Disease,* 169:82–89, 1981. (A concise description of studies documenting problems of communication within schizophrenic families.)
2. Bibring, E. Psychoanalysis and the dynamic psychotherapies. *Journal of the Psychoanalytic Association,* 2:745–770, 1954. (The classic definition and use of basic psychotherapeutic techniques: interpretation, clarification, suggestion, abreaction and manipulation.)
3. Myerson, P. G. Issues of technique where patients relate with difficulty. *International Review of Psychoanalysis,* 6:363–375, 1979. (The underlying causes and the possible solutions to the problem of patients who are difficult to engage in a psychodynamic treatment.)

■ BRIEF REACTIVE PSYCHOSIS

16.   The Case of the Unresurrected Son

Mrs. Z is a 42-year-old housewife who is literally dragged into the emergency room by her husband and two teenage daughters. She is too upset to talk. She moans and screams and beats her head with her fists when simply asked her name and age. While Mrs. Z paces in her housecoat up and down the hospital corridor, her husband explains what has happened.

Several nights ago Mrs. Z's only son, a high-school sophomore, returned home after a party and went straight to bed. He was not up the next morning when Mrs. Z left to do her Saturday shopping, but this was not unusual. It was only when Mrs. Z returned later that afternoon and was putting away the groceries that she realized her son had still not come downstairs to eat. She went upstairs to check, entered his room, and saw her son sprawled naked on the sheets—dead.

The medical examiner's report later disclosed the son had died sometime during the night from an overdose of methaqualone (Quaalude). Mrs. Z could not accept that her son had died. When her husband and two daughters returned to the house late Saturday evening, they discovered Mrs. Z weeping and clinging to her son's dead body. Even when the ambulance drivers arrived, she had to be pried away from the corpse. She then sat up all night in her son's room, praying to herself and seemingly unaware of the turmoil around her. She remained in this daze for four more days, neglecting personal hygiene, refusing to eat, ignoring the clergy who came to speak with her, and refusing to go to the funeral because, in her view, her son was not dead; he was sitting by the right hand of God waiting for the ordained moment to return to earth.

Alarmed by Mrs. Z's "crazy ideas" (she had never before had any psychiatric problems), the family members persistently tried to convince Mrs. Z that her son was not an angel when alive and certainly was not going to be resurrected. These doses of reality were hard for Mrs. Z to accept. Intermittently, when the truth did get through, she would scream that she wanted to be dead herself. Following nightmares in which her son's rigid body gestured for her to join him, she confided to her husband that perhaps her own death is also God's will and that the severe abdominal pain extending upward to her heart is a sign of a fatal cancer.

DSM-III-R DIAGNOSIS

Axis I: Brief reactive psychosis
Axis II: None
Axis III: Chronic cholecystitis
Axis IV: Stress—severe (unexpected death of teenage son)
Axis V: Highest level of functioning past year—very good (efficient homemaker with many pleasurable interests)

TREATMENT PROBLEM

A forty-two-year-old well-adjusted housewife with acute depression, disorganization, and delusions in response to the unexpected death of her teenage son.

DISCUSSION OF TREATMENT SELECTION

Setting. Psychiatric hospitalization for Mrs. Z offers the best protection from her suicidal impulses and may be necessary. However, her wish to be dead is expressed rather passively; she has formulated no specific suicidal plans and has no command hallucinations compelling her to act on her suicidal ideas. In addition, she has a reliable family to stay with and protect her around the clock. It may therefore be possible to use crisis intervention and prevent hospitalization. There are severe disadvantages of a setting that would remove Mrs. Z from her family and home during this time of mutual loss and mourning. Hospitalization would only reinforce Mrs. Z's attempt to avoid reminders of her son's death and might iatrogenically convert a time-limited grief response into what is perceived (by patient, family, and the medical community) as a psychiatric syndrome, refractory to more conservative and less expensive treatments. Even a partial hospitalization has many of these disadvantages. Ideally, the best choice would be crisis intervention conducted in the patient's home, where the memories of the son and the support of the family would be immediately available.

Format. The love and concern within Mrs. Z's family are a powerful asset that must be used. A family format will enable the members to suffer together and support each other, whereas an individual therapy could encourage the view that Mrs. Z is "the sick one" and thereby a target for scapegoating, displacement, and alienation.

Duration and Frequency. By explicitly declaring that the treatment will be intensive and brief, the therapist can convey both a willingness to respond to the crisis and a belief that the problem is time limited. Sessions that are spaced too far apart (e.g., weekly) or are too brief (e.g., 45–50 minutes) will not provide sufficient structure or time for an acutely disorganized patient. If the therapist implies from the start that an extended treatment will be required, both the patient and family are more likely to view the illness as inevitably chronic rather than a circumscribed acute problem.

Approach. Treatment must initially provide a situation in which Mrs. Z can comfortably discuss her personal, even if idealized, view of her son. If this view is prematurely challenged, the need to see her son as a Christ-like figure will only be reinforced. A more accepting stance, which is not at first confrontational, will enable Mrs. Z to begin the mourning process. Gradually, memory by memory, catalyzed by the empathic responses of the therapist and other family members, Mrs. Z can then start to integrate the truth of who her son actually was when alive and of the consequences now that he is dead. At this point, cognitive tasks can be given to Mrs. Z, with family members serving as teachers to ensure that the homework assignments get done, such as describing hour by hour all the traumatic events on that fateful Saturday and looking at photographs and personal items to facilitate the mourning process. Exploratory techniques (such as understanding Mrs. Z's ambivalence towards her son, or her unconscious guilt over how she may have contributed to his problems, or her narcissistic investment in his achievements to increase her own self-esteem) would best be reserved until the final stages of treatment. Though these psychodynamic factors may be contributing to the severity of Mrs. Z's grief response, they will not be well tolerated until she is better integrated and feels support from the family and therapist.

Somatic Treatment. The severity of Mrs. Z's agitation, insomnia and bizarre ideas may require low doses of a sedating neuroleptic at bedtime. When more calm and rested, she may be more receptive to the support of the family and the interventions of the therapist and thereby begin to assimilate her tragic loss. Antidepressant medications are not yet indicated and will become necessary only if the patient's acute symptoms of grief develop into a full-blown affective episode.

CHOICE AND OUTCOME

Mrs. Z responded remarkably well to the treatment plans suggested above. The psychiatry resident in the emergency room contacted a therapist with an expertise and interest in crisis family intervention. That therapist came to the emergency room and introduced herself to Mrs. Z and her family, stated that a hospital setting was neither a comfortable nor an appropriate place for them to talk considering the severe loss they had all suffered, and made arrangements to visit them at their home later that evening. She also suggested that they invite other relatives and close friends to come by as well, both to provide comfort and to share the responsibility of constantly observing Mrs. Z to prevent any self-destructive behavior.

When the therapist arrived later at the home, she found the small group of close relatives and friends gathered in the kitchen and living room sharing memories and commiserating over the loss, while Mrs. Z sat isolated in her son's bedroom with a cousin sitting by the door. The mourners explained that they would prefer to have Mrs. Z join them but, frankly, her talk of the resurrection, of having cancer, or of wanting to die were too upsetting and made them feel helpless and frustrated. The therapist first sat down over coffee and got to know and be known by the family and friends; she then entered the bedroom and spent over an hour listening to Mrs. Z describe and praise her "little angel who will do great things some day." The therapist did not directly challenge the patient's statements that her son was still alive, but she did inquire about various items in the room—posters, pennants, trophies—which were all connected to his memory. A slight crack in Mrs. Z's fragile delusional system occurred when she acknowledged to the therapist and to herself that a treasured fountain pen (a present for graduating from junior high school) would never be used by her son again.

After an empathic understanding had been established with Mrs. Z, the therapist invited Mr. Z, the two daughters, and a few selected friends and relatives into the bedroom, candidly explaining to Mrs. Z that they needed help in learning how to listen and understand what Mrs. Z was describing. As the family and friends all crowded into the room, the therapist encouraged Mrs. Z to share her ideas, however distressing, and by example indicated to others that at this time these ideas need not be confronted. After a half hour, the therapist in front of Mrs. Z arranged around-the-clock assignments so that the patient would never be alone. The assigned relatives and friends were instructed only to sit with Mrs. Z and listen to "whatever ideas and memories were attached to the tears."

When the therapist returned the following evening, Mrs. Z was described by the family as being essentially unchanged in that she was still sitting in her son's room waiting for the resurrection, but the therapist detected some improvement: Mrs. Z had slept for a few hours, was no longer complaining of abdominal pain and cancer, and was holding on to her son's fountain pen. Using this pen, Mrs. Z was then instructed to write down every 15 minutes during the next day whatever thought she was having at that time about her son. To the surprise of her husband, Mrs. Z agreed to this rigid and seemingly arbitrary task, a task that was allegedly to keep the therapist informed but which actually was a first step towards cognitive reframing. During daily visits, the therapist would review the patient's "records" and direct Mrs. Z to elaborate on those selected items that were more rational and accepting of the loss.

Mrs. Z's improvement was rapid and dramatic. By the end of the first week of treatment, she agreed to visit the graveyard with the therapist. Only after placing flowers on the recently dug ground was Mrs. Z able to say aloud and to herself, "Why did he do it—to him, to me?" Over the ensuing few final sessions, now in the therapist's office, this remark was used as an opening to discuss Mrs. Z's resentment and guilt about how the death had occurred. On the final session, Mrs. Z gave the therapist a wallet-sized photo of her son so that he would not be forgotten.

Mrs. Z never contacted the therapist again; however, two years later Mr. Z phoned to say that his wife's mother had died two days before and he was concerned that Mrs. Z would have another breakdown. The husband was instructed to call the therapist if these understandable fears proved true. Mr. Z never called.

SUGGESTED READING

1. Langsley, D. G., Machotka, P., & Flomenhaft, K. Avoiding mental hospital admission: A follow-up study. _American Journal of Psychiatry_ 127:1391–1394, 1971. (Indicates how crisis intervention can diminish the rate of future psychiatric hospitalizations—or at least make them shorter.)
2. Caplan, G. _Principles of Preventive Psychiatry._ New York: Basic Books, 1964. (Rationale and implementation of crisis intervention.)
3. Lindemann, E. Symptomatology and management of acute grief. _American Journal of Psychiatry,_ 101:141–148, 1944. (Documents range of phenomenology [not necessarily psychopathology] that accompanies acute, unanticipated loss.)
4. Raphael, B. Preventive intervention with the recently bereaved. _Archives of General Psychiatry,_ 34:1450–1454, 1977. (Proposes that grieving "normal" widows have a lower morbidity a year later if given a brief supportive treatment immediately following the loss.)

■ SCHIZOAFFECTIVE DISORDER

17. The Case of the Grief-Stricken Daughter

Authors' Note:
Treatment selection is a process that occurs not only during the initial
consultation but throughout the entire course of therapy, at times even
within a given session. Patients and therapists alike often wonder,
aloud or to themselves and for both real and neurotic reasons, whether
the current therapy makes the most sense. Changes that have occurred
because of the therapy or because of external factors in the patient's or
therapist's life may make changes in the treatment selection advisable or
necessary.

Throughout this casebook, in order to present brief and focused discussions, we have primarily dealt with treatment selection in terms of
the initial choices after a consultation. In the following case, necessarily
much longer, we depart from our general approach: The case is presented longitudinally over its entire course. At several points in the account
of the patient's therapy, we pause to discuss possible changes in the
treatment selection and their impact if and when implemented.

Mrs. M was first referred for consultation when she was 38 years old.
At that time she was married to a corporate attorney from a socially
prominent family and was living with their three adolescent children in a
fashionable apartment. The psychiatric referral was recommended by
Mrs. M's neurologist, who admitted that he could no longer stand the
patient's incessant and unexplainable somatic complaints, which included dizzy spells, neck pain, and tingling of the hands. Mrs. M viewed the
recommendation as a rejection from the neurologist for whom, as was
only much later discovered, she had an intense romantic yearning. Out
of desperation and a general tendency to do what she was told, Mrs. M
scheduled an appointment and arrived on time, wearing a gracious
smile and a well-tailored flannel blazer.

Within only the first couple of minutes of the interview, Mrs. M
launched into a rambling, pressured, and tearful saga of how her physical symptoms began when (to paraphrase) she tripped over the edge of a
thick red carpet in a downtown hotel lobby while frantically racing to the
hospital to visit her ailing father who had just been flown in by medical
air ambulance from his pleasant hometown where he had long been
suffering from a slow-growing spinal cord tumor that had been misdiagnosed for two years because of its presentation with neck pain and

tingling of the hands, attributed first to cervical disk disease and then to anxiety—and now here she was with the same complaint and possibly the same disease, wrongly believed to be "just nerves." By the time the consultant had weaved through Mrs. M's pressured and circumstantial account, the session was over. Three more sessions were necessary before a coherent life narrative could be pieced together, and even then the consultant was forced to make many assumptions based on the patient's clinical presentation.

The history, as best the consultant could make out, was that Mrs. M had always been a loner who felt rejected by her mother for being a burden, teased by her brothers for being an oddball, and ignored by her peers for reasons she could never discern (but perhaps was due to her long skirts, high necklines, and lofty standards). Her only companion was her father who, though himself rather cold and forbidding by nature, "at least listened to me even if he didn't understand."

Two weeks after graduation from a small Presbyterian girls' college, Mrs. M married a lawyer in his mid-thirties who bore little of distinction other than his prominent last name and a reputation as a reliable yachtsman. His constrained and colorless manner had kept him from attracting women, including Mrs. M, but she accepted his marriage proposal when her father advised, "Don't look a gift horse in the mouth." The wedding was quickly followed by three children, countless dinner parties, charity balls, functions at the yacht club, and sundry other activities that kept Mrs. M seemingly very involved, but actually friendless and isolated even within the home.

On social occasions her husband avoided Mrs. M by "circulating," and when the two of them could be alone together on a "free" evening, something always came up that would keep Mr. M at the office, at the club, at his parents, wherever. Despite Mrs. M's desire, but never insistence, the couple had not had sex together for years, and by the time of the psychiatric consultation, they shared little other than the morning newspaper and decisions about the children's private schools and summer camps. Mrs. M avoided confronting her husband about his avoidance of her for fear that he would simply leave altogether—and besides, she consoled herself that at least she had her father (though more in fantasy than in fact) as a source of support. This consolation lost its power when her father became deathly ill with a spinal cord tumor.

With the prospect of her father's death, Mrs. M had fallen apart. In a frenzy, she went from one doctor to another—orthopedists, chiropractors, gynecologists, neurologists, physical therapists, neurosurgeons—seeking advice about either her father's illness or her own symptoms. This racing around town was slowed down only by intermittent anxiety attacks that made her afraid to leave the apartment. No matter what time of day, she would try to relieve these symptoms by gulping several stiff highballs, but the drinks did little more than convince her children that their "strange" mother was now turning into a drunk. As for her husband, he simply found more excuses to stay away.

After gathering this information, the consultant was not sure of Mrs. M's diagnosis. She had no apparent history of depression, mania, or psychotic decompensation; but her present panic, disjointed presentation, and conviction that she had a severe physical illness were all worrisome. To gain more information, the consultant had tried to get Mrs. M's permission to contact both her husband and the doctors she had seen over the previous few months. Because Mrs. M was wary of letting anyone know that she was now seeing a psychiatrist, four sessions passed before she finally agreed.

Her medical doctors could provide little additional information, but did confirm that Mrs. M's extensive medical workup was completely normal. One physician, who by chance had seen the patient on a few social occasions, did mention that Mrs. M was generally considered "odd" and that Mr. M was regarded as a bit of a "stodgy bore." It was only the husband's prominent heritage that made the couple acceptable as members of the supporting cast at different social functions.

The attempts to contact Mr. M were less successful. He waited two weeks before returning the consultant's calls and then implied with a rather abrupt and affected British tone that he wanted little to do with psychiatry and, by implication, little to do with his wife as well. He had no intentions of talking with one more doctor about his wife's protracted but unnecessary complaints.

INITIAL DSM-III-R DIAGNOSIS

Axis I: Unclear; possible somatization disorder, conversion disorder, or panic disorder with agoraphobia and hyperventilation syndrome
Axis II: Possible mixed personality disorder with schizotypal and histrionic features
Axis III: None
Axis IV: Stress—severe (father's fatal illness)
Axis V: Highest level of functioning past year—fair

TREATMENT PROBLEM

Anxious housewife with somatic symptoms similar to those of her fatally ill father.

DISCUSSION OF TREATMENT SELECTION (PHASE I)

Setting. Psychiatric hospitalization would provide an opportunity to evaluate Mrs. M more thoroughly and observe her behavior in a structured environment on an hour-to-hour basis. After several sessions, the consultant is still unclear about her diagnosis. Hospitalization might clarify her problems, decompress her anxiety, and prevent her frenetic running from doctor to doctor. On the other hand, Mrs. M has already shown a capacity to regress under stress; hospitalization might foster further regression and make her even more contemptible in the eyes of her husband and children. As long as she continues to keep her outpatient visits and does not further decompensate or become a serious risk to herself or others, it would seem wise to avoid hospitalization unless circumstances dictate its necessity.

Format. Her husband has made it clear that at the present time he is uninterested in being a participant in his wife's treatment. To involve the young adolescent children without the husband's consent would no doubt be divisive. A heterogeneous group might be a possibility in the future to help Mrs. M understand how she interacts with others and why she is perceived as "an oddball"; but currently Mrs. M is so pressured and preoccupied with her somatic problems and her father's illness that she might initially be ostracized from the group for being "selfish," which in turn would only make her feel more rejected. In addition, a heterogeneous group would be incapable of providing the focused attention necessary to meet the current crises in her life. A homogeneous group composed of patients similarly concerned with medical problems might be very helpful in providing support and attention, but Mrs. M is at present incapable of seeing the wisdom of this recommendation.

Duration and Frequency. A time-oriented treatment has many advantages for Mrs. M: it would facilitate a working through of her separation from her father by transferentially working through her separation from the therapist as termination approached; it would impicitly short-circuit whatever secondary gain might be reinforcing her somatic symptoms by indicating that continuous support would not be forthcoming; and it would help prevent a prolonged and refractory regression that might ensue with an open-ended treatment in which the therapist became a surrogate for the lost father. On the other hand, a time-oriented treatment carries certain risks; Mrs. M might feel even more abandoned and frantic if she does not have the reassurance that someone in her life will continue to be available and will not reject her. In addition, many of her problems are not related to the pending loss of her father. A brief treatment might preclude an opportunity to work on these other difficulties.

One problem during the consultation has been that Mrs. M has had so many frenetic day-to-day events to report during her weekly scheduled appointments that more reflective and historical information has not been obtained. Although lengthening the time of individual sessions might be one solution, it runs the risk of fostering more regressive behavior within the session and between appointments. A better alternative might be to see Mrs. M twice or three times per week during this crisis, until the current situation is better understood and can be placed in the perspective of her past.

Approach. Mrs. M does not have the enabling factors at present for an approach that is primarily exploratory. She feels as though, in her words, she is "under attack" and is "desperately searching for an air-raid shelter." She is not in the necessary reflective mood to respond to dynamic interpretations and might regard them as evidence that the therapist is not taking her physical problems seriously. She might respond more positively to a directive approach of a therapist who assumes a "physicianly" stance, i.e., advises the patient about various relaxation techniques she can use to treat the tension that is building up inside her and is causing the somatic symptoms. To facilitate a more adaptive mourning response, Mrs. M might then combine these relaxation methods with structured homework assignments in which she systematically reworks the memories of her father.

Somatic Treatment. A benzodiazepine used for the acute episode in conjunction with hypnosis or another relaxation technique may be helpful in diminishing the anxiety and associated somatic symptoms; but the use of anxiolytics carries the risk that Mrs. M will attribute improvement only to the medication, will not acquire confidence by mastering the current crisis, and will rely on medication in the future in the same way she is currently using alcohol. The use of either neuroleptics or antidepressants should best be deferred until a diagnosis warranting these major psychotropics is more apparent.

Psychological Testing. The diagnosis and the psychodynamic conflicts are not clear. A battery of psychological tests, including the Rorschach and Thematic Apperception Tests, might be helpful; however, Mrs. M is already suspicious that everyone believes her somatic problems are "all in her head" and might refuse or be extremely guarded when taking these tests.

CHOICE AND OUTCOME (PHASE I)

Without an explicit declaration of a therapeutic contract or an open negotiation of a treatment plan, the prolonged consultation with Mrs. M insidiously developed into weekly psychotherapy. The therapist was not sure of the diagnosis, but his working impression was that some of Mrs. M's somatic symptoms (lightheadedness, weakness, paresthesias) were due to a hyperventilation syndrome and some (neck pain, nonanatomical thoracic sensory loss) represented a conversion disorder. He treated the hyperventilation syndrome with psychoeducation, explaining that her overbreathing was a physiological response to anxiety and that the overbreathing, not her imagination, was altering her blood chemistry and causing "real" physical symptoms. To demonstrate to Mrs. M how an alteration in blood gases could produce such symptoms, the therapist instructed Mrs. M voluntarily to overbreathe in the office (about 100 rapid deep breaths) until she actually produced the lightheadedness and paresthesiae. He then advised Mrs. M to practice at home this same "exercise," so that she gradually would become convinced that overbreathing could indeed produce not only the lightheadedness and paresthesiae, but also many of her other symptoms, such as dysphoria, dry mouth, nausea, tightness in the chest, muscular weakness, and spasms. He further explained that when these same symptoms occurred involuntarily, Mrs. M could correct the physiological changes with the combination of breathing into a plastic bag and using abdominal breathing.

Mrs. M responded to these explanations and directives by believing that her physical problems had finally been taken seriously. She followed the therapist's instructions and the hyperventilation syndrome resolved within two weeks. Only then did the therapist introduce a more psychological aspect of the problem, namely, that he suspected that Mrs. M's anxiety and resultant hyperventilation were related to her profound grief over her father's illness. Without her father, she feared she would have no one. Mrs. M accepted this interpretation, as well as the therapist's suggestion that the subsequent sessions be used to help her to master the anticipatory grief. The therapist thereafter encouraged Mrs. M to recall the memories, present and past, of events she had shared with her father. At times, Mrs. M would resist feeling the pain of mourning associated with these memories by complaining of her husband's neglect or her "pain in the neck," whereupon the therapist would redirect Mrs. M's attention to her relationship with her father and, in Shakespeare's phrase, "knit words to the sorrow."

The therapist chose not to deal directly with either the primary or secondary gain of Mrs. M's conversion disorder. He did not interpret the sympathetic identification with her father's somatic symptoms, nor did he interpret how the patient's somatic complaints were reinforced by the attention and care they demanded. Instead, the therapist concentrated on the secondary loss, i.e., how Mrs. M's physical symptoms impeded her caring for her dying father and beloved children. The therapist believed that the conversion disorder would indirectly respond to the patient's work of mourning. As she felt less anxious about losing this one person in her life by whom she felt loved, she would have less unconscious need to "hold" onto him by identifying with him, i.e., imitating his physical symptoms.

If the patient's improvement had not been so prompt and dramatic after the first three months, the therapist might have changed his approach, considered using psychotropic medication, or been more insistent upon Mrs. M's agreeing to psychological testing (which she had previously refused); but because Mrs. M appeared to be improving, the therapist continued with the weekly psychotherapy that was primarily experiential and directive in nature. Far less panic-stricken, she presented herself in a more organized manner during sessions. This organization was reflected in her life as well. She stopped scurrying from doctor to doctor with various physical complaints and instead dealt effectively with her father's prolonged illness and eventual death.

Two months after the funeral, the therapist stated to Mrs. M that her sad feelings associated with memories of her father would no doubt continue to come in waves over the ensuing months as she recalled the many events they had shared together, but because Mrs. M was managing her own affairs so effectively, it was time to begin discussing a date for terminating treatment. Unexpectedly, Mrs. M reacted to the suggestion of stopping treatment by revealing a highly eroticized transference. For the past few weeks, she apparently had developed an intense attachment to the therapist and, with a delusional conviction, was sure that he was thinking only of her when they were apart and that he would marry her at once if it were not for their respective children. She could not imagine stopping treatment and could not believe that the therapist would be so cruel as to even hint at such a possibility. The therapist, quite alarmed at this previously well-concealed psychotic transference, prematurely interpreted Mrs. M's involvement as a substitute for her lost father. The patient responded by sitting sullen and silent for the remaining few minutes of the session, then slammed the door as she left.

The following session, Mrs. M presented all of the original somatic symptoms and also severe symptoms of depression and specific suicidal plans. For the next several weeks, Mrs. M and the therapist were locked into a therapeutic nightmare from which neither could awaken. The therapist, unable to discern from Mrs. M's disjointed presentation whether she did indeed have signs and symptoms of melancholia, decided to start tricyclic antidepressants on a trial basis. A course of imipramine 150 mg/day was begun, but the therapist was never sure whether the pills were being taken reliably. Mrs. M was positive they were unhelpful and only making her dizzy spells much worse. Small doses of thioridazine (25–50 mg) and then haloperidol (2–5 mg) were both rejected because they made her appear "dazed" and because the children were now openly declaring that their mother was both a nut and a drunk.

Psychiatric hospitalization was adamantly refused; despite Mrs. M's well-constructed suicidal plans, she considered hospitalization as the ultimate disgrace and rejection. She was also "too embarrassed" to see any other physician in consultation, including those doctors she had visited prior to psychotherapy. Mrs. M's decision was reinforced by her husband, who not only refused to discuss the problem with the psychiatrist, but also stated that he would marshal the forces of every lawyer in town to prevent an involuntary hospitalization "no matter how much she wants to die."

Session after session, Mrs. M would give a disorganized account of her somatic symptoms, her rage at being rejected by both her father and the therapist, and her conviction that she would be better off dead. Intertwined with her guilt-ridden ruminations would be parenthetical comments about how much she loved or hated or needed the therapist.

REVISED DSM-III-R DIAGNOSIS

> Axis I: Unclear; possible major depressive episode with melancholia, or brief reactive psychosis, and/or transient psychotic transference associated with Axis II diagnosis
> Axis II: Borderline personality disorder
> Axis III: None
> Axis IV: Stress—severe (death of father and potential loss of therapist)
> Axis V: Highest level of functioning past year—poor (deteriorating care of home and self after suggestion that treatment terminate)

TREATMENT PROBLEM (PHASE II)

Profound depression with suicidal plans in a woman refusing the suggestions of a psychiatrist with whom she has an intensely ambivalent relationship.

DISCUSSION OF TREATMENT SELECTION (PHASE II)

It is easy to see, in retrospect, possible errors in Mrs. M's treatment: 1) the failure to document more systematically the psychiatric diagnosis; 2) the failure to clarify during the negotiation phase the specific goals of treatment and the therapeutic options in reaching them; 3) the failure to appreciate that both Mrs. M's past history of being an "oddball" and her presenting symptoms suggested a more malignant process than simply an aberrant grief reaction; 4) the failure to discuss the therapeutic relationship as it was developing to correct possible transferential distortions before they became more fixed; and 5) the poorly-timed and defensive interpretation of how the therapist had become a father surrogate. It is far more difficult to suggest just how these and other possible errors can be corrected by revising the therapeutic approach at this juncture.

Setting. At the present time, outpatient treatment may be the only option. Although the patient threatens that she will kill herself, she has been making these threats for several weeks and, because she is probably not an immediate risk to herself or others, cannot be involuntarily hospitalized. Short of threatening to discontinue treatment altogether unless the patient goes into the hospital, the therapist has already exhausted many methods of persuading Mrs. M that hospitalization offers the best opportunity for her to be treated. Moreover, he has discussed repeatedly with her the distorted fears she has about psychiatric hospitalization. The therapist has also tried unsuccessfully to elicit the support of the husband. Even if the patient were to consent to psychiatric hospitalization, this option has real risks; specifically, the patient has shown a propensity towards psychotic regression, which may become even more pronounced in a hospital where she would be able to relinquish the day-to-day responsibilities that require mature functioning. It would also confirm the stigma attached to her by her family as a behavioral deviant.

Format. A heterogeneous group led by the therapist might defuse the psychotic transference, while at the same time providing Mrs. M with the reassurance that she was not being totally abandoned; however, given the intense attachment she has to the therapist, it is doubtful that she would accept sharing him with others and, in addition, might not be able to weather the initial resentment and rivalry expressed by other group members. In terms of a family or marital format, the husband's refusal (and probable fear) of entering any kind of psychiatric evaluation or treatment precludes this possibility. But the resistance of both Mrs. M and her husband against an alternative format is not the only reason to continue an individual treatment. Mrs. M is in crisis and her problems require focused personal attention.

Duration and Frequency. The therapist has already tried one option with disastrous results, namely, tentatively establishing a termination date. He could stick to this plan, despite Mrs. M's escalating symptoms, in the belief (or at least in the hope) that working through the termination phase of the treatment would in essence be a reworking of the mourning over her father, and that upon completion of this task, she would return to her premorbid functioning. Alternatively, suspecting that Mrs. M's current problems are symptomatic of a severe underlying personality disorder that will not abate or be worked through upon termination, the therapist may choose to go completely in the other direction and reassure Mrs. M that a prolonged open-ended treatment may be necessary and is available. The danger of such a statement is that the erotic and dependent feelings towards the therapist will be fueled by this reassurance, with a resulting increase in the psychotic transference and secondary gain. Another possibility is for the therapist to alter frequency with the same rationale for altering the duration, i.e., a decrease in frequency (less than once a week) to dilute the unmanageable transference feelings, or an increase in frequency (two to four times per week) to reassure Mrs. M that she will not be abandoned and that the intense feelings can be closely monitored and worked through by more frequent appointments. Unfortunately, adjusting the time factors seems in many ways academic in that Mrs. M's symptoms so far have had a life of their own, operating night and day even with the relatively limited contact she has had with the psychiatrist.

Approach. The therapist has already tried an array of different approaches to little avail. Exploratory interventions, such as helping Mrs. M understand that her intense yearning for the therapist is a replacement for the lost father, have so far been met with the patient's bitter resistance, feelings of rejection, and exacerbation of symptoms. A directive approach, such as teaching Mrs. M that many of her somatic symptoms are the result of hyperventilation, is no longer helpful; because of Mrs. M's intensely ambivalent transference, she now rejects whatever suggestions the therapist offers. Similarly, an experiential approach initially seemed helpful in facilitating Mrs. M's grieving over her dying father, but now the therapist's empathic responses and positive regard for the patient are misconstrued and seem to intensify her eroticized dependency.

Somatic Treatment. The same kind of frustration exists regarding a consideration of possible somatic therapies. Mrs. M has not taken psychotropics—both neuroleptics and antidepressants—reliably because the mild side effects are indistinguishable in her mind from the somatic symptoms that frighteningly convince her that she has the same fatal disease as her father. Anxiolytics, such as benzodiazepines, would probably not be effective in treating the psychotic dimensions of the patient's illness and could be harmful in a woman who is noncompliant and has already been abusing alcohol to self-treat her fears.

CHOICE AND OUTCOME (PHASE II)

After reviewing the case with a colleague, including certain countertransference problems, the therapist concluded that Mrs. M's destructive regression in treatment precluded any potential gains and that at this point no interventions within or outside of sessions were likely to be effective in enabling Mrs. M to view the therapist more rationally; therefore, no treatment was the recommendation of choice.

In a definite but tactful manner, the therapist told Mrs. M that treatment would be discontinued. Because of the peer supervision, the therapist was neither tentative nor guilty in making this recommendation. Using a medical analogy to depersonalize the situation, he explained that Mrs. M's therapy was in some respects similar to antibiotic treatment: It had been helpful when prescribed for a limited period of time, but if now used continuously, the risks would outweigh the gains. He added that he was of course well aware that Mrs. M might perceive this recommendation of terminating treatment as one more rejection and that, as a result, her symptoms (including her suicidal feelings) might become temporarily worse. But the therapist believed that Mrs. M now had the capacity to function without him.

In response to this recommendation, Mrs. M smiled graciously, said that she saw no reason to discuss the therapist's decision further at this time, and left the office in a contained manner as though she were politely excusing herself from the dinner table.

Worried about the patient's fate, the therapist phoned her apartment several times, but Mrs. M did not return the calls. He looked in the obituary column to see if his worst fears had been realized. After three weeks of fretting, the psychiatrist received a postcard from the Caribbean: "Kids on spring vacation—me too. Calm seas, beautiful sunsets. Love, Mrs. M." Two months later the psychiatrist learned, by chance and indirectly, that Mrs. M was receiving outpatient physical therapy for suspected cervical arthritis. Nothing else was heard from or about her for a long time.

Four years later, Mrs. M, now age 43, called to arrange an appointment. On the phone she sounded pleasant and eager for a reunion. The session began with her characteristic stilted graciousness as she expressed how nice it was to be back and with someone she could always trust. The chaotic events surrounding her last departure were not mentioned. Before the therapist could even ask Mrs. M about what present problems had prompted the phone call, the patient discarded her social demeanor and erupted into a fragmented and circumstantial description of how her recent civilian secretarial job with the military had placed her in contact with "special people" and "secrets" too important to reveal because they might place the psychiatrist himself in jeopardy. A particular station on the radio was advising Mrs. M how to dispose of the documents, and she wanted the psychiatrist to advise her about what she should do.

This time the psychiatrist had the advantage of having treated Mrs. M in the past. He realized that partly because of her social prominence and grace, he had initially underestimated her psychopathology until a psychotic transference made it all too obvious. He also realized that despite the way the previous treatment had ended and despite Mrs. M's current delusional state, she still retained a modicum of trust, however fragile, in him.

Midway through this session, the psychiatrist told Mrs. M, tactfully but directly, that she was suffering a psychosis and that her imagination was playing tricks on her. He then recommended that because outpatient treatment had been difficult for her in the past and because her situation at home and at work did not offer sufficient support, psychiatric hospitalization could provide the most immediate and intensive help. Realizing that in the past Mrs. M had been reluctant to "humiliate" herself by accepting hospitalization, the psychiatrist added that inpatient care was not absolutely necessary and that the two of them could discuss the matter further in terms of other options which were mutually acceptable.

Mrs. M replied that she had always felt the therapist was the one person she could trust and that if he recommended hospitalization, that was fine with her; she would make the necessary arrangements that night at home and return the following day with her packed suitcase and with insurance forms to finalize the admission plans. She never showed up and never phoned. The therapist chose to let the matter ride.

Two months passed before Mrs. M again scheduled an appointment. It was now July. The children were out of town at college or at summer jobs. Her husband decided to take another apartment and to file for a divorce. She was terrified of the prospects of being alone and even more frightened of "the same secrets." Once again she wanted her "one true friend" (the therapist) to recommend what she should do.

REVISED DSM-III-R DIAGNOSIS

AXIS I: Schizoaffective disorder
AXIS II: Suspected mixed personality disorder with borderline, schizotypal, dependent, hypochondriacal, and histrionic features; but Axis II diagnosis still not adequately documented
AXIS III: None
AXIS IV: Stress—moderate severe (pending divorce, "empty nest")
AXIS V: Highest level of functioning past year—fair (apparently functioning at work and maintaining the household, but still self-treating her fears with alcohol and still visiting various doctors because of persisting somatic delusions)

TREATMENT PROBLEM (PHASE III)

Delusional woman with a propensity to develop a psychotic transference and to take psychotropic medication unreliably. She has little support from her family, has rejected hospitalization in the past, and yet appears to function moderately well with no psychiatric treatment.

DISCUSSION OF TREATMENT SELECTION (PHASE III)

Setting. A major decision is whether or not once again to recommend psychiatric hospitalization for Mrs. M. She vehemently rejected the idea four years ago when first in treatment and, for reasons she cannot make clear, agreed to psychiatric hospitalization two months ago but then never followed through with the plans. If she agreed to an inpatient setting at this time, certainly the therapist would feel relieved: she was difficult to treat, or even evaluate, as an outpatient, was constantly threatening to kill herself, and was resisting all psychotherapeutic and somatic interventions. Yet if the therapist so much as mentions hospitalization at this time, Mrs. M might once again bolt and an opportunity to treat her psychosis will be lost, or at least indefinitely delayed. There is the possibility that Mrs. M may now be more receptive to hospitalization because she is frightened of living alone, because her husband's resistance to it is less of a factor (he is planning a divorce anyway), and because the children have more or less left home and no longer pose obstacles. On the other hand, an inpatient setting may not be the best choice for Mrs. M (although it is perhaps more comfortable for the therapist). She is liable to regress further in the hospital and completely relinquish one of her clearest strengths, namely, to put on a good social front and prevent her illness from totally interfering with her work or home activities. Using the past as a guide, the therapist is now forewarned about the potential for a destructive transferential relationship and he will be able to monitor an outpatient treatment more effectively.

Format. Mr. M would probably be even less willing to attend marital sessions at this time, since he apparently has resolved to leave and to seek a divorce. Conversely, having made this resolution, he may be less threatened by a suspicion that the psychiatrist intends to bring the couple closer together. He may, therefore, be willing to attend at least some sessions to help evaluate the patient's condition and to outline how the divorce might proceed in the best way for both parties. The children may be included in some of these sessions. In a family format, they could be informed about Mrs. M's illness and how best to deal with it and with her.

Duration and Frequency. The therapist is confronted with the same dilemma he encountered four years previously. If the treatment is too intense or prolonged, the patient's propensity to regress and develop an unworkable eroticized dependency might be greater. On the other hand, if the treatment is too infrequent or too short, the time may be too limited to treat Mrs. M's severe psychopathology. With the benefit of past experience, one alternative might be to declare openly from the start that the intensity and duration of treatment will be kept flexible and will depend upon the therapeutic needs on a week-by-week basis. Sessions may be more frequent or more prolonged when the patient's life or therapeutic situation so warrants (e.g., when her disorganization or despair at home is profound or when her medications need to be closely monitored), and may be less frequent or even temporarily terminated altogether when, in the therapist's view, a "cooling-off" period is necessary to diffuse intense transferential feelings that cannot be dealt with effectively within the sessions.

Approach. The therapist has learned that Mrs. M tends to deteriorate further with either exploratory or experiential approaches, so that directive methods would seem most advisable at this time, specifically, explaining to her the nature of her illness, advising her about what situations tend to make her illness worse (e.g., sustained loneliness and unstructured time), correcting any delusional distortions when they occur, and suggesting how she might organize her life and her pending divorce in her best interest.

Somatic Treatment. Psychotropic medication will no doubt be necessary to treat Mrs. M's psychosis. Although she has subjective feelings of depression about the impending divorce and the separation of the children from the home, her delusions do not appear to be mood congruent, and she does not have the vegetative symptoms associated with a major mood disorder. Antidepressants, therefore, would not seem to be the psychotropic of choice. Neuroleptics would appear to be more advisable, with the option of starting antidepressants if the diminution of the psychotic process makes the depression more apparent and more treatable. If she has the same problem of compliance as in the past, the therapist could explain to her the rationale for the use of an intramuscular, long-acting phenothiazine that could be given every two weeks at her scheduled appointments. Electroconvulsive therapy is another option if symptoms persist and psychotropics are not effective, or if Mrs. M becomes so preoccupied with the side effects of medication that consistent adequate dosage is a problem.

Psychological Testing. Many aspects of this case are still unclear: the patient's Axis I and II diagnoses; the psychodynamic determinants; the specific ego strengths and weaknesses, etc. If Mrs. M would agree, psychological testing could be quite helpful in selecting and implementing a treatment plan.

CHOICE AND OUTCOME (PHASE III)

Because of the changes in Mrs. M's home situation and because her delusions and thought-broadcasting were sufficiently ego-dystonic and distressing, the therapist believed that Mrs. M would be more willing at this time to accept hospitalization and that the benefits of her being closely evaluated and treated in a structured setting outweighed any possible risk of an immutable regression. This time Mrs. M accepted the recommendation for voluntary inpatient care.

Hospitalization was helpful diagnostically and, in time, therapeutically. Mr. M remained a phantom who (except for one visit to the hospital's business office) never visited or spoke with his wife or treating psychiatrist. The patient's brothers and mother, however, flew in from out of town and indicated that Mrs. M had suffered bizarre ideas since adolescence, had always been socially isolated, and was secretly regarded by all of them as a "schizophrenic" like her maternal grandmother and a first cousin. They had been delighted when Mr. M had married the patient, and they understood fully why he would want to bail out now that the children were more on their own. Psychological testing indicated an average intelligence, marked subtest variability on the WAIS, no signs of organicity, marked confusion between maternal and paternal roles, and prominent disorganization, depression, and impulsivity on the Rorschach. The diagnostic impression was schizoaffective disorder.

With moderate doses of thioridazine (300 mg/day), Mrs. M's delusions disappeared (or at least were kept quiet from everyone, including the therapist). She stayed by herself and constantly complained of side effects and other somatic problems, but after two months was well enough to be discharged to the care of her original psychiatrist, the only person she was willing to see. He himself had visited Mrs. M about every two weeks for 15–20 minutes while she was in the hospital, but the primary therapist during her stay had been a resident-in-training, whom Mrs. M condescendingly viewed as "a nice young man."

After discharge, Mrs. M at first did well in outpatient treatment with her former therapist. He recommended that in addition to individual treatment with him, Mrs. M consider group therapy to gain the support of others, to learn more appropriate ways of interacting, and to diffuse the intense feelings that tended to become focused on the therapist. Mrs. M vehemently resisted this recommendation, confessing quite frankly that she did not want to share the therapist and was too embarrassed to expose her humiliating problems to others. In other respects, she complied with the therapist's recommendations, took her maintenance dosages of thioridazine reliably, and attended the weekly 45-minute sessions regularly.

Following the therapist's recommendations regarding how she might structure her life, she returned to her secretarial job, stopped discussing her bizarre ideas with others, and followed the therapist's guidelines on how to deal effectively with her lawyer during the divorce proceedings. The therapist had by now learned to point out transferential distortions the moment they appeared to be surfacing; for instance, if Mrs. M mentioned how she imagined the therapist had spent his weekend in some spectacular and idealized way, he would point out that her speculations were not correct and, within limits, would tell her how he actually spent his time. He would also constantly remind Mrs. M of her need to find relationships outside of treatment and not use the therapist as her primary source of friendship and support.

As a result of these interventions, Mrs. M did not become overly attached to the therapist and her psychotic symptoms were well contained; however, with the real appreciation of her chronic illness and with the real loss of her husband and children, she developed a severe depression. At times she would cling unrealistically to the idea of her husband's eventual return, despite all evidence to the contrary, or in the middle of the night she would desperately phone her children at their various colleges and plead for them to return, which would only make them less willing to have anything to do with her.

As the depression increased, Mrs. M found it more and more difficult to concentrate at work, and she spent her evenings wandering in loneliness through the many memories of her apartment, slept fitfully, awakened early to face the gloom of the day, ate only out of habit, and thought frequently of suicide and the eventual reunion with her father. In addition to her despair, Mrs. M's longstanding fears of being alone on the streets had become so severe that during the past couple of weeks she had missed work on occasion because she was too frightened to leave the apartment. She stopped shopping at any stores that were further down the street than the doorman's view for fear that she would be raped or mistaken for a spy or harmed in some unspecified way.

Faced with Mrs. M's increasingly severe depression and the general deterioration in her functioning, the therapist believed that some changes in her treatment were now necessary.

REVISED DSM-III-R DIAGNOSIS

Axis I: Schizoaffective disorder
Axis II: Mixed personality disorder
Axis III: None
Axis IV: Stress—moderate (social isolation, separation of children, and loss of husband)
Axis V: Highest level of functioning past year—poor (erratic attendance at work, no meaningful interpersonal relationships, and no pleasurable activities)

TREATMENT PROBLEM (PHASE IV)

Severe depression and general deterioration in a 44-year-old woman being maintained on low doses of neuroleptics for previous episode of mood-incongruent delusions.

DISCUSSION OF TREATMENT SELECTION (PHASE IV)

Setting. Another psychiatric hospitalization does not appear warranted at this time. Although considering suicide, Mrs. M has no immediate plans. In addition, she is no longer delusionally involved with the therapist. On the contrary, she is far more trusting, has complied with the therapist's recommendations, and has been candid about her fears and despair. If so instructed, she would probably agree to contact the therapist on an emergency basis before acting on her suicidal ideas. If her depression does not respond to other changes in the treatment, a night hospital would be worthwhile to provide structure and support during those lonely hours at home and would not preclude her continuing work. A pronounced regression or feeling of total defeat with another hospitalization would be less pronounced with a partial hospitalization of this kind.

Format. Her resistance to entering a heterogeneous group has been persistent throughout. At this time, the demands of entering such a group might only make her feel more inadequate and, therefore, more depressed. A homogeneous group might be advisable if the interpersonal demands were not too great, perhaps a church-run group for the recently divorced. Such a group might decrease Mrs. M's feelings of alienation and abandonment, while not requiring the kinds of deep interpersonal involvement she finds threatening and disorganizing.

Duration and Frequency. Weekly 45-minute sessions now seem inadequate to follow Mrs. M closely enough to monitor her depression and to provide sufficient support. To achieve the latter, sessions could be two or three times a week but limited to 15 or 20 minutes in hopes of preventing the pronounced regression and psychotic transference that occurred in the past.

Technique. The directive and supportive approach would still seem to be the most advisable.

Somatic Treatment. A possible change in the somatic approach deserves special emphasis. The strongest argument in favor of adding antidepressants to Mrs. M's regimen of maintenance neuroleptics is the presence of a circumscribed depressive syndrome characterized by hopelessness, helplessness, loneliness, suicidal ideation, sleep disturbance with early morning awakening, and loss of appetite. There are two additional advantages of using antidepressants in this particular case: 1) In view of Mrs. M's previous disruptive psychotic transference, the therapist is understandably hesitant about relying on psychotherapy alone to work through Mrs. M's current depression for fear that this kind of intense therapeutic involvement might repeat the nightmare of the past; and 2) the antidepressants could provide an added bonus of treating Mrs. M's agoraphobia and the associated panic attacks.

On the negative side, Mrs. M did not respond to antidepressants in the past. On the contrary, she became delusionally preoccupied with the side effects and was convinced that the associated lightheadedness and lethargy were proof of an underlying neurological disease similar to her father's. The therapeutic situation is now different from when antidepressants were initially prescribed. An ambivalent transference is no longer preventing the patient from trusting the therapist and complying with his recommendations. Moreover, Mrs. M might now be placed on one of the newer antidepressants with fewer anticholinergic side effects. Nonetheless, her adverse response in the past and the possibility of any antidepressant causing an exacerbation of schizophrenic symptoms argue against the use of these drugs unless the depressive syndrome persists and is unresponsive to psychotherapeutic interventions.

CHOICE AND OUTCOME (PHASE IV)

Rather than relying on antidepressants, the therapist chose a psychotherapeutic approach and relied on the positive transference to usher Mrs. M through her current despair, social isolation, and panic attacks. He could not forget how disruptive treatment had become four years previously when he had prescribed various medications, including antidepressants, and how the necessary human and humane relationship with Mrs. M became lost in the process of discussing the shapes and colors and dosages and side effects of one pill as opposed to another. He was wary of jeopardizing Mrs. M's current faith in him and in therapy by once again struggling over her poor compliance with drugs and somatic problems.

To protect against the development of another psychotic transference, he saw Mrs. M frequently but briefly: 15-minute sessions three times a week. He also referred Mrs. M to a weekly homogeneous group that was run by a social worker and occupational therapist for recently discharged patients, and they concentrated on practical issues of daily living and vocational placement. Mrs. M attended only four of these group sessions and rejected the other members for being "too sick"; but in the process of trying out such a group, she recognized her need to be with others and, through her church, became a member of the volunteer corps at a small hospital near where she lived (delivering newspapers and books to patients and working in the gift shop). On four occasions, when Mrs. M was too frightened to leave her apartment to come to a session, the therapist met her at a coffee shop half way between her home and his office and then walked with her into those stores she had been avoiding because of anxiety. On another occasion, when Mrs. M became more severely suicidal on the anniversary of her father's death, the therapist arranged to have Mrs. M's older brother come to the city for a weekend visit.

These changes proved effective. Over the next two years, although Mrs. M gained considerable weight and lost her aristocratic appearance, and although she continued to believe that inevitably she would one day develop a "nerve tumor" like her father's that would cause her to faint in the street and be run over, she nevertheless was able to accomplish the following: hold her job as a secretary, continue her volunteer jobs, participate in activities at the church that allayed her loneliness, and manage the prolonged divorce proceedings proficiently and without jeopardizing the final settlement. The frequency of sessions was gradually decreased to monthly appointments during which she and the therapist would discuss the understandable pain of her being completely rejected by her husband and children.

After four years of supportive psychotherapy and maintenance thioridazine, Mrs. M, now age 48, was told by the therapist that he had decided to accept an academic position in another area and in three months would be discontinuing his private practice. Though upset, Mrs. M appeared to accept this "final blow" with resignation and, during the last session, finally agreed to follow through with the therapist's referral. The final parting seemed sad and caring, yet incomplete, as if the last chord had not yet been struck.

FINAL OUTCOME (PHASE V)

Mrs. M phoned a month later, as previously arranged, and told the therapist that the new doctor had switched her medication to thiothixene in hopes that she could tolerate higher dosages of this antipsychotic medication and thereby finally get over some of her "funny ideas," such as developing a brain tumor. She added that she yearned nostalgically for her previous therapist but was willing to comply with her new doctor's recommendations. A phone call six months later was less reassuring: Mrs. M had stopped treatment with the recommended therapist shortly after her previous call, was hospitalized overnight two months later at the city hospital, and was now in a "drug clinic" connected with that facility. She had stopped working and for financial reasons could no longer continue in private treatment. In addition, she would probably be forced to sell her apartment in a high rent district within the next few weeks.

Nothing was heard from or about Mrs. M for about three years until, out of the blue, the therapist received a phone call from her brother. Mrs. M, now at age 51 (13 years since the original consultation) had been in a state hospital for two months and had not responded to an array of different medications. The physicians were recommending electroconvulsive therapy and the brother wanted advice. The brother was advised not to give informed consent until the therapist had spoken with the treating physician, but the phone calls to the doctor in charge were not returned. When the therapist was finally able to talk with a member of the hospital staff two weeks later, he was told by an administrative nurse that Mrs. M had improved rapidly without ECT and had been discharged to be followed at the clinic in her catchment area.

Two months later the brother called to say that Mrs. M had been killed by a transit bus while walking to her outpatient clinic. He wanted to know if the cause could possibly have been suicide. The therapist had no answer.

SUGGESTED READING

1. Cavenar, J. O., Nash, J. L., & Maltbie, A. A. Anniversary reactions masquerading as manic-depressive illness. *American Journal of Psychiatry,* 134: 1273–1276, 1977. (Review of literature and several clinical examples that resemble Mrs. M.)
2. Horowitz, M., Wilner, N., Marmar, C., et al. Pathological grief and the activation of latent self-images. *American Journal of Psychiatry,* 137:1157–1162, 1980. (How depressive feelings are held in check by a loved one, then reemerge when the loved one dies.)
3. Asch, S. S. Varieties of negative therapeutic reaction and problems of technique. *Journal of the American Psychoanalytic Association,* 24:383–407, 1976. (Extends Freud's original explanations to include problems in separation–individuation; also suggests how this humbling and difficult situation can be handled clinically.)
4. Horowitz, M., Krupnick, J. L., Kaltreider, N., et al. Initial psychological response to parental death. *Archives of General Psychiatry,* 38:316–323, 1981. (A systematic study reminding us that we are never too old to experience parental loss as if we were a helpless child.)

VI

Mood Disorders

■ BIPOLAR DISORDER, MANIC

18. The Case of the Music Student

(Historical Case: Emil Kraepelin)

Authors' Note:
One of Kraepelin's lasting contributions was the objective clinical data
he accumulated at the Research Institute of Psychiatry in Munich. On
the basis of his detailed observations, he was able to differentiate dementia praecox from manic-depressive psychosis. An example of the
latter is presented here.

You see here before you a student of music, aged 19, who has been ill
for about a year. The highly gifted patient, without any tangible cause,
while studying music, became depressed, felt ill at ease and lonely,
made all manner of plans, which he always gave up, for changing his
place of residence and his profession, for he could come to no fixed
resolutions.

During a visit to Munich, he felt as if people in the street had something to say to him, and as if he were talked about everywhere. He heard
an offensive remark at an inn at the next table, which he answered
rudely. Next day he was seized with the apprehension that his remark

might be taken as *lèse majesté*. He heard that students asked for him at the door, and he left Munich posthaste with every precautionary measure, because he thought himself accompanied and followed on the way. Since then he overheard people in the street who threatened to shoot him, and to set fire to his house, and on that account he burned no light in his room. In the streets voices pointed out the way he ought to go so as to avoid being shot. Behind doors, windows, hedges, pursuers seemed to lurk everywhere. He also heard long conversations of not very flattering purport as to his person. In consequence of this, he withdrew altogether from society, but yet behaved in such an ordinary way that his relatives, whom he visited, did not notice his delusions. At last the many mocking calls which he heard at every turn provoked the thought of shooting himself.

After about six months he felt more free, "comfortable, enterprising, and cheerful," began to talk a lot, to compose, criticized everything, concocted great schemes, and was insubordinate to his teacher. The voices still continued, and he recognized in them the whisperings of master spirits. Hallucinations of sight now became very marked. The patient saw Beethoven's image radiant with joy at his genius; saw Goethe, whom he had abused, in a threatening attitude; masked old men and ideal female forms floated through his room. He saw lightning and glorious brilliancy of colors, which he interpreted partly as the flowing out of his great genius, partly as attestations of applause from the dead.

He regarded himself as the Messiah, preached openly against prostitution, wished to enter into an ideal connection with a female student of music, whom he sought for in strange houses, composed the "Great Song of Love," and on account of this priceless work was brought to the hospital by those who envied him, as he said.

The patient is quite collected, and gives connected information as to his personal circumstances. He is clear as to time and place, but betrays himself by judging his position falsely, in as much as he takes us for hypnotizers, who wish to try experiments with him. He does not look upon himself as ill; at the most as somewhat nervously overexcited. Through diplomatic questions we learn that all people know his thoughts; if he writes, the words are repeated before the door. In the creaking of boards, in the whistle of the train, he hears calls, exhortations, orders, threats. Christ appears to him in the night, or a golden figure as the spirit of his father; colored signs of special meaning are given through the window. In prolonged conversation the patient very quickly loses the thread, and produces finally a succession of fine phrases, which wind up unexpectedly with some facetious question.

His mood is arrogant, conceited, generally condescending, occasion-ally transitorily irritated or apprehensive. The patient speaks much and willingly, talks aloud to himself, and marches boisterously up and down the ward, interests himself more than is desirable in his fellow patients, seeking to cheer them and to manage them. He is very busy, too, with letter writing and composing, but only produces fugitive, carelessly jotted down written work, with numerous marginal notes.

KRAEPELIN'S DIAGNOSIS

Manical-depressive insanity

DSM-III-R DIAGNOSIS

Axis I: Manic episode, with mood-congruent psychotic features

TREATMENT PROBLEM

A young man with grandiose delusions who does not recognize that he is ill and who is too suspicious of caretakers to accept their opinion.

DISCUSSION OF TREATMENT SELECTION

Setting. As is so often true with manic patients, the choice of thera-peutic setting—or at least the implementation of that choice—may be the most important consideration in the treatment of Kraepelin's music stu-dent. Inpatient care is clearly the preferred choice. This setting is most likely to ensure that the patient remains available for treatment, takes his medication, and avoids potentially dangerous behavior and financial or professional transgressions that might be irreversible blots on his life or reputation. Outpatient management for the music student, in his current state, would probably be unsuccessful. He does not recognize that he is ill, would not keep his appointments or take his medication reliably, and at a moment's notice might once again respond to a grandiose or perse-cutory delusion by leaving town as he has in the past when he moved away from Munich.

But suppose the student suddenly decides to leave his hospital ward and submits a signout letter demanding that he be released. In the present day, many jurisdictions would not enable the therapist legally to keep the patient in the hospital against his will. Although the patient is obviously disturbed, he has not said or done anything up to this point that provides clear and convincing evidence that he is an immediate risk to himself or others. Unfortunately, he may need to exhaust the family's financial resources, terrorize relatives, and irreparably endanger his social and professional life, before his condition deteriorates to the point where involuntary commitment becomes legally possible. Manic and hypomanic patients often present the most painful of situations for physician, patient, and families because the definition of "dangerousness to self or others" does not include other justifiable reasons for hospitalizing these patients involuntarily.

Format. Kraepelin does not mention this patient's family; but if they are available, they might be helpful in providing much-needed structure for this patient during his psychotic turmoil. Relatives are often reluctant to set firm limits for manic or hypomanic patients because initially they do not realize that the patient's elated mood is secondary to a serious illness ("he's just feeling his oats"); and when they then do come to realize that the patient is seriously ill, they continue to avoid confronting him or her for fear of an unmanageable rage that can become dangerous.

A family format is difficult because the patient is likely to ignore, resent, or attack his relatives; but often even a few family sessions are helpful in both showing and explaining how one can best respond to the provocations of a manic patient. Family sessions, possibly without the patient present, become absolutely necessary in those unfortunate situations in which an outpatient setting is the only alternative. The family's structure, support, guidance, and monitoring of medication will be essential during the early phases of treatment. Neither a heterogeneous nor homogeneous group nor a community meeting on the hospital ward is advisable for patients who are as acutely disturbed and provocative as is this patient presented by Kraepelin; they simply disrupt the group and remain impervious to the interventions of the other members, who then become enraged and frustrated.

Duration and Frequency. Sessions should be brief when the patient is acutely manic or hypomanic. Usually 15 or 20 minutes is as much as the patient (and therapist) can tolerate. Longer sessions are too demanding on these patients with limited concentration and frustration tolerance. Although the duration of individual sessions should be brief, they should occur frequently, ideally a few times each day, in order to evaluate fluctuations in the course of the illness and to maintain a presence with a patient who is so easily distracted and forgetful. The duration of treatment will in many cases be lifelong, but intermittent. Even during remissions the patient should be followed regularly (about every few months) to monitor medication and to ensure that a hypomanic, manic, or depressive episode is not emerging. Patients with bipolar disorder tend to have relatively frequent episodes and the course and eventual outcome will depend on careful management over the years and the prevention of serious exacerbations which tend to worsen the overall prognosis.

Approach. Exploratory treatments are contraindicated during the acute episodes. Patients simply do not have the insight or motivation to understand their behavior and often experience any interpretation or even clarification as ridicule, which, in turn, only further motivates them to ridicule others. Experiential techniques are also ill-advised. Although the therapist should relate empathically to the patient and resonate with those infrequent moments when genuine feelings break through the colorful façade, the therapist cannot merely accept the patient's behavior with unconditional positive regard. This approach can both further escalate the patient's grandiose delusions and make it difficult for the over-tolerant therapist to convey the seriousness of the illness and the need for hospitalization or medication. If the therapist has not taken a firm stance from the beginning but instead has merely spent most of the session laughing in response to the patient's humor, it will be hard to switch gears from being an entertained member of the patient's audience to being a concerned clinician. In such case, the manic patient may dismiss whatever the overaccepting therapist has to say. Directive techniques are therefore usually the best approach, i.e., setting well-defined limits, attempting to correct those hallucinatory and delusional experiences that are not fixed and appear to be only mood-congruent responses to misperceptions, and repeatedly advising the patient that his behavior is an inappropriate response caused by an illness that has temporarily elevated his mood.

Somatic Treatment. The major modality for Kraepelin's music student would now be psychotropic medication, most notably lithium carbonate alone or perhaps in combination with a neuroleptic for the management of the acute episode. Most therapists would choose to prescribe lithium alone unless they are uncertain of the diagnosis of mania, are eager to reduce psychotic symptoms quickly, or are unable to manage the patient's symptoms without combined treatment. For this particular patient, whose symptoms have been persisting for at least several weeks without complication, the urgency of rapidly removing the psychosis seems less than the need to determine the degree to which the disorder is responsive to lithium prescribed alone.

There is considerable controversy about the prophylactic use of lithium to prevent future recurrences after the current acute episode is in remission. After the current episode resolves, we would maintain the patient on lithium for six to nine months in order to ensure that the episode has been treated thoroughly and to reduce the documented high risk of relapse when lithium is discontinued prematurely in the continuation phase after treatment of acute symptoms. We would provide long-term maintenance or prophylactic treatment only after a patient has already had two episodes spaced fairly close to one another. Lithium prophylaxis is much more necessary in bipolar than in unipolar affective disorders, depressed, for which the usefulness of lithium has generally not been as well established. Since this patient will no doubt need to be maintained on lithium after discharge from the hospital, this medication should be prescribed at some point during the hospital stay (with appropriate medical screening tests).

SUGGESTED READING

1. Janowsky, D., Leff, M., & Epstein, R. Playing the manic game. *Archives of General Psychiatry,* 22:252–257, 1970. (Clinical advice on how to manage the enraged and enraging manic patient.)
2. Jefferson, J. W., & Griest, J. M. *Primer of Lithium Therapy.* Baltimore: Williams & Wilkins, 1977. (Exactly what the title indicates, with an emphasis on the practical.)
3. Reisberg, B., & Gershon, S. Side effects associated with lithium therapy. *Archives of General Psychiatry,* 36:879–887, 1979. (Reviews effects, both toxic and clinically insignificant, on every organ system, including cardiac, endocrinologic, renal, and CNS.)
4. Ballenger, J. C., & Post, R. M. Carbamazepine in manic-depressive illness: A new treatment. *American Journal of Psychiatry,* 137:782–790, 1980. (This anticonvulsant remains a possible alternative to those who fail to respond to lithium.)

■ MAJOR DEPRESSION, RECURRENT, WITHOUT MELANCHOLIA

19. The Case of the Disappointed Decorator

(Guest Expert: Robert Hales, M.D.)

Authors' Note:
Robert E. Hales, M.D., is Chairman, Department of Psychiatry, Pacific-Presbyterian Medical Center, San Francisco. In this case he discusses the efficacy of combining psychotherapy and pharmacotherapy for a highly functioning woman whose depression did not have prominent endogenous features.

Mrs. B is a 57-year-old woman who presents with dysphoria, tearfulness, suicidal ideation, loss of energy and sexual interest, and insomnia. Although she feels hopeless about the future and worries that she will never get better, Mrs. B does accept reassurance that her pessimism is exaggerated and results from her depression. She feels that she is a great burden on her family and blames herself for letting them down and for not bearing her difficulties with dignified stoicism. Her recent inability to achieve orgasm also convinces Mrs. B that her sexual life and femininity are things of the past.

The patient's symptoms began rather suddenly three weeks ago after an unusually unpleasant argument with her husband. Mrs. B had been trying to establish a greater intimacy in their marriage and he rebuffed her in no uncertain terms, making clear that he was and would remain totally preoccupied with his business activities and had no supply of time or emotion left for her. This disappointment was made even more poignant by the concomitant departure for college of the patient's youngest daughter. Mrs. B contemptuously described herself as "an old bird with an empty nest."

Mrs. B has always been a highly competent, popular, and attractive woman. She is widely regarded as an ideal wife, mother, and friend and has also managed a successful side career as an interior decorator. She would never have dreamed of seeing a psychiatrist until, at age 48, she had a depressive episode similar in its presentation to the one described above. This lasted for three months and was treated with a brief, psychodynamically oriented therapy. The focus of this treatment was the patient's excessively high self-expectation. It became clear that Mrs. B experienced considerable self-loathing because she found unacceptable her anger towards her husband, her dependency on her daughter, and her illicit sexual feelings about other men. The patient attributed her improvement to the insights gained in the therapy and to the warm and open relationship with the therapist. She felt less inhibited and guilt-ridden than ever before in her life and was generally well and happy until the current episode.

Mrs. B has a strong family history of depressions, including a maternal grandmother who killed herself. She grew up in a stern and demanding environment and was expected to be a letter-perfect little lady. She was a hardworking student, a dutiful wife, and a devoted mother, but never felt satisfied with her performance. She now feels trapped in an unhappy and unfulfilling marriage and also feels that she has wasted her life. She would like to leave her husband but does not believe in divorce; and she would like to have affairs but believes this to be sinful. Her husband is not willing to participate in her treatment. The patient does not appear to be acutely suicidal. She is able to relate to the therapist and brightens in response to a joke.

DSM-III-R DIAGNOSIS

> Axis I: Major depression, recurrent, without melancholia
> Axis II: None (though some features of both dependent and compulsive personality disorders)
> Axis III: None
> Axis IV: Stress—moderate (unhappy marriage, daughter leaves home)
> Axis V: Highest level of functioning past year—superior

DISCUSSION OF TREATMENT SELECTION

The primary question is what type of therapy we should prescribe for Mrs. B: psychotherapy, pharmacotherapy, or a combination of treatments. A secondary question is the extent to which Mrs. B's personality may have contributed to the development and expression of her depressive symptoms and how it may affect her treatment and recovery.

Mrs. B displays several personality characteristics commonly seen in depressive-prone individuals: dependence, lack of self-confidence, non-assertiveness, and pessimism. For instance, the development of depressive symptoms coincidental with the husband's rejection of her attempts to establish greater intimacy and with her daughter's departure for college gives evidence of her dependence upon both of them for her self-regard.

In an evaluation it is often difficult to distinguish actual symptoms of depression from longstanding personality features that may have predisposed to depression or influenced the presentation of symptoms. The protocol shows evidence of Mrs. B's normal and superior functioning but also suggests compulsive perfectionism and dependency, a combination of traits particularly prominent in persons prone to depression. Such individuals look to others to provide emotional supplies and for a meaning they so desperately yearn for in their lives. Their lifelong dependency on others leaves them rudderless, with impaired capacity for self-direction and happiness.

We also see how her compulsive personality features may modify the expression of her affective symptoms. Mrs. B feels she is "a great burden on her family" and blames herself for "letting them down." Instead of believing herself to be ill, she characterizes herself as weak and failing her family. She reports considerable self-loathing when she experiences "forbidden" feelings, such as anger towards her husband or sexual attraction towards other men. We learn that she grew up in a "stern and demanding" environment, but we know little about whether, as a child, she was shown love or encouragement for nonachievement behavior.

A related issue is whether Mrs. B actually recovered from her previous depressive episode nine years ago. Weissman, Klerman et al.[1] found that 15% of patients who had experienced an acute depression continued to experience chronic depressive symptoms or social maladjustment. Furthermore, they reported that the best predictor of chronicity was the patient's "neuroticism"—a measure of underlying personality characteristics and adaptive functioning.

During her first episode, Mrs. B had received only three months of psychotherapy, without antidepressants and without follow-up psychotherapy. She did not have the opportunity to work through the "neurotic source" of her difficulties. If she never recovered, she may have been quite vulnerable to moderate stress (an "unpleasant argument with her husband" and her daughter's departure for college). As Metcalfe has concluded, the depressive person is not necessarily the one who is prone to the development of depression but the one who has difficulty recovering from it.[2]

We have a patient whose personality may predispose her to depression, modify the symptomatic expression of the depressive episode, and complicate her treatment and recovery. Mrs. B may not have fully recovered from her previous depression and has not resolved her marital conflicts. Additionally, she exhibits symptoms suggestive of a major depressive disorder. Should we begin Mrs. B on tricyclic antidepressants?

Several factors seem to weigh against an initial psychopharmacologic approach. First, in spite of her "strong family history of depression" and a previous depressive episode, we have no personal or family history of a positive antidepressant response. The protocol notes that the maternal grandmother committed suicide, but we don't know whether she was suffering from an affective illness or other psychiatric disorder. Furthermore, Mrs. B's previous depression, which reportedly presented in a fashion similar to her current episode, responded well to a brief psychodynamically oriented psychotherapy. Since an insidious onset of depressive symptoms has been correlated with response to tricyclics, the presence of well-defined precipitating events for Mrs. B provides additional support for not using pharmacotherapy. Endogenous symptoms, poor appetite, weight loss, mild insomnia, and early morning awakening have also been reported to predict response to tricyclics.[3] We know that Mrs. B has insomnia, loss of libido, and loss of energy, but the presence of other endogenous symptoms is less clear.

Mrs. B's prospects for psychodynamic psychotherapy are more clear-cut in that she fulfills several of the criteria usually associated with a successful outcome. She responded well to this form of psychotherapy during her previous depressive episode. She currently is able to "relate to the therapist and brightens in response to a joke." Finally, she appears psychologically minded, is partly aware of the nature and origin of her psychological conflicts, and is motivated for psychological change. However, we know little about the history of her object relations, her capacity to love, and her ability to think about her own psychological contribution to her difficulties.

What about combining psychotherapy with antidepressants? Rounsville, Klerman, and Weissman[4] recently tested six hypotheses about negative interactions between pharmacotherapy and psychotherapy and found no support for any. If there are no negative interactions, would there be an added benefit to including antidepressants in a psychotherapeutic treatment approach? The study by Weissman and colleagues[1] found that patients who received interpersonal psychotherapy, with or without antidepressants, were doing significantly better on several measures of social function than depressed patients treated only with medication. Consequently, pharmacotherapy for Mrs. B may be less important than psychotherapy.

In summary, I would initially treat Mrs. B with dynamically oriented psychotherapy without antidepressants. The overall goal would be to protect Mrs. B from rash and irreversible decisions (such as divorce or separation) that may be influenced by her current depressed mood. I would focus psychotherapeutic work on her excessively high self-expectations and abundant self-criticism. Additional goals would be to promote communication with her husband and to attempt to resolve interpersonal conflicts that may hinder recovery from her depressive episode. Resolving marital discord and other social maladjustments is particularly useful in decreasing postdepressive personality disturbances before they crystalize into chronic maladaptive patterns.

If Mrs. B responded well to individual therapy, I would anticipate that she might develop an interest in dealing with her marital problems. If appropriate, I would recommend couples therapy. On the other hand, if she exhibited no response to individual psychotherapy or if she began to exhibit additional endogenous depressive symptoms, I would begin her on a course of tricyclic antidepressants.

Finally, her previous short-term psychotherapy was not enduring in its effect; consequently, I would seriously consider long-term intensive psychotherapeutic work until Mrs. B is able to consolidate her capacity for self-direction and is able to get her needs satisfied in a culturally acceptable and personally satisfactory manner. I would also consider long-term follow-up at regular intervals to consolidate therapeutic gains, whether achieved from psychotherapy alone or in combination with antidepressants.

REFERENCES

1. Weissman, M. M., Klerman, G. L., Prusoff, B. A., et al. Depressed outpatients. *Archives of General Psychiatry*, 38:51–55, 1981.
2. Metcalfe, M. The personality of depressive patients. In A. Coppen & A. Walk (Eds.), *The Psychology of Depression: Contemporary Therapy and Research*. New York: John Wiley & Sons, 1974, pp. 97–104.
3. Bielski, R. J., & Friedel, R. O. Prediction of tricyclic antidepressant response: A critical review. *Archives of General Psychiatry*, 33:1479–1489, 1976.
4. Rounsville, B. J., Klerman, G. L., & Weissman, M. M. Do psychotherapy and pharmacotherapy for depression conflict? *Archives of General Psychiatry*, 38:24–29, 1981.

■ MAJOR DEPRESSION, RECURRENT, WITH MELANCHOLIA

20. The Case of the Childless Mother

Mrs. W is a 54-year-old mother of four grown children. She is referred for consultation by her youngest son, a second-year medical student. The son's current course in psychopathology has led him to believe that his mother has not been receiving the best treatment for her depression over the past 10 years. Mrs. W, always willing to appease her children, agrees to the consultation, although she herself is quite satisfied with her present psychotherapist and attributes her profound despair to her own failings.

Her current depression began five months ago following a minor quarrel at the airport with her daughter who was leaving for college. Mrs. W worried during the next several weeks that she had irreparably damaged her relationship with this child and that the daughter's distress would lead to problems in her studying, and perhaps to an eventual failure and need to return home. The psychotherapist, whom Mrs. W had been seeing weekly for many years, suggested the patient was overreacting to the airport incident, and he interpreted Mrs. W's reaction as guilt over an unconscious wish to hurt her child for leaving home.

The therapist's attempts at both support and understanding were to no avail. Mrs. W's depression insidiously gathered momentum. She stopped attending social functions, lost interest in her housecleaning (an ominous sign for Mrs. W), found preparing meals or even sitting still with her husband a chore, rejected comforting from him and her children, and couldn't concentrate on TV sitcoms or even short articles in the newspaper. Over the past several weeks, she picked at her food, lost 15 pounds, went to bed early and to sleep late, and woke before dawn to stare into the darkness, wondering if her wish to be dead might eventually lead to suicide. On a few occasions she stood at the medicine cabinet with an overdose of pills in her hand, but stopped at the last minute for fear of how her suicide might scar the children; however, just yesterday, following a session with her psychotherapist, the idea entered her mind that perhaps the children were so tired of her complaining and of her being a burden that they would be more relieved than hurt by her death.

Alarmed by the severity of Mrs. W's depression, the consultant asked for permission to contact her psychotherapist. She agreed and now sits in the waiting room while the consultant makes the call. He learns from the therapist that Mrs. W has had three similar episodes of depression in the past 10 years, all of which lasted between three and six months and resulted in complete remissions. When well, Mrs. W was an extremely conscientious and meticulous woman, dedicated to the care of her children, but lately she has been somewhat at a loss, now that the children have become more emotionally and geographically separate from her.

For two of the past three depressions, the therapist had placed Mrs. W on antidepressant medication in small doses, but because she complained of the anticholinergic side effects and because he had little expertise in using these drugs, the medication was discontinued. Mrs. W now takes an occasional hypnotic or benzodiazepine for insomnia and agitation. The therapist had not been told by Mrs. W that she was seeking a consultation, but he nonetheless was appreciative and welcomed any advice. Because he had seen the patient recover so well in the past and because she always phoned him whenever she felt particularly desperate, he was not so worried about her current suicidal risk.

DSM-III-R DIAGNOSIS

Axis I: Major depression, recurrent, with melancholia
Axis II: Possible obsessive and/or dependent personality disorder
Axis III: Hysterectomy for fibroids six years ago; paroxysmal atrial tachycardia found on routine life insurance exam, not currently requiring medication
Axis IV: Stress—mild (youngest child leaving for school)
Axis V: Highest level of functioning past year—very good (inability to manage own affairs and household chores is relatively recent)

TREATMENT PROBLEM

Recurrent depressions in a 54-year-old woman that remit within a few months either spontaneously or because of supportive psychotherapy.

DISCUSSION OF TREATMENT SELECTION

Setting. Psychiatric hospitalization is a worthy consideration for Mrs. W. Her depression is profound; her family is understandably distraught and burdened; her suicidal ideas are worrisome; and in consideration of her cardiac arrhythmia and her intolerance of psychotropic medication in the past, a hospital setting may be necessary to monitor her antidepressant medication.

But the disadvantages of hospitalization are also noteworthy and probably outweigh the advantages. She has no previous history of suicide, has sought help rather than acted on suicidal impulses in the past, is faced with no external crisis at this time that is likely to throw her over the edge, and has a family able and willing to provide support at home. She is also a cooperative patient who is likely to comply with medications and with daily monitoring of her heart condition, should this prove necessary. Furthermore, a hospitalization might disrupt the long-term relationship with her current psychotherapist, a relationship which, despite its shortcomings, is perceived as supportive and must be respected until further evidence indicates otherwise. If hospitalization can be avoided during this depression, it might prevent an automatic resort to inpatient care when and if Mrs. W's depressions recur in the future.

Format. Mrs. W is too depressed to deal with the demands of a group at this time. Her inability to rise to the challenge of interacting with others would only increase her feelings of inadequacy and might thereby make the depression worse rather than better. Even a family format might be too distracting and deflect attention onto interpersonal issues and away from more primary concerns, such as the assessment of Mrs. W's mood, current suicidal ideation, and response to medication. However, since Mrs. W's family is particularly concerned and well-meaning, a family format could serve as a useful adjunct, particularly to provide psychoeducation about her condition.

Duration and Frequency. During the time that Mrs. W is profoundly depressed, the duration of individual sessions may need to be shortened to 30 minutes or less. Longer sessions may be experienced by her as an overwhelming strain because of her diminished capacity to concentrate and respond. The sessions should be scheduled frequently, however, to monitor closely Mrs. W's suicidal risk and her response to psychotropic medication. Regarding duration of treatment, a fixed and final termination date would be contraindicated in that it would be experienced by Mrs. W as the very kind of separation she finds so difficult. Moreover, given a 10-year history of depression, the likelihood of recurrence in the future is high. Some provisions will need to be made to ensure that a therapist is always readily available to help Mrs. W to intercept these depressions before they become severe. The contact with this therapist may be intermittent if the patient is good at spotting her depressive symptoms in their early stages and seeking help promptly; or the contact may need to be continuous if outside monitoring or maintenance medication is required.

Approach. A combination of experiential, exploratory, and directive approaches will be helpful for Mrs. W. With regard to experiential techniques, the reasonable optimism, encouragement, and empathy of the therapist can often help to reverse demoralization and provide a supportive holding pattern while pharmacologic and other psychotherapeutic maneuvers are applied. Considering Mrs. W's deep attachments to her family and to her therapist of 10 years, the importance of this empathic bond cannot be overestimated. However, given the present severity of Mrs. W's depression, experiential techniques alone will probably not be sufficient to alter the course of the illness. In addition, because many depressed patients like Mrs. W feel unworthy, they may actually experience the therapist's positive regard as false or unworthy flattery and, as a result, may feel even more guilty and depressed for receiving what they believe they do not deserve.

With regard to exploratory techniques, Mrs. W will feel less bewildered and more understood if she is given some opportunity to examine her overreaction to current events in her life and to place these events into the context of her past. However, here again, some caution is necessary. Explorations cannot be conducted in a field of complete abstinence, neutrality, and free association; the resulting lack of structure and of direct engagement is likely to make Mrs. W feel rejected and leave her to wallow unproductively in her own ruminations. Whereas clarifications can be helpful, interpretations of unconscious wishes have definite risks usually labeled as "negative therapeutic reactions." Depressed patients may react by feeling even more guilty and inadequate for having forbidden ideas and feelings outside their awareness and control (such as Mrs. W's depressive response to the interpretation made by her psychotherapist that the preoccupying concern about her daughter actually reflected an underlying resentment). Explorations are usually best made after the patient has recovered from the acute phase of the depression.

With regard to directive techniques, the first part of such an approach would be to teach Mrs. W and her family about the nature of her condition and its presumed causes, course, and treatments. An important aim in this psychoeducation would be to relieve Mrs. W's sense of responsibility for the depression and to reverse her secondary guilt about it and her consequent demoralization. Though she blames herself for her despair and feels that she should be able to snap out of it by an act of will, the therapist can explain that at this point the depression has a life of its own—like a pneumonia or an appendicitis—and that willpower alone cannot reverse the course of the biological illness. The therapist can also explain that her reaction to the illness can be as problematic as the condition itself and, for that reason, learning about the condition and its treatment are important steps toward recovery. He will point out that because hopelessness and helplessness are common symptoms of depression, Mrs. W will inevitably but incorrectly feel that her condition will last forever. She will not be totally reassured when reminded that she has recovered from similar depressions in the past, but this realistic perspective should be offered nonetheless, over and over again if necessary. Later in treatment, after Mrs. W's depression has lifted, she and the family should be informed about the early signs of depression so that treatment can be started promptly in the future. Earlier interventions can diminish the severity and the duration of the depressive episodes. Mrs. W and her family should be partners in decisions about how long treatment should be continued and whether a maintenance therapy is indicated. A cognitive approach may be effective for both the acute and the recovery phase. It will focus on those irrational, automatic thoughts that fuel depressive feelings, particularly Mrs. W's need to be perfect and to take care of others. A behavioral approach will focus on helping Mrs. W increase the percentage of her time spent in experiences that are rewarding and pleasurable. An interpersonal treatment will focus on Mrs. W's sense of loss of her children, on ways of maintaining her alliance with them, and on developing alternative sources of interpersonal gratification.

Somatic Treatment. Mrs. W requires one or more trials of antidepressant medication prescribed in adequate doses. If drug A is not effective, as is the case 30%–40% of the time, she should be tried on an antidepressant of another class. Several different medication trials with monitoring of blood levels may be necessary before she has a response. If her suicidal risk increases and/or she fails to respond to medication and/or her cardiac condition precludes adequate dosaging, electroconvulsive therapy should be considered as an effective and safe alternative. Within days after starting the antidepressant medication, Mrs. W can be tapered off the hypnotics and benzodiazepines which, at best, will no longer be necessary and, at worst, may be actually worsening the depression and establishing a dependency pattern.

Because Mrs. W's own psychotherapist has admitted that he is not an expert in psychobiological methods of assessment and treatment of depression and because he has not supported their use in the past, considerable tact will be required on the part of the consultant to enlist his cooperation in the medication trials. One possibility is for Mrs. W to continue in psychotherapy with this therapist and simultaneously to receive psychotropic medication from someone else with greater expertise in this area. There is no reason to suspect that she will "split" the transference in a disruptive way. Because the supportive relationship offered by her therapist is important to Mrs. W, she might disregard the other therapeutic recommendations if they involve being abandoned by her current therapist.

CHOICE AND OUTCOME

Mrs. W recovered dramatically. Because so many changes were made in her treatment, it is difficult to weigh their relative impact. The consultant assumed an adjunctive therapeutic role and met with the entire family during the children's semester break. These sessions clearly had a therapeutic value that went beyond a psychoeducational process. As Mrs. W herself stated as she looked around at her husband and her four children, "I no longer feel like a childless mother." She was also relieved when informed about the biological component of her depression and how she need not assume full responsibility for either its cause or its cure. In addition, Mrs. W was referred to a psychopharmacologist, who prescribed a tricyclic antidepressant with fewer anticholinergic side effects (desimipramine). The drug was rapidly increased to therapeutic blood levels with minimal and well-tolerated side effects and without any cardiac complications. After six months the desimipramine was tapered over a five-week period, then discontinued. Because of Mrs. W's history of recurrent depressions, the psychopharmacologist considered maintenance antidepressants or lithium, but at that point Mrs. W was insistent upon discontinuing all medications. She was apprised of the advantages and disadvantages of the various options and her wishes were respected.

In a way that at first seemed remarkable, Mrs. W's psychotherapist was quite accepting of the referral to a psychopharmacologist and of the consultant's family therapy interventions. A few months after Mrs. W's depression lifted, a contributing reason for the therapist's noncompetitive and accepting attitude was disclosed. At a professional meeting he confided with the consultant that he and Mrs. W had developed an erotic transference-countertransference relationship that neither could openly discuss. Both therapist and patient were therefore relieved when the intensity of that relationship was somewhat diminished by the other therapeutic interventions.

Three years later, coincident with the marriage of Mrs. W's younger son, she again became depressed. This time the prodomal signs—changes in sleep pattern, loss of interest in housework—were detected early and she was immediately started on antidepressant medication with a prompt response. Her psychopharmacologist has continued antidepressant maintenance and has followed her monthly. These meetings, though only 10–15 minutes long, became a replacement for her appointments with the psychotherapist, whom she eventually stopped seeing altogether. Her son, who became a psychiatrist and from time to time sees the consultant at annual meetings, reports that his mother has had no depressions while being maintained on lithium for the past four years.

SUGGESTED READING

1. Haas, G., Clarkin, J. F., & Glick, I. D. Family treatment of depression. In J. Jeffers (Ed.), *Handbook for the Diagnosis and Treatment of Depression*. Homewood, IL: Dow Jones-Irwin, in press. (The value and methods of family therapy for even those with "biological" depressions.)
2. Freud, S. (1917). Mourning and melancholia. In J. Strachey (Ed.), *Standard Edition*, 14:239–258, 1957. (Although today most would dispute Freud's view that Mrs. W's depression was primarily a result of anger turned against the self, his description of how pathological depression can be distinguished from normal grief remains clinically useful.)
3. Akiskal, H. S., & McKinney, W. T., Jr. Overview of recent research in depression: Integration of ten conceptual models into a comprehensive clinical frame. *Archives of General Psychiatry*, 32:285–305, 1975. (Explains how psychobiological, psychosocial, and psychodynamic models can be integrated in designing a treatment plan for depression.)

21.   The Case of the Exhausted Executive

Mr. O is a 65-year-old corporate executive referred for consultation by a junior colleague because the patient's depression has not responded to psychotherapy. The consultant obtained the following history by piecing together information from the referring psychotherapist and from the patient.

Mr. O was first seen by the junior psychiatrist three years ago. At that time Mr. O was in a general hospital to determine the cause of two distressing symptoms that had developed over the previous months: 1) a generalized feeling of exhaustion; and 2) an altered taste and smell in which particular foods, like vinegar, made the patient feel nauseated. The extensive workup revealed no physical problems other than relatively mild diabetes that had begun two years before and had been well controlled, at first by diet alone, then by oral agents. In the absence of any other detectable cause, diabetes was considered to be the presumed cause of the changes in taste and smell; but because the fasting and postprandial blood sugars were consistently within an acceptable range, the internist doubted that the relatively mild diabetes could explain the profound feelings of exhaustion. A psychiatric consultation was therefore requested to determine if the problem might be "psychosomatic." Though neither the internist nor the patient knew of any significant emotional problems, each felt a psychiatric assessment was a good idea, for, as Mr. O stated, "God knows, they've tried everything else."

After three interviews in the hospital, the psychiatrist also was uncertain whether Mr. O's symptoms were psychogenic. The patient, a distinguished-looking man with silver gray hair and an eloquent manner, was at first quite pleasant and proper with the psychiatrist, but not especially revealing. Even after an empathic resonance developed and Mr. O divulged a "personal matter" he had never told anyone before, the psychiatrist was not sure whether these longstanding character problems were the basis of Mr. O's present complaint of exhaustion.

The "personal matter" was Mr. O's homosexuality. Raised in Austria by a conservative and harsh "peasant" family, Mr. O concealed his sexual preferences from them. A precocious child, he pursued intellectual and aesthetic interests that isolated him further from his many siblings and from his peers. The sense of shame and guilt about his homosexuality became all the more intense after a few secret encounters with clergymen.

In late adolescence, Mr. O's mother died during an operation for colonic cancer. With this loss, he saw no reason to remain at home and, with minimal financial resources, immigrated alone to the United States, where he worked during the day and attended college at night. His academic and later business successes were countered by personal failures. Time after time he would fall in love with a beautiful young man. Even if the relationship became briefly sexual, it inevitably ended in Mr. O's feeling unrequited and unfulfilled. The anguish over these relationships was compounded by their secretiveness; as Mr. O proceeded up the corporate ladder, no one suspected that his private life was so despairing nor that he was homosexual. Even his closest colleagues regarded him as a most eligible bachelor and were constantly arranging dinner parties to match Mr. O with beautiful and rich women, who were not interesting to him.

On his fiftieth birthday, Mr. O took stock of his life. Almost as if making a New Year's resolution, he decided that the quest for a loving relationship with a man was futile. It would only color the remaining years of his life with more frustration. He realized that his entire adult life was punctuated by transient affairs followed by a few weeks of profound despair. He resolved to give up the search.

For the next 10 years, this resolution worked fairly well. With more concentration on his profession, Mr. O became even more financially successful and, though still a lonely man, became a prominent patron of the arts and various charities. Now that he was no longer suffering from unrequited love affairs, his more profound periods of depression had not recurred. Both the highs and the lows were now gone.

All of this changed five years ago when Mr. O, now 60, once again fell in love. This time the object of his desire was V, a strikingly handsome 30-year-old waiter, whom Mr. O met while on a business trip in another town. They locked eyes while Mr. O was being served at dinner and they secretively arranged a rendezvous that night; thereafter, Mr. O's life was irreversibly changed. His infatuation over V was hard to understand. Except for his looks, V had little going for him. He was not intelligent, ambitious, or caring. On the contrary, he conveyed an air of being indifferent to the needs of others, and to his own needs as well. He was imperturbable. When asked to make a decision, his typical reply was, "Do whatever you want." He simply did not seem to care who came, who went, who felt what about what, and why people did what they did. As a sexual partner, however, V was far from complacent. He made it clear from the start that there would be no fondling and no kissing. Instead, he would perform brutal and painful anal intercourse on Mr. O while shouting, "Shut up! Shut up!"

Although Mr. O was bewildered about why V should have such great appeal, his love was not completely blind. Mr. O was well aware of V's limitations and was openly contemptuous of his friends; yet he yearned for V morning and night, arranged his schedule around daily long-distance phone calls, and was often too distracted and preoccupied at work to plan corporate matters. As was typical of V, he was unimpressed by Mr. O's attentiveness, neither rejecting nor accepting, just "making do." Even when Mr. O would fly long distances to be with V for a weekend, V's response remained one of indifference.

Coincident with the relationship with V, Mr. O developed polydypsia and polyuria. He characteristically ignored these symptoms, but when they became severe, consultation with a physician friend confirmed the diagnosis of diabetes and the need for continuing medical care. Two years later, Mr. O developed the changes in taste and smell and the generalized fatigue that eventually led to the medical hospitalization and the psychiatric referral.

Although the psychiatrist admitted to the referring internist and to Mr. O that he was unsure whether the current symptoms could be attributed to an emotional cause, he felt that a trial of exploratory psychotherapy might be helpful because no physical cause for the exhaustion had been found and because in the past Mr. O's moods had been markedly influenced by homosexual relationships that were neither caring nor well understood. Although Mr. O had always before resisted revealing his personal life, he was quite receptive to this opportunity for the first time in his life to discuss candidly his self-doubts and private longings. Twice-weekly sessions were arranged.

During the first four months of treatment, even though Mr. O had spent most of his life suppressing painful memories, he now became committed to the uncovering process and developed a deep attachment to the therapist, for whom he struggled to contain homosexual desires. Despite this commitment to the therapy and fondness for the therapist, Mr. O's exhaustion did not improve.

On the contrary, his feelings of weakness became worse and were now accompanied by more well-defined psychological and vegetative symptoms of depression. He doubted his professional competence and held no hope that he would ever again be the energetic and dynamic force in the firm. Typically, he would awaken early, then lie in bed all day, stare at the ceiling, ignore calls and visits from friends, piddle around the kitchen with no taste for food, try to read but put down the book after a few pages, or try to listen to the opera but turn off the stereo in the middle of the first aria. He went to bed early, not because he was tired but because there was nothing else to do; he would then toss and turn through the night, awaken with dreams he could not remember, and greet the next morning with the same sense of weariness. The only pleasure in his entire day was the long-distance calls to V. Mr. O had no idea what was overcoming him. He had at long last found a man whom he could love and a therapist with whom he could share his deepest feelings, so why should he now lose his health, his energy, his ambition, his confidence, and his self-respect?

The therapist attempted to interpret the current and past psychodynamic determinants of Mr. O's depression—the unconscious resentment towards V, the early loss of Mr. O's mother, the longing for an affectionate father, and the absence of enduring intimate relationships throughout Mr. O's life. These interpretations were to no avail; they only seemed to increase Mr. O's despair. The therapist therefore changed to a more directive and experiential approach. Since Mr. O was surprisingly ill informed about homosexuality, he was advised to read about it rather than avoid the subject. Mr. O was also given various reframing homework assignments to "silence" the constant self-ridiculing of his "inner voice." In addition, the therapist no longer adhered so strictly to rules of neutrality and abstinence, and instead offered emotional encouragement, emphasized Mr. O's assets, sided against Mr. O's harsh conscience, and when indicated, the therapist revealed certain facts about himself that were designed to strengthen the friendly relationship.

After a six-week trial of this new approach, Mr. O's symptoms continued to worsen. The therapist therefore began desimipramine and maintained this tricyclic antidepressant at therapeutic blood levels for four months; but the depression, though no worse, was also no better. The therapist then switched to another medication, trazadone. When Mr. O found the sedating side effects of this drug intolerable, the therapist switched again to an MAO inhibitor, which Mr. O felt made him too agitated and "confused."

The therapist was confused as well, and following this one-year trial on various antidepressant medication, stopped all drugs except for an occasional short-acting hypnotic at night. Discontinuing the medication also seemed to have no effect one way or the other. Mr. O's depression remained quite serious and, although not suicidal, he wondered aloud how much longer he could endure the exhaustion and despair. By now the phone calls to V were less and less frequent and the occasional rendezvous held little of the previous pleasure. V, of course, was indifferent to Mr. O's depressions and, partly as a result of the therapist's pointing out how Mr. O was being exploited in the relationship, the patient decreased the phone calls to no more than once a month.

By this time Mr. O had been in treatment for 18 months and both he and the therapist were at a loss. In desperation, he tried various less conventional methods—dextroamphetamine, vitamin therapy, and aerobic exercise. When the depression did not respond, the therapist then recommended electroconvulsive therapy (ECT). Six bilateral treatments produced no improvement in the depression.

Session after session, Mr. O talked about the emptiness in his life, the meaninglessness of his days, and the inability to work. The company by now had learned to function fine without his presence, and he saw no reason to return even if his mood should lift. Finally, Mr. O gathered the courage to ask the therapist if he too might not be losing hope and patience. Though the therapist denied these feelings, the discussion which followed led to the two of them agreeing that Mr. O should see a senior psychiatrist in consultation.

DSM-III-R DIAGNOSIS

Axis I: Major depression, recurrent, with melancholia
Axis II: Mixed personality disorder (avoidant, narcissistic, obsessive)
Axis III: Diabetes mellitus, adult onset
Axis IV: Stress—moderate (unrequited love affair; loneliness of advanced age without a family)
Axis V: Highest level of functioning past year—fair (managing personal affairs while living alone, but unproductive at work and able to extract no pleasure from life)

TREATMENT PROBLEM

Sixty-five-year-old homosexual man with a chronic history of intermittent depressions following brief love relationships. He now presents with a major depression that became more severe after beginning psychotherapy three years ago. This depression has been refractory to exploratory, cognitive, directive, and experiential techniques, to antidepressant medications, and to a brief course of ECT.

DISCUSSION OF TREATMENT SELECTION

Setting. Although Mr. O is not so seriously depressed or suicidal that hospitalization is a necessity, an inpatient setting offers certain advantages that could change the course of his depression. Antidepressant medication, including a combination of MAO inhibitors and tricyclics, could be increased to maximum levels if closer monitoring is available. In addition, the staff could provide more hour-to-hour support and encourage Mr. O to come out of his shell by interacting with more people. A strong feature weighing against hospitalization is the defeat and exposure Mr. O might feel by such a recommendation, which in turn would only increase his demoralization. Throughout his life, he has struggled to deal with his problems alone and preserved his pride by not leaning on or even sharing with others. Hospitalization would run counter to all these efforts he has made over the years. Mr. O has already become worse during the course of treatment, perhaps because therapy fostered a regression and futile longing for unqualified love. Hospitalization might further this regression with an iatrogenic worsening of his state.

Format. Self-help groups, such as those run by the Gay Alliance Task Force, are enormously helpful for individuals ashamed of their homosexuality. Unfortunately, at the beginning of treatment Mr. O probably would have been so wary of exposing himself that he would have refused to attend a homogeneous group, and at this stage a self-help group might be too narrow in scope and might require more interaction than Mr. O could endure. A heterogeneous group would place even greater demands on Mr. O in a situation that might be even less accepting of his "weaknesses" (his homosexuality and his social reserve). Remaining with an individual format would, therefore, appear to be the best option at this time to provide the focused attention his depression requires.

Duration and Frequency. Until now, Mr. O has been seen once or twice a week in conventional 45-minute sessions. Since this time frame has not worked, a change would seem advisable. The question then is whether the change should be more or less. Increasing the frequency of sessions could overcome the inertia in treatment and reverse the increasing demoralization. Another credible possibility is to decrease the intensity with the rationale that even weekly therapy is too intimate for Mr. O and too potentially regressive, given how distant he has stayed from others during most of his life. Although an abrupt termination or even a time-limited treatment might be too upsetting for a man who is seriously depressed and very attached to his therapist, a gradual weaning from treatment with sessions spaced further and further apart might enable Mr. O to resume using the defensive mechanisms of suppression, avoidance, and disavowal, which, though limiting, at least prevented the despair he has felt over the past few years. This decrease in intensity might also covertly diminish whatever secondary gain Mr. O is extracting from psychotherapy without an explicit and demeaning interpretation that he has been unconsciously "using" his symptoms to receive the desired attention and caring.

Approach. Mr. O has already received a trial of many different approaches. He became worse coincident with, and perhaps because of, the exploratory psychotherapy conducted during the first few months. He then did not respond when other techniques were introduced, such as education about homosexuality, assignment of homework for cognitive reframing, and provision of friendly emotional support. A difficult question for the consultant is whether any of these approaches were given with sufficient quantity and quality, that is, whether the duration and intensity of each approach constituted an adequate trial and whether the psychotherapist was sufficiently skilled for a given approach to have a good chance of its working. If the consultant concludes that the psychotherapist's ineptness or inexperience or countertransference problems are impeding an approach that might otherwise be effective, the consultant is then faced with an equally difficult question: Should Mr. O switch doctors or can the psychotherapist, with advice and supervision, improve the provision of the suggested technique?

Somatic Treatment. As discussed in the section on therapeutic techniques, although Mr. O has received many different somatic therapies, he may not have received them in sufficient amounts or with sufficient expertise. Both the quantity and the quality of delivery may have been inadequate. For instance, although he was maintained on therapeutic blood levels of desimipramine for several weeks, the dosage was not maintained for a sufficient number of weeks to ensure that he is a nonresponder. Similarly, although he received six ECTs without discernible benefit, these treatments may have been stopped prematurely, as suggested by the complete absence of any memory loss. Another possible somatic treatment would be to switch Mr. O from his oral diabetic agents to insulin. Although his blood sugar levels suggest that he is in good control, these values could be misleading if he is in a catabolic state and unable to raise his blood sugar. If such is the case, Mr. O's fatigue and secondary demoralization may be mainly the result of an underlying metabolic problem.

CHOICE AND OUTCOME

The consultant was quite alarmed by Mr. O's deterioration during the course of treatment. He arranged to meet with the psychotherapist and made the following recommendations:

First, he reminded the therapist that Mr. O had been able to rebound from previous depressions. The problem now was to discern why this depression had not remitted after three years. The two main factors that were present at this time and not in the past were: 1) the patient's diabetes, and 2) the patient's entering psychotherapy. Modifying these two possible contributing factors seemed the best approach in trying to change the course of Mr. O's depression.

Regarding the diabetes, even though Mr. O's blood sugars were not dangerously high, his requirement of high dosages of oral diabetic agents and his changes in taste and smell suggested that the disease might be more severe than his blood sugars indicated. The consultant therefore recommended: 1) that the patient's glycosylated hemoglobin and not his blood sugars be followed to assess how well the diabetes was being controlled; and 2) that a trial of insulin therapy be instituted. Within a few weeks the therapist would be able to tell whether the introduction of insulin seemed to improve Mr. O's feeling of exhaustion and despair.

Regarding the psychotherapy, the consultant stated that he considered recommending that Mr. O gradually be weaned from this treatment since nothing seemed to be helping and possibly it was making Mr. O worse; however, before weaning Mr. O from treatment, the consultant thought it most advisable to make some modifications in the treatment and see if they were helpful. One modification would be a more concentrated and systematic application of cognitive therapy, which was compatible with Mr. O's attempts in the past to use intellectual control. Although some reframing techniques had been tried before, in the consultant's view they had been given insufficient emphasis.

The consultant also advised the therapist to discontinue explorations of the patient's past. However, one "here-and-now" clarification needed to be made: Because the therapist was wary of a homosexually eroticized transference (and countertransferentially wary of his own unconscious homosexual feelings towards the patient), no mention had been made up until this time of Mr. O's longing for the therapist and the resulting frustration when this longing remained unfulfilled. The therapist needed to discuss these homosexual elements within the therapeutic relationship more openly, and to point out that unconsciously Mr. O was being sexually frustrated by the therapist in the same way he had been frustrated by other men whom he desired. The consultant also recommended that these modifications initially be done in the hospital, where a more concentrated effort could be made. Hospitalization would also provide a "fresh" ancillary staff, while still maintaining Mr. O's relationship with the therapist.

The tactfulness and the careful reasoning of the consultant were helpful in enabling the therapist to accept the recommendations without being overly defensive. Mr. O was hospitalized and was seen daily for half-hour sessions, in which the therapist used a more systematic and focused cognitive therapy (under the supervision of a colleague with more expertise in this approach). Exploratory techniques were deemphasized, except for clearing the air by discussing the homosexual aspects of the transference. During a long holiday weekend towards the end of Mr. O's hospitalization, the therapist took an opportunity to discuss Mr. O's longings for the therapist and how this too stirred up unrequited homosexual feelings. Because the glycosylated hemoglobin levels were indeed elevated, Mr. O was placed on insulin. Though his blood sugar levels were slightly more elevated (a result of switching from a catabolic to an anabolic state), his fatigue improved dramatically starting within just a few days after taking insulin.

Because so many changes were made in the treatment at the same time, it is difficult to know which particular factor played the most significant role in Mr. O's improvement. Following his hospitalization, Mr. O continued to be seen in twice and then once weekly psychotherapy, which comprised more or less review sessions of his cognitive training. By three months following the consultation, Mr. O had improved remarkably, was back at work, was no longer feeling exhausted, and was looking forward to an extended holiday—alone. Once again, he had completely given up the idea of ever having a successful love affair. When he returned from his holiday, he announced (rather than asked) that his termination of treatment would be in six weeks. During the final six sessions, Mr. O appropriately grieved over what price the depression had taken in his professional and personal life and grieved as well over losing the therapist, feeling similar to when he had lost loved ones in the past.

Not surprisingly, after extending a warm hug at the end of the last session, Mr. O left and was never heard from again. The therapist did learn from the endocrinologist who was following Mr. O for his diabetes that the patient was continuing to do well, and two years following the termination of treatment, he was actively involved in a merger of two major corporations.

SUGGESTED READING

1. Beck, A. T., Rush, A. J., Shaw, B. F., & Emery, G. *Cognitive Therapy of Depression*. New York: Guilford Press, 1979. (Theoretical rationale is complemented by specific protocols for application of this treatment.)
2. Rush, A. J., Beck, A. T., Kovacs, M., & Hollon, S. Comparative efficacy of cognitive therapy and imipramine in the treatment of depressed outpatients. *Cognitive Therapy and Research*, 1:17–37, 1977. (Confirms efficacy of this nonsomatic treatment.)
3. Jacobson, E. Transference problems in the psychoanalytic treatment of severely depressive patients. *Journal of the American Psychoanalytic Association*, 2:595–606, 1954. (Distinguishes potentially harmful from beneficial effects of exploratory techniques for depressed patients.)

■ CYCLOTHYMIA

22. The Case of the Love Junkie

(Guest Expert: Michael R. Liebowitz, M.D.)

Authors' Note:
Dr. Liebowitz is Associate Professor, Clinical Psychiatry, Columbia University College of Physicians and Surgeons, New York City; and Director, Anxiety Disorders Clinic, New York State Psychiatric Institute. As illustrated in this case, he is interested in how a treatment plan must often consider the complex mixture of affective and character pathology.

Ms. C is a 35-year-old single unemployed commercial artist who presents for consultation after her boyfriend has abruptly walked out. She is disconsolate, pulls at her hair, and says she wants to die. However, her symptoms remit rapidly as she becomes increasingly interested in and seductive towards the male consultant.

Apparently, this sequence of events repeats a pattern that has occurred quite frequently in Ms. C's life. She falls quickly and deeply in love, soon becomes a "love junkie" who can't stand being away from her latest boyfriend, and then can't tolerate the "cold-turkey" withdrawal of love that seems to follow inevitably from relationships that are too intense and torrid to have any staying power.

Ms. C has already been in psychotherapy many times in her life and is aware of the self-defeating and self-destructive nature of her love relationships. Moreover, she is an extremely bright and psychologically sophisticated woman who can provide a very detailed and convincing psychodynamic formulation for her behavior. None of her apparent insight has any perceptible effect once she leaves the office, a fact that she also recognizes and points out with a combination of thoughtfulness, regret, and insouciance.

Ms. C is remarkable for the lability of her mood, attitudes, and behavior. In response to good news and attention she can become expressive, energetic, excited, sleepless, and even giddy. This mood will ordinarily last for no more than a day or two and will be followed by a letdown. When Ms. C is disappointed or feels rejected, she becomes severely depressed and listless, can't get out of bed, sleeps and eats too much, and feels like dying. There are periods when she is euthymic, but they also tend to be fleeting. The patient manipulates her mood with cocaine, which almost always makes her feel better.

The patient has a strikingly erratic work history. She has abruptly started and stopped a number of different careers and is as fickle in work as she has been in love. She starts a job with tremendous commitment and initially does very well, but after a few months she is off to something else.

The youngest and prettiest of three sisters, the patient was prized and pampered by both of her parents. She was always considered to have great promise and encouraged to cultivate her charm and feminine appeal. She matured early and began her many erotic adventures at the tender age of 12. Ever since, she has experienced her life as an unhappy but exciting melodrama.

Ms. C begins her many psychotherapies with her usual enthusiasm and ends them with her usual sense of disappointment or rejection. She typically falls in love with male therapists and has trouble keeping them out of her mind. She feels frustrated when her affection is not reciprocated, even though she knows it would be inappropriate and unprofessional. She has never received medication.

DSM-III-R DIAGNOSIS

Axis I: Cyclothymia (some might say she is best described by the term, hysteroid dysphoria)
Axis II: Histrionic personality disorder
Axis III: None
Axis IV: Stress—moderate (losing boyfriend)
Axis V: Highest level of functioning past year—fair

DISCUSSION OF TREATMENT SELECTION

A patient like Ms. C is familiar to most mental health practitioners. Those with a psychoanalytic orientation tend to focus on oedipal, and more recently on preoedipal, disturbances in such cases, while descriptive psychiatrists would traditionally classify such patients as neurotically or reactively depressed. Unfortunately, the therapeutic interventions that are implied by these kinds of psychodynamic formulations are not often successful. At the other extreme, viewing cyclothymia merely as a subtype of bipolar illness can also lead to poor results.

To call Ms. C cyclothymic is to not recognize that her mood swings are almost always precipitated by attention or rejection, of either a real or an imagined nature. Cyclothymia usually is thought of as a dilute variant of bipolar illness and would suggest unprecipitated mood shifts that might respond to lithium. There are no controlled trials of lithium with patients such as Ms. C, but anecdotal data suggest that it is not terribly effective, at least in preventing depressive mood crashes.

Similarly, to diagnose Ms. C as having a histrionic personality disorder is to ignore the affective basis for her symptomatology. It also reinforces the tendency to treat such patients exclusively with psychotherapy or, in the face of several unsuccessful psychotherapy trials, to view them as untreatable.

What these formulations ignore is that Ms. C is often depressed, that when depressed she shows atypical vegetative signs (overeating and oversleeping), that her mood remains reactive (she can be cheered up), and that her mood state and sense of well-being are greatly lowered by rejection (either real or imagined). These features are important because they roughly fit the British notion of atypical depression,[1] more precisely fit Klein's[2] notion of hysteroid dysphoria, and strongly suggest that the patient would benefit from a trial of monoamine oxidase inhibitors (MAOIs).

Klein has hypothesized that, since all human beings tend to feel better with positive attention and worse with rejection, these reactions must reflect neurochemical changes in the brain that occur quite rapidly in response to environmental stimuli. Patients like Ms. C appear to overreact to such stimulation, becoming elated and giddy with positive (especially romantic) attention, and suicidally despondent in the face of severe (especially romantic) rejection.

One can thus postulate an unstable biological "social approval-disapproval" apparatus in such patients. While the precise mechanism remains a mystery, the symptom pattern of energized euphoria that occurs with positive attention and of hungry lethargy with rejection are similar, respectively, to the effects of amphetamine ingestion and withdrawal, suggesting that reactions to social approval and disapproval are mediated by some amphetamine-like substance in the brain. (Phenylethylamine is one possible candidate.)

Treatment of hysteroid dysphoria with an MAOI such as phenelzine (Nardil) seems to prevent or mute the depressive reaction that follows rejection. In my experience, MAOIs also allow patients like Ms. C to feel okay when not romantically involved, reducing the frantic search for relationships and permitting better choice of partners. Our experience in a controlled trial of phenelzine plus twice-weekly psychotherapy was that hysteroid dysphoric patients who did not meet DSM-III-R criteria for borderline personality disorder seemed to benefit from drug plus psychotherapy, but could continue to progress in therapy or at least maintain their gains after discontinuing phenelzine at the end of three months.[3] On the other hand, hysteroid dysphoric patients who were also borderline had more trouble stopping phenelzine, and when they did, they were harder to treat with psychotherapy alone.

In terms of which pharmacological agents to use, our clinical experience, supported by preliminary data from a controlled trial, suggests that hysteroid dysphoric patients do better with MAOIs than with tricyclics or placebo. However, lithium may also have a role. Lithium can block stimulant drug highs and, therefore, might diminish a hysteroid dysphoric patient's tendency to be too easily or excessively excited by romantic attention, which seems to contribute to poor partner choice. MAOIs would be expected to block depressive swings, and might even augment upward mood swings. Therefore, phenelzine plus lithium may be useful for some patients. The role of lithium alone requires further assessment.

The same mechanisms that destabilize the romantic relationships of hysteroid dysphorics also affect vocational adjustments. Many of the hysteroid dysphorics we see thrive on, and often require, constant admiration and applause, and have sought careers as performing artists. They tend to become stalemated in their careers, often because they find rejection at auditions too traumatic to endure.

In fact, any vocational adjustment may be harder for an hysteroid dysphoric. They begin work with a bang, and thrive on the attention usually given to newcomers. Then they become restless or bored as the novelty wears off, and find it hard to take even the normal amount of criticism one gets at work.

What I would recommend is that a patient such as Ms. C be offered a trial with phenelzine. If she agreed, I would start her on phenelzine with the understanding that certain dietary restrictions have to be rigidly followed. I would prescribe as a starting dose phenelzine 15 mg/b.i.d. for one week, then raise her to 45 mg/day. Effective dose is usually 45 to 90 mg/day. Signs of hypomania, which usually begin with a decreased need for sleep, need to be watched for, and dosage titrated accordingly.

As to why phenelzine is suggested, it is the MAOI with which we have the most clinical experience. The next is tranylcypromine, which may be slightly more energizing, but in my experience puts the patient at greater risk of hypertensive reactions. Actually, while hypertensive reactions are the most serious potential adverse reaction to a MAOI, the side effects that cause us the most trouble are insomnia, daytime drowsiness, sexual dysfunction, postural hypotension, and peripheral edema, all of which one encounters fairly frequently.

We tend to view hysteroid dysphoria as one subtype of atypical depression, which in turn is defined as episodic, intermittent, or chronic depression with preservation of mood reactivity and two of four of the following features: overeating, oversleeping, leaden fatigue, and chronic oversensitivity to rejection. While the specific MAOI responsivity of this depressive subtype remains to be demonstrated, through double-blind placebo-controlled comparisons with tricyclics, preliminary data from an ongoing study suggest that patients meeting the above criteria do respond preferentially to treatment with MAOIs.

REFERENCES

1. West, E. D., & Dally, P. J. Effect of iproniazid in depressive syndromes. *British Medical Journal*, 1:1491–1494, 1959.
2. Klein, D. F., Gittelman, R., Quitkin, F., et al. *Diagnosis and Drug Treatment of Psychiatric Disorders: Adults and Children* (2nd ed.). Baltimore: Williams & Wilkins, 1980.
3. Liebowitz, M. R., & Klein, D. F. Hysteroid dysphoria. *Psychiatric Clinics of North America*, 2:555–575, 1979.

■ DYSTHYMIA

23. The Case of the Lonesome Mistress

Miss R is a 35-year-old salesmanager who arranges a private psychiatric consultation because she is "numb and confused." Although she sounded quite assertive on the phone and although she arrives for her first appointment appearing professional and confident in a well-tailored grey flannel suit, she dissolves into tears as soon as she sits down and begins to discuss her problems.

She is having an affair with a married man and wants to end the relationship, but cannot. The affair began two years ago after she returned to the metropolitan area following six years of a childless marriage to her high school sweetheart. She had drifted into that marriage with no passion or direction and seemingly had ended the marriage on the same bland note. Feeling adrift and doubting her ability to love anyone deeply, she took a menial job at a large department store and spent her nights alone in her small apartment, sipping wine in front of the TV until sleep would finally come. Her isolation was filled with vague fantasies that some man might some day enter her life and make it all better.

These daydreams were in part fueled by Miss R's mother who would telephone frequently during the week and ask in one way or another, "Why aren't you doing something to find a man?" The mother would berate her daughter for not dressing more attractively, for not accepting invitations from old high school and college friends, and in general for not making herself more available and receptive. The implication was that the right man was all that was needed to provide happiness.

The "right" man turned out to be all wrong. He was her boss, a powerful and crass man 20 years older than Miss R. During her first few weeks at work, she had little contact with him and had no indication that he was particularly attracted to her. As her ability in purchasing and marketing became more apparent, she gradually came more into his view—first, at business meetings and individual conferences, then at lunch dates or drinks after work. Finally, they began seeing and sleeping with each other at her apartment, while he lied to his wife and said he was out of town on business.

Just as Miss R had no idea how to get out of the relationship, she has no clear idea of how she got into it. She does not find this man particularly attractive and, although he is bright and powerful, she is not swept away by his charm. When he does not phone, she stays at home feeling distraught, berating herself for ever getting into such a relationship in the first place and vowing that she will reject him at the next opportunity and send him onto other women in his long chain of widely known extramarital affairs. But when he does call, she inevitably gives in and finds herself first at dinner and then in bed with a man whom she does not love and does not even really like.

Miss R is doubtful that she is capable of genuinely loving anyone. Her marriage had been one more of convenience than of passion and ended simply because she and her husband had so little to talk about rather than because of any strong disagreements: "It just went flat." She characterizes relationships in her childhood with the same blandness: Her mother tolerated her father's criticism and devaluation because she felt cared for; her father was "never around but his money was"; and her relationship with her older sister was based on simply getting along so that they could "share clothes" rather than because of affection for one another.

Whatever intrapersonal or interpersonal conflicts might have been present during her upbringing are now forgotten. Miss R's past is a vague and distant memory, with her recalling only isolated events—e.g., the fury of her father when her sister needed an abortion or her mother's frustration when the patient would not wear her orthopedic shoes. Dreams and fantasies are also generally not remembered, but during the interview Miss R did recall one dream: she was thinking of buying a very powerful and fancy car, then changed her mind because the paint job was secondhand and cheaply done.

Miss R had tried psychotherapy briefly at various times during her marriage. Typically, she would see a male therapist four or five times, then stop treatment abruptly for no apparent reason. She is not even sure why she sought psychotherapy other than because she felt "depressed." She cannot now recall her therapists' names but offers to look them up in her old checkbook. All she knows is that for a long time she has found little interest or pleasure in life, finds it hard to sleep without drinking, feels generally tired, does not know why anyone would ever want to be with her, gets annoyed at the slightest inconveniences, and feels trapped in an unfulfilling relationship.

DSM-III-R DIAGNOSIS

  Axis I: Dysthymia
  Axis II: Possible dependent personality disorder
  Axis III: None
  Axis IV: Stress—mild (affair with married man)
  Axis V: Highest level of functioning past year—fair (outstanding work performance but limited pleasurable activities)

TREATMENT PROBLEM

A 35-year-old accomplished salesmanager who has drifted in and out of a childless marriage, as well as a few short-lived attempts at individual psychotherapy; she now wants help getting out of an unloving affair with her married boss and getting into something that will fill the void in her life.

DISCUSSION OF TREATMENT SELECTION

Setting. The consultant is confronted with many difficult decisions regarding Miss R, but the choice of setting is not one of them. Hospitalization is neither necessary nor desirable; outpatient therapy is clearly the preferred choice.

Format. The choice of therapeutic format is far more difficult. Considering how much Miss R appears to be influenced by her mother's notion that all life's problems can simply be solved by "getting a man," it is tempting to suggest a few family sessions in which this view could be directly examined and challenged. Nonetheless, a family format is almost certainly not indicated for this 35-year-old woman. The recommendation alone would probably be experienced by Miss R as infantilizing, and the process of family meetings is likely to bring Miss R back into the family fold instead of helping her acquire more autonomy.

Miss R's own preference would doubtlessly be an individual format, in part because she would be understandably reluctant to discuss the intricacies and intimacies of an extramarital affair in the presence of her family or of anyone else. To provide this confidentiality, some adjunctive individual sessions will probably be necessary.

But there are reasons why an individual format might not be the best choice as the primary format. This format has already been attempted several times in the past and quite unsuccessfully. Although one could argue that with a different therapist, perhaps a woman instead of a man, Miss R's pattern of uninvolvement and early dropout might not be repeated, nevertheless, a patient's previous response to therapy is a powerful predictor of future response and therefore a persuasive guide to treatment selection. Even if Miss R were to succeed in becoming engaged in an individual treatment, the therapy might serve to reenact her desire to be rescued by another rather than to resolve this very problem.

Given the limitations of both a family and an individual format, a heterogeneous group must be granted serious consideration. The kinds of dynamic issues present in the family would no doubt be revealed by Miss R's ways of relating to other group members and could be worked out there with less risk of her devaluing or idealizing the therapist.

Duration and Frequency. Miss R has indicated that she tends to drift along, living day by day and putting emotional problems aside until circumstances force her to change her situation. This tendency is illustrated by the fact that she stayed in an unfulfilling marriage with little attempt to alter its course and also that she can only vaguely remember her developmental years and what transpired in psychotherapy. For this reason, therapy sessions initially may need to be relatively frequent (perhaps twice a week) and recapitulatory. Otherwise, important material will surface, then immediately become repressed before a change occurs. The same kind of rationale would justify a time-limited treatment, so that Miss R does not believe that she can live day by day and maintain her extramarital affair indefinitely while she is "working on" her problems. Having a fixed termination date would set a time limit on resolving her conflicts. On the other hand, many of her problems are not specifically related to the extramarital affair and may require a more open-ended treatment to be uncovered, then resolved.

Approach. Because Miss R is verbal, attractive, intelligent, and relatively young and psychologically healthy, and because the psychodynamic determinants of her problems seem so apparent, one is tempted to recommend that the basic approach be exploratory in nature. Miss R could thereby come to understand how unresolved oedipal struggles are contributing to her illicit involvement with an older married man and her resulting depressive feelings. For example, if Miss R developed an eroticized attachment to a male therapist, transference interpretations could be used to point out multiple intrapsychic conflicts inherent in such an attachment—the wish to replace (kill) the wife-mother and the associated guilt; the identification with a mother who lives through and for a man and the concomitant devaluation of that inferior, beholden position; the envy of the therapist-father's power and stature, yet the underlying rage and resentment, and so forth.

However, despite the potential value of Miss R understanding and working through within the transference these and other unconscious conflicts, the recommendation of exploratory techniques as the primary intervention must be seriously challenged for at least two reasons. First, Miss R is not by nature psychologically minded; she is more inclined to look at her life as a series of situations and events that have happened to her and is not invested in looking at her role in what has occurred or at the underlying meanings. Second, repression is one of her prominent defense mechanisms; she can barely recall the events of her marriage and remembers far less about her formative years. In time an exploratory treatment might be able to overcome this global repression, but in her situation time is an important consideration. Any treatment that requires a prolonged latency before external changes are realized would be poorly matched to a 35-year-old woman in the midst of a crucial developmental period. Important opportunities might pass her by (e.g., marriage, motherhood, professional advancement) if she remained enmeshed in her current relationship while the resistance to an exploratory treatment was gradually being overcome.

For these reasons, rather than relying primarily on psychodynamic interventions, the therapist would be advised to include additional strategies. For example, cognitive restructuring could help modify Miss R's belief that a man is the solution to her every problem; assertiveness training would help Miss R to be more direct and autonomous in her personal and professional decisions; and supportive interventions would advise and encourage the patient to interact less diffidently with others and to pursue more fulfilling professional and personal relationships. And perhaps most important would be the development and maintenance of a genuine, involved therapeutic relationship that would contrast with the selfish, exploitative and self-preoccupied relationships she has experienced with her family, her former husband, and her current lover.

Some recent studies indicate antidepressants may be helpful for Miss R even though she experiences mild depressive symptoms without florid episodes, but the efficacy of these drugs for "neurotic depression" awaits further investigation to predict which patients do or do not respond. For Miss R, who is inclined to delegate rather than share responsibility, it would be best to inform her of the current dilemma about the efficacy of antidepressants for her kind of depressive symptoms and have her participate in the decision regarding whether or not a period of drug therapy should be tried. She would also be informed why it is desirable not to confound psychotherapy and drug effect. The mutual decision could then be made with the understanding that the choice would be given a trial period, after which the degree of improvement would be assessed and the alternative choice could be reconsidered. Combined treatment is often useful but usually best reached in steps.

CHOICE AND OUTCOME

At the end of the first session, the consultant informed Miss R that he would like to think about what she had said and meet with her the following week to discuss various treatment possibilities—what kind of treatment and with whom. When Miss R returned the following week, her spirits were remarkably brighter and her manner was notably seductive as she coyly greeted the consultant and complimented him on his choice of tie as she entered his office. She continued on this theme during the first few minutes of the session, saying that the initial appointment had helped her understand the necessity of ending her destructive relationship with her boss and that she was eager to begin treatment with the consultant and do whatever he advised.

The consultant had tentatively considered what he was going to advise Miss R about her therapy. Her presentation at the beginning of this second appointment reinforced his choice: He told Miss R in a frank but tactful way that he believed the best treatment for her at this time would consist of participation in group therapy. This format would prevent her from using treatment—and the therapist—as a replacement for her current lover and would not actualize her tendency to wait to be rescued by another person. He pointed out that Miss R clearly had the capacity to interact with others, as was illustrated by her success in sales and marketing. This asset could be used to her advantage in interacting with the group and learning how she affects others and how she is inclined to become overly dependent on them.

As might have been predicted, Miss R felt rejected by this recommendation and initially rejected the advice; but the consultant stood his ground. During the remaining portion of the second visit, as well as during the third, he continued to negotiate with Miss R, finally reaching an agreement that she would be seen individually as an aid to induction during early phases of the group therapy. The consultant also confronted Miss R about her presumption that it would have been a good idea for him to have been her therapist in an individual treatment. He pointed out that once again she was rapidly committing herself to a man and then was feeling hurt when he did not come through as she had hoped. Miss R, although still feeling rejected, was able to express these feelings in a direct manner rather than withdrawing into a depressive void. She then agreed to the group format.

Miss R met in adjunctive individual treatment once a week for the first few months, while simultaneously beginning group therapy. She remained in the group for three years. The group leader has since informed the consultant that the group process proved to be very beneficial for Miss R. Within several months she changed to a job with a large increase in salary and responsibility, and left her boss-lover. Eventually she married an older psychologist and was pleased to assume care of his three young children from a previous marriage. Medications had not been necessary.

SUGGESTED READING

1. Akiskal, H. S. Dysthymic disorder: Psychopathology of proposed chronic depressive subtypes. *American Journal of Psychiatry,* 140:11–20, 1983.
2. Klerman, G. L., Endicott, J., Spitzer, R. L., et al. Neurotic depressions: A systematic analysis of multiple criteria and meanings. *American Journal of Psychiatry,* 136:57–61, 1979. (Both of the above articles wrestle with the difficult relationship between affective illness and personality conflicts, the problem presented by Miss R.)
3. Stein, A., Kibel, H. D., Fidler, J. W., et al. The group therapies. In J. M. Lewis & G. Usdin (Eds.), *Treatment Planning in Psychiatry.* Washington, D.C.: American Psychiatric Press, 1982. (A useful guide for determining the indications, composition, and process of a group treatment for different kinds of patients and problems.)
4. Kocsis, J. H., Frances, J. J., Voss, C., et al. Imipramine for treatment for chronic depression. *Archives of General Psychiatry,* 45:253–257, 1988. (Supports antidepressants for dysthymics.)
5. Frances, A. J., Manning, D. W. *Combination Drug and Psychotherapy in Depression.* New York: Spiegel, 1990. (Treatments once considered strange bedfellows do remarkably well together.)

■ DEPRESSIVE DISORDER NOT OTHERWISE SPECIFIED

24. The Case of the Suicidal Senior

A 17-year-old female high school senior was referred for evaluation following an attempted suicide with an overdose of pills. Earlier during the night of the suicide attempt, she had been involved in an angry fight with her mother over a request for pizza. The patient remembers her mother saying that she was a "spoiled brat" and asking if she would be "happier living elsewhere." The patient recalls that, feeling rejected and despondent, she wrote a note in the kitchen saying that she had had a mental breakdown and was going to a friend's house. Then she went upstairs to her room and left another note stating that she loved her parents but could not communicate with them. She added a request that her favorite glass animals be given to a particular friend. The parents returned home later that evening to find their daughter lying comatose on her bed, whereupon they took her to a hospital emergency room.

Upon evaluation, it was apparent that this adolescent teenager, the youngest of three children of upper-class and very accomplished parents, believed that she was less bright, clever, and attractive than her older brother and sister, whom she bitterly referred to as "college all-stars." She felt ignored and therefore rejected by her "workaholic" father and, in contrast, felt her mother was omnipresent and overbearing, constantly offering suggestions about everything—hairstyles, clothes, friends, evening arrangements, even the daughter's choice of toothpaste or kind of pizza. These suggestions were experienced by the daughter as intrusive demands that were interfering with her adolescent efforts to become her own person. Every declaration of independence seemed to require a revolutionary war, and the daughter, on the night of the diazepam overdose, simply felt too depressed and inadequate to continue to wage this battle for autonomy.

The daughter, drowsy but medically stable, was admitted from the emergency room to a general hospital for overnight observation. Prior to discharge the following afternoon, now alert, cooperative, and ashamed about what she had done, the daughter was seen with her father and mother to discuss future treatment. This evaluation took a strange twist. Though the daughter, sitting up in her hospital bed, was clearly the designated patient, within minutes of the evaluation the focus of concern shifted as the daughter poignantly described how her mother had seemed increasingly depressed over the past year, following the family's move from one urban center to another as a consequence of the father's recent promotion. The daughter, with a worried and pained expression, confronted the mother for the first time and reminded her of how she (the mother) had become irritable and ruminative and had stopped dressing attractively. In response, the mother tearfully "confessed" that she had indeed been very upset ever since the move, frequently crying herself to sleep, but that she had mistakenly believed that these feelings of despair had been kept from the view of others. She realized that part of her depression was due to resentment, for while her husband's career was moving forward she was being left behind without friends and without any opportunity for her own professional advancement. The mother also admitted that she had never considered it legitimate to ask for psychiatric help since she felt that "people should pull themselves up by their own bootstraps" and not depend on others.

DSM-III-R DIAGNOSIS (DAUGHTER)

    Axis I: Depressive disorder not otherwise specified
    Axis II: None
    Axis III: None
    Axis IV: Stress—moderate (move to new location, change of school, mother's depression)
    Axis V: Highest level of functioning past year—good

DSM-III-R DIAGNOSIS (MOTHER)

    Axis I: Possible major depression requiring further evaluation
    Axis II: None
    Axis III: None
    Axis IV: Stress—moderate (move to new location)
    Axis V: Highest level of functioning past year—fair

DISCUSSION OF TREATMENT SELECTION

This case has intentionally been presented in a schematic form so that we can focus on one central issue regarding treatment selection, namely, the decision of a family versus an individual format for this depressed and suicidal teenager. In deciding whether a family format is indicated, it is helpful to answer the five following questions:

1) Is the presenting problem directly related to current interactions within the family?
2) Does the presenting problem help maintain the current family homeostasis?
3) Will the family's need to maintain the homeostasis prevent individual therapy from being effective?

4) What interventions would initially be implemented to reduce symptoms and alleviate the crisis?

5) What motivation and capacity does the family have to participate in a family format?

1) *Relationship of presenting problem to current family interactions.* The daughter's depression and suicide attempt are both temporally and dynamically related to family problems. The adolescent, clearly upset about her mother's depression, appears to be offering herself as a suicidal victim to gain attention for the mother's plight. At the same time, the daughter's expressed resentment at the distant father appears to reflect the mother's latent resentment towards her husband who is pursuing his own career at the expense of his wife's advancement. Because the daughter's problems are so interwoven with the problems of the mother and father, it is difficult to understand the meaning and goal of the suicidal behavior without considering the family system.

2) *Role of pathology in stabilizing current family homeostasis.* The daughter is approaching the end of her senior year in high school after which she is expected to leave the family and go off to college. If she pursues this normal and healthy path, she will leave her parents to themselves for the first time in many years; but if she remains sick, she can stay home and serve as a buffer for her parents. The daughter's depression deflects attention from the parents' interpersonal struggles and thereby maintains the current family homeostasis.

3) *Is individual intervention possible?* So far there are no indications that the daughters depression serves such an important family function that the parents will prevent individual therapy or will sabotage its gains. Although the initial family consultation has revealed that the daughter's depression and the mother's depression are both related to family issues, this evaluation has also disclosed that each family member is viewed by other members with sufficient self-object differentiation, that is, the father and the mother and the daughter are all perceived as persons with their own individual wishes and needs. In other cases, where the ego capacities of major family figures are low and where the interrelationships are parasitic or even symbiotic, individual treatment cannot be implemented until substantial gains have been made using a family format.

4) *What will most likely be the initial therapeutic interventions?* To reduce the current crisis, a three-pronged attack will be required. The daughter will need to believe that a solution other than suicide is available for her to express her frustrations, her mother's depression, and their combined resentment towards the aloof father. The mother will need to acknowledge her own depression to herself and to others and to confront her

husband more directly rather than taking out her own professional frustrations on herself and on her daughter. The father will need to become
more appreciative of the family's difficulties and more available for their
resolution. Clearly, a family format is the most efficient and economical
way of accomplishing these interrelated goals. Furthermore, the daughter is at this point so enmeshed with the family dynamics and so involved with how her mother and father are treating her that she might
believe that the consultant was ignoring her parents' role in her problems if he were to recommend only an individual therapy. At a later
time, when the daughter is able to perceive her own problems more
separately from the problems of others, the therapist could recommend
an individual format. This recommendation would then be an actual as
well as a symbolic step towards becoming more autonomous and eventually leaving home.

5) *What are the enabling factors for family intervention?* Based on the
initial productive consultation, the daughter and mother and father appeared capable and motivated to meet in a family format. No family
member was defensive or disruptive in a way that precluded discussion
of interpersonal problems that were contributing to the present difficulties. The daughter was not totally dumping her behavior in her parents'
lap, and the father and mother were both willing to reflect honestly on
the roles they may have played in the current crisis. This openness,
though at times quite painful, seemed genuine and potentially useful. In
contrast, some families are so replete with severe chaotic pathologies
that they are incapable of meeting in the same room with enough equanimity to provide a treatment milieu that will make the format viable.
Moreover, extremely paranoid families may appear initially very well
organized and not at all chaotic, but they are too suspicious to "let in"
the therapist and, through projections, rigidly force the identified patient into the sick role while disavowing their own contribution to the
problem. Fortunately, neither severe psychopathology nor extreme paranoia appear to be operating in this case—but one potential difficulty is
worth noting, namely, the geographical (and perhaps emotional) distance of the two other children. If more available, they might diffuse the
current intense triangular interaction and might serve as models for
identification to help the daughter individuate.

COURSE AND OUTCOME

At the beginning of the second family session, the consultant was
prepared to recommend family therapy and to explain the rationale for
this choice; but before he could begin, the father preempted this discus-

sion by announcing that after the first family meeting in his daughter's hospital room, he recognized that unless he was part of the solution he was part of the problem. In a surprisingly touching and revealing way, he explained that his own aloofness was not primarily due to professional obligations but rather due to his feeling incapable of dealing with his wife's irritable outbursts and his daughter's diatribes. His response was to withdraw even further, which of course only worsened the resentment of both his wife and his daughter.

In response to these revelations, both the mother and the daughter felt closer to the father than they had in years, and their own interpersonal tensions (between mother and daughter) were temporarily put aside. Of course, not all the family's problems were thereupon magically resolved. In fact, over the next three months in weekly family sessions, while the mother discussed her plans to return to graduate school and the daughter made more specific plans for college, ironically the father began to feel rejected and to make thinly veiled hints that he was planning on having extramarital affairs. These threats typically infused the family sessions with anger and fear and temporarily stalled the daughter's and mother's quests for greater self-worth; but gradually the father was able to feel more comfortable, as he put it, "holding on and letting go."

Several months after termination of the family therapy, while the daughter was home from college for semester break, she dropped by to have coffee with the family therapist and to talk over "old times." She was most grateful and doing well—and reported that her parents were busily going their own ways but seemed happier with themselves and with each other.

SUGGESTED READING

1. Davidson, J. R. T., Miller, R. D., Turbull, C. D., et al. Atypical depression. *Archives of General Psychiatry,* 39:527–534, 1982. (Discusses why depression, such as the daughter's in this case, would diagnostically be regarded as "atypical".)
2. Miller, D. Adolescent suicide: Etiology and treatment. *Adolescent Psychiatry,* 9: 327–342, 1981. (Categorizes suicidal behavior among adolescents and, relevant to this case, discusses how the familial and personal dynamics can be considered in treatment planning.)
3. Blos, P. The second individuation process of adolescence. *Psychoanalytic Study of the Child,* 22:162–186, 1967. (A theoretical construct [similar to Mahler's description of the separation-individuation process of early childhood] is described to explain dynamically this daughter's struggle to separate from her parents and develop a more solid sense of autonomy.)

VII

Anxiety Disorders

■ **PANIC DISORDER WITH AGORAPHOBIA**

25. The Case of the Schoolmaster

(Historical Case: Emil Kraepelin)

Authors' Note:
Janet and Freud were primarily responsible for altering the 19th-century view of neurotic symptoms. By describing and explaining the psychological mechanisms underlying these disorders, they proposed that irrational feelings, ideas, and behaviors may be generated by psychodynamic forces and are not always a result of an hereditary degeneration of the central nervous system. Although Kraepelin was not a proponent of this psychodynamic view, he complemented his contemporaries by providing a system of classification and thoughtful, detailed, and colorful clinical descriptions, as this case illustrates.

First you see a schoolmaster, aged 31, who came to the hospital of his own accord four weeks ago in order to be treated here. The patient was, in fact, violently agitated when he had to come here, sank down on his bed, and said that the discussion in the hospital would cost him his life. He begged to be allowed to sit in the hall before the lecture began, so that he could see the audience come in gradually, as he could not face a number of people so suddenly.

The patient is quite collected, clear, and well ordered in his statements. He says that one of his sisters suffers in the same way as himself. He traces the beginning of his illness back to about 11 years ago. Being a very clever lad, he became a schoolmaster and had to do a great deal of mental work to qualify. Gradually he began to fear that he had a serious disease and was going to die of heart apoplexy. All the assurances and examinations of his doctor could not convince him. For this reason he suddenly left his appointment and went home one day, seven years ago, being afraid that he would die shortly. After this he consulted every possible doctor and took long holidays repeatedly, always recovering a little, but invariably finding that his fears returned speedily. These were gradually reinforced by the fear of gatherings of people. He was also unable to cross large squares or go through wide streets by himself. He avoided using the railway for fear of collisions and derailments, and he would not travel in a boat lest it might capsize. He was seized with apprehension on bridges and when skating, and at last the apprehension of apprehension itself caused palpitations and oppression on all sorts of occasions. He did not improve after his marriage three years ago. He was domesticated, good-natured, and manageable, only "too soft." On the way here, when he had finally made up his mind to place himself in our hands, he trembled with deadly fear.

The patient describes himself as a chicken-hearted fellow who, in spite of good mental ability, has always been afraid of all sorts of diseases—consumption, heart apoplexy, and the like. He knows that these anxieties are morbid, yet cannot free himself from them. This apprehensiveness came out in a very marked way while he was under observation in the hospital. He worried about every remedy, whether it was baths, packs, or medicine, being afraid it would be too strong for him and have a weakening effect. He always wished to have a warder within call in case he got agitated. The sight of other patients disturbed him greatly, and when he went for a walk in the garden with the door shut, he was tormented by the fear of not being able to get out of it in case anything happened. At last, he would hardly venture in front of the house and always had to have the door open behind him so that he could take refuge indoors in case of necessity. He begged to have a little bottle of "blue electricity" that he had brought with him to give him confidence. Sometimes he was seized with violent palpitation of the heart while he was sitting down. Some little acne spots gave him so much alarm that he could neither go for a walk nor sleep. It struck him that his look had got very gloomy, and he thought it was the beginning of a mental disturbance which would certainly seize upon him while he was here.

KRAEPELIN'S DIAGNOSIS

Insanity of irrepressible ideas

DSM-III-R DIAGNOSIS

AXIS I: Panic disorder with agoraphobia and hypochondriasis
AXIS II: Probable avoidant personality disorder
AXIS III: Mild acne
AXIS IV: Stress—moderate (psychiatric hospitalization)
AXIS V: Highest level of functioning past year—fair (apparently re-
           sponsible in his marriage and profession, but crippled by
           excessive fears and somatic preoccupations)

TREATMENT PROBLEM

Thirty-one-year-old man with an 11-year history of incapacitating
fears and hypochondriacal preoccupations, including fears of going crazy.

DISCUSSION OF TREATMENT SELECTION

Setting. As soon as possible, this patient should be discharged from
the hospital and followed as an outpatient. The patient has already
shown signs of regression and further avoidant behavior since being
hospitalized. A longer inpatient stay is likely to confirm his fears about
mental illness and increase his self-absorption and dependence.

Format. Since this schoolmaster is disturbed by even the sight of
other patients, group therapy would probably be intolerable to him at
the present time. A marital format, however, might be helpful in both
educating his wife about the nature of the illness and advising her how
not to become a crippling and crippled phobic partner by infantilizing
her husband and by arranging their lives so that neither must deal with
life's anxieties. An individual format will be the mainstay of his treatment.

Duration and Frequency. The patient has indicated that he is exquisitely sensitive to separation and potential rejection. The thought of
either one is enough to bring on a panic attack. He will therefore be
keenly aware of how frequently sessions are scheduled, how long they
last and how termination—of both individual sessions and of treatment

itself—is managed. Accordingly, the therapist must deal with the issue of time explicitly and thoughtfully. No matter how frequently sessions are scheduled, the schoolmaster will experience anxiety between visits. The solution is for the therapist not to increase the frequency (which is likely to foster further regression), but instead to acknowledge the anxiety and to take care, especially during the induction phase of treatment, to be absolutely punctual and, if possible, to schedule appointments consistently at the same time on the same day each week. A few minutes before the individual sessions come to a close the patient should be informed of the pending separation, allowing some time to deal with the mounting anxiety. However, even if the patient's distress makes it difficult to end on time, again the therapist should stick to the specified time frame, thereby indicating that anxiety is not in itself a reason to avoid painful tasks.

This method of ending individual sessions can be viewed as a paradigm for terminating treatment itself. The patient should be informed from the start that although some continuing follow-up visits may be scheduled at infrequent intervals over the ensuing years, the bulk of treatment will occur within a relatively compressed period of time—perhaps four to eight months—and that anxiety about concluding treatment will not in itself be a reason to delay termination. The therapist can be quite candid about the rationale for arranging the duration in this manner, namely, to avoid the therapist's becoming a phobic partner and to convey the expectation that the patient's well-defined disorder is indeed treatable within a circumscribed period of time.

Approach. A first step would be psychoeducational, an approach compatible with the schoolmaster's profession. For example, he could read the relevant sections of the DSM-III-R to relieve the sense of being alone in his fears. A component of this psychoeducation would also be to have the schoolmaster hyperventilate in the presence of the therapist. The associated cardiovascular symptoms could then be explained in terms of their psychological triggers and their physiological results.

After the schoolmaster has a better appreciation that he suffers from a definable disorder, a behavioral therapy can be implemented. One advantage of the behavioral approach for this patient is that he has a view of himself as "chicken-hearted. " By gradually confronting those situations that produce anxiety and reducing the fear of panic by graded exposure, this negative view of himself will diminish and in turn instill greater confidence to confront the next anxiety-laden task.

Though empathy will be an important ingredient in whatever approach is used, relying only on nonspecific support and encouragement is likely to fail. This approach has not worked up until now, and Kraepelin indicates that the patient is somewhat ambivalent towards his caretakers, wanting them in sight yet suspicious about their remedies. Similarly, although exploratory techniques might appeal to the schoolmaster's wish to gain intellectual mastery over his problems, exclusive reliance on understanding may provide the schoolmaster with rationalizations for not approaching the situations that make him anxious. In a subtle way, the therapist would then be colluding with the patient's avoidance and become a phobic partner. However, as the incapacitating anxieties are faced, the patient may benefit from psychodynamic inquiries into the fantasies and fears that are generated. For instance, he apparently became more phobic at the very time he was obtaining recognition; perhaps an unconscious fear of retaliation for success is contributing to his agoraphobia. This irrational expectation can be identified and worked through after he does once again become successful.

Somatic Treatment. Some therapists would rely primarily on medication alone to treat the schoolmaster's symptoms. This approach has some disadvantages for this particular patient. First, Kraepelin indicates that like many phobics, this patient is "worried about every remedy." The likely side effects of medication (e.g., tricyclic antidepressants) might compound these fears and impede compliance. Second, the schoolmaster has a tendency to develop magical thinking about medication (i.e., his little bottle of "blue electricity"). The risk of using medication is that the schoolmaster will attribute all the possible gains to the pills themselves, will acquire little confidence in his own ability to tolerate anxiety, and will relapse if and when the medications are withdrawn. For these reasons, we would recommend beginning with the behavioral approach and adding medication only if the patient is too terrified to participate in a behavioral treatment without pharmacological assistance, or if the patient does not respond to a program of graded exposures.

SUGGESTED READING

1. Group for Advancement of Psychiatry. *Pharmacotherapy and Psychotherapy: Paradoxes, Problems and Progress. GAP,* 9 (Report no. 93): 260–434, 1975. (Chapter 5 of this report discusses the biological and psychological factors that would be considered in designing a treatment plan for this schoolmaster's panic attacks.)
2. Barlow, D. H. (Ed.). *Behavioral Assessment of Adult Disorders.* New York:

Guilford Press, 1981. (Provides both the rationale and the specific therapeutic maneuvers for a behavioral treatment of phobic disorders.)
3. Marks, I. M. Drugs combined with behavioral psychotherapy. In A. S. Bellak, M. Hersen, & A. E. Kazdin (Eds.), *International Handbook of Behavior Modification*. New York: Plenum Press, 1982, pp. 319–345. (Points out how the use of drug-behavioral combinations remains controversial and must be guided by clinical judgment.)

26.   The Case of the Homebound Son

(Guest Expert: Charlotte M. Zitrin, M.D.)

Authors' Note:
Dr. Zitrin is Associate Professor of Psychiatry, Albert Einstein College of Medicine; and Director Emeritus of the Phobia Clinic, Long Island Jewish-Hillside Medical Center, New Hyde Park, New York. She has been the senior investigator in a series of unusually well-designed studies to determine the specific effects of medication and behavior therapy in the treatment of various types of phobic patients, one of whom is presented here.

Mr. A is a 28-year-old unemployed accountant who has become increasingly incapacitated by panic attacks, agoraphobia, and somatic preoccupations to the point that he can no longer tolerate being alone and cannot go out without accompaniment. The patient has had similar symptoms on and off for many years, but he now fears that he is losing his mind and that he is experiencing a schizophrenic deterioration. The symptoms worsened three months ago when his girlfriend suddenly left him because of his "passivity." The patient is now spending most of his time at his parents' home, where he behaves and is treated like an invalid.

The patient was an only child born to parents who were already in their late thirties and had expected to be childless. As an infant he had considerable separation anxiety and could not be left with babysitters. He developed into a shy boy who was subject to many minor illnesses and was much more comfortable with adults than in the rough-and-tumble of peer relationships. Mr. A developed mild school refusal in the first and fourth grades and was never willing to try summer camp. He attended college and business school locally so that he could continue to live at home, and then went into the family business. He was interested in dating, but was usually too shy to initiate his own relationships with women and depended on his mother to serve as matchmaker.

The patient's symptoms have exacerbated and remitted throughout his twenties. On and off he has tried to establish his separateness in various ways: taking trips overseas, moving into his own apartment, dating a girl of his own choosing, and even quitting his father's firm and finding a job on his own. Each effort has ended in failure and humiliation because the patient becomes anxious, ruminates that he is doing the wrong thing, and finally gives up and returns to the "family routine."

The patient feels especially bound to his physically ailing mother, and she is equally bound to him. She cannot tolerate his "suffering" and is willing to sacrifice her relationship with her husband and her social life to be with him. On his side, Mr. A worries that his mother will die soon and is troubled by the thought that she gets lonely without him, just as he feels lonely without her. When apart, they call each other several times a day. At the same time, he is angry at both parents and blames them for his difficulties, for not loving him enough and also for loving him too much, for not taking care of him and for making him dependent. He is particularly contemptuous of his father, who also has some mild phobias.

Mr. A feels defective and inferior. He expects to be criticized by others and is sensitive to rejection. He is also highly critical of others and constantly feels let down. He has had close friends in the past but is now too embarrassed to call them.

Mr. A has been in psychotherapy on several different occasions, each of which lasted for about a year. Typically he becomes demanding, becomes disappointed with his therapist, and feels that things are going nowhere. He has a strong tendency to addiction to minor tranquilizers and shows little ability to use them within the recommended dosage. He has received neuroleptics with poor results. Antidepressants in low dosages have not been helpful. He is bright and perceptive about his motivations and behaviors, but seemingly unable to change them.

DSM-III-R DIAGNOSIS

Axis I: Panic disorder with agoraphobia
Axis II: Avoidant personality disorder, dependent personality disorder
Axis III: None
Axis IV: Stress—moderate (losing girlfriend)
Axis V: Highest level of functioning past year—fair

DISCUSSION OF TREATMENT SELECTION

This patient's case is typical of agoraphobia in some respects and atypical in others. A typical aspect is the separation anxiety with school refusal in childhood. Although we do not have a complete history, there are clues suggesting that his separation anxiety may have been fostered by his mother: He is an only child, born to parents late in life, which may have led them to be overprotective; his mother sacrifices her social life to be with him (and possibly did so during his developmental years); he feels bound to his ailing mother, yet is angry with her and his father (suggesting a hostile-dependent relationship, which may have been a factor in his developing separation anxiety and school phobia).

Also typical is that Mr. A's present illness was precipitated by a loss, and that he shows remissions and exacerbations. It is also common for such patients to fear they are going crazy. An atypical aspect is that the patient is a man: the vast majority of agoraphobics are women (from 68%–90%, depending upon the study). In the differential diagnosis, it would be necessary to consider a schizophrenic process, which can be ruled out through the psychiatric examination.

I believe the treatment of choice for agoraphobic patients is supportive psychotherapy combined with desensitization. If at all possible, the desensitization should be done *in vivo*, using the actual phobic situations. Some patients who are too frightened to agree to this technique can be treated with desensitization through mental imagery until they feel ready to participate in *in vivo* therapy.

The first therapeutic task with a patient like Mr. A would be to reach agreement with all members of the family to cooperate in his treatment. One must not only establish a therapeutic alliance with the patient, but also get the parents to thwart his demands that one of them stay home with him and take care of him. The task of having him stay home alone for increasing periods of time must be agreed on by the patient and his parents in a conference held with the family. Sometimes the time alone is as little as one minute at first; sometimes the patient can tolerate staying home alone for hours. Thus, we must individualize the treatment to meet the patient's requirements. However, once the principle of separation is established, the time that the patient spends at home alone is increased as quickly as possible.

Concurrently, Mr. A would be placed in a therapy group of agoraphobic patients. In our view, group therapy is preferable to individual therapy for many reasons. The members of the group are enormously helpful to each other. Many of them fear that they are crazy or going crazy, and they are tremendously relieved to meet other people who express similar concerns and who are obviously not insane. The patients immediately establish identifications with each other and pour out feelings, help each other with coping mechanisms and empathy, and quickly coalesce into a functioning therapeutic group.

In the first stage of group treatment, the patients go out immediately after the group session for *in vivo* desensitization exercises. Their first task would be to walk alone to a local shopping center five blocks away, with each group member taking a different route. Patients are reassured that their therapist will be there to meet them when they reconvene at the shopping center. The next task is to go unaccompanied into a department store, while the therapist waits outside. It is important for the patients to spend a prolonged period of time inside the store. We have found that initially the patient's anxiety level increases, and it requires 30 minutes or more for it to decrease to a low level or subside entirely.

For patients who do not wish to be in a group, the principle of desensitization *in vivo* is the same, but he or she works individually with the therapist. For patients who are too anxious to commit themselves to an *in vivo* procedure at all, we start with desensitization in fantasy, composing a hierarchy of imagined scenes. After they complete a hierarchy in imagination, they are given *in vivo* homework assignments.

The second stage of treatment consists of using public transportation and cars to travel farther away from the treatment facility and eventually to the center of the city. As we know, the farther agoraphobic patients travel from home, the greater their anxiety. Ideally, the second stage is also carried out within the context of the group.

Both of these stages require several weeks, since each *in vivo* exercise may need to be repeated several times before the anxiety abates. Patients are also asked to practice similar exercises between sessions, with friends or family members helping them.

By the end of the second stage of treatment, many patients have attained greater self-esteem and self-confidence. Therefore, the third stage involves widening their horizons, both in functioning and in socialization. For patients who don't need help with socialization, the group experience, with homework assignments and, when indicated, the use of modeling and role-playing, are now emphasized. For patients who seek to return to work, improve their work situations, or change jobs, these factors are stressed. The group, under the therapist's supervision, can be enormously helpful and supportive during this critical period.

Whenever possible, we treat patients without medication. However, for patients whose panic attacks do not subside with the above treatment after four to six weeks, we add medication that is specifically designed to ameliorate the attacks. In our experience, both the tricyclics and the MAO inhibitors are very effective. Usually, we start with a tricyclic like imipramine rather than an MAO inhibitor because of the strict diet required with the latter and the danger of hypertensive crisis. If imipramine is not helpful or produces unpleasant side effects, we try another tricyclic. If that, too, is unsatisfactory, we then switch to an MAO inhibitor.

A word of caution: About 20%–25% of patients with panic disorder are exquisitely sensitive to tricyclics and get an immediate amphetamine-like reaction. Therefore, we routinely start with a small dose (25 mg) and increase gradually to 150 mg over the next 10–14 days. Thus, if there is an untoward reaction, it is likely to be less severe and the dose can be lowered to 10 mg. Some patients require even smaller doses initially, but with time are gradually able to tolerate increasing amounts. Many of these patients never require large doses, yet show a favorable response.

SUGGESTED READING

1. Mavissakalian, M., & Barlow, D. H. *Phobia: Psychological and Pharmacological Treatment*. New York: Guilford Press, 1981. (Describes the many kinds of behavioral treatments besides those suggested above by Dr. Zitrin.)
2. Wolpe, J. *The Practice of Behavior Therapy* (2nd Ed.). New York: Pergamon Press, 1973. (The application of systematic desensitization, as well as alternative behavioral treatments, elaborated in detail by the primary founder of this technique.)
3. Bowlby, J. *Attachment and Loss: Vol. II. Separation, Anxiety and Anger*. New York: Basic Books, 1973. (In this controversial revision of psychoanalytic theory, Bowlby provides one way of understanding this patient's phobic avoidance of separation from his mother and his response to losing his girlfriend.)

■ OBSESSIVE COMPULSIVE DISORDER

27. The Case of the Plagued Perfectionist

Mr. S is a 22-year-old black first-year graduate student referred to a psychiatric clinic by the Dean of Students, who suspects emotional problems are interfering with Mr. S's academic performance. Although Mr. S would never have thought of seeking psychiatric help on his own—where he grew up "shrinks were for nuts"—he agrees to the referral and arrives for his first appointment dressed in a three-piece suit as if attending a job interview. Within a few moments, he feels more comfortable, loosens his tie, and describes the facts about his current situation.

He is likely to fail his semester exams and has no idea what to do or to whom to turn. The problem does not stem from his lack of ability. He was first in his high school class, was third in his graduating class from a prestigious college, had outstanding board scores, and received distinguished prizes along the way. All of these kudos indicated that he was destined for success. Nor is the problem his laziness. On the contrary, since entering graduate school three months ago, he has never worked harder in his life, and never so ineffectively. The problem is (and here Mr. S blushes with embarrassment) a time-consuming need to perform ridiculous rituals in preparation for studying at his desk. In high school and college, the rituals were rather minor: wiping his desk with a clean rag; sharpening seven colored pencils; aligning the blotter and notebooks at perfect right angles; and washing his hands before and after completing the assignment in each course.

In the past, Mr. S had simply rationalized that these rituals helped remove distractions and prepared his mind for concentrating. After entering graduate school, however, Mr. S found that the rituals were becoming more and more of a burden rather than a helpful habit. By the time of mid-semester exams, they were seriously impeding his studies. It took him a half hour to prepare his desk before he could even open a book; he had to sharpen pencils after he read each chapter and, eventually, after he read each page; and if the slightest smudge appeared on his study outlines or diagrams, he had to recopy that portion of the assignment.

Mr. S realized that these rituals were excessive; yet, if he did not play out the medley, the resulting anxiety would be intolerable. He would have even more doubts about his capacities, would wonder if for intellectual and social reasons attending graduate school was a mistake, and in his worst moments would consider calling the Dean of Students to say he was dropping out. To gain control over such anxiety and doubts, Mr. S would then increase his rituals. These compulsions would interfere with his studying, give more reason for the anxiety and more cause for rigorous study habits, and the problems would crescendo.

After failing two of his mid-semester exams, Mr. S stopped attending all classes and locked himself in his room day and night to prepare for finals, which were weeks away. His instructors, aware of his academic difficulties, misinterpreted Mr. S's absenteeism as defiance because in class Mr. S never appeared that anxious, but rather overly casual and at times tactlessly argumentative about insignificant points. At the instructors' insistence, the Dean of Students met with Mr. S, but the Dean was reluctant to discuss any specific personal problems for fear that racial issues might emerge, issues which the Dean characteristically chose to avoid. In a rather perfunctory manner, the Dean referred Mr. S for psychiatric evaluation on the assumption that even if Mr. S were not having emotional problems, the threat of having to see a psychiatrist would straighten him out and make him work harder. Mr. S recognized that "being sent off to the spooks" was a threat, but inwardly he also saw the Dean's requirement as a face-saving way of finally getting help.

Although the Dean had warned the psychiatrist that Mr. S might try to avoid facing his problems by blaming everything on racial prejudice, nothing during the evaluation supported this concern. Instead, Mr. S was eager to discuss his incapacitating rituals (e.g., how he must now always read the last seven pages of a book before turning to the assigned section and how he must proceed through a given chapter by first reading the top lines of each page from right to left).

During the interview, Mr. S tended to dwell on the details of these compulsions and appeared hesitant about discussing his past and his present family difficulties. When the consultant pointed out this hesitancy, Mr. S acknowledged that he hated to bad-mouth his family, but he then agreed to reveal his unusual background. He was born "as an afterthought" into a poor working-class family with many much older siblings and half siblings. He grew up in a neighborhood that was a training ground for the local penitentiary. In fact, two of his older stepbrothers had served time for drug-related problems. Instead of following this career pattern, Mr. S became a model student, but his accomplishments were not really appreciated by the other family members. They did not even remotely understand what he had achieved and regarded him as excessively ambitious—and, ironically, as a rather wayward son and a bit of a disappointment. By the time Mr. S had completed college, all his siblings were in various stages of marriage or divorce with many children of their own. They were living either at home or nearby and tended to view the rest of the world with suspicion.

Throughout his college years and even now while attending graduate school, Mr. S has continued to return home every weekend. He has no friends outside the family and though he has had several girlfriends in the past, because they were always of another race he could never allow himself to take the relationships very seriously, and certainly could never take his girlfriends home to meet his family. They were always "weekday" dates. As a result, the women typically felt rejected and ended the relationship on a bitter note.

DSM-III-R DIAGNOSIS

Axis I: Obsessive compulsive disorder
Axis II: Compulsive personality disorder with both avoidant and dependent features
Axis III: Asthma, in remission
Axis IV: Stress—moderate (first semester of graduate school)
Axis V: Highest level of functioning past year—good

TREATMENT PROBLEM

A 22-year-old graduate student with crippling compulsive rituals which may lead to dismissal from graduate school; he also has long-standing difficulty in separating from his family and establishing both a coherent personal identity and meaningful interpersonal relationships.

DISCUSSION OF TREATMENT SELECTION

Setting. Of the various components of treatment, the easiest to decide for Mr. S is the therapeutic setting. Neither hospitalization nor partial hospitalization is indicated; an outpatient setting is clearly the preferred choice.

Format. Choosing the most effective therapeutic format is somewhat more of a problem. An argument could be made that because Mr. S's anxiety at school and his limited social life both derive from a failure to resolve intrafamilial conflicts, a family format would bring these issues immediately into focus where they could be dealt with most directly and where distortions and scapegoating could be corrected. On the other hand, this format might bring the family more immediately into Mr. S's other world and might only reinforce his difficulty in separating from them. In addition, the prospects of Mr. S's psychiatrically unsophisticated and suspicious family engaging in such a treatment are poor.

Others might argue, somewhat less persuasively, that regardless of the source of Mr. S's compulsive anxiety, the end result has been an embedded sense of alienation. A heterogeneous group could therefore offer the support and encouragement of a surrogate family. This support would in turn diminish his anxiety and the compulsive rituals, which are merely futile attempts to master a mounting panic. A problem with this recommendation is that time is short; Mr. S's dismissal from school is imminent. A group with its other concerns and with Mr. S's tendency to cover his problems with feigned casualness might not be able to act rapidly enough to reverse the acute situation. For these reasons, an individual format would be preferred; it offers a focused and immediate opportunity to address the current crisis. A family treatment and heterogeneous group are options to reconsider in the future.

Duration and Frequency. Sessions must be scheduled close enough together to provide sufficient intensity to resolve or at least quell the current critical situation, yet sessions cannot be so frequent that Mr. S feels forced to develop a more intimate relationship than he has until now been able to tolerate. An involvement that is too intense and, for example, quickly uncovers a deep resentment towards his family might increase Mr. S's anxiety and be counterproductive. Two times a week would tentatively be a reasonable choice, with the option to increase or decrease this frequency as circumstances warrant.

Sessions of approximately 45–60 minutes would be the preferred length—sufficient time for the discussion of more than a superficial recount of day-to-day activities and for performing exercises that require graded exposure. Occasional longer exposure sessions may be desirable.

Because Mr. S's characterological problems may require a more prolonged treatment after the current anxiety decreases, the duration should at this time be left open-ended. A time-oriented or time-limited treatment might increase Mr. S's anxiety if he perceived a set termination date as one more deadline he must meet.

Approach. Mr. S has the enabling factors and the indications for many treatment techniques. Exploratory treatment could diminish his anxiety by helping him understand intrapsychic conflicts (e.g., that he is ambivalent about asserting himself academically and personally because any such assertion unconsciously means leaving home, "killing off" his family, and being abandoned).

A behavioral treatment might have more appeal to Mr. S because of his sociocultural doubts about "head shrinkers." The general approach of the behavioral treatment would be to expose Mr. S systematically to those situations which produce anxiety, an anxiety he either avoids or attempts to control with compulsive rituals. While exposing himself to these situations, he would be prohibited from his usual avoidance or compulsive behavior. For example, he might be instructed to work for increasing amounts of time at a sloppy desk or to read pages only forward.

Depending on Mr. S's motivation and capacity to tolerate anxiety, other methods could be used in conjunction with this type of graded exposure (e.g., self-relaxation techniques or assertiveness training).

Finally, an experiential treatment which conveyed support and positive regard for Mr. S would help decrease his demoralization and sense of alienation, and his compulsive rituals might decrease as he became less anxious about losing either his family or his academic goals.

Somatic Treatment. Tricyclic antidepressants may be useful for obsessive-compulsive disorders, especially when the syndrome is accompanied by symptoms of depression. The drug that has been most tested in this regard (chloripramine) is not currently available in the United States.

CHOICE AND OUTCOME

Towards the end of the first session, the consultant recommended that Mr. S be seen once a week in a behavioral treatment. He explained to Mr. S that although the acute crisis was superimposed on longstanding problems, the first goal of treatment must be to rapidly decrease compulsions, improve study habits, and thereby prevent dismissal from school. In the consultant's view, behavioral treatment was the preferred choice to achieve these immediate goals in the briefest period of time and avoid failure at a crucial phase of Mr. S's development.

Mr. S agreed with the consultant's recommendations and returned two days later to begin a systematic behavioral treatment with the consultant as the therapist. In just the short interval since his first session, Mr. S had already improved remarkably. He spontaneously explained this improvement was a direct result of feeling less alone and more understood. Although a few behavioral interventions were suggested (e.g., that Mr. S force himself to read the book frontwards rather than backwards, first within the therapy sessions and then alone in his room), Mr. S's rapid improvement over the next few weeks probably had more to do with interpersonal and experiential factors, namely, an empathic relationship that reduced Mr. S's sense of isolation and of being a misfit.

After the immediate crisis was over and Mr. S passed his semester exams, the therapist recommended that Mr. S consider a twice weekly, psychoanalytically oriented psychotherapy. Mr. S agreed that understanding the basis for his fears of success and his fears of outdoing his fathers and brothers might help him meet the challenges of early adulthood, might increase his confidence, and might reduce his compulsive symptoms and avoidant lifestyle. For logistical and financial reasons, in order to receive an extended exploratory treatment, Mr. S was referred to a senior psychiatry resident.

Four years later, the original consultant-therapist literally bumped into Mr. S on the street. In this brief encounter, he learned that Mr. S had completed his doctoral thesis and was now working in a laboratory for a renowned professor who was also black. The patient said he was happily married and had benefited greatly from the treatment which had lasted three years and was now terminated because "the work was done. " He graciously thanked the consultant once again for the help he had given.

SUGGESTED READING

1. Beech, H. R., & Vaughan, M. *Behavioral Treatment of Obsessional States.* New York: Wiley, 1978. (Exceptionally helpful in describing how the therapist can approach the oppositionalism many obsessives present when behavioral strategies are recommended.)
2. Salzman, L., & Thaler, F. H. Obsessive-compulsive disorders: A review of the literature. *American Journal of Psychiatry,* 138:286–296, 1981. (Includes sections on both psychodynamically oriented and pharmacological approaches to patients similar to Mr. S.)
3. Gendlin, E. T. Experiential psychotherapy. In R. Corsini (Ed.), *Current Psychotherapies* (2nd Ed.). Itasca, IL: Peacock, 1979, pp. 317-352. (Articulates concisely and precisely how and why experiential factors may catalyze therapeutic change in patients like Mr. S.)

28. The Case of the Rat Man

(Historical Case: Sigmund Freud)

Authors' Note:
This famous case treated by Freud needs no introduction.

A youngish man of university education introduced himself to me with the statement that he had suffered from obsessions ever since his childhood, but with particular intensity for the last four years. The chief features of his disorder were *fears* that something might happen to two people of whom he was very fond—his father and a lady whom he admired. Besides this he was aware of *compulsive impulses*—such as an impulse, for instance, to cut his throat with a razor, and further he produced *prohibitions*, sometimes in connection with quite unimportant things. He had wasted years, he told me, in fighting against these ideas of his, and in this way had lost much ground in the course of his life. He had tried various treatments, but none had been of any use to him except a course of hydrotherapy at a sanatorium. . . .

The next day I made him pledge himself to submit to the one and only condition of the treatment, namely, to say everything that came into his head, even if it was *unpleasant* to him, or seemed *unimportant* or *irrelevant* or *senseless*. I then gave him leave to start his communications with any subject he pleased:

"When I was six years old I already suffered from erections, and I know that once I went to my mother to complain about them. I know, too, that in doing so I had some misgivings to get over, for I had a feeling that there was some connection between this subject and my ideas and inquisitiveness, and at that time I used to have a morbid idea *that my parents knew my thoughts; I explained this to myself by supposing that I had spoken them out loud, without having heard myself do it.* I look on this as the beginning of my illness. There were certain people, girls, who pleased me very much, and I had a very strong wish *to see them make it.* But in wishing this I had *an uncanny feeling, as though something must happen if I thought such things, as though I must do all sorts of things to prevent it."*

(In reply to a question, he gave an example of these fears: "for instance, *that my father might die."*)

" . . . I think I will begin today with the experience which was the immediate occasion of my coming to you. It was in August, during the manoeuvres. . . . During a halt . . . I sat between two officers, one of whom, a captain with a Czech name, was to be of no small importance to me. I had a kind of dread of him, *for he was obviously fond of cruelty.* I do not say he was a bad man, but at the officers' mess he had repeatedly defended the introduction of corporal punishment, so that I had been obliged to disagree with him very sharply. Well, during this halt we got into conversation, and the captain told me he had read of an especially horrible punishment used in the East. . . . The criminal was tied up . . . a pot was turned upside down on his buttocks . . . some *rats* were put into it . . . and they . . . *bored their way in.*

" . . . At that moment the idea flashed through my mind *that this was happening to a person who was very dear to me."* In answer to a direct question he said that it was not he himself who was carrying out the punishment, but that it was being carried out as it were impersonally. After a little prompting I learnt that the person to whom this "idea" of his related was the lady whom he admired.

. . . So far we have heard only of one idea—of the rat punishment being carried out on the lady. He was now obliged to admit that second idea had occurred to him simultaneously, namely, the idea of the punishment also being applied to his father. As his father had died many years previously, this obsessive fear was much more nonsensical even than the first, and accordingly it had attempted to escape being confessed to for a little while longer.

FREUD'S DIAGNOSIS

Obsessional neurosis

DSM-III-R DIAGNOSIS

Axis I: Obsessive compulsive disorder
Axis II: Compulsive personality disorder
Axis III: None
Axis IV: Stress—moderate (proposed marriage)
Axis V: Highest level of functioning past year—poor (unable to work, complete his education, or enjoy people and life)

TREATMENT PROBLEM

This young military officer presents with the persistent and terrifying obsession that rats will bore up through the anus of his lady love and of his father (long since dead). This obsessional fear occurred immediately after the patient heard about a method of using rats to torture prisoners. The patient has had a number of compulsions and prohibitions since childhood. These became more frequent and intense after his father's death. For the last four years, he had been particularly debilitated by compulsive rituals that are intended to undo the harm he expects to befall his loved ones. Because the patient has been unsuccessful in fighting these rituals and intrusive ideas, he has lost much ground in life and has been unable to complete his education, to work, or to enter marriage (a marriage arranged by his mother in accordance with his father's wishes). Many different treatments have been tried, and have failed.

DISCUSSION OF TREATMENT SELECTION

Freud's treatment in 1907 consisted of a yearlong psychoanalysis. The patient came five times a week, used the couch, and through free association traced the roots of his unconscious ambivalence towards his father. Interpretation of dreams and transferential distortions facilitated the recovery of repressed memories and impulses. By the end of treatment, Freud reports "the patient's rat delirium disappeared." Freud does not mention whether the patient's character problems also improved.

If the Rat Man presented today, he probably would be prescribed a somewhat different treatment. If an exploratory approach were recommended, the three choices would most likely be: a contemporary form of psychoanalysis, a psychoanalytically oriented psychotherapy, or a brief focal therapy. The contemporary psychoanalysis would last much longer (at least three years), would attempt to resolve character problems as well as symptoms, and would use the transference neurosis as a paradigm. A psychoanalytically oriented psychotherapy would be longer than one year but less intense than Freud's treatment (perhaps one to three times per week for several years). This form of treatment would also have the ambitious goal of improving character problems, but would not use the couch or encourage the development of a regressive transference neurosis. A brief dynamic focal therapy would meet once or twice a week for less than a year and would restrict attention to the conflicts, fantasies, and experiences that constitute the patient's ambivalence towards his arranged marriage and towards his father.

But these three forms of psychodynamic treatments are not the only options for the Rat Man. Today, there is an extensive literature on the behavioral treatment for compulsions and, though the reports are somewhat less impressive, of behavioral treatment for obsessions as well. For example, a patient reports that one day he was out with his girlfriend in a boat, there was a stiff breeze blowing, and he was compelled to make her put on his cap so that, magically, nothing would happen to her. The patient would be instructed that when similar occasions occurred in the future, he should prohibit himself from compulsively acting on this belief and instead expose himself to the surges of anxiety that he would feel as a result of this prohibition. He would be reassured that the anxiety would eventually extinguish so long as he did not attempt to avoid the unpleasant affect by performing some obsessive or compulsive ritual.

Flooding would be another kind of behavioral treatment: The Rat Man would be given an opportunity to come into contact with rats either in thought or in reality. If not allowed to avoid this terrifying situation, the anxiety would gradually extinguish and lose its connection to the assuaging obsession or ritual. These kinds of behavioral interventions obviously require that the patient have enough confidence in the treatment and the therapist to confront the anxiety directly.

A third approach for the Rat Man would be the use of psychotropic medication. The intermittent course of his symptoms resembles that of an affective disorder. In a number of clinical trials, antidepressant medication has been found to be effective in reducing obsessive-compulsive symptoms, even with patients like the Rat Man who do not present with a clear-cut affective syndrome.

Occasionally, when a patient presents with devastating and crippling obsessive-compulsive symptoms that have responded to nothing else, psychosurgery is indicated, and good results have been reported, particularly from Great Britain. But for the Rat Man this approach would only be recommended as a last resort and only if his symptoms became far more severe and incapacitating than they have been up until now.

What would we do if the Rat Man presented today? We would recommend a combination of behavioral and exploratory approaches. His motivation for treatment, his willingness to confront his anxiety, and his trust in the therapist suggest that he would be a good candidate for exposure techniques. However, in addition to the need for symptom removal, he also has characterological problems that could benefit from exploratory psychotherapy. Of the three options, we would suggest a brief focal therapy, but admittedly this choice is influenced by our knowledge that the Rat Man responded previously within one year (of course, Freud was a particularly charismatic therapist and a hard act to follow). We would not prescribe psychotropic medications for the Rat Man, at least not initially, for he appears willing and able to participate in the rather rigorous demands of our recommended behavioral and psychodynamic approaches without the necessity of using a pharmacological intervention. If he did not respond to these methods, a trial of antidepressant medication would be indicated.

SUGGESTED READING

1. Freud, S. (1909). Notes upon a case of obsessional neurosis. In J. Strachey (Ed.), *Standard Edition*, 10:153–318, 1955. (Freud includes in this marvelous account his therapeutic interventions and his daily notes.)
2. Zetzel, E. R. Additional notes upon a case of obsessional neurosis. *International Journal of Psychoanalysis*, 47:123–129, 1966. (The author discusses the Rat Man 60 years after the original publication and indicates how the psychodynamics would be viewed differently by contemporary analysts, especially the mother's role, which Freud ignores.)
3. Shapiro, D. Obsessive-compulsive style. In *Neurotic Styles*. New York: Basic Books, 1965, pp. 23–53. (This chapter explains not only who these individuals are [emotionally, cognitively, dynamically, and interpersonally], but also why they can be so frustrating to treat.)
4. MacKinnon, R., & Michels, R. *The Psychiatric Interview in Clinical Practice.* Philadelphia: Saunders, 1971, pp. 89–109. (The authors' chapter on the obsessive patient is a gem, especially in the way a psychodynamic understanding can be used to tailor psychotherapeutic responses.)
5. Perry, S., Frances, A., Klar, H., & Clarkin, J. Selection criteria for the dynamic

psychotherapies. *Psychiatric Quarterly,* 55(1):3–16, 1983. (Suggests enabling factors, indications, and contraindications for 1) dynamically based supportive psychotherapy, 2) focal dynamic therapy, 3) psychodynamically oriented psychotherapy, and 4) psychoanalysis.)

■ POST-TRAUMATIC STRESS DISORDER

29. The Case of the Burned Fireman

Mr. R, a 37-year-old burly, full-bearded Irish fireman, was hospitalized for second- and third-degree burns over a third of his body. During his month on the burn unit, he was the model stoic patient, but when seen a week after discharge for his first appointment in the surgical clinic, he was tremulous, stammering, and unresponsive to the surgeon's reassurance. Deeply concerned, the surgeon paged the consultation-liaison psychiatrist on the burn unit and introduced him to Mr. R, who shook hands and mumbled, "I sort of expected you'd be calling the shrinks."

Although Mr. R tried to appear confident, he chain-smoked, glanced around furtively, squirmed in his chair, and at times burst into tears. He explained that he was just a little upset because two months ago his wife announced to his complete surprise that after 18 years of marriage and raising two children, she had filed for a divorce. Making no connection between the two events, Mr. R went on to say that his near-fatal burns occurred only a week after his wife's announcement: For the first time in his distinguished career, he entered a burning building alone and in a manner contrary to the safety procedures he was responsible for teaching.

His hospitalization had been bearable because the burn unit team had been very supportive, but now that he was home, he admitted to becoming a nervous wreck, taking drinks to calm his nerves and to get to sleep, and feeling humiliated about his silly mistake at the fire. He could not stop thinking and dreaming about his error. He was most ashamed about the prospect of facing his co-workers, who would see him shaky, sweating, and frightened instead of characteristically brash and brave. When alone the previous night while his wife was out with her new "feminist girlfriends," he felt that he was cracking up as he paced the floor, afraid to leave the house on his own, and feeling dizzy, numb, and detached. For the first time he wondered whether life was worth living.

Mr. R said that he could now see things more rationally. His plans were to live at home for two more months (his wife had granted him that much) and then to move into an apartment with his elderly mother, who currently lived in a basement apartment in Mr. R's house. In fact, Mr. R, an only child, had never lived *without* his mother. The two of them had been, in his words, "a team" ever since his father died when Mr. R was five. After graduation from high school, Mr. R married the first woman who agreed that his mother could live in the house. He believed his mother's presence had never posed much of a problem, and that the real cause for the divorce was his admittedly harsh and critical attitude towards his wife for little things, such as not serving food in the traditional family style.

Over the years, Mr. R's wife had pushed for them to see a marriage counselor, but Mr. R had adamantly refused to have anything to do with psychiatry. He preferred to get advice from the guys at the firehouse with whom he worked, talked, joked, played, and drank (to the exclusion of his wife and children). He wondered aloud where he would get the same kind of support now, and whether he would ever be able to return to work.

While the psychiatrist was writing up the interview in the surgical clinic, the head nurse on the burn unit informed him that one of her staff nurses was distraught. This nurse had become close to Mr. R during his hospitalization, and later she had spent one night with him in a hotel. The head nurse wanted advice about how this delicate matter should be handled.

DSM-III-R DIAGNOSIS

AXIS I: Post-traumatic stress disorder
AXIS II: Diagnosis deferred
AXIS III: Status post 35% second- and third-degree burns
AXIS IV: Stress—extreme (burns, illness, potential loss of job, impending divorce)
AXIS V: Highest level of functioning past year—fair

DISCUSSION OF TREATMENT SELECTION

Setting. The psychiatrist chose an outpatient setting, with the option of introducing day or night hospital treatment if it turned out that more structure and support were needed. An office in the surgical rather than psychiatric clinic would be used in hopes of helping Mr. R save face, of increasing his compliance, and of conveying concretely that his illness was largely a reaction to an overwhelming stress and not an indication of an irreversible mental condition. The psychiatrist was well aware of Mr. R's potential to transform a psychiatric facility into a chronic replacement for the support he had received from his marriage and the firehouse; the surgical setting would be less likely to foster such a replacement.

Format. Given the pending plans for divorce, the psychiatrist believed that marital or family sessions might only produce an exchange of accusations rather than provide reassurance and support. He therefore decided to have the attending surgeon meet once with Mr. and Mrs. R to educate them about Mr. R's stress disorder, and to advise them that "until the pieces settle back into place" during the next two or three months, neither partner should make any irreversible moves. The surgeon was advised to emphasize that he was only suggesting a moratorium and was not advising either partner what ultimately should be done in terms of the marriage.

The psychiatrist also recommended that Mr. R attend a homogeneous group of former burn victims that was conducted by a nonpsychiatric nurse. The group would give Mr. R the same kind of support he had received over the years from his fellow firemen and reinforce the notion that his reactions were common, self-limited, and not necessarily an indication of chronic mental illness. In addition, individual psychotherapy to deal with issues more specifically related to Mr. R was arranged.

Approach. The psychiatrist recommended that Mr. R's dependency needs be supported by having the individual treatment done by the burn unit's social worker. This caring female therapist would be a transferential replacement for the separating wife, and would not be viewed as a "shrink" who might probe and destroy Mr. R's façade.

For this reason, the psychiatrist also recommended that exploratory techniques not be used at this time, that regression or dynamic uncovering be discouraged, and that adaptive defenses of repression, suppression, and displacement be reinforced. He suggested the social worker use directive and cognitive techniques to educate Mr. R about his stress disorder and to help him solve logistical problems involving his finances, disability compensation, return to work, and divorce proceedings. His "military" style would respond well to the use of a hierarchy and behavioral modification to overcome his phobic avoidance of work; such techniques would also facilitate his return to work before the gratification of secondary gain and financial compensation became fixed and perhaps irreversible.

Somatic Treatment. Initially, benzodiazepines were recommended to reduce Mr. R's nervousness and his need for alcohol, with the option of later introducing imipramine for his associated panic disorder.

Duration and Frequency. The psychiatrist recommended that Mr. R should be seen by the surgeon once a week for routine follow-up care (in addition to the one-time meeting with Mr. and Mrs. R), should attend the burn group once a week, and on the three remaining weekdays should see the social worker for 20-minute sessions to discuss immediate problems, have his medication adjusted, and receive the next directive in the behavioral modification hierarchy. A specific date for termination was not established at the start of treatment, but the patient was explicitly told that the frequency of sessions would diminish over the coming weeks as the end of treatment grew near. This schedule was intended to give Mr. R sufficient day-to-day support without the threat of a premature termination, and at the same time prevent regression or sustained dependency.

Liaison Management. The surgeon felt unreasonably guilty about not having predicted Mr. R's serious emotional problems. The psychiatrist dealt with the surgeon's reactions by making him an active participant in the treatment, such as by meeting with Mr. and Mrs. R. The burn unit staff's concern about Mr. R, a man whom they admired and had worked hard to save, was handled by a discussion of post-traumatic stress disorders at the weekly staff conference; the purpose was to increase the staff's objectivity and intellectual mastery of the problem and to help them predict the occurrence of such problems in other patients before they were discharged from the unit. The psychiatrist chose to avoid dealing with the nurse who had become intimate with Mr. R but did suggest that the head nurse not tell her any confidential psychiatric material.

CHOICE AND OUTCOME

Mr. R initially accepted the treatment plan in its entirety. After the meeting with the surgeon, Mrs. R agreed to postpone any plans for irreversible moves. Mr. R attended the weekly burn group and was relieved that he was not "alone." The brief triweekly sessions with the social worker were used to establish a behavioral modification regime, which Mr. R followed religiously. He used small doses of diazepam during the first two weeks and thereafter discontinued all medications and stopped abusing alcohol. After an informative conference on post-traumatic stress disorder, the burn unit staff became more aware of the genesis of this problem and its early symptoms. The issue about the staff nurse was not raised.

After three months of treatment, Mr. R's acute symptoms had diminished to the point where he was able to move out of his home and, with the help of his firemen buddies, into an apartment with his elderly mother. He did not show signs of a panic disorder or any hesitancy about returning to work in another couple of months, when his burn wounds would be healed more fully. Both group and individual treatment were stopped by mutual agreement, and the treatment was considered a success.

Three months after termination of treatment, the psychiatrist was told by the burn unit's head nurse that the staff nurse who had been involved with Mr. R had quit her job unexpectedly and had moved in with Mr. R and his mother. One year later the psychiatrist learned from another fireman admitted to the burn unit that Mr. R had not in fact returned to the fire department and was working part-time with the post office.

SUGGESTED READING

1. Horowitz, M. Stress response syndromes: Character style and dynamic psychotherapy. *Archives of General Psychiatry,* 31:768–781, 1974. (How a psychodynamic approach would be matched to this particular fireman's character style.)
2. Schnaper, N., & Cowley, R. A. Overview: Psychiatric sequelae to multiple trauma. *American Journal of Psychiatry,* 133:833–890, 1976. (How a consultant can approach the psychiatric sequelae in patients who have suffered severe trauma and been treated in intensive care units.)
3. Moses, R. Adult psychic trauma: The question of early predisposition and some detailed mechanisms. *International Journal of Psychoanalysis,* 59:353–363, 1978. (Though primarily addressing combat reactions, the author points out that one's vulnerability to post-traumatic complications is increased by character traits exemplified by the fireman presented above [poor self-esteem, estrangement, dependency, narcissistic preoccupation, etc.].)

VIII

Somatoform Disorders

■ SOMATIZATION DISORDER

30. The Case of the Suffering Lady

(Historical Case: Emil Kraepelin)

Authors' Note:
As mentioned earlier, Kraepelin is primarily acclaimed for distinguish-ing manic-depressive illness from dementia praecox and criticized for viewing the latter (schizophrenia) as an untreatable deteriorating ill-ness. He is less known for his detailed clinical descriptions of other kinds of psychiatric disorders, another one of which is presented here.

The young lady, aged 30, carefully dressed in black, who comes into the hall with short, shuffling steps, leaning on the nurse, and sinks into a chair as if exhausted, gives you the impression that she is ill. She is of slender build, her features are pale and rather painfully drawn, and her eyes are cast down. Her small, manicured fingers play nervously with a handkerchief. The patient answers the questions addressed to her in a low, tired voice, without looking up, and we find that she is quite clear about time, place, and her surroundings. After a few minutes, her eyes suddenly become convulsively shut, her head sinks forward, and she seems to have fallen into a deep sleep. Her arms have grown quite limp, and fall down as if palsied when you try to lift them. She has ceased to answer, and if you try to raise her eyelids, her eyes suddenly rotate upwards. Needlepricks only produce a slight shudder. But sprinkling with cold water is followed by a deep sigh; the patient starts up, opens her eyes, looks round her with surprise, and gradually comes to herself. She says that she has just had one of her sleeping attacks, from which she has suffered for seven years. They come on quite irregularly, often many in one day, and last from a few minutes to half an hour.

Concerning the history of her life, the patient tells us that . . . she was educated in convent schools, and passed the examination for teachers. As a young girl, she inhaled a great deal of chloroform, which she was able to get secretly, for toothache. She also suffered from headaches, until they were relieved by the removal of growths from the nose. She very readily became delirious in feverish illnesses. Thirteen years ago she took a place as governess in Holland, but soon began to be ill, and has passed the last seven years in different hospitals, except for a short interval when she was in a situation in Moravia.

It would appear from the statements of her relations and doctors that the patient has suffered from the most varied ailments, and been through the most remarkable courses of treatment. For violent abdominal pains and disturbances of menstruation, ascribed to stenosis of the cervical canal and retroflection of the uterus, recourse was had five years ago to the excision of the wedge supposed to cause the obstruction, and the introduction of a pessary. At a later period loss of voice and a contraction of the right forearm and the left thigh set in, and were treated with massage, electricity, bandaging, and stretching under an anaesthetic. Heart oppression and spasmodic breathing also appeared, with quickly passing disablements of various sets of muscles, disturbances of urination, diarrhea, and unpleasant sensations, now in one and now in another part of the body, but particularly headaches. Extraordinarily strong and sudden changes of mood were observed at the same time, with introspection and complaints of want of consideration in those about her and in her relations, although the latter had made the greatest sacrifices. Brine baths, Russian baths, pine-needle baths, electricity, country air, summer resorts, and, finally, residence on the Riviera—everything was tried, generally with only a brief improvement or with none at all.

The immediate cause of the patient being brought to the hospital was the increase in the "sleeping attacks" two years ago. They came on at last even when the patient was standing, and might continue for an hour. The patient did not fall down, but simply leaned against something. The attacks continued in the hospital, and spasmodic breathing was also observed, which could be influenced by suggestion.

After spending eight months here, the patient went away at first to her sister's. But after a few months she had to be taken to another asylum, where she stayed about a year, and then, after a short time spent with her family, came back to us.

During her present residence here, so-called great attacks have appeared, in addition to her previous troubles. We will try to produce such an attack by pressure on the very sensitive left ovarian region. After one or two minutes of moderately strong pressure, during which the patient shows sharp pain, her expression alters. She throws herself to and fro with her eyes shut, and screams to us loudly, generally in French, not to touch her. "You must not do anything to me, you hound, cochon, cochon!" She cries for help, pushes with her hands, and twists herself as if she were trying to escape from a sexual assault. Whenever she is touched, the excitement increases. Her whole body is strongly bent backwards. Suddenly the picture changes, and the patient begs piteously not to be cursed, and laments and sobs aloud. This condition, too, is very soon put to an end by sprinkling with cold water. The patient shudders, wakes with a deep sigh, and looks fixedly round, only making a tired, senseless impression. She cannot explain what has happened.

The physical examination of the patient shows no particular disturbances at present, except the abnormalities already mentioned. There is only a well-marked weakness, in consequence of which she often keeps to her bed or lies about. All her movements are limp and feeble, but there is no actual disablement anywhere. She often sleeps very badly. At times she wanders about in the night, wakes the nurses, and sends for the doctor. Her appetite is very poor, but she has a habit of nibbling between her meals at all kinds of cakes, fruit, and jam, which are sent to her, at her urgent request, by her relations.

With her growing expertness in illness, the emotional sympathies of the patient are more and more confined to the selfish furthering of her own wishes. She tries ruthlessly to extort the most careful attention from those around her, obliges the doctor to occupy himself with her by day or by night on the slightest occasion, is extremely sensitive to any supposed neglect, is jealous if preference is shown to other patients, and tries to make the attendants give in to her by complaints, accusations, and outbursts of temper. The sacrifices made by others, more especially by her family, are regarded quite as a matter of course, and her occasional prodigality of thanks only serves to pave the way for new demands. To secure the sympathy of those around her, she has recourse to more and more forcible descriptions of her physical and mental torments, histrionic exaggeration of her attacks, and the effective elucidation of her personal character. She calls herself the abandoned, the outcast, and in mysterious hints makes confession of horrible, delightful experiences and failings, which she will only confide to the discreet bosom of her very best friend, the doctor.

KRAEPELIN'S DIAGNOSIS

Hysterical insanity

DSM-III-R DIAGNOSIS

Axis I: Somatization disorder
Axis II: Histrionic personality disorder
Axis III: Retroflection of uterus with cervical stenosis; contraction of right forearm and left thigh
Axis IV: Stress—none known
Axis V: Highest level of functioning past year—poor (inability to meet even minimal responsibilities of hospital environment)

TREATMENT PROBLEM

Thirty-year-old former governess who since adolescence has suffered multiple somatic problems that have been primarily psychogenic in origin. For the past seven years she has been unable to function for any sustained period outside a hospital environment and even in the hospital finds the minimal demands at times intolerable.

DISCUSSION OF TREATMENT SELECTION

Setting. The history suggests that hospitalization has been more harmful than helpful in treating this patient. It has permitted her to relinquish daily responsibilities, maintain a sick role, and focus on her somatic problems. This regression, despite limit-setting and prodding by the staff, is likely to continue in an inpatient environment. Although outpatient treatment is the eventual goal, a day hospital and then a halfway house will probably be necessary as transitional settings. If the discharge from the hospital is too abrupt a "weaning," the patient may experience more or new somatic complaints which will perhaps make her, the doctors, and her family insist on another hospitalization and make all concerned even less willing to face the problems of remobilizing her to more independent living.

Format. The patient's family has shown a continuing concern. Over the years they have provided her with private hospitalization, summer resorts, and a residence on the Riviera. They have even responded to her "urgent requests" for cakes, fruit, and jam. Family sessions are clearly indicated to inform these relatives that despite their good intentions, the patient's psychological need to assume a sick role may actually be reinforced by their generous response to her demands. The family will also need to be taught specifically how to deal with the patient when she has "a sleeping attack" or a similar kind of psychologically induced symptom. They should not assume responsibility for either preventing the illness behavior or relieving the distress; rather, they should indicate to the patient in an empathic and concerned way that while they are sorry she is suffering and hope she manages a recovery soon, they also have other responsibilities and must live their own lives despite her illness. The family may view this approach as cruel and as if they are "ignoring" the patient's problems. The therapist can then explain that infantilizing the patient in the end will be even more cruel because she will continue to lead a limited and suffering existence, and that limit-setting can be done in a gentle and loving way if one doesn't feel guilty about it.

Including the patient in some of these family sessions will indicate to her what she can expect and will provide an opportunity for the therapist to point out how the family instantly tries to relieve the patient's suffering. Using the therapist as a model, the family will learn to tolerate the anxiety and anger that occur when the patient's unreasonable demands are not met. Unless the family can tolerate these feelings within sessions, they are unlikely to participate in a treatment plan that will necessarily at times make the patient anxious and resentful. The family has the potential of sabotaging any treatment by indefinitely providing for the patient and supporting her hospitalization and medical care. The patient will probably accept changes in her treatment only after family members indicate to her in no uncertain terms that they will no longer continue to support the current infantilizing approach.

In addition to family sessions, group therapy will be helpful for this patient. Since her current "illness behavior" is so demanding, she would probably not accept or be accepted by a heterogeneous group. Such a group might ridicule the patient for her irresponsibility and immature self-preoccupations. A homogeneous group consisting of hypochondriacal patients might offer more compassion and understanding for this patient and, at the same time, would broaden her interpersonal sharing so that she is no longer only confiding "to the discrete bosom of her very best friend, the doctor." Clearly these individual sessions with the doctor may fuel the regression. Although such sessions may never be totally eliminated, they should probably be used more sparingly and not as the primary mode of intervention.

Duration and Frequency. This young woman has spent over half her life seeking and receiving medical care. Although one is tempted (partly out of frustration) to design a time-limited treatment in hopes that a set date of termination will force the patient to relinquish her regressive behavior, it is unlikely that she now has the capacity to tolerate this plan. Years of hospitalization and assuming the sick role have restricted her internal and external resources. The threat of being forced "to grow up" may make her so overwhelmingly anxious about being abandoned that her somatic symptoms will only increase.

An alternative approach would be to relieve any fears of abandonment by indicating that the duration of treatment will be "as long as necessary," but that the frequency of sessions will be reset at fixed intervals and will not be increased even if psychosomatic complaints arise during the interim between sessions. However, if the patient wishes to try something new and difficult or discuss some accomplishments she has achieved that are unrelated to medical complaints (resuming her job as a governess, beginning to date, living apart from her family, applying for a teaching position, etc.), an increased frequency of sessions will make sense and will reinforce this more adaptive behavior.

Approach. Every effort should be made to address this patient's strengths and not her weaknesses. She apparently is a bright woman (she passed the examination to become a teacher) so that appealing to her intellect might provide a good start. Specifically, she could be told her DSM-III-R diagnosis and how her loss of voice, loss of consciousness, loss of memory, loss of appetite, seizures, muscle weakness, dysuria, dysmenorrhea, abdominal pain, chest pain, and shortness of breath are all consistent with a somatization disorder. If interested, she could read the research literature regarding her illness and negotiate more actively in the treatment plan. This didactic approach would help form a working alliance with the therapist on a more mature level.

Predictive interpretations might also be helpful in indicating to the patient that she is experiencing a well-described syndrome as opposed to a diagnostic dilemma. For example, the therapist could state in advance that in the future he will not be responding to many of the patient's physical complaints because any response might reinforce her maintaining the sick role and accruing its secondary gain. The therapist could also state that he predicts that when he does not respond to her somatic complaints, the patient will feel rejected and present with more somatic complaints and/or seek attention elsewhere. The value of this kind of predictive interpretation is that if and when this behavior does occur, the therapist will have some leverage; he can remind the patient that this pattern had been forecasted and often occurs with her particular kind of emotional illness. In this way, the therapist grants the patient her illness (somatization disorder), does not appear cold and rejecting, and yet prevents reinforcing the patient's sick role.

In addition to not responding automatically and immediately to the patient's somatic complaints, the therapist can try to limit physical examinations, doctor's appointments, and even discussion of somatic complaints. Instead, he can concentrate on other aspects of the patient's external and internal life. Although the therapist will need to be empathic, especially in regard to the secondary loss that has resulted from her psychological illness, he should try to avoid being too warm and sympathetic. Being too responsive might encourage the very regression that treatment is designed to prevent. Furthermore, the patient is capable of providing a myriad of psychological symptoms to compound her somatic complaints. Nothing will be gained if she changes labels from a medical to a designated psychiatric patient, but remains stuck in a sick role. For this reason, an exploratory approach that encourages the patient to reflect too much on herself—her feelings and fears and fantasies—should be postponed until she is more engaged in the real world with a job, relationships, and pleasurable activities. Prevocational training and role-playing both can be helpful in teaching the patient those professional and social skills she has never acquired, or lost, due to her lengthy hospitalizations and the doting care provided by family and medical personnel.

Somatic Treatment. At present the patient has no psychiatric disorder for which psychotropic medications are indicated. Even starting a benzodiazepine for her anxiety runs the risk of reinforcing illness-seeking behavior and dependency rather than helping her master life's inevitable struggles.

SUGGESTED READING

1. Woodruff, R. A., Clayton, P. J., & Guze, S. B. Hysterical studies of diagnosis, outcome and prevalence. *Journal of the American Medical Association*, 215:425–

428, 1971. (Summarizes the research that clustered various symptoms and signs into Briquet's syndrome, a somatization disorder.)

2. Maxmen, J. S., Tucker, G. J., & LeBow, M. *Rational Hospital Psychiatry: The Reactive Environment.* New York: Brunner/Mazel, 1974. (Describes specifically how the inpatient staff can be instructed to reverse the regressive and reinforcing patterns established by Kraepelin's suffering lady.)

3. Sacks, M. H., & Carpenter, W. T. The pseudotherapeutic community: An examination of anti-therapeutic forces on psychiatric units. *Hospital & Community Psychiatry,* 25:315–318, 1974. (Describes how a psychiatric inpatient staff can covertly sabotage an effective therapeutic milieu.)

■ CONVERSION DISORDER

31. The Case of the Powerless Priest

Father A, a 37-year-old priest at a metropolitan parish, was admitted to a general hospital for the first time after the sudden onset of numbness and weakness in both arms. Because the "long-sleeve" distribution of sensory loss was nonanatomical and because an exhaustive search failed to disclose a neurological cause, psychiatric consultation was requested.

During the evaluation, Father A was seen to be a soft-spoken, effeminate man whose solicitous manner conveyed a boyish quality. With notable detachment bordering on indifference, he gave a tediously detailed account of how his symptoms began: After conducting early morning mass and having "a few words" with the elderly senior priest, Father A was returning to his study when suddenly he felt "powerless" in both arms, whereupon he informed the senior priest that he would be unable to conduct services until further notice. Father A was especially apologetic because the senior priest would now not be able to leave for an extended vacation that was planned to begin that evening. When his symptoms failed to resolve the following day, Father A took a taxi to the emergency room where the diagnostic possibility of a serious spinal cord disease led to his prompt admission.

Two additional psychiatric interviews with the patient and a telephone conversation with the senior priest were necessary before some of the determinants of the patient's symptoms could be clarified: Whereas Father A described himself as a "thorough" worker, he was regarded by others as a colorless plodder whose procrastination and adherence to detail were infuriating—though his meek and polite manner made him seem well intentioned and prevented others from getting angry at him in any face-to-face confrontations. After many months of seething, the senior priest admonished Father A for his many delays in filing a particular financial report and suggested that he would spend his vacation deciding whether Father A would be recommended to assume the responsibility of the senior priest as originally planned or whether a replacement should be found. This unusual encounter occurred only a few minutes before the onset of symptoms.

Although Father A acknowledged during the psychiatric interview that he might have been "slightly annoyed," he saw no connection between the "words" of the senior priest and the ensuing weakness which had rendered him powerless. On the contrary, Father A recalled that at the time the symptoms began, he suspected that they were due to either a flareup of the poliomeylitis he had as a child or perhaps a heart attack—he remembered that his father had strange feelings in his arms a few hours before he died of a myocardial infarction. In recalling his father's death, Father A became quite tearful. Further exploration disclosed that Father A has always felt guilty because a bitter argument (in which he almost struck his father) had occurred the day before his father died.

Despite some obvious parallels between the patient's relationship with his father and with the senior priest (resentment of a harsh authority figure; a wish to strike out angrily but a fear of causing harm and of retaliation; a passive-aggressive expression of defiance; a longing for a tender relationship to replace the chronic bitterness), Father A was impervious to psychological issues. In fact, he was by nature a man who thought and lived in only the most concrete terms, a characteristic which no doubt contributed to his limitations as a priest.

DSM-III-R DIAGNOSIS

 Axis I: Conversion disorder
 Axis II: Passive-aggressive and compulsive personality disorders
 Axis III: None
 Axis IV: Stress—moderate (argument with authority figure)
 Axis V: Highest level of functioning past year—fair

TREATMENT PROBLEM

Acute psychogenic numbness and weakness of the arms in a man who lacks psychological insight.

DISCUSSION OF TREATMENT SELECTION

Unlike many patients with suspected psychogenic symptoms, Father A's conversion disorder is diagnostically straightforward: An extensive neurologic evaluation has ruled out a pathophysiological mechanism, and there is a close temporal relationship between the onset of symptoms and the environmental stimulus (a confrontation with the senior priest the day of his pending vacation). Moreover, in terms of primary gain, the "powerlessness" of the arms unconsciously resolves several intrapsychic conflicts: It prevents the "son" from hitting the "father" which would lead to both guilt and fear of retaliation; it also enables the "son" to be cared for by the "father" and not be abandoned, while at the same time the symptoms passive-aggressively frustrate the "father" and express the hostility towards him. In terms of secondary gain, the symptoms provide attention and care from surrogate figures and excuse Father A from those responsibilities he finds burdensome. The past determinants are also apparent in this case: somatic compliance (childhood polio) and sympathetic identification (father's weakness in the arms).

Although the diagnosis and psychodynamics are unusually clear in this case, selection of an effective treatment presents more of a problem. The therapeutic aim is first to find a face-saving way of promptly removing the symptoms before the secondary gain reinforces the conversion disorder and makes it more refractory to treatment, and before the secondary loss (such as the resentment of others towards him and the inability to work) complicates the problem and possibly leads to demoralization and a secondary depression.

Setting. The setting will initially be in the general hospital with plans for outpatient treatment as soon as possible to diminish the secondary loss and gain.

Format. The format will be an individual treatment. Although some might consider involving the senior priest in one or two "family" sessions, this format increases the risk of revealing deep resentments in both parties that would jeopardize their future working relationship. Furthermore, the "family" format might further infantilize the patient. Because the patient's problem primarily involves the intrapersonal system, an individual format is the preferred choice.

Duration and Frequency. By indicating that treatment for the numbness and weakness will require "a matter of days," the therapist can intercept any possible regression and indirectly diminish the potential secondary loss and gain. If the patient accepts the recommendation for psychotherapy to work on his underlying characterological problems, the duration of treatment will be extended—but this recommendation to extend treatment would best be made after the immediate conversion reaction has resolved. Sessions during the initial phase of treatment should be scheduled frequently, consistent with the treatment of an acute medical problem that requires prompt daily visits of limited duration (15–20 minutes). Longer sessions scheduled less frequently would be used if and when the patient entered psychotherapy for his more chronic interpersonal difficulties.

Approach. In the initial stages of treatment, neither exploratory nor experiential methods are likely to be effective. The patient is not at all psychologically-minded and may only experience psychodynamic interpretations as a belittling way of not taking his "illness" seriously. Those experiential treatments which rely primarily on empathy and positive regard might foster further regression and provide reinforcing secondary gain without directly addressing the secondary loss. Directive medical and behavioral techniques would therefore be the preferred approach; by having Father A play a role in his recovery, these techniques would provide him with a face-saving means towards recovery and a sense of mastery, and would not be infantilizing. The behavioral techniques would need to be presented in a rather objective, even detached, fashion; if the directives are presented too personally by an authority figure, Father A's passive-aggressive defiance might be mobilized, and any treatment would be sabotaged. In the event that Father A is unwilling or unable to actively participate in any directive approaches and instead remains passively and concretely fixed in the sick role, then hypnosis or amytal interviews may be used to facilitate a catharsis and suggest away the conversion symptoms. These techniques might be more acceptable to Father A because they appear to be impersonal somatic methods performed "on" him without his having to assume direct responsibility.

CHOICE AND OUTCOME

Assuming a matter-of-fact stance, the psychiatric consultant informed the patient that neurologic and psychiatric evaluations had concluded that the "illness" was the result of "bodily tension" that was caused by "certain stresses." Sensing no interest in the patient to explore what those "stresses" were, the psychiatrist did not elaborate further, but simply stated that Father A's kind of problem in most cases responded promptly to physical therapy and relaxation techniques. Accordingly, with the understanding and support of the hospital staff, Father A was transferred to the rehabilitation service where he was given deep massage and placed in a comprehensive exercise program. While avoiding any discussion of Father A's personal problems, the physical therapists constantly offered encouragement and told him how well he was doing.

In addition, a psychologist with an expertise in biofeedback was introduced to the patient by the psychiatrist and appointments were made for outpatient treatment. Biofeedback met many of the therapeutic objectives: It provided an intervention that was both face-saving and acceptable to the patient; it provided a transition from an inpatient to an outpatient treatment so that an early discharge from the hospital could be implemented; it provided a surrogate father figure (the psychologist) to be available during the senior priest's vacation; it provided a detached "objective" treatment that would not be perceived as "psychiatric" and that would not mobilize the patient's passive-aggressive defenses; it forced the patient to be a participant in the treatment and thereby not foster further regression; it offered a somatic treatment that would appeal to the patient's concrete cognitive style in place of other kinds of somatic treatment (e.g., mild tranquilizers), which might only reinforce his chronic dependency and feelings of being inadequate; and finally, most ambitiously, the biofeedback treatment offered the possibility of being a preliminary step towards engaging the patient in a longer-term exploratory treatment to help him with his characterological problems.

The patient was discharged from the rehabilitation service after three days with a 70% reduction in his weakness and numbness. Over the next three weeks, Father A attended seven biofeedback sessions. As he focused on the galvanic meter and auditory signals to "learn" how to reduce tension in his neck and arms, Father A was reassured by the psychologist that this capacity to "relieve spasm" would soon resolve any residual weakness in the arms. Indeed, his symptoms were gradually "cured." Though the suggestion was then made that the patient examine the "stresses" that had led to the "tension," Father A decided instead to terminate treatment, feeling fully satisfied with the results. No further follow-up is available.

SUGGESTED READING

1. Freud, S. (1893). Some points for a comparative study of organic and hysterical motor paralyses. In J. Strachey (Ed.), *Standard Edition*, 1:160–172. London: Hogarth Press, 1966. (Though written almost a century ago, this article remains a helpful clinical guide for distinguishing physical from psychogenic disorders.)
2. Chodoff, P., & Lyons, H. Hysteria, the hysterical personality, and "hysterical" conversion. *American Journal of Psychiatry*, 144:734–740, 1958. (As is true with the patient presented above, the authors demonstrate that so-called "hysterical" reactions occur frequently in patients who do not have hysterical personality traits.)

3. Haley, J. *Uncommon Therapy: The Psychiatric Techniques of Milton H. Erickson, M.D.* New York: Norton, 1973.
4. Grinder, J., Delozier, J., & Bandler, R. *Patterns of Hypnotic Techniques of Milton H. Erickson, M.D.* Vol. II, pp. 1–115. Cupertino, CA: Meta Publications, 1977. (These last two references describe the indirect, nonverbal strategies prescribed by Erickson—how they are used and why they work.)

■ HYPOCHONDRIASIS

32. The Case of the Complaining Civil Servant

Consultation was requested for Miss K, a 47-year-old civil servant admitted to a general hospital because of epigastric pain. The written reason for the psychiatric consultation was: "Please evaluate for supratentorial overlay" (medical jargon for physical complaints that are presumed to have a major psychological component). The unstated problem became immediately clear when the psychiatrist arrived on the ward and spoke with the staff. The patient was a "crock" and "driving everyone up the wall." The head nurse was angry that the patient had ever been hospitalized. She believed Miss K had been "dumped" by the patient's private physician who had pressured the residents to admit Miss K and now wanted no part in her hospital care or following her after discharge.

According to the treating intern, throughout her week of hospitalization the patient had shown no physical signs to indicate an acute abdomen, only severe unrelenting pain which was variably described as burning, cutting, piercing, and which varied as well in location from moment to moment. The intern described how Miss K moaned and groaned about the pain during the entire time the medical history was being taken. These complaints would stop only when the patient was given an opportunity to complain about some other vague and chronic problem in another organ system. Indeed, her entire life consisted of an endless series of evaluations, physicians, hospitalizations, and medications to the point that she had a four-volume medical chart and was diagnosed as having sinusitis, hiatus hernia, irritable colon, hemorrhoids, low back pain, contact dermatitis, tension headaches, varicose veins, and adhesions secondary to exploratory abdominal surgery. For these problems she was taking buffered aspirin, diazepam, various laxatives, chloral hydrate, "allergy shots," Fiorinal, antacids, codeine, and a pharmacopoeia of topical lotions.

During at least three of her previous hospitalizations, she had been seen by psychiatric consultants but had refused to follow through with their recommendations for outpatient psychotherapy. On this occasion, she had screamed the intern out of the room when he informed the patient that "somebody to talk to" would be dropping by.

The consultant suspected that the patient's outrage at seeing a psychiatrist might be due to her perception (in part correct) that all the medical staff wanted was to get rid of Miss K by sending her off to psychiatry. To counter this suspicion, the psychiatrist asked the intern to introduce him to the patient and sit with him for at least some of the evaluation. He agreed.

Miss K was not much different from the way she had been described. With grey hair knotted back tightly in a bun, she had the manner and appearance of an irate school teacher demanding attention from an unresponsive class. She considered psychiatry in general and the consultant in particular to be irrelevant to her many somatic problems. Her dismissal of any psychological issues in her life was indicated by her complete disavowal that stress might make her symptoms worse, or even that her many physical problems might from time to time have made her feel either discouraged or upset. On the contrary, every distressing affect was only experienced in physical terms—an ache here, a tightness there.

During the history-taking, a slight suggestion of sadness did surface as she talked about the prolonged fatal illess of her mother when Miss K was in her early adolescent years, and later during the interview the patient also acknowledged that she was occasionally "lonely" living by herself, working in an isolated small office, and having no friends. The acknowledgment of this loneliness was perfunctory and, in her view, absolutely no reason to change her lifestyle. All she wanted was relief from her many medical problems: "Just 24 hours of relief! Is that too much to ask?"

DSM-III-R DIAGNOSIS

AXIS I: Hypochondriasis; possible "masked" major mood disorder
AXIS II: Possible schizoid personality disorder
AXIS III: Multiple minor medical problems
AXIS IV: Stress—mild (recent hospitalization)
AXIS V: Highest level of functioning past year—fair (isolated and friendless life, frequent medical appointments interfering with job performance)

TREATMENT PROBLEM

A middle-aged single woman preoccupied with real or imagined physical problems. She is constantly dissatisfied with her medical care ("doctor-shopping"), feels rejected by her medical caregivers, and does not acknowledge possible psychogenic determinants of her complaints and the need for psychiatric help.

DISCUSSION OF TREATMENT SELECTION

Miss K presents a problem all too familiar to the medical profession. She wants to be cared for by doctors, yet she behaves in such a way that doctors do not want to care for her. Furthermore, she is unable to acknowledge that she develops physical complaints partly for psychological and interpersonal reasons and that her behavior with physicians must change if she is ever going to elicit a different response. This situation is made worse because Miss K views any contact with psychiatry as a rejection by her medical doctors. She is convinced that by making such a referral, they believe she is either crazy or feigning her symptoms. For this reason, if possible, a nonpsychiatric physician should be designated as the primary physician responsible for treating both her physical and psychological problems. This physician could then consult with a psychiatrist as necessary. If Miss K is sufficiently reassured that she will not be abandoned by the primary physician, she may agree to see a psychiatrist in consultation for specific problems, such as adjustment of psychotropic medication.

Setting. There is no doubt that the patient should be treated whenever possible as an outpatient. Repeated hospitalizations are destructive. They frustrate the patient, enrage caregivers, limit her vocational and personal life, are not cost-effective, and help maintain a lifelong pattern of seeking a relationship through physical complaints.

Format. In the most narrow sense, individual treatment is the only option. Miss K has no relatives to participate in any kind of family treatment and at this time she would never agree to be in either a heterogeneous group or a homogeneous group composed of psychosomatic patients (the latter would probably be the best choice if only she would agree to it). In a broader sense, however, the format might be a kind of "surrogate family treatment" if the psychiatrist in a liaison capacity could monitor the doctor-patient relationship and help it proceed more smoothly.

Duration and Frequency. These aspects of treatment deserve particular attention. For patients such as Miss K, the time component may
have the strongest therapeutic impact. Because hypochondriacal patients are usually not psychologically-minded and can rarely become
engaged in an exploratory treatment, little is known about their psychodynamics and why they choose physical symptoms to sustain a hostile-
dependent relationship with physicians.

It is known, however, that the history of many hypochondriacal
patients reveals a serious childhood illness or a relationship during childhood with an important figure who was chronically ill and perhaps died
(such as Miss K's mother). One dynamic speculation is that Miss K
identifies with her lost mother to maintain a relationship with her.
Whenever a physician offers reassurance that the symptoms are "nothing to worry about," the patient unconsciously hears this statement as, "I
am well; I am not like the loved one I have lost; I therefore am a separate
person and am alone." To counteract this form of "separation anxiety,"
the patient then produces other symptoms to try to convince the care-
giver that one or another illness is still present and that she still requires
attention.

No doubt other psychodynamic explanations for hypochondriacal
behavior are more or less operative in each individual patient (learned
helplessness, narcissistic preoccupation, self-boundary diffusion, etc.).
The advantage of the "separation anxiety" dynamic is that it not only
explains the behavior, but also suggests a possible therapeutic approach
for some patients. Specifically, if Miss K is concerned about being abandoned and if she uses physical symptoms to maintain an attachment, it
follows that she will be more relieved if "guaranteed" a prolonged relationship with a physician than if proclaimed as "cured." For this reason,
the implied duration as established early in treatment should go beyond
being openended and, by implication, should be lifelong. Miss K may
have far less need to experience somatic complaints if she is reassured of
a continuing relationship with the physician even when her complaints
and pains are not prominent. A more ambitious goal—changing her
need to maintain this attachment—can be deferred (perhaps indefinitely)
until a sustained relationship has been established.

In terms of frequency of sessions, until the patient becomes convinced that she will not be abandoned, sessions may need to be quite
frequent, as often as two or three times a week, so that ideally the patient
will be seen by the physician *before* rather than *after* new symptoms arise.

In terms of duration of individual sessions, the time can be quite
brief. Typically, hypochondriacal patients have a difficult time leaving
the doctor's office. They come up with a new complaint or question to

prolong the contact no matter how long the doctor has already spent with them. There is little value in spending extended periods of time with these patients. Regardless of the length, they will rarely feel that they have gotten enough. Furthermore, as the individual sessions drag on, the doctor is understandably liable to become frustrated and annoyed and then indicate his anger directly or indirectly (which, of course, only increases the patient's fear of being rejected and need to experience physical symptoms). A preferable approach is to indicate right from the start that sessions will only be 10-20 minutes. When a patient tests this limit by presenting a new complaint, the doctor can reassuringly but firmly state, "Fortunately, we will have an opportunity to talk about that question next time. We will have to stop for now."

Approach. Exploratory treatments are rarely effective until a prolonged and trusting relationship has been established. Premature interpretations, or even clarifications of psychological issues, will at best be dismissed and at worst make the patient suspicious that the doctor is not taking the somatic complaints seriously. In the same way, behavioral techniques are usually unacceptable to these patients because their maladaptive behavior is ego-syntonic and does not produce sufficient psychic pain to motivate them to change these behaviors. Experiential and interpersonal techniques are therefore the preferred choice; specifically, the physician can indicate an empathic understanding of the patient's physical distress and worries while making few interventions that indicate that the cause might be psychological or that a particular kind of behavior should be changed. Again, techniques aimed at changing character style and behavior can be tried at a future date when and if the patient appears more receptive.

Somatic Treatment. Antidepressants are an important consideration even if the patient does not describe the dysphoria associated with a major mood disorder. Miss K may have what has been termed a "masked" depression. Because at least some of these patients seem unable to describe their psychological state ("alexithymia") and because their description of possible vegetative symptoms and signs are suspect, the effectiveness of antidepressants—or any other psychotropic medication—is hard to assess directly and may have to be determined indirectly by such changes as a diminution in physical complaints, medical appointments, or irritable behavior.

The risk of a trial of antidepressants also must be considered. Hypochondriacal patients often exaggerate the mild side effects and/or do not comply with the therapeutic regimen, unconsciously fearing that the drugs will remove the physical symptoms they maintain for psychological reasons. Conversely, once this or any other medication is started, hypochondriacal patients may become magically attached to it and are reluctant to stop the drug, symbolically viewing any discontinuation as another abandonment. For this reason, any new medication for Miss K must be prescribed cautiously, especially for those drugs that can produce physical dependence (such as the benzodiazepines or opioids) or can produce somatic problems from chronic misuse (such as laxatives or steroid topical creams).

CHOICE AND OUTCOME

Fortuitously, the psychiatric consultant who saw Miss K happened to be writing his residency graduation paper on hypochondriasis and was far more interested in the management of her problems than the average psychiatric consultant. Applying the psychodynamic speculations outlined above, he agreed with Miss K that psychiatric treatment would most likely not be acceptable or helpful at this time. What she needed was a continuing relationship with an internist who would see her regularly to make sure that her physical symptoms were being closely watched. He added that up until now she had not been able to establish this kind of working relationship with a physician and that he was not sure exactly why. He asked Miss K if he might be permitted to attend her visits with the medical doctor in order to help the *doctor* sustain an adequate working relationship. Though skeptical, Miss K consented. The intern, somewhat intrigued by this manipulation, agreed to follow Miss K in his outpatient clinic (the intern was also influenced by what he perceived to be coercion from Miss K's former private internist, a prominent figure in the training hospital, who no longer wanted to follow the patient himself).

For several months Miss K's treatment went well. She left the hospital shortly after the treatment plan was arranged and at first saw the intern with the psychiatrist three times a week for 20 minutes. When Miss K felt more reassured that she would not be abandoned, the frequency of sessions was gradually decreased over a period of months to one session every other week. In her view, the sessions were never long enough. At times she had to be taken by the arm and actually ushered from the office. Miss K otherwise was more pleased with the treatment than any she could ever recall.

In an attempt to decrease the number of medications she was taking, new safer "medications" were substituted for old, less safe medications; for example, she was given a multivitamin tablet in place of her diazepam.

No "p.r.n." medications were prescribed in the belief that she should take the medications regularly (such as relatively inert creams and lotions) rather than "having to get sick" in order to take a drug. Under this plan, eventually she was taking one or another vitamin in safe dosages throughout the day at rigidly scheduled times rather than a random, haphazard array of unnecessary and potentially dangerous drugs.

With the help of the psychiatrist, the intern learned how to respond to Miss K's many somatic complaints. Instead of stating that her symptoms were nothing to worry about, he learned to respond by saying, "Yes, that is something we will have to keep a close eye on to make sure it does not become any more serious." By the third month of treatment, the psychiatrist did not attend these medical visits, and there was no indication that his presence was missed by Miss K. The intern, too, was now comfortable applying this treatment approach with its limited goals, namely, to decrease her absenteeism from work and her intermittent hospitalizations. Even when the intern became a resident the following year and had a choice to stop following Miss K, he continued to see her, for he, too, found the treatment rewarding.

Miss K's list of complaints and medications continued to decrease as the relationship with the intern developed further. For the first time in many years, Miss K had gone over six months without presenting herself in the emergency room or being admitted to a general hospital for a suspected acute illness or for a surgical procedure. During her visits she even seemed relatively pleasant and would from time to time talk about something other than her physical problems, e.g., staying with a distant aunt over the holidays.

Unfortunately, the case does not have a very happy ending, but it does illustrate how the availability of a caring therapist (or lack thereof) can make all the difference: Miss K and the intern did not grow old together. Instead, the doctor eventually left the city to pursue further training. Despite his attempts and the attempts of the psychiatrist to convince another physician to assume a similar kind of therapy with Miss K, there were no takers. She began showing up more and more frequently in the emergency room complaining of this or that, was evaluated in a cursory fashion by the resentful physicians on call, and eventually (to the satisfaction of all concerned) decided to seek help for her problems elsewhere.

SUGGESTED READING

1. Barsky, A. J., & Klerman, G. L. Overview: Hypochondriasis, bodily complaints, and somatic styles. *American Journal of Psychiatry,* 140:273–283, 1983.

(An excellent review of the literature that summarizes the confusing conceptual, diagnostic, and therapeutic approaches towards those with "amplifying somatic styles.")

2. Richards, A. D. Self-theory, conflict theory and the problem of hypochondriasis. *Psychoanalytic Study of the Child*, 36:319–337, 1981. (How the fragility of hypochondriacal patients must be considered in designing a treatment plan.)

3. Meador, B., & Rogers, C. R. Client-centered therapy. In R. Corsini (Ed.), *Current Psychotherapies* (2nd ed.). Itasca, IL: Peacock, 1979, pp. 119–165. (Describes this form of experiential therapy and how it contrasts with the manipulative or rejecting approaches often attempted with hypochondriacal patients like Miss K.)

IX

Sexual Disorders

■ **MALE ERECTILE DISORDER**

33. The Case of the Frustrated Sports Fan

Mr. Y, a 53-year-old shipping clerk, was referred for psychiatric consultation by his endocrinologist because of sexual impotence. In making the referral, the endocrinologist explained that Mr. Y was originally seen three years ago because of visual changes secondary to a benign pituitary tumor. After two surgical procedures and replacement medication, Mr. Y's hormonal status was now considered normal but his sexual impotence, which had begun insidiously 15 years before, had not improved.

Mr. Y greeted the consultant in the waiting room with a firm handshake. He did not look like a man who was physically ill. In fact, his bulky build and gruff voice gave him a rather formidable appearance. When Mr. Y came into the office, however, his manner changed. He took a distant seat in the corner and, obviously anxious, waited for the consultant to take the lead.

On the basis of the referral, the consultant presumed Mr. Y had come to discuss his impotence and therefore spent the first half of the session taking a sexual history. The impotence had begun insidiously 10 to 15 years ago for no known reason. As was his style, Mr. Y dealt with the problem by not dealing with it. He simply stopped attempting to have sex with his wife and did not discuss the problem with her. After several months without any sexual relations at all, his wife made some tentative inquiries. When Mr. Y confessed to "a little trouble," she suggested that he have a medical evaluation.

Many more months passed without sex, without further discussion, and without a search for the cause of the problem. A few times Mr. Y tried to masturbate, but when he was impotent with self-stimulation as well, he just tried to put the difficulty out of his mind and to proceed through the day-to-day course of his life—going to the factory, then to the bar for a few beers with the guys, then home for dinner with his wife and two teenage sons, then typically out to some sports event or watching one on television. He became even more resigned to his impotence a few years later when, at the age of 45, he saw an internist for a required physical examination when switching from one factory to another. He mentioned his impotence to the doctor, who could find nothing wrong and recommended a psychiatric evaluation. Mr. Y reflexively dismissed the idea of seeing a "shrink" and, though inwardly disheartened that no pill could solve the problem, kept these feelings to himself.

Five years later, now age 50, Mr. Y began to suffer excruciating headaches, which he again characteristically tried to ignore. When he also began to notice at ball games that he could not see the entire field of play (because of a peripheral visual field deficit), he was significantly frightened over the idea of going blind that he did seek medical help. After a series of evaluations and referrals, a pituitary brain tumor was diagnosed and surgically and medically treated. When last tested several months ago, his hormone levels were normal, but the impotence had not improved. At the time the diagnosis of a pituitary tumor was originally made, Mr. Y believed that the impotence would no longer be a problem after treatment was completed. That wish has not come true. Mr. Y still does not have erections during sleep or at least he has not awakened with an erection in over 10 years.

The consultant, after acquiring this information by structured questions throughout the first portion of the interview, felt fairly confident about how to proceed and shared these ideas with Mr. Y. The first step would be a review of the medical report to ensure that the necessary tests, including androgen levels, were normal. Some of these tests might have to be repeated since Mr. Y had not had a complete evaluation in the past few months. Other new tests might need to be conducted as well, including sleep studies to determine if an erection was present at night. If the tests indicated the problem was physical, the next step would be to treat the underlying cause. Even if these treatments were unsuccessful, perhaps Mr. Y would consider a urological procedure to insert one of the newer prosthetic devices for his problem. On the other hand, if the problem also had psychological components, the evaluation would include the consultant's meeting with Mr. Y and his wife to obtain a more detailed sexual history. Recommendations for psychotherapy could then be made.

Mr. Y appeared somewhat distracted as these various options were being outlined. He waited for the consultant to finish before mentioning "another slight problem": Three weeks ago his wife had unexpectedly asked for a separation; a few days ago, at her insistence, he had moved out of the house and now was temporarily living with his elderly mother. With this confession Mr. Y erupted into tears and sobbed intermittently throughout the rest of the interview as the consultant learned, too late, the real reason Mr. Y had come. The endocrinologist had actually recommended months before that Mr. Y see a psychiatrist for his impotence. As in the past, Mr. Y had rejected the idea but now, out of desperation, he hoped that if he could find a rapid solution to his impotence, he might be able to convince his wife the marriage was not over.

Other than his prolonged sexual problem, Mr. Y could imagine no other reason why she would leave. Her only stated reason was that they had "grown apart over the years." Mr. Y was not even sure what his wife meant by such a comment, except that she preferred to go to concerts rather than sporting events. Only when asked specifically did Mr. Y mention that his wife had left once before several years ago when he got in serious debt because of gambling on sporting events. After they both attended meetings of Gamblers Anonymous together for several months, he stopped betting, his wife returned, and now, through regularly scheduled monthly payments, he had almost cleared his debts.

The consultant sensed that he was not getting the full story; it was as though suddenly out of the blue his wife after 26 years of marriage decided to leave without any clear reason. When the consultant shared this impression, Mr. Y simply shrugged and said that he was answering the questions as best he could. The consultant then asked for permission to contact Mrs. Y and tried to phone her at work while Mr. Y was still present in the office. He learned that Mrs. Y, an executive secretary, would not be available for a couple of hours, so he left a message for her to call back.

The remaining few minutes of the first session were spent obtaining a personal history to put Mr. Y's problems in perspective. He had been raised in a large Polish, Catholic family during the Depression. His father, a bitter and rageful alcoholic, died when Mr. Y was in his early teens—a death that was more a relief than a loss. For financial reasons, Mr. Y quit high school to work, then enlisted in the army at age 17. There he had his first sexual encounters, "one-night stands" during his leaves. He met and married his wife during his mid-twenties and had never been unfaithful, or even thought of it, through all these years. Along with the current threatening loss of his wife, he also feels sad that his two sons, now in their early twenties, have less and less to do with their father, no longer respect his authority, and do not accept his extremely conservative political views. The consultant, convinced that Mr. Y does not have a major depression or suicidal ideas in reaction to the separation, ended the session with arrangements for an appointment the following week.

Mrs. Y phoned the consultant a few hours after Mr. Y left. On the phone she sounded like an articulate, candid, and distraught woman who was pleased that her husband was now making some attempt to get help. She confided at once that she had been dissatisfied with the marriage for years but chose to stay with Mr. Y until the children had finished high school. Her secret plans were then changed; only months before the younger son graduated, Mr. Y became ill with his brain tumor and Mrs. Y decided that she could not in good conscience leave until he was in better health. When the endocrinologist recently pronounced Mr. Y as "cured," she felt less guilty about now separating from a man for whom she had lost all tender feelings. Although she loved her husband during the early phases of the marriage, she found his hard-nosed and bitter attitude—towards work, the privileged class, the spoiled kids of the me-generation—intolerable. She appreciated that his machismo, his fanaticism over sports and his extreme right-wing beliefs were no doubt partly due to his occupational and sexual failures, but she nevertheless resented his demeaning attitude towards her, his lack of interest in anything aesthetic, and his inability to be "more imaginative" in his lovemaking despite the impotence. She now needed to get away from him to save her own soul. She was, however, willing to come with her husband to next week's appointment.

DSM-III-R DIAGNOSIS

Axis I: Male erectile disorder
Axis II: None documented
Axis III: Status—post pituitary tumor
Axis IV: Stress—severe (recent recovery from medical illness followed by separation from wife)
Axis V: Highest level of functioning past year—good (has continued to work, pleasurably attend sporting events, and socialize)

TREATMENT PROBLEM

A middle-aged man, faced with marital separation, is now belatedly seeking help for chronic impotence. The cause of his impotence is not clear, but it may be a residual effect of a treated benign pituitary tumor.

DISCUSSION OF TREATMENT SELECTION

Setting. Mr. Y has presented no psychiatric problem that warrants hospitalization at this time. An overnight hospitalization may be necessary in the future for more sophisticated sleep studies to determine if Mr. Y has erections during the REM phases of sleep, but at present, outpatient care is the preferred choice.

Format. The consultant's decision to have at least one evaluation with both Mr. and Mrs. Y seems wise. This format will enable the consultant to obtain a fuller history than Mr. Y is able to supply. This information plus an opportunity to observe how the two of them interact will give important clues regarding the present and future state of the marriage and will help the consultant determine what is likely to become the main therapeutic task: i. e., whether to attempt to repair the marriage and treat the sexual dysfunction or to help Mr. Y cope with a separation that in Mrs. Y's mind is already final and satisfactory.

Though the reasons for seeing Mr. and Mrs. Y together in consultation are persuasive, the reasons for not seeing them in treatment are also noteworthy. Mr. and Mrs. Y have functioned for 26 years without directly confronting each other or sharing emotional problems. A format that changes this pattern may be more disruptive than helpful. If the marriage is left alone, perhaps Mr. and Mrs. Y will once again end the separation as they did once before in the past. Moreover, by prematurely recommending a marital format, the consultant may be conveying the message to Mrs. Y that she should not leave, thereby colluding with Mr. Y in using psychiatric treatment as a way of forcing Mrs. Y to return.

Regarding a family format, the argument in favor of involving the children at this time is far less compelling. The children are now in the process of leaving home and developing their own identities. They probably would resent being brought back into the nest, and if they felt they were being coerced into participating by their father, their presence might be more divisive than helpful. Furthermore, Mr. Y's difficulty with the children seems to be symptomatic of other problems. Including the children might prevent a more focused approach on the current difficulties and would preclude an open discussion of the marital sexual dysfunction. Depending on how the current crisis in the marriage is resolved, family sessions might be scheduled in the future either to help Mr. Y form a closer relationship with his sons and/or to have the sons participate in arranging a more amicable and mutually supportive separation.

Another consideration for the future is a heterogeneous group for Mr. Y. This format might enable him in time to see that his inability to discuss emotional problems and his rigid conservative attitude prevent the development of intimate relationships. This understanding might in turn enable him to recognize that the rejection by his wife and sons is in part due to his own manner of relating and not entirely their fault. The group, along with confronting Mr. Y about his characteristic way of dealing with emotions and with others, could at the same time provide support and prevent an extreme sense of isolation if and when Mrs. Y left for good. A group format, however, would not be a suitable recommendation at the present time. Mr. Y is extremely reluctant to discuss his feelings, especially the humiliation associated with his impotence. The very suggestion of a group might send him running, and many more years might pass before he ever agreed to another psychiatric consultation. In addition, a group format would probably not be able to provide the focused attention to deal with the current marital crisis which, if rapidly reversed, might prevent a more chronic disability.

Duration and Frequency. The duration of treatment at the present time should probably be left open-ended. Mr. Y has given no indication that he is likely to regress or become overattached to the therapist; on the contrary, it may take some time before he develops enough trust for any attachment at all. A predetermined date of ending treatment might only make Mr. Y feel that there is no reason to open up if he will only reexperience the same pain he is currently suffering with the separation from his wife.

The preferred frequency of sessions will be easier to determine after seeing Mr. Y in the second consultation and learning how he does or does not continue to think and work with the material between sessions. The history would suggest his style is "out of sight, out of mind"; if this proves to be true and he does not "remember" the issues discussed in the previous session, the sessions may need to be frequent so that momentum of treatment is not lost. Similarly, Mr. Y revealed in the first consultation that he is very guarded about revealing even the most distressing problems. Some time elapsed before he even mentioned his recent marital separation. To deal with this difficulty, the first few sessions with Mr. Y may need to be extended beyond the traditional 45–50-minute hour.

Approach. The therapeutic approach will depend to a large extent on whether the consultant discovers that the marriage should be over, is already over, or is viable. The consultant may come to feel that a separation and eventual divorce would be best for all concerned. It would enable Mrs. Y to leave a relationship she has found oppressive instead of continuing to act like the martyr, and it would force Mr. Y to act more autonomously and modify his rigid style, a style that has hampered his vocational and social growth as well as the relationship with his two sons. If this conclusion is reached or if the combined consultation indicates that the marriage is already over, the main therapeutic task in working with Mr. Y will be to help him deal with the loss. Supportive techniques will include: decreasing his isolation by allowing him to share feelings with another; suggesting ways to develop a closer relationship with his sons despite the marital separation; eventually encouraging him to develop an intimate relationship with another woman; and pointing out his tendency to be opinionated and autocratic (as a means of compensating for his inner sense of failure and impotence).

If the marriage appears potentially viable, the therapeutic approach will be different, or at least will proceed in a different sequence. Exploratory efforts, rather than supportive techniques, would seem a more advisable first step, specifically, clarifying why Mr. (and perhaps Mrs.) Y have avoided dealing with their emotional and sexual problems for so many years. Once this fear is better understood and worked through, then the couple would be more receptive to educational and behavioral techniques for their sexual problem.

Somatic Treatment. No psychotropic medications appear to be warranted at this time. If further evaluation indicates that Mr. Y's impotence is primarily of a physical nature and will not respond to hormonal replacement therapy, one of the prosthetic devices might be considered, but only after the marital difficulties have been addressed. Neither Mr. nor Mrs. Y should view a prosthetic device as a way of repairing many years of discord, disappointments, and bitterness.

CHOICE AND OUTCOME

The day before the scheduled consultation, Mrs. Y telephoned to say she still wanted more time "away from everybody" to think about her future and had therefore decided not to keep the appointment. She had also phoned her husband, who was still staying at his mother's, to let him know of her decision. He had told her that if she were not going to keep the appointment, neither was he. Mr. Y never phoned himself to cancel the appointment. The scheduled hour came and went without a word from him.

Three weeks later Mrs. Y again phoned the consultant, this time to say that she was worried about her husband. He was still living outside the home, now at his sister's, and was apparently starting to gamble again, staying out later with the guys to have more than just one or two beers. He had missed a few days of work and, when he came by to visit the children, looked disheveled and depressed. Knowing her husband over the years, Mrs. Y was convinced that he would agree to come for an appointment if she came as well. An appointment was scheduled for the following day.

Mr. and Mrs. Y arrived together at the scheduled hour. Mr. Y sat dejectedly and waited for either his wife or the consultant to take the lead. After gathering more information about what had transpired since the first appointment, the consultant indicated that although Mr. Y's sexual impotence had contributed to the strained relationship with his wife, this problem should be further evaluated and treated in the future, and that the more pressing problem at present was the state of the marriage.

He therefore recommended that the first phase of treatment should address this problem in a marital format. Mr. Y lit up with this recommendation, believing that the format itself would be enough to bring his wife "back to her senses." Mrs. Y was far more hesitant in accepting the recommendation. She agreed that the sexual impotence at this point was "immaterial," but wondered aloud how she could possibly help treat Mr. Y's "depression." Besides, she was just now beginning to feel "free." In response, the consultant told Mrs. Y that a marital format was not a commitment to her husband, but rather a commitment to a better understanding of the issues, an understanding which they could both use to decide upon their future and which could result in a confirmation of her decision to separate. Reluctantly, Mrs. Y agreed.

The couple was referred to a female marital therapist. In 15 90–minute sessions over the next three months, Mr. and Mrs. Y gradually and very cautiously inched their way towards a more open discussion about the chronic resentment each held for the other. Though many of these issues were aired and though Mr. Y moved back into the house, the couple was not coming any closer together, nor was Mrs. Y coming any closer to a final resolve to end the marriage. The turning point came when, after three months, the two children were invited to attend a session. The younger son, obviously upset by the pain he sensed in both his mother and father, sat throughout the session with feigned indifference. The older son was far more assertive and stated directly that the problem was that his mother always needed someone to take care of. With the children leaving home and with Mr. Y no longer physically ill, the only person she now had to take care of was her boss. To this statement, Mr. Y perked up and spontaneously replied, "But I *still* need her!"

This brief exchange revealed an important interpersonal dynamic that had not previously been appreciated: Despite Mrs. Y's proclamations about wanting to be "free," what she really wanted was to be needed and appreciated for what she was providing. The real resentment about Mr. Y's cantankerous manner—and even his impotence—stemmed from the frustration she felt in being turned away and not being allowed to help. Paradoxically, she felt useless and discouraged at the very times when Mr. Y needed her the most. The problem was made all the worse because when Mr. Y was depressed or concerned about his personal and professional problems, he tended to gamble, drink with the guys, or talk about nothing but sports. He thereby never made himself available to the care his wife wanted to give.

Further exploration of this dynamic brought the couple closer together. The therapist then recommended that the chronic sexual dysfunction be dealt with in a more direct and specific way. She indicated that it was not clear to what extent Mr. Y's pituitary tumor had caused the sexual impotence and was now contributing to the problem, and she described how sleep studies could be used to determine Mr. Y's capacity to have an erection. Mr. and Mrs. Y mutually decided to defer such a procedure because of its time and costs; they would begin a behavioral sex therapy program, and if Mr. Y remained unresponsive, they would agree to further diagnostic tests.

The sex therapy was successful. To relieve Mr. Y of any pressure to "perform" after years of sexual impotence, intercourse was prohibited during the first seven weeks of the sex therapy while Mr. and Mrs. Y proceeded in a systematic step-by-step program of mutual fondling. Because Mr. Y began to have erections during this fondling phase, no additional medical tests were considered necessary. Interestingly, even during this phase, as Mr. Y became more potent, Mrs. Y openly expressed concerns that her husband might now start "running around." She realized that over the years she had not been more adamant about their getting treatment for her husband's impotence because, unconsciously, she saw his weakness as a way of keeping him around and ensuring that she would always have someone to care for. Another interesting note was that Mr. Y insisted upon terminating treatment (alleged-ly for financial reasons) two weeks before the predetermined "schedule" was set to begin intercourse. The therapist was unsuccessful in dealing with this resistance in what appeared to be a premature termination.

As it turned out, the therapist's fears, though understandable, were wrong. Mr. Y, for reasons outside of his own awareness, actually wanted to stop treatment so that he could have the satisfaction of performing on his own. There was also some indication that he had developed an erotic attachment to the therapist and, by stopping treatment, he was able to resolve this potential conflict.

Mrs. Y called the therapist several weeks after the last appointment, saying that she was most appreciative of the help the two of them had received and that their sexual life was "extraordinarily satisfying," al-though she provided no details over the phone other than that Mr. Y's impotence was no longer a problem. Mr. Y never again contacted the therapist directly, but two years after stopping treatment, he sent her an announcement card of the birth of his new grandson.

SUGGESTED READING

1. Kaplan, H. S. *The New Sex Therapy*. New York: Brunner/Mazel, 1974. (De-scribes the rationale and specific interventions for sex therapy.)
2. Sager, C. J. The role of sex therapy in marital therapy. *American Journal of Psychiatry*, 133:555–558, 1976. (Discusses how sex therapy can be integrated into an ongoing marital therapy [as was done in the case above].)
3. Wagner, G., & Green, R. (Eds.). *Impotence (Erectile Failure): Physiological, Psy-chological and Surgical Diagnosis and Treatment*. New York: Plenum Press, 1981. (Integrates the multidimensional view required for assessing and treating pa-tients like Mr. Y.)

■ INHIBITED FEMALE ORGASM

34.   The Case of the Failing Teacher

(Guest Expert: Helen Singer Kaplan, M.D., Ph.D.)

Authors' Note:
Dr. Kaplan is Clinical Professor of Psychiatry at Cornell University Medical College and Director of the Sex Therapy Program at Payne Whitney Clinic. She is one of the leading experts in the treatment and diagnosis of sexual disorders and has written widely on both topics.

Ms. G is an attractive 28-year-old school teacher who presents now because she is unsatisfied with her sexual life with her husband. Before they were married six years ago she was "wildly in love" and they were both "forlorn" if intercourse was not possible almost every night. His desire remained high after marriage but for Ms. G "things were somehow different." She began to avoid sexual encounters with her husband, to go to sleep early or late, to feel tired or sick, and so forth. Recently matters have deteriorated such that they make love less than once a week and only on his insistence.

Ms. G comes from a rigidly proper and religious family. She was therefore surprised and mortified when her brother, who was 13 at the time and six years her senior, began to regularly expose his penis to her and to touch her genitals. In spite of herself, Ms. G simultaneously enjoyed these experiences and knew that they were sinful. She tried to confess them to her mother and at church but could not, both because she was so ashamed of them and because her brother threatened to hurt her. Intermittent sexual contact with her brother continued for about a year and ended only when he was sent away to boarding school because he was having other behavioral troubles as well.

Ms. G was slow to enter puberty and did not date until age 18. Her future husband was the boy next door. She felt surprised that anyone would find her attractive, was quite taken by his attentions, and soon they were inseparable. He is still her best friend and, as she puts it, "we live like brother and sister."

Even at the height of their sexual activity, Ms. G never experienced an orgasm and she regards this as the major failing in her life and proof that she is not sufficiently feminine. Whenever they have sex, she tries very hard to have an orgasm and feels disappointed and inferior when she doesn't. She also tries very hard to fake having an orgasm for her husband's benefit and is apparently quite convincing. Ms. G is very self-conscious about her body and does not let her husband see her undressed except in very dim light. She is also shy about looking at him. Intercourse is, in her view, meant to be done quickly and to focus on genital contact, not on other touching or looking.

Lately Ms. G has felt aroused sexually by men at work and has been quite flirtatious with one of them. She wonders if her "failures" in bed might not be at least partly her husband's fault and is tempted to try out someone else to see if she can achieve orgasm under different circumstances. She feels very guilty about this inclination and this is one reason that she has come for assistance at this time. She has never masturbated and believes that to do so would be proof that she is sexually inadequate.

DSM-III-R DIAGNOSIS

> Axis I: Inhibited female orgasm
> Axis II: None (based on two interviews)
> Axis III: None
> Axis IV: Stress—none
> Axis V: Highest level of functioning past year—good (but sexual functioning is poor)

DISCUSSION OF TREATMENT SELECTION

I have found it useful to formulate the treatment plan for a sexual disorder around the following questions: 1) What is the exact nature of the patient's complaint? 2) What are the immediate antecedents or causes? 3) Are there deeper causes? If so, what are they? and 4) Are problems in relationships playing a role? If so, in what manner?

1) *What is the exact nature of the patient's complaint?* It is essential to describe sexual problems in precise detail because some sexual disorders are amenable to brief behaviorally oriented interventions while others are not, and also because the different psychosexual dysfunctions require different and specific treatment tactics. The patient in this case history has two sexual symptoms: *inhibited orgasm*, which is global and primary, and secondary *inhibited sexual desire* (ISD) specifically towards

her husband. It is not clear which of these is really the patient's chief complaint. Nonetheless, since anorgasmia is often rapidly responsive to sex therapy and has a much better prognosis than ISD, it would make sense to treat this symptom first and wait to see if (a) the patient's ability to climax will increase her sexual desire automatically or (b) her avoidance will have to be addressed as a separate therapeutic issue later on.

2) *What are the immediate antecedents and causes?* The immediate causes that are currently instrumental in blocking this patient's sexual responses would have to be assessed precisely and in detail before a rational treatment strategy could be devised. Inadequate stimulation, obsessive self-observation ("spectatoring"), excessive self-control, and failure to communicate her sexual needs to her partner are common immediate defenses against orgastic release. A phobic avoidance of sexual stimulation, the focus on negative thoughts ("anti-fantasies"), and the withholding of erotic imagery may also constitute the defenses currently operating in the avoidance-desire elements of this case.

The behavioral components of sex therapy are used to modify the patient's immediate defenses against sexuality, and must be individualized for each case. With this patient it would be my inclination first to resolve her resistance to self-stimulation and then prescribe self-induced clitoral stimulation accompanied by erotic imagery. Masturbation provides patients the opportunity to learn to become comfortable with their previously avoided erotic sensations; the concomitant focus and erotic fantasy are used to distract them from their obsessive self-observations which block the release of the orgasm reflex.

3) *Are there deeper causes? If so, what are they?* If the currently operating causes or antecedents that were mentioned above were the sole etiological factors in this case, simple behavior modification would be indicated. But two "deeper" or more complex psychopathological processes are probably also contributing to this patient's sexual inhibition and these may pose obstacles to the direct removal of her symptoms.

These deeper issues, which generally operate outside of the patient's awareness, derive from the past and have cultural as well as neurotic origins. First, it may be speculated that antisexual "messages" (the sense transmitted to the child by her family that sexual gratification is wrong or shameful) may still be operative in this case. Second, it can be inferred that the incestuous abuse she experienced in childhood was sufficiently traumatic to set into motion neurotic conflicts and defenses against sexual pleasure and gratification. Because of these considerations, an argument could be made for dynamically oriented psychotherapy with the objective of fostering insight and resolving underlying sexual conflicts. However, research evidence, as well as extensive clinical experience, suggests that while psychodynamic modalities may yield substantial benefits in terms of improving patients' lives and even though patients may attain excellent insight into their past and the dynamics of their problems, specific sexual symptoms are cured in only a small proportion of patients with this approach. A more promising treatment alternative is to employ a sex therapy that combines behavioral techniques with psychodynamically oriented interventions which will specifically address those underlying sexual conflicts that create resistances to the resolution of sexual symptoms.

More specifically in this case, in conjunction with the behavioral program described above, I would use the power of a positive transference to give this woman "permission" and strong encouragement to allow herself to experience sexual sensations and pleasure, and I would attempt to work through her guilt in this area. The extent to which I would be obliged to confront her sexual avoidance and explore her deeper conflicts would depend on the intensity and nature of the resistances, which would most probably emerge during the treatment process.

4) *Are problems in relationships playing a role? If so, in what manner?* Clinicians who follow the Masters and Johnson model emphasize the systems aspect of sexual problems and only accept couples for treatment. In this model, the marital unit is "the patient." This position often makes good sense, except in those cases where the patient has an intrinsic sexual problem which would surface with any partner. Although more detailed data are needed to be certain in this case, this patient's sexual inhibition appears to be the product of the interplay between both intrinsic and dyadic problems. In other words, while it is unlikely that this woman would be able to experience orgasms with even the most skillful partner because of her own problems, this couple's sexual interactions may also be inadequate. Her husband may not provide sufficient clitoral stimulation for any woman; in addition, the couple's lovemaking seems tense, emphasizing performance rather than an intimate exchange of pleasure.

Although the husband may be contributing to the problem, it is easier to conduct the initial phase of the treatment for anorgasmia with an individual format. The partner's presence may heighten a woman's performance anxiety and interfere with her concentration on her erotic sensations and imagery. For these reasons it is my practice to first work with an anorgastic woman alone, including the partner (if she has one) in the second phase of treatment, which emphasizes the sharing and mutuality of sexual pleasure.

In sum, during the initial phase of therapy the patient would work on her orgasm inhibition. This part of treatment can be effectively conducted within a brief sex therapy group or individual sessions. After she has learned to have orgasms by herself, I would work with the couple conjointly in order to improve their specific sexual interactions and to deal with any deeper problems and ambivalences in their relationship if such should surface.

In regard to prognosis, psychosexual disorders are frequently amenable to brief psychosexual therapy, and this patient's chances of becoming orgastic are excellent with these techniques. However, the prognosis for improvement of her sexual avoidance and lack of desire for her husband is less favorable and more problematic and will depend in part on the husband's psychological and sexual status and in part on the quality of this couple's relationship.

SUGGESTED READING

1. Barbach, L. G. *Women Discover Orgasm: A Therapist's Guide to a New Treatment Approach*. New York: Free Press, 1980. (A detailed guide of the women's group approach to nonorgasmic response.)
2. Levay, A., & Kagle, A. A study of treatment needs following sex therapy. *American Journal of Psychiatry*, 134:970–973, 1977. (Sex therapy may only be the first phase of the required treatment.)
3. Munjack, D., Cristol, A., Goldstein, A., et al. Behavioral treatment for orgasmic dysfunction: A controlled study. *British Journal of Psychiatry*, 129:497–502, 1976. (Systematic study indicating the effectiveness—and limitations—of sex therapy.)

35. The Case of the Frigid Housewife

Mrs. A is a 35-year-old suburban housewife who seeks treatment because she is anxious about a possible divorce. She arrives promptly for her first appointment dressed in a turtleneck sweater and slacks, looking more like a graduate student than the mother of two grade-school children. Seemingly well rehearsed, she presents her story in a carefully measured manner that conceals her underlying anxiety.

For 15 years Mrs. A has lived through and for her husband, a research scientist, whom she viewed as "infallible." She raised their children (now ages 12 and 10) as the model mother, rehearsed what she would say to her husband before they took a walk, planned to the last detail any social encounter, and stereotypically performed sex once a month without orgasm. Mrs. A is an inhibited woman who has no rough edges but who seems to lack the capacity for spontaneous fun or deep friendship.

A year before the consultation, her husband became more preoccupied with problems in the lab and even less emotionally available. Mrs. A was concerned that she might be losing her attractiveness and asked for the first time, "Is there anyone else?" To her surprise, Dr. A admitted to a current affair as well as previous brief encounters (which in retrospect should have been obvious to Mrs. A).

The lid had come off the "perfect marriage" and Mrs. A was devastated. For the next few months there were several brief separations during which Mrs. A wrestled with her bitter yet frightened feelings. When Dr. A was away, she would be numb, with no idea how to manage without him. She pleaded for him to see a marriage counselor with her, but her husband ridiculed this suggestion as foolish, expensive, and one more attempt to make everything intellectual. As Dr. A's emotional withdrawal and disinterest in the marriage increased, so did Mrs. A's panic. Finally, she sought psychiatric consultation for herself.

During the first interview, the consultant found it difficult to learn much about Mrs. A. She was much more interested in giving the details of her husband's indifference and neglect. For example, when the consultant asked Mrs. A to place the present problem in perspective and tell him about her past, she dismissed the question as though it were irrelevant: "My childhood was typical for a poor Irish girl." She would then resume discussing the "abandonment" by her husband.

A second session was necessary before the consultant learned that Mrs. A's childhood was anything but typical. Her father, an ineffectual factory worker, was totally dominated by Mrs. A's mother, a sexy and dynamic woman who used the patient as a confidante. She would secretly describe in detail sexual encounters with her employers and suggested that the patient's younger sister was the illegitimate product of one such affair. During her adolescence, Mrs. A was stimulated by these detailed accounts and yet, privately, vowed that she herself would never act so immorally. Indeed, Mrs. A shunned passionate relationships, avoided sexually provocative movies, condemned pornography, and never masturbated or permitted herself to fantasize "unclean" thoughts. She married her husband because in part he was "nice" (and not sexy) and she never gave much thought to the fact that their sexual life was stilted and unpleasurable. In fact, when she sensed that the consultant was indicating by his questions that Mrs. A might have some sexual dysfunction, she jokingly but defensively retorted, "George Bernard Shaw once said that the most overrated thing in the world is sex and the most underrated is a satisfactory bowel movement. Don't you agree?" At this point, the consultant chuckled and let the dynamically laden question go unanswered.

DSM-III-R DIAGNOSIS

Axis I: Inhibited female orgasm
Axis II: Obsessive compulsive personality disorder
Axis III: None
Axis IV: Stress—severe (pending divorce)
Axis V: Highest level of functioning past year—very good

TREATMENT PROBLEM

Sexually and emotionally inhibited woman very worried about a possible divorce.

DISCUSSION OF TREATMENT SELECTION

Setting. Of all the decisions the consultant must make, choosing the therapeutic setting is by far the easiest. Hospitalization is unnecessary; outpatient treatment is the only reasonable option.

Format. Choosing the most effective therapeutic format is more of a problem. Available research indicates that when the chief complaint involves a problem between couples or within a family, a couple or family format is more effective than an individual treatment. The value of a conjoint format is particularly well supported when, as with Dr. and Mrs. A, there is a sexual dysfunction within the marriage.

Although Mrs. A states that her husband is unwilling to participate in treatment, the consultant cannot take this statement at face value. Perhaps Mrs. A presented the possibility to her husband more as a threat or a punishment than an opportunity for both of them to work through their difficulties and improve the marriage. Automatically excluding the husband early in treatment might implicitly convey that the marriage was irreparable, when in fact a marital treatment had not yet been tried.

Another danger of prematurely excluding the husband is that Mrs. A will simply turn to the psychiatrist and live through and for him the way she did with her husband. Many months of treatment might pass before Mrs. A was able to understand this passive-dependent character trait; meanwhile, irreversible damage may have been done to the marriage and the children. In terms of the children, family therapy might also be helpful in conjunction with marital treatment. The children are at an age when they might be able to participate actively in solving at least some of the current problems. By including the children in the treatment, whatever its outcome, they might be less inclined to feel like the passive victims of their parents' difficulties (the way Mrs. A felt when she was growing up).

Although Mrs. A sees her problems as focused within the home and would no doubt be reluctant to discuss her difficulties with others, the format of a heterogeneous group cannot be discounted. In the early stages, the group could offer support for Mrs. A who feels abandoned without her husband. In time, the group could point out to Mrs. A how she herself must bear some of the responsibility for her husband's leaving, specifically, her cold and methodical way of relating to others. The problem with group treatment is that at the present time Mrs. A will probably view such a recommendation as both threatening and off the mark. Given her proclivity to exclude both others and herself from intimate revelations, an individual format will probably be the only choice acceptable to all parties—and this format does have the advantage of dealing most directly and promptly with Mrs. A's intrapsychic and behavioral problems that are contributing to the current crisis.

Duration and Frequency. These components of treatment will depend largely on the therapeutic goals and on the therapeutic techniques and formats used to reach them. If the aim is to focus on the current crisis within the family, a brief targeted treatment (10–20 sessions) is usually sufficient; but if the aim is also to work on Mrs. A's longstanding characterological difficulties, an open-ended prolonged treatment might be necessary as well. A time-oriented treatment with a set termination date would certainly focus on Mrs. A's difficulty in separating and feeling autonomous when on her own, but given the state of her anxiety at present, this kind of treatment would probably be too overwhelming and therefore unacceptable. The initial evaluation indicates that she will need the reassurance that even if her husband leaves, she will not be completely alone. She is not a good candidate for focal therapy because she does not see her problems psychologically and is not greatly motivated for autoplastic change. Mainly, she just wants her husband back and will settle for the way things used to be.

Approach. Despite Mrs. A's own disparaging view of her capabilities, she has the enabling factors for most therapeutic approaches. She also has the indications for many kinds of treatment. In some ways this is reassuring; no matter what technique the consultant chooses, his choice is likely to be helpful. On the other hand, choosing the *best* technique presents more of a problem. An exploratory treatment will no doubt be beneficial; Mrs. A is verbal, intelligent, and could probably in time become sufficiently reflective to examine her past and its relationship to the present. This examination would help her understand how her inhibited, compliant behavior is a maladaptive defense against unconscious sexual and aggressive impulses and is a reaction against an identification with her sexy, dominant mother. A problem with an exploratory treatment is that given her current tendency to attribute her distress to external events (e.g., her husband's leaving) rather than internal dynamics (e.g., exaggerated fear of abandonment), many months are liable to pass before Mrs. A is able to hear and respond to interpretations; in the meantime, her marriage and children may suffer in ways that could have been avoided by a more direct and explicit approach. It may be best to address specific target problems first and gradually develop the atmosphere and motivation for a psychodynamic treatment aimed at character change.

Of the directive treatments, one strong possibility is sex therapy, assuming Dr. A would agree and is not already too far out of the door. Mrs. A, all too willing to follow directions, would probably accept behavioral techniques to improve her sexual performance; and possibly Dr. A would reveal that his interest in extramarital affairs was prompted by his wife's chronic sexual inhibitions. Considering how much turmoil and dissention are now occurring in the marriage, neither partner may at first be inclined to believe that an improvement in their sexual relations should be the focus of treatment. They may need to be informed that sex therapy is often very successful in situations like theirs, particularly if the problem is one of performance and not desire. Furthermore, an initial therapeutic success in this one area is likely to have ripple effects both by benefiting other aspects of their relationship and by increasing motivation for treatment of those problems that do not resolve from sex therapy alone.

An experiential, interpersonal approach that conveyed an uncritical positive regard and an appreciation for Mrs. A might provide sufficient reassurance for her to feel less frightened and more spontaneous, both within sessions and with her husband.

Somatic Treatment. Small doses of benzodiazepines may be necessary in the very early stages of treatment to take the edge off Mrs. A's anxiety so that she can cope effectively with the logistics of running her home and not appear so distraught that her husband becomes even more eager to leave.

CHOICE AND OUTCOME

With the consultant's direction and encouragement, Mrs. A spoke with her husband, who agreed to attend the next consultation. Within minutes after this session began, Dr. A made it clear why he had agreed to come: He wanted a third party present when he told his wife that the marriage was absolutely over and that he already had rented an apartment in the city and was planning to live with his most recent girlfriend. Furthermore, he had no interest in discussing any of these matters with the children with or without the psychiatric consultant and would leave this difficult task in the hands of his wife. Dr. A stated these decisions as though reading the conclusions from a scientific paper, then left the session before it was over, informing the consultant on the way out of the door that "this kind of medical expense would not be covered in the divorce settlement."

The remainder of that session was spent consoling Mrs. A. As the end of the hour approached, Mrs. A, hurt but reconciled to the fate of her marriage, stated that she now saw no need for treatment. If it would not bring back her husband, what was the use? The consultant suggested that she not make such a decision prematurely and arranged another session for the following week. A time was set, but Mrs. A canceled the appointment.

Six months passed before Mrs. A called again for another consultation. During the interim Dr. A had left the home. Legal separation plans had been finalized and Mrs. A, finding a strength she had never before realized, had taken a job as an executive secretary and had enrolled in evening courses to become a hospital administrator. She explained to the consultant that although she had been able to alter the external structure of her life, she still had the same internal doubts about her worth as "a professional woman and lover." In particular, she had continued to reflect on the question posed earlier by the consultant regarding why she had accepted such an unfulfilling marriage for so many years with such blind compliance.

Because Mrs. A's problems were now more characterological than situational and because she herself, having done some reading about therapeutic options, believed an exploratory treatment offered the best chance of resolving lifelong problems that largely derived from unconscious conflicts, the consultant concluded that Mrs. A had not only the enabling factors but also the indications for psychoanalysis. A referral was made to a male psychologist with extensive training and expertise in this form of treatment.

During the first few months of psychoanalysis, Mrs. A would usually begin with a tense greeting, then lie stiffly on the couch citing a prepared rendition of the day's events. Running dry after 20 minutes, she would try to have the analyst define his expectations for her. When structure was not provided, she would go blank. Fantasies were sparse and unelaborated; historical data were in headline form; and dreams were presented as gifts to be opened and played with by the analyst without Mrs. A's own associations.

By the sixth month of treatment, Mrs. A's global repression could no longer hold. The analytic situation had catalyzed an intense erotic transference and, with it, the recovery of many previously repressed memories and stimulating sexual feelings that psychogenetically related to her mother's clandestine affairs. As a result, Mrs. A shifted identifications from her ineffectual father to her dynamic mother, finalized the divorce, became an administrator in the hospital where her analyst worked, and resolved never again passively to submit to a man. By her own description, she had become "an ardent, hardened feminist." She was, however, still troubled by her inability to have orgasms during intercourse with the many men she was now dating, and wondered aloud if sex therapy might be more effective for this problem than lying on a couch "sifting and sorting."

The analyst was in a dilemma. He was aware that sex therapy might very well be effective for Mrs. A's sexual dysfunction, but he was also aware that Mrs. A's rapid shift from passivity to a zealous declaration of feminine independence had many elements of a fragile reaction formation. Because she was still repressing many childhood memories and was avoiding any discussion of her feelings about the analyst, he was concerned that she was introducing the notion of sex therapy at this time as a way of acting out rather than working through the transference neurosis.

The analyst openly raised this possibility with Mrs. A and they agreed that even if the motivation for sex therapy was stemming in part from unconscious factors that had not yet come fully into view, these could be analyzed during and after the sex therapy. Accordingly, Mrs. A and her current lover arranged for a behaviorally oriented sex therapy. After 15 conjoint sessions over a three-month period, her frigidity improved to the point where she was able to experience orgasms consistently with manual stimulation by herself or her partner during intercourse. Mrs. A was delighted with the results of the sex therapy and continued to work in the psychoanalysis. There was no indication that the concomitant treatment had split the transference or in any other way precluded an effective working-through of unconscious conflicts.

During the next four years of psychoanalysis, Mrs. A gradually stopped trying to be a "Wonder Woman." She realized that her frenetic behavior and provocations were desperate attempts to conceal her intense yearnings for the analyst to be her caretaker. Long-repressed, painful memories accompanied this yearning. She recalled how she felt abandoned at age four, when her mother returned to work and left the patient with "a withered toothless grandmother" who wandered around the sparse apartment with her varicose legs wrapped in rags; and she remembered how her mother would return from work and "bored with the family" would prepare canned food from which each member would eat alone at different times. Frequently during the analysis, as this childhood affective deprivation was remembered and reexperienced, an intense negative maternal transference would mount, but the therapeutic alliance remained strong. In general, she experienced the analytic situation as a cocoon that gave her a second chance to develop a loving view of herself and others, instead of using a fragile reaction formation to contain her rage under an infallible, unruffled manner.

By the time the analysis terminated, Mrs. A had advanced to an executive position at work and had married a man whom she found socially, emotionally, and sexually fufilling. In her view, of even greater importance was the realization that she had at last gained a sense of self-worth and a capacity to function autonomously.

SUGGESTED READING

1. Bieber, I. The psychoanalytic treatment of sexual disorders. *Journal of Sex & Marital Therapy*, 1:5–15, 1974. (Relevant to the case above, the author discusses an approach to sexual issues that arise during a psychoanalysis.)
2. Greenacre, P. Certain technical problems in the transference relationship. *Journal of the American Psychoanalytic Association*, 7:484–502, 1959. (The author describes how certain real situations can have an impact on the therapeutic alliance and the transference.)
3. Deutsch, H. (Ed.). (1930). The part of the actual conflict in the formation of neurosis. In: *Neuroses and Character Types*. New York: International Universities Press, 1965, pp. 3–13. (As true in the case presented here, the author explains how childhood experiences and unconscious dynamics directly relate to conflicts in the patient's current life.)

X

Factitious Disorders

■ **FACTITIOUS DISORDER WITH PSYCHOLOGICAL SYMPTOMS**

36. The Case of the Nightly Caller

Mrs. H, a divorced woman presumed to be in her late forties, has been the scourge of psychiatry clinics and emergency rooms for many years. Night after night she telephones the doctor on call in one or more of the various emergency rooms around the city and complains of an unendurable loneliness that she states is driving her to suicide. When the doctor suggests that Mrs. H's situation and feelings are too important to discuss over the phone and that she should come to the hospital, Mrs. H not only refuses, but launches into a litany of additional complaints—some accurate, some exaggerated—against emergency rooms in particular and the medical profession in general. Depending on the doctor's willingness to debate the various points raised by Mrs. H, these entangled explanations for her refusal to come to the hospital usually last between five and 30 minutes.

Just as the discussions seem to be winding down and Mrs. H senses the doctor is losing interest, the patient once again implies that suicide is the only way out of her desperate situation. Alarmed and concerned, the doctor will at some point try to obtain Mrs. H's address, but no matter how subtle and indirect this attempt may be, Mrs. H is well aware of the doctor's intentions and states that if the police are sent to bring her to the hospital, she will act completely sane when they arrive, will sue the hospital, will write letters to the directors of the hospital, and will do everything else in her power to expose the doctor for the complete fool he or she so clearly is.

These phone conversations have been known to go on for over an hour, especially with an anxious psychiatry resident during the first months of training. The calls typically end with Mrs. H making inflammatory personal accusations against the doctor whom by now, in her own uncanny way, she has gotten to know so well. When she hangs up the phone, the doctor is left feeling both frustrated and frightened about what Mrs. H might do to herself or to him.

As might be imagined, Mrs. H has not been easy to treat. She refuses to accept scheduled outpatient appointments. Instead, she periodically drops into the emergency room or the walk-in clinic and, using different pseudonyms, complains of unmanageable suicidal ideas. Even if the more experienced staff recognizes Mrs. H as the nightly caller, the patient still manages to absorb a remarkable amount of staff time and interest. In the end, the staff's concern does nothing more than provide a stage for Mrs. H to reenact the notion of herself as a deprived and tormented orphan. When the play ends and Mrs. H is sent home from the clinic, she often does not leave at once, but rather lingers around the waiting area talking with patients and with ancillary staff members, such as aids, clerks, and security guards, who are touched by her pathetic but crusty loneliness. Mrs. H has also been seen spending hours at a time in the hospital cafeteria, either sipping tea alone in the corner or engaging hospital personnel and visitors in the alleged saga of her life and miseries.

It is striking that despite the many hours Mrs. H has spent talking to doctors and despite the volumes of her medical and psychiatric charts at several different hospitals, no one knows very much about her background, her present living circumstances, or even the specific nature of her psychiatric symptomatology. The hospital records are filled with her complaints and threats, often in colorful language, but no one has recorded a clear and useful description of her history or a complete mental status. On two occasions, social workers attempted to make a home visit, only to learn after a wild goose chase that Mrs. H had given the wrong address. On another occasion a hospital cafeteria employee arranged to meet Mrs. H at church for a Sunday service, but the patient never showed up. Despite the genuine efforts of many competent people over the years, Mrs. H remains the phantom on the phone.

DSM-III-R DIAGNOSIS

Axis I: Factitious disorder; possible major psychiatric disorder
Axis II: Mixed personality disorder
Axis III: Presumed medical conditions (arthritis, hiatus hernia, colitis, tinnitus, headaches, low back pain, etc.), all of which await adequate documentation
Axis IV: Stress—none known
Axis V: Highest level of functioning past year—presumed to be very poor

TREATMENT PROBLEM

A middle-aged woman who apparently experiences a restless and continuous dysphoria. She feels like a victim of the medical system, which pays insufficient attention to her needs, but she is also a victimizer of the system by absorbing enormous amounts of staff time and by refusing to accept medical and psychiatric recommendations.

DISCUSSION OF TREATMENT SELECTION

In the case of Mrs. H, any discussion of therapeutic setting, format, duration, and possible somatic interventions will no doubt be an irrelevant academic exercise unless the entire clinic staff adopts a more thoughtful and unified approach. At present, Mrs. H is able to mount a formidable (though unconsciously determined) "attack" on the medical system, whereas the response to this attack has been disorganized, inconsistent and, so far, ineffective. This problem in management is particularly apparent during the summer months when Mrs. H performs her initiation ceremony with each new rotation of medical and psychiatric residents at each available hospital. Their naive eagerness to help selects for the most regressed and "suicidal" aspects of Mrs. H's behavior. The first step in Mrs. H's treatment must therefore be to present the staff (i.e., ideally at all of the various hospitals she patronizes) with an approach that is perceived by them (and perhaps ultimately by Mrs. H) as firm but not punitive. Since Mrs. H will be adroit at finding any flaws in the approach and will test for its weaknesses, the entire staff and new trainees must be oriented to the plan, then reoriented in the ensuing months to maintain consistency.

CHOICE AND OUTCOME

After a new group of psychiatry residents expressed particular confusion and frustration about the management of Mrs. H, the director of
the outpatient clinic held a staff conference with all available staff to
outline a unified approach, which was then presented as well by a mem-
orandum to all concerned staff members. The approach was quite simple: Any time Mrs. H telephoned or appeared in one of the clinics she
was to be told that her case was now the personal responsibility of the
director of the outpatient clinic and, under his instructions, all other staff
members had been strictly prohibited from spending more than five
minutes with her. She was then to be given the telephone number of the
director and instructed to call him (and no one else) whenever she wanted to negotiate for treatment.

Though some staff members felt the approach was too harsh, it
served several purposes: 1) It enabled those staff members who might be
inclined to get more involved with Mrs. H to avoid pathogenic interactions without feeling guilty or angry at her; they could honestly say they
were just doing their job; 2) it made one person responsible for any
additional therapeutic steps, thus reducing Mrs. H's ability to test and
split the system; 3) it made Mrs. H feel important that the director
of the clinic was now personally responsible for her care; and 4) it
made the clinic's most experienced clinician responsible for its most
difficult patient, a fair matchup under the circumstances.

Three weeks after this approach was implemented and after a dwin-
dling frequency of nightly calls, Mrs. H phoned the director and point-
edly asked what he was going to do for her. He replied that he would not
even make any tentative recommendations until he had met with her
and more thoroughly assessed the problems. She refused and began to
bombard him with phone messages which he ignored. On the rebound,
Mrs. H next tried to engage various staff members and trainees on the
phone or through emergency room visits. The staff consistently stuck
with its mandate and told Mrs. H that these contacts were not part of her
treatment plan.

More than two months passed during which Mrs. H undoubtedly
was phoning or visiting other hospitals. But then, out of the blue, she
called to arrange an appointment with the director, which she then
missed. A month later when she called for another appointment, she
was given a time to meet three weeks in the future. When she complained of the delay, the director responded that Mrs. H could not expect
to keep missing appointments and then have immediate service. Mrs.
H's view of the director seemed to be that he was some combination of

fool and devil. She threatened him with a malpractice suit, a letter to the chairman of psychiatry, and a suicide attempt.

The director's response to these threats was that it would be silly to hurt herself over him and for something so trivial. The director's air of imperviousness (though not indifference) was disarming. He went on to explain that having reviewed her records thoroughly, he was not convinced that previous efforts on the part of the hospital had helped her and that he feared that some of the staff's responses may have even made things worse. He was determined not to allow staff members to participate in her decline and he personally would do his best to correct what seemed to be a bad treatment situation. Although she might find some of his actions arbitrary and unfair, his approach was not intended to be punitive but rather an attempt to do what he thought was best—even so, he was still not sure what if anything the hospital could do to help. Consoled, or perhaps only intrigued and challenged, Mrs. H agreed to meet with the director in three weeks. She kept that appointment.

The consultation involved three visits over a six-week period. The director took a methodical psychiatric history, completed several rating scales, and using a semistructured interview, consistently interrupted Mrs. H whenever she drifted away from the questions at hand.

He discovered that the patient had been raised in a small rural community by a foster family, in which sexual and physical abuse were frequent. There Mrs. H learned to live by her wits and admittedly to "trap" an older man into marriage by becoming pregnant at the age of 14. Three years later, she told her husband and young child that she was going out to get some cigarettes; she left the small housetrailer, took a bus to a big city and has not seen or heard from them since. Over the past 25 years (as much as her story could be believed), she has worked as a clerk, waitress, metermaid, nurse's aide, and call girl, and has had many shortlived relationships that typically end when the man's physical abuse becomes unbearable. She was quite evasive when asked about her current living arrangements and financial situation, as well as about her contact with physicians and mental health professionals over the years, but her mental status exam revealed no evidence of disordered thinking, substance abuse, or specific symptoms of an affective illness.

After this careful assessment, the director concluded that Mrs. H did not have a treatable psychiatric condition and that the patient's flirting with psychiatric treatment had been harmful rather than helpful. He suggested that at least for the present Mrs. H should give up the idea that psychiatrists could help her and instead plan a life that did not require her round of desperate phone calls.

The last session was spent with the director explaining his reasons for his recommendations. He pointed out that during the past several years Mrs. H had declined in her social and vocational functioning as well as in her appearance and feelings about herself. He assured her that she could be doing much better and fortunately had no major psychiatric problem that would prevent her from pulling herself together. To buffer any perceived rejection, the director offered Mrs. H a monthly phone conversation with him to discuss both how her life was progressing and any changes in her condition that warranted a reconsideration of psychiatric treatment.

The director's interventions did not produce an immediate and dramatic cure. Mrs. H continued her phone calls at night and her appearances at walk-in clinics; but these diminished remarkably in number as did Mrs. H's sense of desperate deprivation and the staff's frustrated, guilt-ridden reactions. Two years later she got a job as a receptionist after which, except for occasional phone calls each July to a new group of psychiatry residents, she no longer contacted the hospital (although from time to time she was seen in the cafeteria).

SUGGESTED READING

1. Spiro, H. R. Chronic factitious illness: Munchausen's syndrome. *Archives of General Psychiatry,* 18:569–579, 1968. (By providing an historical and dynamic perspective, the article helps diminish the frustration of dealing with those who are compelled to make themselves ill.)
2. Main, T. F. The ailment. *British Journal of Medical Psychology,* 30:129–145, 1957. (Illustrates how one patient's psychopathology can have an impact on an entire psychiatric staff.)
3. Bassuk, E., & Gerson, S. Chronic crisis patients: A discrete clinical group. *American Journal of Psychiatry,* 137:1513–1517, 1980. (Management of emergency room "repeaters.")

XI

Impulse Control Disorders
Not Elsewhere Classified

■ **INTERMITTENT EXPLOSIVE DISORDER**

37. The Case of the Explosive Mechanic

Mr. W, a 34-year-old divorced auto mechanic, is brought to the emergency room by the hospital security guards after explosively threatening a nurse on a medical ward when she told him that visiting hours were over and he must leave. Mr. W continues to scream angrily at the guards as he is placed in restraints, but mounts only a half-hearted physical struggle. Within a few moments after being left in an isolated room, he calms down and tells the intern his side of the story.

Six days ago his girlfriend was suddenly rushed to the hospital after a subarachnoid hemorrhage which left her in a coma until earlier this morning when she became arousable. After days of vigil at the bedside, Mr. W was eager to be with her now that she was more alert. Already less than satisfied with the nursing care, he became enraged when he was told to leave in what seemed to him a perfunctory manner. He admits that screaming, disrupting the entire ward, and threatening to kill the nurse was an overreaction, but "that's just the way I am."

Overreacting has been a problem throughout Mr. W's life. In grade school he was considered unmanageable and unable to concentrate. Although not diagnosed at the time, in retrospect he probably had both hyperactivity and a learning disability. As a teenager, he settled down somewhat in class and did well in vocational school, but he was still

273

prone to violent outbursts when even minimally provoked. As a result of the same problem, he lost several jobs after graduation while working as a gas station mechanic. On one occasion, he lost a lawsuit after striking a customer; and on another occasion, he was imprisoned for six weeks after fracturing his employer's kneecap with a tire iron. In addition, he was investigated by the bureau of child welfare for suspected child (and wife) abuse, but the case was dropped after his wife took the children and left three years previously. Since then, Mr. W has been running his own back alley garage with fair success. He is apparently a superb mechanic and able to hold a loyal clientele.

Mr. W has never seen a psychiatrist for his problems—in fact, the idea has never occurred to him—and except for chain-smoking, he has never abused drugs and dislikes the taste of alcohol of any kind.

DSM-III-R DIAGNOSIS

AXIS I: Intermittent explosive disorder
AXIS II: None
AXIS III: Chronic bronchitis; recurrent respiratory infections
AXIS IV: Stress—moderate (illness of girlfriend)
AXIS V: Highest level of functioning past year—good (successful mechanic, pleasurable love relationship, accomplished bowler)

TREATMENT PROBLEM

Thirty-two-year-old man with history of impulsive violent episodes that have impaired his vocational life and destroyed the relationship with his previous wife and children. Apart from these fits of violence, he functions well and cares deeply about his job performance and for others.

DISCUSSION OF TREATMENT SELECTION

Mr. W's treatment can be viewed as having three phases: first, controlling the violent outburst; second, assessing immediate risk of harm to himself or others; and third, preventing future violent episodes or at least reducing their frequency and severity.

To the relief of everyone involved, the first phase of Mr. W's treatment is already over. The security guards, following the explicit directions of the staff on the medical ward, have successfully placed Mr. W on a stretcher in four-point restraint without causing physical harm to the

patient or to others. In addition, the guards have searched for any potentially dangerous items, removed Mr. W from the provoking stimulus,
and placed him in a quiet room, where he has been observed, had vital
signs monitored and, while still restrained, been given a chance to calm
down on his own without medication. In this case the use of tranquilizers against Mr. W's will might not have been legally justified, might have
made him feel even more helpless (and provoked a counterattack), and
might have caused a sedation which would have delayed and perhaps
complicated the neuropsychiatric evaluation. Immediate control of a violent episode, especially when the patient is a stranger and the underlying cause is unclear, can usually be more safely and promptly accomplished by physical and not pharmacological interventions.

Regarding the second phase of Mr. W's treatment, several factors
indicate that he is no longer an immediate risk to himself or others. He is
not psychotically disorganized, is not being controlled by a paranoid
belief system, and is not intoxicated or an abuser of drugs that diminish
impulse control. Furthermore, now that he has been removed from the
provoking stimulus, he has gained control without tranquilizers, has
cooperated with the intern, and has not expressed any desire to get back
at the security guards or the medical staff. For these reasons, having Mr.
W committed to a hospital involuntarily would not appear justified either for prevention or for treatment of his violent episodes which, given
our current knowledge, remain unpredictable. If Mr. W does not wish
further evaluation and treatment for his problem, he may simply go
home. The hospital administrator or the nurses involved may perhaps
wish to press charges for the disruption and verbal assault (they probably won't), but these choices are not medical and should remain outside
the purview of the treating physician.

Regarding the third phase of treatment, the first step towards reducing the frequency and intensity of Mr. W's violent episodes is to motivate
him to accept help. This is no easy task. Mr. W has been inclined over the
years to dismiss his problem as nothing more than a "short fuse." No
doubt he will be even less interested in recognizing the severity of his
difficulty at the present time, when he is far more concerned about his
girlfriend's illness and about his being released from the emergency
room where he feels trapped, resentful, and humiliated. Moreover, like
many others with his disorder, Mr. W does not feel deep remorse for his
explosive behavior and will feel scorned rather than hopeful if the therapist attempts to motivate him either by reminding Mr. W of all that he
has lost in his life as a result of losing control or by trying to make him
feel guilty and ashamed of his actions. Instead, Mr. W may be more
receptive towards treatment if the therapist uses psychoeducation to

explain that the attacks are not the result of his being basically "a bad guy" but rather are symptoms of a known syndrome. Advising Mr. W to read about the disorder (e.g., the section in the DSM-III) may help reinforce this view and make his violent outbursts more ego-dystonic.

Assuming Mr. W does accept a treatment plan, he should be informed from the start that many different treatments are available but the best one for him may not be readily apparent and therefore a trial of different approaches over time may be necessary. This explanation might decrease the chances of Mr. W's becoming discouraged and quitting treatment if he does not receive immediate improvement. The evaluation can then proceed including a neurological examination (to detect possible "soft" signs, such as a left-right ambivalence or a perceptual reversal), an electroencephalographic (EEG) study (to detect a possible underlying seizure disorder), and psychological testing (to determine if a subtle organicity is present). If these tests are normal (and they usually are), anticonvulsant medication is less likely to be effective; other kinds of medications should therefore be tried first, e.g., beta blockers, benzodiazepines, and even neuroleptics, antidepressants, or lithium (as long as a trusting relationship has developed and compliance can be reasonably assured). Unfortunately, the specific indications and efficacy of these drugs for violent behavior remain uncertain, but the reported possibility of their usefulness warrants a clinical trial.

While different drugs, alone and in combination, are being given an extended trial, the therapist can concomitantly evaluate what particular situations tend to provoke Mr. W. The patient can then be informed both how to avoid those situations and how to use relaxation techniques and behavioral modification to deal with those situations which have not been avoided. Surprisingly, some patients respond remarkably well to the simple advice of being taught to count to 10 or to walk away from their troubles. More formal assertiveness training and stress management are often helpful. Finally, patients like Mr. W tend to elicit negative countertransference reactions. The therapist will need to keep a medical model in mind and remain nonpunitive when outbursts do occur.

CHOICE AND OUTCOME

Because the intern felt unqualified to assess either the severity or the management of Mr. W's violent behavior, a psychiatric consultant was called. Based on experience and intuition, she discerned that Mr. W was not at present a risk to himself or others. While removing the restraints, she informed Mr. W that he was free to leave the hospital and to return during visiting hours the following day. In the same reassuring and nonpunitive manner, she informed Mr. W that his so-called short fuse should be further evaluated after the current crisis had passed. She explained that the "short circuit" in his brain might respond to medication that would act as a modulator. She emphasized that there was no hurry for a neuropsychiatric evaluation and that the problem with his girlfriend should certainly be given top priority at the present time. She scheduled an appointment for Mr. W in five days.

Mr. W did not keep his follow-up appointment. Three months later he phoned the consultant to ask what kind of medication she had in mind. The consultant replied that the matter was too important to discuss over the phone and that no medication should be given before certain tests had been performed. Mr. W said that he would think about what the consultant had said and would arrange for an appointment when he had the time.

The consultant herself never heard directly from Mr. W. She did see him by chance one day in the hospital corridor taking a young woman in a wheelchair, presumably his girlfriend, into the elevator to the rehabilitation service. Mr. W avoided the consultant's eyes, so she did not press the matter. Of interest, one year after the episode in the hospital, a neurologist phoned the consultant and explained that Mr. W had contacted him to try medication for his "fits." Mr. W had mentioned to the neurologist that the idea of medication had been planted by the psychiatrist's comments, but that Mr. W was unwilling to see a "shrink" for the problem.

A neurological evaluation revealed a normal exam and EEG; the patient was prescribed propanolol on a trial basis. He tolerated the medication well, complied with treatment and though an extended follow-up is not available, the neurologist reports that for the past two years Mr. W subjectively believes that he has "flown off the handle" far fewer times and far less extremely. The relationship with the girlfriend and the residual effects from her hemorrhage are not known.

SUGGESTED READING

1. Perry, S., & Gilmore, M. M. The disruptive patient or visitor. *Journal of the American Medical Association*, 245:755–757, 1981. (How this mechanic's explosive episode on a medical ward could have been managed in terms of restraints, medication, medical and psychiatric evaluation, and legal considerations.)
2. Lion, J. R., & Reid, W. *Assaults Within Psychiatric Facilities.* New York: Grune & Stratton, 1984. (Series of clinical papers discuss the epidemiology, etiology,

and management of violence within various settings, including general hospitals and emergency rooms.)
3. Lion, J. R., & Monroe, R. R. (Eds.). Special section: Drugs in the treatment of aggression. *Journal of Nervous and Mental Disease*, 160:75–155, 1975. (Effectiveness of neuroleptics, anxiolytics, lithium, psychostimulants, hormones, and anticonvulsants in the treatment of aggression.)

■ IMPULSE CONTROL DISORDER NOT OTHERWISE SPECIFIED

38.   The Case of the Violent Plumber

(Guest Expert: Henry Weinstein, M.D.)

Authors' Note:
Dr. Weinstein is Clinical Associate Professor of Psychiatry, New York University Medical Center, New York City; Director of Forensic Psychiatry Services, Bellevue Hospital; and Adjunct Professor of Law, New York University Law School. His interests and expertise are illustrated by this case, which involved a difficult decision regarding whether or not the patient should be involuntarily committed and whether the therapist has a legal duty to warn a threatened third party.

Mr. P is a 46-year-old unemployed plumber who comes to the emergency room because "I don't want to hurt nobody." This has not been a good year for Mr. P. Six months ago he lost his job because of a recession in the construction industry. He began to drink heavily and to beat his wife. She also began drinking, and three months ago left him for another man.

Mr. P has nightmares in which he is shooting his wife or running over her with his car. He has become irritable, has been involved in several barroom skirmishes, and has occasional blackouts. He keeps having the thought that the only way he can regain peace of mind is to kill his wife and perhaps also the other man. He does not know precisely where his wife is living now, but he does know the general neighborhood and feels he could find her without any great effort. He is a hunter and has several weapons at home with ammunition, and he fears that he may use them against her.

Mr. P has never previously seen a psychiatrist and has never been arrested. However, he does have a lifelong history of impulsive and at least mildly dangerous behavior. As a child he was frequently truant, smoked and drank at an early age, and was finally suspended during his junior year of high school. He was honorably discharged from the Army, but not before he had incurred numerous fines and reductions in rank for drinking while driving, vandalism, and going AWOL. He settled down a good deal with marriage and steady work, but would occasionally "go on a toot" of drinking, rowdiness, and barroom fighting. He has broken several noses and jaws (and his own nose is now well out of joint), but until the present time he has never come close to killing anyone.

Mr. P comes for assistance now because he is afraid that he is losing control and may actually stalk and kill his wife. He has been drinking a fifth of bourbon a day for the past month but does not appear to be intoxicated, unclear in sensorium, or impaired on mental status testing. He is open and cooperative with the consultant, but adamantly refuses hospitalization with such comments as, "I'd rather kill myself" and "I came here for help and now you want to put me in jail." He promises not to harm his wife and to keep whatever outpatient appointments the consultant feels are necessary.

The consultant is unsure what to do next. He is reasonably confident that Mr. P will not commit murder in the next day or so, but worries about the longer haul, especially if Mr. P runs into his wife. The consultant is not at all sure that Mr. P will keep the next appointment and is concerned about his ability to be detoxified from alcohol as an outpatient.

DSM-III-R DIAGNOSIS

Axis I: Impulse control disorder not otherwise specified; adjustment disorder with disturbance of conduct
Axis II: None
Axis III: None
Axis IV: Stress—severe (loss of job, marital separation)
Axis V: Highest level of functioning past year—good

DISCUSSION OF TREATMENT SELECTION

Mr. P has come to the emergency room in crisis. Having exhausted his somewhat limited resources, he is about to test our resources and our resourcefulness. We should not be surprised that the consultant is "unsure what to do next"—whether or how he should or can intervene. The case encompasses a series of difficult issues and complex dilemmas related to some of the thorniest problems in modern psychiatry: the prediction of violence; the involuntary hospitalization of the dangerously mentally ill; the treatment of impulse disorders; and the duty to warn potential victims.

The magnitude of the stressors and Mr. P's impulsivity, his tendency to resort to violence, and his serious problem with alcohol lend a particularly threatening aura. When the consultant suggests hospitalization, Mr. P adamantly refuses. He promises not to kill his wife. He is cognitively intact, but can we rely on his protestations and promises when we know he is under such severe stress and has not been able to control his violent impulses in the past?

We certainly do not wish to traumatize Mr. P further, but there are many factors weighing in favor of involuntary hospitalization. It may be necessary to accept the responsibility that society has thrust upon us to protect Mr. P from himself and to protect others. Involuntary hospitalization would provide Mr. P with necessary external controls, would permit detoxification, and would facilitate the development of a comprehensive treatment plan.

Do the factors that suggest involuntary hospitalization meet the necessary criteria? Is there a major mental disorder? Does the fact that Mr. P has an impulse disorder and a problem with alcoholism suffice?

Ordinarily when involuntary hospitalization is being considered, we are dealing with severe psychotic symptomatology. However, a famous 1962 case, *McDonald v. U.S.*, stated that a mental disease or defect was to be defined broadly as "any abnormal condition of the mind which substantially affects mental or emotional processes and substantially impairs behavior controls." While our case meets these minimal requirements, it is questionable whether a court reviewing the case would agree that Mr. P meets the criteria for a major mental disorder and would permit his retention.

Is Mr. P dangerous to himself or others? Can we justifiably predict violence or dangerousness in this case? Probably yes. The hazards of predicting are well-known, but research has shown that violence is considerably more likely if there are severe stressors, a problem of alcohol abuse, and a history of violent acts. All those factors are present here, and I believe Mr. P is "dangerous," but I have serious doubts about whether he could be involuntarily committed. Like many others walking the streets, he is dangerous but not committable.

In light of those doubts about his committability, we must consider alternatives. Would Mr. P be agreeable to admission to a "medical" service for detoxification? As for outpatient treatment, might we increase the likelihood that he would keep appointments by enlisting the help of relatives or friends? Could we assert that if he does not appear for appointments, we will try to reach him and perhaps then involuntarily hospitalize him?

Mr. P's coming to the emergency room to seek help appears to be evidence of his better judgment. On the other hand, we can assume that it was also a characteristically impulsive act, and that Mr. P is not psychologically-minded; he would probably prefer a "quick fix," perhaps a pill to help him sleep. However, he is also quite upset and anxious to talk to someone, and we can define long-term goals for him that will require his active participation.

For the long haul, it is crucial that Mr. P establish some form of therapeutic relationship with an individual he can trust and also with an institution. If the consultant is able to spend more time with Mr. P in the emergency room, he can further explore Mr. P's situation (including what outside supports are available), as well as begin therapeutic efforts.

Individual outpatient therapy could be useful to Mr. P, but group therapy could also be quite helpful. However, group therapy is usually regarded as more appropriate for a person who has difficulties controlling impulses. Various organic therapies have been tried for violent and impulsive patients but have not proven efficacious.

We know that alcoholism has been a problem throughout Mr. P's life, and we wonder whether he has ever sought help from Alcoholics Anonymous. The social network and support provided by the other members of the group would probably be beneficial.

If we decide not to hospitalize Mr. P, are we required to locate Mrs. P and warn her that her husband has thoughts and dreams about killing her? This case nicely illustrates the dilemmas caused by the notorious *Tarasoff* decision in California, which established the precedent that a therapist who determines that a patient poses a serious threat to a third party has a duty to warn the intended victim. This principle has been followed in only a very few jurisdictions. I do not believe Mr. P's situation warrants a warning. The patient is not psychotic; he is frightened by his homicidal thoughts and dreams and has sought help; and our consultant does not think there is an imminent danger.

Some final words illustrate the complexity of this case. When I presented Mr. P's situation to a group of senior psychiatric residents, they were evenly divided between the view that he should be committed and the view that he could not be involuntarily committed. During the course of a rather heated discussion, a number of the residents changed their positions; however, when another vote was taken, the group remained evenly divided.

Similarly, I had occasion to discuss the case with a number of lawyers. All agreed that as long as supporting arguments were carefully documented in the chart, either the decision to involuntarily hospitalize Mr. P or the decision to refer him to an outpatient clinic would be legally defensible.

SUGGESTED READING

1. Monahan, J. *The Clinical Prediction of Violent Behavior: Crime and Delinquency Issues.* Rockville, MD: NIMH, 1981. (Discusses those factors to be considered in trying to predict future risks of violence.)
2. Skodol, A. E., & Karasu, T. B. Emergency psychiatry and the assaultive patient. *American Journal of Psychiatry,* 135:202–205, 1978. (A successful approach to patients like Mr. P who have violent ideation.)
3. Shah, S. Dangerousness and mental illness: Some concerns, predictions, and policy dilemmas. In: *Dangerous Behavior: A Problem in Law and Mental Health. Crime and Delinquency Issues.* Rockville, MD: NIMH, 1978, pp. 153–191. (The consultant's dilemma when asked to predict dangerousness and to inform others of that possibility.)

XII

Adjustment Disorder

■ ADJUSTMENT DISORDER WITH PHYSICAL
COMPLAINTS

39. The Case of the Suspected Detective

Miss I is a 33-year-old policewoman with a long and complicated medical history. As a result of an on-the-job auto accident three years before, she suffered a nearly fatal hemothorax, a spinal cord concussion, and bilateral femoral fractures. After many hospitalizations and procedures, she made a remarkable recovery, but three months ago she began suffering chronic pain in her right leg. This pain began when a femoral steel plate was surgically removed. The pain varies in intensity and quality. Sometimes it is sharp, piercing, brief, and severe; at other times it is a persistent burning that is mild, but nevertheless so distracting that it interferes with her ability to concentrate at work. The captain of her precinct has recommended Miss I be placed on chronic disability or at the very least be given an extended leave of absence.

Miss I's many doctors disagree about her pain problem. Some believe the pain is not that severe and Miss I is merely seeking chronic disability; others believe the pain is real but the main problem is the patient's hostile attitude; and still others maintain that the patient was a bit "strange" from the start and, since the accident, has become a true "hysteric"; and finally, two of her orthopedists suspect that the patient is planning a malpractice suit and is exaggerating the pain if it exists at all.

The final blow came when her neurologist discovered that the patient had been obtaining prescriptions for narcotics (meperidine, oxycodone, codeine) from three different physicians, who were not aware of what the others were prescribing. This neurologist demanded that the patient be seen by a psychiatrist. Afraid to further jeopardize her case by not complying, Miss I reluctantly arranged for a consultation.

The consultant had been informed by the neurologist about the circumstances leading to the referral. He was therefore not surprised at Miss I's angry tone during the beginning of the session. In an outspoken manner, the patient explained how much she resented all the doctors and nurses who expressed doubt about the genuineness of her pain. After all, for three years she had endured multiple procedures stoically, even heroically, without once indicating that the ordeal was too much for her to handle. And besides, her record on the force for the past eight years had been exemplary with a minimum of sick days and with one glowing report after another, including one of the earliest promotions to detective for either a male or a female. The idea that she would fake pain to get drugs is ridiculous, she argued. Any cop can get her hands on drugs without having to go through the ritual of seeing doctors. Furthermore, the last thing she wanted was disability or compensation. She wanted to get back and do the job she was trained to do and took pride in doing well.

After hearing the patient's bitter, sarcastic, yet persuasive, argument, the consultant asked Miss I why she thought the doctors had become suspicious about her pain complaints. Miss I replied that she had already given this question some thought and believed the reasons were obvious: The doctors felt responsible for causing the pain when they removed the steel plate and they also felt helpless about how to relieve it; guilty and frustrated, they preferred to blame the patient rather than themselves. With only a brief hesitation, Miss I added that she was homosexual and thought the doctors knew it, or at least sensed it, and were therefore additionally prejudiced against her. For instance, she noted how the neurologist's attitude seemed to change ever since he saw her with her lover in the waiting room; and in subtle ways, during her hospitalizations, the nurses treated her visitors in a slightly condescending and distant manner.

After a second appointment to learn more about Miss I's past and after conferring with several of the specialists who had been involved with Miss I's care, the consultant concluded that the pain itself was not psychogenic and that the patient's current emotional difficulties were a reaction to the pain and its management and not the cause of the pain.

This conclusion did not mean that there were no significant psychological conflicts. On the contrary, the patient was in the dilemma of being enraged at those whose care and support she needed most: her doctors and her supervisors. And though none of those involved had specifically mentioned the patient's homosexuality, the consultant inferred that Miss I's outspoken and even abrasive manner had probably antagonized others and interfered with her care.

DSM-III-R DIAGNOSIS

Axis I:	Adjustment disorder with physical complaints
Axis II:	None
Axis III:	Causalgia
Axis IV:	Stress—severe (multiple hospitalizations and procedures, chronic pain, threatened disability and unemployment)
Axis V:	Highest level of functioning past year—fair (has maintained a loving relationship and has adequately complied with necessary medical care, but work performance has been substandard)

TREATMENT PROBLEM

Thirty-three-year-old policewoman whose frustrated and angry response to postsurgical causalgia has disrupted the relationship with her supervisors and her caregivers to the point that they have begun to doubt the severity of her pain and her real intentions.

DISCUSSION OF TREATMENT SELECTION

After a thorough evaluation, the consultant has concluded in this case that Miss I's emotional problems are mainly a reaction to, rather than the cause of, the pain. The presence of dysphoria (anxiety, depression, or anger) does not necessarily mean that the pain is not "real." Furthermore, the patient does not have the past history nor the present mental status to meet the diagnostic criteria for psychiatric disorders that commonly present with complaints of pain (depression, conversion reaction, somatoform disorder, malingering, factitious illness, schizophrenic somatic delusion, and so on). In short, the diagnosis of any psychogenic pain disorder is not simply one of exclusion. Just because the pain has not responded to medical management and has an unclear etiology does not mean that the cause of the pain is primarily psychological.

With this in mind, the first therapeutic task will be to establish an alliance with this discouraged and bitter patient by explicitly indicating that the psychotherapist has no doubts that the pain is genuine. Taking the time and effort to obtain a detailed pain history will reinforce this statement and help convince the patient that the pain itself is viewed as a significant problem which must be taken seriously.

After a therapist-patient alliance has been formed around the issue of pain (which after all is what most bothers Miss I), the next task is to make the patient appreciate that her current way of coping with the pain can be improved by specific therapeutic interventions. Miss I already feels harshly criticized for the way she is handling her pain problem; the therapist will therefore need to be extremely tactful when suggesting ways she might cope with the pain in a more effective manner. The emphasis must be on what she can do in addition, rather than on what she is doing wrong. Although some experiential techniques will be necessary (such as letting Miss I express her spite and helplessness), these methods alone will probably be insufficient in that Miss I is a "doer" and will no doubt be looking for specific directives on how to change her behavior and the pain's intensity. For the same reasons, exploratory techniques that examine what the pain means to her at this time will at best hold no interest for her and will at worst convey that the therapist does not consider the pain to be the primary problem.

Along with using directive techniques to help the patient cope with the pain, the therapist will need to help the patient reestablish a working relationship with her doctors and supervisors. A statement to them that the patient is not hysterical or malingering or an addict will probably not be sufficient because others may understandably believe the diagnosis of an adjustment disorder is simply a matter of opinion and not based on a thorough assessment and specific criteria. The disagreements among the various specialists regarding both the cause and the management of the pain are perhaps unavoidable but nevertheless are interfering with effective care and with the doctor-patient relationships. Rather than expect all the physicians to unite around the psychiatric opinion (an unlikely possibility), the consultant would be better advised to suggest that one of the current physicians assume full responsibility for the pain management. This will prevent the suspicion that emerged when three physicians independently prescribed three different narcotic analgesics and blamed the patient for the polypharmacy. If no suitable physician is available for this task, a pain expert or pain clinic could be added to the repertoire of Miss I's caretakers. The patient's working relationship with her current physicians may return when the responsibility for pain management is placed elsewhere.

CHOICE AND OUTCOME

By mutual agreement, the consultant became the patient's therapist. He spent the first four sessions gathering a precise and detailed pain history, especially clarifying the exact nature of the patient's pain and the response to the various analgesics. Between the sessions, the patient was given visual analogue scales and categorical scales to document at various points in the day the severity of her pain and the response to medication. Though tedious, this careful assessment served several purposes: 1) It provided a background to measure treatment response; 2) it transposed the pain into a definable, quantified, and less impressionistic problem; 3) it implicitly indicated that the pain was being taken seriously and the patient's subjective response was not being challenged; and 4) it diffused Miss I's sense of angry helplessness and dependence because she was now being viewed as a respected and active participant in the treatment process.

Once the nature and intensity of the causalgia were documented, the therapist appealed to the patient's inclination to "attack" problems by explaining that different approaches for chronic pain were available but at present no one knew how to determine which method was best for which patient. Miss I would therefore need to make herself "an experiment of one" and investigate the array of alternative methods. Though total and continuing relief of pain was probably an unrealistic goal, techniques were available to make the pain less severe and more tolerable. Miss I and the therapist would need to compare a given method's effectiveness, using the original assessment for comparison. Both professional and lay texts were read to acquaint Miss I with the non-pharmacological methods available for treatment. The therapist also provided adequate prescriptions for narcotic and nonnarcotic analgesics to take concomitantly to achieve a synergistic effect, but he advised Miss I that taking any medicine might interfere with "the study." In this way, the therapist sidestepped any power struggle over the issue of drugs and correctly conveyed that the fear of iatrogenic substance abuse was not an important issue (see suggested reading). This approach also changed the patient's perception of pain; its presence was no longer perceived as a failure on her part or an indication of chronic disability and dependence.

Of the many approaches described in the books on chronic pain given to Miss I, she chose a method consistent with her aggressive approach to problems, namely, a modified yoga program that combined active aerobic exercise with stretching and meditation. Using both distraction and dissociation, she found the severity of the pain decreased and her tolerance of the pain improved. Ironically, she also then became adamantly against what she called "chemicals." She improved her general nutrition, increased her vitamin intake, and stopped using all medication. Miss I's relationship with her physicians improved. They stopped asking about the pain and she stopped complaining about it. After five months, Miss I felt her pain was now a manageable problem and, by mutual agreement, she discontinued psychotherapy.

But that was not the end of it. Over the ensuing months, Miss I's relationship with her supervisors deteriorated at work. She found them unaccepting and inconsiderate in making her assignments. They found her abrasive, argumentative, and no longer a cooperative member of the team. Push came to shove and, after various arbitrations, Miss I was dismissed from the police force with chronic disability and compensation but with little hope for a satisfying future. She became depressed, returned to the original consultant, and was referred for exploratory psychotherapy.

During the first three months of this treatment Miss I vacillated, often within the same session, between a despairing resignation and a spiteful bitterness—towards her former supervisors, doctors, bigots, and eventually the therapist himself. She would berate him for not solving her problems by "doing something." The therapist felt the brunt of Miss I's attacks, for she could be quite incisive in identifying the limitations of the mental health profession in general and the therapist in particular. Despite Miss I's contentious arguments, the therapist stuck to his treatment plan. He knew that Miss I was prone to externalize her problems by blaming them on circumstances and not acknowledging her own contribution to her difficulties.

After a stormy induction phase, Miss I gradually became more reflective. With the therapist's encouragement and support, she began to explore childhood memories she had long suppressed and the relationship of these early experiences to her current character traits and difficulties. She recalled her mother's alcoholic rages, the physical abuse and negligence inflicted upon her and her younger sister, and the feelings of abandonment and humiliation when her common-law father was imprisoned. For a time, Miss I's depression actually became worse as she worked through these painful recollections; but after nine months of this exploratory psychotherapy, her mood gradually began to lift as she realized that her angry, abrasive style had been acquired to defend herself as a child and that her present resentments were compounded by early experiences.

These realizations were facilitated by transference interpretations. Acting on intense transference feelings, Miss I would anticipate that she would be angrily attacked by the therapist (the mother) or that treatment would be abruptly terminated and she would be "left hanging" (by the father). To defend against these expectations, Miss I would look for any minor inconsistencies in the therapist's explanations or behavior and then, having "gotten the goods" on him, would attack him before he (in her view) attacked her; and in anticipation of being abandoned, especially before the therapist's summer vacation, Miss I would act surly and indifferent, and bad-mouth men for being so selfish and callous. Although these transferential reactions were at times very pronounced, Miss I retained sufficient ego-observing capacities to see her distortions and to respond to psychogenetic interpretations.

After one year of treatment, and now resolved to stop wallowing in bitterness over the past she could not change, Miss I decided to use her outspoken manner to her advantage and the advantage of others. She became actively involved in labor negotiations and gay rights. After two years of psychotherapy and two years of follow-up, she is known to be doing well. Physical and emotional distress exacerbate her causalgia, but nonpharmacological methods have continued to increase her tolerance of the pain and decrease its severity and secondary psychological effects.

SUGGESTED READING

1. Perry, S. The undermedication for pain. *Psychiatric Annals,* 14:808–811, 1984. (Pharmacological and psychological reasons for ineffective prescribing patterns.)
2. Marks, R. M., & Sachar, E. J. Undertreatment of medical inpatients with narcotic analgesics. *Annals of Internal Medicine,* 78:173–181, 1973. (Overconcern about iatrogenic addiction at two teaching hospitals.)
3. Roberts, A. H. The behavioral treatment of pain. In J. M. Ferguson & C. B. Taylor (Eds.), *The Comprehensive Handbook of Behavioral Medicine.* New York: Spectrum Publishers, 1981. (Nonpharmacological methods for acute and chronic pain.)

XIII

Psychological Factors

Affecting Physical

Condition

■ PSYCHOLOGICAL FACTORS AFFECTING
PHYSICAL CONDITION

40. The Case of the Pain-Ridden Politician

Ms. E, a city official in her late forties, was referred for emergency consultation by her orthopedist whom she had called in the middle of the night because of uncontrollable suicidal impulses. When she arrived at the consultant's office early the next morning, she did not appear to be the desperate woman one might have expected by the nature of the referral. On the contrary, she looked like the same attractive and articulate woman seen occasionally on the evening news. She took charge of the interview immediately by tracing her problems from early childhood to the current crisis. Her history was reported in such a concise and detached manner that the real seriousness of her problems did not emerge until much later in the session.

Ms. E was raised in an upper-class family. Her only sibling, an older brother, was institutionalized during his youth with the diagnosis of schizophrenia and later committed suicide. Her father, an internationally renowned physician, was remembered as a hard-driving man who was never able to accept having "a mental cripple" in the family. In fact, after the brother was sent away, his very existence was never mentioned in the family. Ms. E recalled that at an early age she consciously decided that she would need to be exceptional if she were not to be "discarded" in a

291

similar way. Accordingly, she rejected the traditional female role represented by her mother and attempted to match her father's accomplishments, determined to gain his favor. She never did. When the father
himself suicided when Ms. E was in her late thirties (10 years ago), his
will stated that she was to receive no inheritance, ironically because she
had pursued a career and had not borne him a grandson.

The desire to have children had never been a prominent desire for
Ms. E. She was far more interested in becoming a Congresswoman,
Senator or even President. After graduating from law school in the top of
her class, she entered a prestigious law firm. After becoming more financially secure, she became a district attorney and then, by her mid-thirties, a politician. Her reputation as a hard worker was widely heralded,
especially her capacity to manage on only a few hours of sleep while
"red-lining" to meet various deadlines. Although Ms. E's highly productive periods would last for several months, they would be followed, in
predictable fashion, by an eventual "crash" in which she would awaken
alone at 3:00 in the morning and stare into the loneliness of her apartment and of her life. She never considered these cycles as "sick" but
only as the price a woman must pay to succeed in a man's world.

Despite these mood swings, Ms. E never thought of getting psychiatric help until her late thirties when (shortly after her father's suicide)
she saw a psychologist because of depression following rejection by a
married lover. After only three sessions, she concluded that therapy was
an unnecessary distraction from her rapidly escalating career. She
pushed aside her grief, abruptly quit treatment, and reentered the fast
lane, racing towards success.

A year later, at age 40, Ms. E's ambitions were impeded by an unfore-
seen event. While helping her mother move her father's belongings out
of the attic, Ms. E's back went into a severe spasm. She had experienced
intermittently over the years some mild back pain that she had for the
most part simply ignored, but this pain immobilized her for several
days. Even when she was able to return to work, the pain was so bother-
some that she was forced to overcome her usual reluctance to see any
doctors.

She consulted an orthopedist and, in her view, this visit was the
beginning of a nine-year nightmare from which she had still not awakened. She underwent every possible kind of treatment—two laminecoto-
mies, a spinal fusion, physical therapy, chiropractic realignment, acu-
puncture, hypnosis, bed rest with prolonged traction, muscle relaxants,
podiatry, transcutaneous nerve stimulator, megavitamins, etc.—but her
chronic back pain not only remained refractory to these efforts, but often
became worse after each new prescription failed. No one doubted the

existence of a real physical problem. Repeated X rays and scans had confirmed disc disease and neurological examinations showed sensory, motor, and reflex changes. But even with these findings, the doctors suspected that Ms. E had "an emotional overlay." This belief was based primarily on Ms. E's frustrated and angry reaction when none of the various treatments provided any relief. Accordingly, in the midst of this "nightmare" when Ms. E was 45, she was told by her orthopedist that she must "stop doctor-shopping" and "see someone to talk to."

Willing to give psychotherapy a try but resentful that her persistent search for pain relief was misinterpreted as neurotic, Ms. E began a twice-weekly psychotherapy. She found the exploration of her psychodynamics intriguing but essentially unhelpful for either her frustrations or her pain. The therapist, admittedly also frustrated by Ms. E's seeming resistance to receive any benefit from his interpretations, decided after three months to place Ms. E on amitriptyline 25 mg three times a day. Ms. E did not like the idea of taking any psychotropic medication because it suggested a "moral weakness," and she found the dry mouth and lightheadedness an intolerable obstacle to her job performance. She discontinued the antidepressant after only a few days and when the therapist learned of her noncompliance, she felt that he became openly hostile and contentious. An argument ensued and Ms. E abruptly stopped treatment.

During the next four years until the present time, Ms. E continued to struggle with her chronic pain for the most part on her own except for occasional visits to the orthopedist for hypnotics and nonnarcotic analgesics. She would carefully arrange her schedule to allow for three one-hour blocks each day to do her back exercises and apply ice packs. Despite the distraction and anguish produced by the chronic pain, she managed to conceal her problem from the public, her coworkers, and her friends. Her involvement with men continued its former pattern of brief affairs with VIPs who were usually married and who also wanted to keep these affairs private. Professionally, her usual frenetic pace was interrupted only by her annual "crashes," which she would hide by taking "an unscheduled vacation" that was actually a retreat to her country home. There she would stay drunk for two weeks until her mood again began to lift; but during her last crash, Ms. E felt she had hit the bottom of the barrel and could not bounce back up. Instead she continued to sink into despair, lost her capacity to concentrate at work, and was unable to attend committee meetings, meet with the public, or see friends. Even after a few nightcaps and painkillers, she was unable to sleep through the night. She would be awakened by nightmares followed by wishes "to get some rest once and for all."

This entire account was reported by Ms. E so articulately that only when the consultant began to inquire about the specific events of the previous night that led to the emergency referral did he discover the severity of Ms. E's despair. After a dinner engagement and sexual encounter with her orthopedist, Ms. E had returned to her apartment, had a few more drinks, and began taking stock of her life. Her fiftieth birthday was only a month away, and though successful, Ms. E knew that she was no longer on the fast track and that her grand childhood expectations to be a prominent political leader would never be realized.

At first "just for fun" but then more seriously, she sat down in her despairing and intoxicated state and wrote a revealing exposé to the orthopedist's wife and then prepared for the Associated Press her "obituary," which was actually a list of every physician with whom she had slept for the past 30 years. Her motivation at the time was that her death would "take all you medical bastards with me." After completing the letter and obituary, she opened a cherished bottle of 1957 burgundy (a gift from her father years before) and intended to drink the wine with an overdose of hypnotics. Instead, she impulsively phoned the orthopedist who promptly came and stayed with her through the night.

Even when describing these events, Ms. E appeared confident and self-assured. She looked piercingly at the consultant and wondered aloud, "The pills were in my hand. I don't know what it was that stopped me and made me phone. The pain, it's just too much. I wish I had ended it."

DSM-III-R DIAGNOSIS

AXIS I: Major depressive episode; cyclothymia; psychological factors affecting physical condition; possible alcohol abuse
AXIS II: None documented
AXIS III: Chronic back pain unresponsive to surgical and nonsurgical interventions
AXIS IV: Stress—severe (unrelenting back pain, also approaching fiftieth birthday)
AXIS V: Highest level of functioning past year—very good (although at times profoundly depressed and although interpersonal relationships remain transient, patient's work performance has been extraordinarily productive)

TREATMENT PROBLEM

A city official with a history of moderate mood swings. As she approaches her fiftieth birthday, she has become severely depressed, partially because of unrelenting back pain and partially because professional ambitions have not been realized. She has not responded well to previous psychiatric treatments and has a general hostility towards physicians who have, in her view, exploited her personally and sexually and have not relieved her chronic pain. Though she presents in a well-organized and controlled manner, she came close to killing herself only hours before the consultation.

DISCUSSION OF TREATMENT SELECTION

Setting. Ms. E is at a high risk for suicide. Both her father and her brother killed themselves, and she herself came dangerously close when under the influence of alcohol, which she abuses. These worrisome features combined with the fact that Ms. E lives alone and has no supportive family or friends strongly suggest that psychiatric hospitalization is indicated. But hospitalization carries its own risk, including a public exposure that might irreversibly jeopardize the patient's political career. Furthermore, she is so suspicious of doctors in general and psychiatrists in particular that she probably would not consent to voluntary admission. Even if she were committed, the procedure might impede establishing a working alliance and might deprive her of the one aspect of herself in which she takes the greatest pride—a sense of control. For these reasons, the best setting might be crisis intervention, perhaps with around-the-clock private nurses to offer structure and support and to protect her from acting on suicidal impulses.

Format. An individual treatment is clearly the only option.

Duration and Frequency. Ms. E, despite her appearance and manner, is severely ill and a continuing high suicidal risk. Sessions must be sufficiently intense to convey that her depression is taken seriously. Given the need she has to feel in control, she no doubt will object to any indication that she is out of control and requires close attention. Tactful but firm confrontation may be necessary to point out that her behavior, like someone with a high fever, is being dictated by her depressive illness and that one goal of treatment will be to treat this illness quickly so that she may resume control of her life. The current crisis makes it difficult to predict the duration of treatment, but to relieve her fear of becoming overdependent on psychiatrists, she may feel reassured if informed that most major depressions are time-limited. However, though the frequency of sessions may be gradually decreased, Ms. E will certainly need to be followed for several months, especially since the risk of suicide may actually increase during the recovery period. Whether she requires some form of continual therapy will depend on several factors: 1) the use of maintenance antidepressants or lithium; 2) the role the therapist takes, if any, in helping manage her chronic pain; and 3) the likelihood of Ms. E seeking psychiatric treatment promptly if and when another major depression recurs.

Approach. Ms. E is by temperament a woman of action, not reflection. In order to engage her effectively, the therapist will need to point out what needs to be done and how this can best be implemented. At the same time, the therapist will need to avoid being experienced by Ms. E as controlling. Her own sense of autonomy can be preserved if the therapist, assuming the stance of an expert, educates Ms. E about her illness and advises what *she* can do to facilitate recovery. Some of these suggestions may need to be quite specific and concrete: rearranging her hectic schedule; discontinuing alcohol; avoiding unnecessary public appearances for the time being; avoiding being alone, and temporarily allowing herself to be cared for by another. Though she may secretly yearn for a nurturing relationship, the therapist will need to be cautious in expressing concern and empathizing with her pain. Ms. E may experience such remarks as condescending and demeaning. She is determined not to feel sorry for herself and certainly will not wish to be "pitied" by another.

Finally, although the psychodynamic determinants of her depression and even her back pain are noteworthy, an exploratory approach at this time is ill-advised. She has not responded to similar techniques in the past, is wary of anyone "getting inside her head," and may become more depressed as she ponders the conflicts and losses throughout her life.

Somatic Treatment. Electroconvulsive therapy (ECT) has many advantages as a treatment for Ms. E's major depression: It is fast and effective, reduces the suicidal risk, and may not require the same kind of ongoing compliance as outpatient antidepressant medication (although informed consent is of course necessary). But the disadvantages are also formidable: Hospitalization would probably be necessary and if the public should become aware that she received "shock treatment," this exposure might jeopardize her political career. Although antidepressant medications were tried in the past, she did not have an adequate trial at adequate dosage of a medication that did not produce intolerable side effects. Furthermore, the administration of medication in the past was contaminated by a negative therapeutic relationship.

Countertransference. Ms. E's VIP status as well as her challenging attitude present special problems for the therapist. On the one hand, the therapist should not be intimidated and unable to assume the authoritative stance that will be necessary to convey an air of expertise and responsibility; on the other hand, the therapist cannot react to Ms. E's controlling manner by becoming too controlling himself. This stance will only make Ms. E feel that her autonomy is being threatened and, in response, make her more hostile and suspicious towards the psychiatric treatment she so urgently needs. Ms. E has had erotic-hostile-dependent relationships with scores of doctors, including her father, and will be difficult to engage in a neutral, collaborative professional relationship. Under these circumstances, a female therapist may be preferable.

CHOICE AND OUTCOME

The initial interview with Ms. E took a dramatic turn when the consultant asked how the patient felt about the sexual indiscretions of the orthopedist, someone Ms. E knew was a professional colleague and friend of the consultant. She replied, "Why do you think I'm here?" She then revealed her secret though quite conscious delight in presenting herself to "psychiatry" as an intelligent, prominent, and articulate woman who could not be helped and who would inevitably kill herself despite the profession's best efforts. This private determination to commit suicide was seen by her as the last laugh against a profession (and father) that had not responded to either her physical or emotional pain. In essence she was saying, "You could have helped me with my pain and you didn't, now you want to help me and you can't."

The consultant was in a bind. He feared that at any moment, with the slightest provocation, Ms. E would leave the office and continue on her destructive path. At the same time, he knew it would be difficult to establish a working relationship under great pressure in this initial encounter. He therefore chose what might be regarded as a manipulative intervention by using a paradoxical injunction that nonetheless also expressed an essential truth about the current situation. He stated that he was convinced Ms. E was absolutely correct in distrusting doctors in general and him in particular; she had no reason to trust a stranger and under no circumstances should be too quick to trust him. He then added that although most "ordinary" people with her kind of depression respond quite well and promptly to treatment, she probably would not respond so well because hers was such an exceptional case and because she would have such difficulties participating well in the treatment. Then, as though making a parenthetical remark, the therapist stated that of course no one would ever know whether or not Ms. E would have been refractory to all treatments because she would be too angry at psychiatrists and too frightened to let them try.

Ms. E, certainly no fool, probably recognized the intent of the therapist's manipulation and no doubt detected the tongue-in-cheek presentation of his observations; but nevertheless she was engaged. She asked what treatments "ordinary" people would find beneficial. The consultant replied that ECT was by far the fastest, safest, and most potent treatment. He had never seen anyone with a depression like Ms. E's who did not respond.

Perhaps the strange admixture of Ms. E's willingness to be exploited by physicians as well as her wish to prove them ineffective led her to agree to give ECT a try. The therapist then presented the various ways this treatment could be implemented. Ms. E listened attentively, then assumed control: Rather than be hospitalized, she would arrange for outpatient treatment and for around-the-clock psychiatric nursing care in her apartment. She explained that over the years she had become very adroit at protecting her privacy and would be far better than the consultant at making arrangements that would prevent any leaks to the media. To preserve the patient's need for control, the consultant did not challenge Ms. E on this point and instead, with little participation on his part, listened to Ms. E make arrangements on his phone for the outpatient treatment, transportation, and nursing care. Only towards the end of the two-and-a-half-hour crisis intervention session, after all the arrangements had been made, did Ms. E once again expose the severity of her despair and indicate that she believed that all these efforts would be to no avail for she would probably kill herself, if not now, then in the near future.

Ms. E's response to ECT was prompt and dramatic. After nine treatments she not only experienced an improvement in her mood but also in her back pain. Except for a mild loss of memory for the events during the course of treatment, no side effects were apparent and she was able to return to work from her four-week "vacation." Because of her previous history of moderate mood swings and because of a mild hypomanic episode following the treatment, she was then started on lithium maintenance therapy and followed at weekly intervals in a psychodynamically based psychotherapy for the next two years. She approached these scheduled appointments as though she were bringing in her car to be tuned and even teasingly referred to the psychiatrist as her "mechanic." However, when the frequency of her appointments was decreased to every other week, Ms. E began to miss some of her appointments (a previously unprecedented event) and to experience more incapacitating back pain, which during the previous year had become far less of a problem. Although she herself offered real and practical reasons why it had been necessary for her to cancel or reschedule visits, in a session that followed a series of missed appointments the therapist (perhaps erroneously) interpreted the cancellations and the exacerbation of her pain as her response to his decision to make their visits less frequent. He stated that she would prefer "to leave rather than to be left." Ms. E was enraged at this interpretation, left the office before the end of the hour, and when telephoned by the therapist that evening, said she had no need for further treatment and had already begun to discontinue the lithium.

The therapist did not press the issue, in part for countertransferential reasons. Three months later when he saw on the news that Ms. E had experienced a political defeat, he called her, apologized for his clumsy handling of her missed appointments, commiserated with her loss, and suggested that if she should need someone to talk to, he was available. Ms. E did not acknowledge the therapist's apology and concern for her welfare, but in a perfunctory manner she did schedule an appointment. Lithium maintenance was resumed, and the back pain once again improved. Her seemingly detached and mechanical sessions continued on a weekly basis for the next several years. Despite occasional political disappointments and the need for Ms. E to make the transition into an administrative career, her severe depressions did not recur.

SUGGESTED READING

1. Kendall, R. E. The present status of electroconvulsive therapy. *British Journal of Psychiatry,* 139:265–283, 1981. (Thoroughly reviews the efficacy, ethics, techniques, and adverse effects of ECT.)
2. Bernstein, N. R. Chronic illness and impairment. *Psychiatric Clinics of North America,* 2:331–346, 1979. (How chronic illness [like Ms. E's back pain] can disrupt the doctor-patient relationship.)
3. Kane, J. M., Quitkin, F. M., Rifkin, A., et al. Lithium carbonate and imipramine in the prophylaxis of unipolar and bipolar II illness: A prospective placebo-controlled comparison. *Archives of General Psychiatry,* 39:1065–1069, 1982. (Supports the indications and value of maintaining patients like Ms. E on lithium.)

XIV

Personality Disorders

■ SCHIZOTYPAL PERSONALITY DISORDER

41. The Case of Harry the Turtle

Mr. L is brought to a psychiatry clinic for the first time at the age of 36 by his mother who would like him "fixed." He is a pudgy, short fellow in a striped T-shirt and carpenter's overalls. This outfit, along with his unbrushed bushy hair and whimsical distant stare, gives the appearance of an overgrown boy. When Mr. L enters the consultant's office, he looks bewildered and slumps down in a corner chair as though he would be content to sit there for hours if left undisturbed.

The history, obtained mostly from the mother, reveals that this kind of inertia has been a lifelong problem for Mr. L. Born out of wedlock in a remote rural area when his mother was only 15, Mr. L was raised first by his grandparents while his mother worked as a waitress in a nearby town. When Mr. L was seven, his mother left the area to waitress in a larger metropolitan area, leaving Mr. L to stay with his cousins and to drift through a small country school, where he was accepted with benign neglect simply as a creature who could not pull his weight or earn his feed.

Sixteen years ago when the cousins sold their farm, Mr. L (now age 20) was "shipped" to the city to stay with his mother. She had been married a couple of times during the interim but was once again living alone. With little choice, she agreed to make room in her small apartment for her son, a relative stranger. The original plan was that when Mr. L got used to the city and found a job, he would live at a place of his own—but he never made even a tentative first step.

The mother soon resigned herself to the situation, viewing Mr. L not as a son but more as a strange pet (she teasingly called him "Harry the Turtle"). Mr. L was content with this view. He never liked people and believed they did not like him. To avoid their ridicule, real or imagined, he kept to himself, closing himself up in his small room, eating his meals alone while listening to talk shows or country music on the radio, and avoiding even his mother whenever she tentatively challenged some of his unusual ideas. These beliefs, though not frankly delusional, centered on nutrition and the prevention of disease, such as the benefits of drinking ocean water in large volumes and the value of darkness during the day for improving dreams at night. These ideas were apparently elaborations and distortions of opinions he had heard expressed on late night radio programs.

The psychiatric evaluation had proceeded for over a half hour (first with the patient alone then with the mother present), but the consultant was still not clear what had changed recently that prompted Mr. L's mother to bring him to the clinic. Mr. L himself believed that he was perfectly fine, and most of the problems described by the mother were longstanding, not acute. The incident that had occurred recently was a rather casual comment made by Mr. L to his mother regarding reincarnation and the virtues of suicide, death being merely a transitional phase towards a higher order. Mr. L mentioned these ideas first in relationship to his pet turtle (which he had named Harry). He told her that Harry might have to be sacrificed and "become less to be more." The mother had become accustomed to Mr. L discussing his own feelings in relationship to this turtle because, as Mr. L admitted during the interview, "We're a lot alike except Harry doesn't have to talk."

The search for other signs of depression besides possible suicidal ideation was difficult because of Mr. L's unusual eating and sleeping habits and because Mr. L would simply hide behind his shell whenever asked directly about what he was feeling. For example, when asked if he had been feeling sad, he would reply in a vague and general way that he did not know why people cried or laughed or why they said the strange things that they did or why they "go out." The best the consultant could discern was that at least in the mother's opinion Mr. L's appetite had decreased over the past few months, he had lost a few pounds, his sleep had become more restless, and he was now pacing around his room more than ever. She did not recall any similar episode previously in her son's life.

DSM-III-R DIAGNOSIS

> Axis I: Possible major depression with melancholia
> Axis II: Schizotypal personality disorder
> Axis III: None
> Axis IV: Stress—none known
> Axis V: Highest level of functioning past year—very poor

TREATMENT PROBLEM

Possible depression or impending disorganization in a chronically suspicious, reclusive man who has no interest in obtaining help for his problems.

DISCUSSION OF TREATMENT SELECTION

Setting. Psychiatric hospitalization, or at least a partial hospitalization, may be necessary to evaluate Mr. L adequately, reduce the risk of suicide, determine if a depression or psychotic disorganization is present, and provide a sustained and reliable treatment with both psychotropic medication and prevocational training. A major problem with this recommendation is that Mr. L probably would not agree and could not at this juncture be hospitalized against his will. Moreover, the intense and intimate involvement with staff and patients in a hospital setting may be extremely threatening to him and thereby make the situation worse, not better. On the other hand, an outpatient setting cannot offer the sustained hour-by-hour structure and observation that Mr. L's problems may require. A possible compromise might be a day hospital with an emphasis on concrete impersonal tasks for prevocational training and avoidance of close interpersonal contact with the staff and other patients. Or Mr. L could be followed as an outpatient initially and hospitalized only if this setting seemed insufficient and/or he became willing to participate in a more structured program.

Duration and Frequency. The same dilemma is posed by the decision about duration and frequency. If sessions are scheduled too closely together, Mr. L may be threatened by the intensity and intimacy and, like Harry, retreat back into his shell. On the other hand, if the sessions are scheduled too infrequently, it may be impossible either to evaluate Mr. L's problems adequately or to mobilize change. As a possible compromise, to prevent Mr. L from feeling gobbled up or harmed by the therapist and to enable him to maintain a modicum of control, Mr. L might be given some latitude in deciding upon frequency and whether he would come for sessions in the morning or in the afternoon. In addition, on a given day the session length and training program could be brief or extended depending upon what Mr. L and the therapist felt was tolerable and helpful.

The same balance might be found in determining the duration of treatment. A compromise might be to treat the acute problem and then set up six-month blocks between evaluations for Mr. L to be on his own and to consolidate whatever gains had been made with the option of scheduling additional appointments at his request.

Format and Approach. Mr. L will clearly need to be involved in some kind of family treatment. Little progress is likely to be made without some participation on the part of the mother, both in informing her about her son's problems and in advising her how little or how much to push at a given time. The majority of the sessions, however, should use an individual format to convey that Mr. L must assume responsibility on his own and should not expect his mother to continue to infantilize him. These responsibilities will need to be listed, perhaps even written, in the most specific and concrete terms (e.g., make bed, empty garbage, keep radio turned down after 10 p.m.). Individual sessions will also enable the therapist to understand the nature of Mr. L's bizarre ideas and whether or not a deterioration is occurring which would warrant either a change of setting or the prescription of a somatic treatment.

Somatic Treatment. If further evaluation discloses that a major depressive episode with melancholia is indeed present, then antidepressants may be started, but only with the assurance that compliance is likely. In the same way, further evaluation may disclose that the mother's intuition is absolutely correct and that Mr. L is becoming more disorganized and bizarre. In that event, neuroleptics may be the first psychotropic of choice. Even in the absence of an acute disorganization, neuroleptics may be helpful. There is some preliminary evidence that low doses of neuroleptics reduce the thought disorder and other symptoms of schizotypal personalities. The risk of either kind of drug cannot be discounted. Antidepressant medications may provoke or expose a psychosis in Mr. L, and the use of neuroleptics without clear indications would be unwise, considering the possibility of tardive dyskinesia. For these reasons, the therapist will need to discuss the medicines thoroughly with Mr. L and start with low doses.

CHOICE AND OUTCOME

The negotiation phase of the treatment was unsuccessful. The consultant was concerned that Mr. L would not comply with outpatient medication and was also alarmed by Mr. L's combination of strange suicidal ideas and bizarre beliefs. Without having a firm foundation for his hunch, the consultant worried that Mr. L might kill himself in some particularly bizarre way or that violent impulses might erupt. He therefore presented to Mr. L in no uncertain terms that psychiatric hospitalization was necessary. In response, Mr. L refused hospitalization in no uncertain terms of his own and argued with surprising persuasiveness that locking him up in close contact with many other people would drive him crazier than he already was and that he would have to kill himself in the hospital for this reason alone if he were admitted against his will.

With no choice but to concede this argument, the consultant then turned to the issue of medication and recommended that Mr. L take antidepressants to reverse his current sense of despair. Mr. L replied that the doctor did not have any idea what he was talking about. How could he understand the situation in any depth after only one interview? And after all, hadn't "Harry and I" managed to cope with life's problems without needing doctors or pills? Mr. L was convinced that nature's way was best; perhaps the best treatment would be to increase his daily intake of ocean water from two to three quarts. The consultant, the patient, and the patient's mother then became involved in a strangely circumstantial and inconclusive debate about turtles, nutrition, and medication. Whatever chance there might have been for establishing a therapeutic alliance was now lost as each camp stood its ground.

Finally, another concession was made. Mr. L would take the written prescription blank, would give the idea of antidepressants more thought, and would discuss the issue with his mother (who herself was worried that Mr. L would become hooked on drugs). At some level, the consultant realized that this concession was being made more as a way of ending a fruitless argument than beginning treatment. He sensed that he would never see Mr. L again. In this respect, the consultant was absolutely correct. Mr. L's mother called to cancel the next two appointments, explaining that her son was determined to cure himself. The patient and mother never returned.

SUGGESTED READING

1. Siever, L. J. Schizoid and schizotypal personality disorder. In J. R. Lion (Ed.), *Personality Disorders: Diagnosis and Management* (2nd ed.). Baltimore: Williams & Wilkins, 1981. (Addresses the current controversies regarding the diagnosis and management of patients like Mr. L.)
2. Guntrip, H. J. The schizoid problem. In *Psychoanalytic Theory, Therapy and the Self.* New York: Basic Books, 1971, pp. 145–173. (Describes, from an object-relations point of view, the internal life of severely disturbed schizoid patients.)
3. Adler, G. Helplessness in the helpers. *British Journal of Medical Psychology,* 45:315–326, 1972. (How and why primitive personality disorders can stimulate intense negative countertransference reactions.)

■ NARCISSISTIC PERSONALITY DISORDER

42. The Case of the Ambitious Law Student

Mr. N is a 24-year-old unmarried law student who seeks psychiatric treatment because he feels like "a complete failure." His appearance, however, does not match this chief complaint. A tall, dark, and strikingly handsome man in a pin-striped suit and expensive silk tie, he has the appealing manner of a man destined for success. From the articulate and engaging way Mr. N presents his problems, the consultant feels intrigued by Mr. N and has trouble believing that the depression is very severe, even though the patient describes difficulty falling asleep, avoidance of classmates, trouble preparing studies, and, for the first time in his life, doubts about his intellectual capacities.

All these problems began only two weeks before when Mr. N received his first-semester grades and learned that he had received only two "excellents" in his four courses. Although this level of performance put him near the top of his class, he was devastated that he did no better than "very good" for the two other courses. When the consultant points out the great expectations Mr. N has for himself, the patient responds without the slightest degree of self-consciousness that he had hoped some day to become Attorney General of the United States. His first semester performance now throws this ambition into doubt. Demoralized and disillusioned, he wonders whether he made the right decision by going to law school and would like "psychiatric expertise" to help him redesign his future.

Mr. N admits that he has always had a need to achieve special distinction, a need he was almost always able to meet: president of his high school class, voted most likely to succeed in college, and seemingly always in the right place at the right time with the right things to say to the right people. When asked what setbacks—if not failures—he had experienced growing up, Mr. N has to think for a moment before finding an example, then recalls that as a high school tennis champion, he was invited to an important junior tournament. Although he made it to the semifinals, after a narrow defeat he became convinced that he would never achieve top junior ranking and would never be "good enough." On the way home from the tournament, he decided to give up tennis altogether and can now not play it even for fun.

Although Mr. N has been admired from a distance, he has never developed any sustained friendships. Those who are drawn to him by his attractiveness and charismatic appeal invariably begin to sense a subtle contemptuousness from Mr. N and an attitude of indifference to the interests and desires of others. Throughout college Mr. N had an endless series of love affairs with extraordinarily beautiful women, but he never got to know them very well or be known by them. The women (whom Mr. N refers to as his "string of pearls") would typically be discarded whenever they began to express any personal needs of their own. These needs (perhaps no more than wishing Mr. N would return their phone calls or remember their birthdays) were viewed by Mr. N as weaknesses and failings. For instance, a few weeks before semester exams Mr. N broke up with a fellow law student whom he had begun dating the first day of classes. After initially being swept away by her great beauty and intelligence, he became disappointed when she no longer seemed so infatuated by his charm. Whereas at first she would drop everything just to be with him, she later began refusing his demand that she stop studying and go out with him for a late night snack and sex. When he accused her of being selfish, she retaliated, calling Mr. N a pompous bastard who always insisted upon having things done his own way. Mr. N was not really hurt by these remarks (he had decided to stop seeing the girl anyway), but he was bewildered why she and others did not appreciate him more and would view him as pompous.

DSM-III-R DIAGNOSIS

Axis I: Adjustment disorder with depressed mood
Axis II: Narcissistic personality disorder
Axis III: Psoriasis, mild
Axis IV: Stress—mild (disappointment in grades)

Axis V: Highest level of functioning past year—very good

TREATMENT PROBLEM

Exaggerated sense of failure in a 24-year-old man who has a profound difficulty in accepting the limitations of himself and others.

DISCUSSION OF TREATMENT SELECTION

Setting. Mr. N's depression (more accurately labeled disappointment and demoralization) certainly does not require hospitalization. An outpatient therapy is the only reasonable choice.

Format. An individual treatment is the only option at this time. Because Mr. N has so much difficulty sharing and appreciating the needs of others, a heterogeneous group is a temptation; but Mr. N would never accept such a recommendation and might initially have great difficulty in the rough and tumble of group therapy. He wants the "expertise" and focused attention that only an individual format can provide.

Approach. There is considerable debate on how best to treat patients like Mr. N. Two competing forms of long-term intensive psychodynamic therapy have been suggested. In the more confronting approach advocated by Kernberg,[1] the patient's unrealistic demands of himself and of others are consistently pointed out as these occur in his life and in the transference. The major tool is interpretation of the conflicts and defenses that lead to inflated expectations and intolerance of personal needs and limitations, both in oneself and in others. In the second approach, advocated by Kohut,[2] narcissistic pathology is seen less as a result of conflict and more as a failure of development; early traumas and unempathic responses from significant figures have impeded the development of a more mature and reasonable view of oneself and others. So as not to repeat these early difficulties, the therapeutic situation is designed to encourage the patient to express freely his grandiosity and his childhood need to idealize both himself and the therapist. As opposed to confrontation and interpretation, the major therapeutic tool is an empathic resonance and a sensitive exploration of the patient's narcissistic disappointments as these occur in life and within the transference.

Since no studies have compared these two approaches, one is forced to rely on clinical judgment and take certain clues from the patient. Often the two approaches are combined in the treatment of a particular patient, depending on the needs of the moment. In Mr. N's case, he felt horribly rebuffed when the consultant even tentatively suggested that the patient's expectations were extraordinarily high, whereas there was a suggestion of therapeutic engagement when Mr. N plaintively commented on how others do not appreciate him for who he is and what he is trying to accomplish. On the basis of these preliminary data, an experiential (empathic) rather than an exploratory (interpretative) approach might be more acceptable, at least in the early stages of treatment.

A third approach, which falls outside the current debate in the psychoanalytic literature, might be the use of more directive methods. Although cognitive therapies have not yet been applied consistently to the treatment of narcissistic personality disorders, aspects of this approach might be helpful. For example, cognitive techniques could be designed to gradually diminish Mr. N's remarkably high ambitions (i.e., to become Attorney General). These goals are harmful and paralyzing if, instead of settling for less, he gives up his ambitions altogether (as he did in the past with tennis and as he is about to do with law school). Graded exposure both in fantasy and in vivo to the anxiety accompanying those situations in which he is not the best would be an interesting behavioral approach to narcissistic personality disorders, but this exposure would require a patient with greater motivation for change and with a stronger resilience to letdowns than Mr. N presents.

Psychoeducation might be more acceptable to Mr. N and fits with his request for "psychiatric expertise." He could be informed about the characteristics of his type of personality, such as a vulnerability to damaged self-esteem and a tendency to avoid or withdraw from situations in which he fears he will not excel. The therapist could then help Mr. N identify the particular stressors which are most likely to cause severe disappointment. If forewarned is forearmed, this information might help him endure without great despair whatever potentially demoralizing episodes should occur in the future.

Duration and Frequency. These time factors will to some extent depend on the therapeutic approach and goals. Though the treatments advocated by Kernberg and Kohut differ in both their theoretical and clinical view of narcissism, they share one feature: They are both intensive, long-term, open-ended treatments. More recently, a variation of the Kohutian approach has been used in a briefer psychodynamic treatment: The therapist empathizes with Mr. N's current disappointment without challenging its reasonableness and, at the same time, expresses admiration for what Mr. N has already achieved. The aim is to prevent an irreversible response to the present demoralization (such as quitting law school), but without trying to greatly modify the underlying character pathology. The patient's particular vulnerability to specific stressors can also be pointed out in this form of time-limited psychodynamic therapy.

Somatic Treatment. Mr. N's distress appears neither severe nor prolonged enough to warrant psychotropic medication at this time. Antidepressant drugs might be considered if a depressive syndrome develops.

CHOICE AND OUTCOME

Because Mr. N's stated reason for seeking help was to acquire "psychiatric expertise," the consultant followed this lead and midway through the second session presented Mr. N a "psychiatric brief" on the phenomenology of narcissistic personality disorders, the debate about methods of treatment, and the expected prognosis. Mr. N responded by feeling slighted that he could be so easily categorized. He was most upset about the prognosis, that is, a life punctuated by inevitable disappointments when grand expectations could not possibly be met and a tendency, often not recognized until the mid-forties, to fail to succeed in the manner anticipated by himself and by others. Towards the end of this discussion, Mr. N's charming glibness faded and he looked a bit sad.

The agreement was that Mr. N would think about what had been presented and return for a third appointment to "negotiate" a treatment program. He canceled the third appointment because of "a cold" and canceled the rescheduled third appointment as well, phoning the following day to say that he was now so enmeshed in trying to catch up on his studies that he had "forgotten" his appointment. He said that he would call the following week when things settled into place. He didn't.

Two years later Mr. N called to say he would like another appointment for further "career counseling." He began the session by explaining that he was in a dilemma as to whether or not to pursue a career in a prestigious law firm or to establish a small specialized corporate law firm with two colleagues who were also on the Law Review. Since the consultant presumably understood Mr. N in depth, he should be able to offer some sage advice.

The consultant did not challenge Mr. N's idealized view but did challenge Mr. N's stated reasons for seeking advice. He wondered aloud if Mr. N might perhaps have suffered another disappointment for which he would now like some consultation. Only then did Mr. N admit that as he approached graduation from law school, he had not received the numerous and enthusiastic invitations he had expected from prominent Wall Street firms, even though he had performed extraordinarily well academically. While Mr. N's demoralization was not as profound as during the first consultative visits, he was in sufficient distress to reconsider the various therapeutic options. He himself chose the more confronting approach, perhaps to prove that he was strong enough to endure the confrontations and interpretations.

Mr. N was referred to a psychoanalyst with a particular interest and expertise in narcissistic personality disorders. Several years later a disguised version of the patient's case was published in a psychoanalytic journal, summarizing how Mr. N's narcissism had arisen in part because of an illusory oedipal triumph in early age. The therapeutic process had been characterized by many storms and prolonged interruptions, but gradually resulted in Mr. N acquiring by his mid-thirties a more cohesive sense of himself and a greater tolerance for limitations in both himself and in others. Of note, he finally married towards the end of treatment, but never resumed tennis.

REFERENCES

1. Kernberg, O. *Borderline Conditions and Pathological Narcissism.* New York: Jason Aronson, 1975. (The diagnostic criteria, development, and treatment rationale for these patients.)
2. Kohut, H. *The Analysis of the Self.* New York: International Universities Press, 1971. (The empathic approach and resulting transferences with narcissistic characters.)
3. Akhtar, S., & Thompson, J. A. Overview: Narcissistic personality disorder. *American Journal of Psychiatry,* 139:12–20, 1982. (Article reviews prevailing [and controversial] theoretical and clinical approaches.)

■ ANTISOCIAL PERSONALITY DISORDER

43. The Case of Tom

(Historical Case: Hervey Cleckley)

Authors' Note:
The Mask of Insanity, by Hervey Cleckley, was an influential attempt to clarify issues about what we today would call antisocial personality disorders. In the introduction, Dr. Cleckley observes, "Although still in

the unspectacular and perforce modest position of one who can offer neither a cure nor a well-established explanation, I am encouraged by ever increasing evidence that few medical or social problems have ever so richly deserved and urgently demanded a hearing." The case of Tom, presented in part below, supports this observation.

This young man, 21 years of age, does not look at all like a criminal type. . . . In his face a prospective employer would be likely to see strong indications of character as well as high incentive and ability. He is well informed, alert, and entirely at ease, exhibiting a confidence in himself that the observer is likely to consider amply justified. . . .

This poised young man's immediate problem was serious but not monumental. His family and legal authorities were in hope that if some psychiatric disorder could be discovered in him, he might escape a jail sentence for stealing. . . .

Evidence of his maladjustment became distinct in childhood. . . . He was frequently truant from school. . . . Though he was generously provided for, he stole some of his father's chickens from time to time, selling them at stores downtown. Pieces of table silver would be missed. These were sometimes recovered from those to whom he had sold them for a pittance or swapped them for odds and ends which seemed to hold no particular interest or value for him. He resented and seemed eager to avoid punishment, but no modification in his behavior resulted from it.

Often when truant from high school classes, Tom wandered more or less aimlessly, sometimes shooting at a Negro's chickens, setting fire to a rural trivy around the outskirts of town, or perhaps loitering about a cigar store or a pool room, reading the comics, throwing rocks at squirrels in a park, perpetuating small thefts or swindles. . . . He lied so plausibly and with such utter equanimity, devised such ingenious alibis or simply denied all responsibility with such convincing appearances of candor that for many years his real career was poorly estimated. . . .

At 14 or 15 years of age, having learned to drive, Tom began to steal automobiles with some regularity. . . . After he had tried to sell a stolen car, his father consulted advisors and, on the theory that he might have some specific craving for automobiles, bought one for him as a therapeutic measure. On one occasion while out driving, he deliberately parked his own car and, leaving it, stole an inferior model which he left slightly damaged on the outskirts of a village some miles away. . . .

Private physicians, scout masters, and social workers were consulted. They talked and worked with him, but to no avail. . . . He was usually polite, often considerate in small, appearing ways, and always seemed to have learned his lesson after detection and punishment. . . .

When he drove a stolen automobile across a state line, he came in contact with federal authorities. In view of his youth and the wonderful impression he made, he was put on probation. Soon afterward he took another automobile and again left it in an adjoining state. . . . Tom was sent to a federal institution in a distant state where a well-organized program of rehabilitation and guidance was available. . . . The impression he made during confinement was so promising that he was pardoned before the expiration of the regular term and he came home confident, buoyant, apparently matured, and thoroughly rehabilitated. . . .

He found employment in a drydock at a nearby port. His employers found him at first energetic, bright, and apparently enthusiastic about the work. Soon evidence of inexplicable irresponsibility emerged and accumulated. Sometimes he missed several days and brought simple but convincing excuses of illness. . . . Later he sometimes left the job, stayed away for hours, and gave no account of his behavior except to say that he did not feel like working at the time. . . .

The theft of an automobile brought Tom to jail again. He expressed remorse over his mistake, talked so well, and seemed so genuinely and appropriately motivated and determined that his father, by making heavy financial settlements, secured his release. . . .

Reliable information indicates that he has been arrested and imprisoned approximately 50 or 60 times. It is estimated that he would have been put in jails or police barracks for short or long periods of detention on approximately 150 other occasions if his family had not made good his small thefts and damages and paid fines for him. . . .

This young man apparently has never formed any substantial attachment for another person. Sexually he has been desultorily promiscuous under a wide variety of circumstances. A year or two earlier he married a girl who had achieved considerable local recognition as a prostitute and as one whose fee was moderate. He had previously shared her offerings during an evening (on a commercial basis) with friends or with brief acquaintances among whom he found himself. He soon left the bride and never showed signs of shame or chagrin about the character of the woman he had espoused or of any responsibility toward her. . . .

On returning from his trips during the war, he sometimes told interesting stories of having been for a time in the Navy, narrating with vivid and lifelike plausibility action in which he had participated and which led to the destruction of a German submarine off Jamaica or the pursuit of a raiding warship off the coast of Greenland. . . . None of these fraudulent stories had a real element of delusion. When really caught in the lie about any of them and confronted with definite proof, he often laughed and passed it off as a sort of joke.

After these events and many others similar in general but differing in detail, Tom seemed modestly pleased with himself, effortlessly confident of the future. He gave the impression of a young man fresh and unhardened, in no respect brutalized or worn by his past experiences.

CLECKLEY'S DIAGNOSIS

Psychopathic personality

DSM-III-R DIAGNOSIS

Axis I: None
Axis II: Antisocial personality disorder
Axis III: None
Axis IV: Stress—mild (once again caught for stealing)
Axis V: Highest level of functioning past year—poor (unable to hold a job, sustain relationships, or avoid criminal behavior)

TREATMENT PROBLEM

This 21-year-old man is hopeful that his current legal problems will be resolved when authorities are informed that a psychiatric disorder accounts for his behavior. He has already been arrested 50 times and been in scrapes with the law on another 150 occasions. He is a barroom brawler, a thief, and a runaway who has never formed meaningful attachments to anyone. He is skillful in presenting himself as an appealing, energetic, and motivated young man and has no trouble finding jobs; but soon he becomes irresponsible, frequently misses work, and eventually loses his jobs when elaborate and convincing excuses no longer are tolerated.

His behavioral problems have a long and consistent history. In childhood he couldn't or wouldn't tell the truth. He was truant from school and stole from both his family and others. He set fires, killed animals needlessly, and frequently vandalized property, always covering his tracks with alibis. Throughout his childhood and during his entire adolescence, multiple attempts have been made to alter his behavior by psychiatric treatment or confinement. All these efforts have failed.

DISCUSSION OF TREATMENT SELECTION

Cleckley's case of Tom illustrates one situation in which no psychiatric treatment is the prescription of choice. Because Tom has limited control of his behavior, the consultant might understandably wish to protect him from legal action and to help him overcome rather than be punished for emotional problems. At present, however, there is no treatment for Tom's disorder that is very effective—and the provision of an ineffective treatment will make it even worse. Once Tom is offered the opportunity to become a psychiatric patient as a refuge from legal responsibility, he will have even less reason to apply whatever controls are within his power. In addition, if Tom is sent to a hospital instead of a jail, he is likely to become a wolf, preying on the weaknesses of mental patients who are especially unable to protect themselves. He might also study the other patients to learn the particular signs and symptoms of mental illness that will provide him with even more convincing excuses in the future and enable him to be transferred to a hospital and avoid going to jail.

Rather than offering Tom psychiatric treatment instead of imprisonment, the consultant might suggest psychiatric treatment only if he still needs it after he is placed in a highly controlled and structured correctional setting. He might then be more receptive to a behavioral or an exploratory psychotherapy program. The consultant's best contribution in this case is to make clear to the legal and correctional authorities that our capacity to treat antisocial personality disorders is extremely limited and that these individuals should not avoid punishment by being referred for a treatment that does not exist.

SUGGESTED READING

1. Cleckley, H. *The Mask of Sanity* (5th Ed.). St. Louis: C. V. Mosby Co., 1976. (This pioneering book is filled with detailed clinical descriptions of "psychopathic personalities" in an effort to document and understand this disorder.)
2. Vaillant, G. E. Sociopathy as a human process. *Archives of General Psychiatry,* 32:178–183, 1975. (After presenting a psychodynamic perspective of antisocial personality disorders, the author optimistically describes how a strict hospital setting can be used to treat these individuals.)

44. The Case of the Unabashed Raconteur

Mr. U is a 32-year-old man referred by his lawyer for documentation of a presumed mental disorder. From the relaxed way Mr. U chats with the consultant, no one would suspect that he is now on bail and is scheduled to appear in court in two weeks for embezzling $30,000 from the restaurant he has been managing over the past several months. Mr. U readily admits that he juggled the books to steal the money, but explains that he cannot reasonably be held accountable since emotional problems forced him into a dark hole and he had no other way to climb out.

As Mr. U tells the story—and he seems only too willing to let the story be told—he has needed to live "on the edge" since early childhood. An incident amusingly recounted by his parents is the way Mr. U walked into kindergarten the first day, decided in an instant the teacher was unacceptable, and walked out of the classroom's back door and went home. Little did the parents know that breaking the rules would later become Mr. U's coping style. After recurring serious disciplinary problems in grade school, he was referred to a child psychiatrist and was labeled hyperactive.

During adolescence the problems remained basically the same—truancy and insolence—but the label was changed by the next psychiatrist to "identity crisis." After a few arrests for drug-peddling on the school grounds, the judge gave Mr. U the option of jail or military service. Mr. U chose the latter and was in the army for only a few months before "a difference of opinion" with the commanding officer eventually led to court charges. The testimony by a civilian psychiatrist hired by Mr. U was largely responsible for Mr. U's escaping punishment and being granted a general administrative discharge from the service.

After leaving the military, Mr. U "tried on a few colleges to see if they'd fit," and when his parents would no longer pay the tuition, he was "forced" to go to work. Over the past 10 years he never held a job for very long and was in and out of two brief marriages because, as Mr. U put it jokingly, "My wallet and my charm wore thin." Because of "financial reasons" (i.e., unpaid bills), he then drifted from city to city without any long-term plans. He was delighted when a year ago he was able to talk himself into a job as manager of a restaurant by using forged references and claiming an experience with the business that he didn't really have. Although he was superb at engaging and intriguing (and at times hustling) the restaurant's patrons, he lived with the fear that the owners might discover that as a manager he was inexperienced, inefficient, and incompetent and relied heavily on the head cook, bartender, and maitre d' to bail him out of jams.

In Mr. U's view, this "nervousness" over his job performance was the reason he began to abuse alcohol, barbiturates, and cocaine, though he concedes that he had "a little problem" with these and other drugs in the past. To support his growing habit, he began dealing in drugs (especially with the patrons of the restaurant) and when these sales could not support his expensive cocaine habit, he began borrowing from loan sharks to stay afloat. As the debts mounted further, and "the fellows with the bulging coats" became impatient and threatening, Mr. U felt he had no other choice but to alter the private charge accounts and the food order sheets at the restaurant to escape physical harm. Having tried to convey that "this so-called crime" is really the result of a nervous condition and unfortunate circumstances, Mr. U concludes his tale by reassuring the consultant that despite his current financial problems, the cost of the entire psychiatric evaluation will most certainly be paid "sometime after the trial."

DSM-III-R DIAGNOSIS

Axis I: Mixed substance abuse (mainly cocaine, also alcohol and barbiturates)
Axis II: Antisocial personality disorder
Axis III: Two prior episodes of hepatitis; no known residua
Axis IV: Stress—moderate-severe (pending criminal trial)
Axis V: Highest level of functioning past year—fair (through exploitation and manipulation has been able to remain employed and socially active)

TREATMENT PROBLEM

Thirty-two-year-old man with an antisocial personality disorder who is attempting to avoid punishment for admitted embezzlement by having a psychiatrist document his emotional problems. The patient does in fact have an Axis I psychiatric disorder (multiple substance abuse), but is not physically dependent on these drugs at the present time.

DISCUSSION OF TREATMENT SELECTION

The consultant has a difficult decision. On the one hand, realizing that Mr. U is manipulating to escape criminal charges, she may choose to recommend no psychiatric treatment as the prescription of choice in this situation. This recommendation, explained to Mr. U in a nonpunishing manner, would have three points in its favor: 1) It would acknowledge that although Mr. U is indeed compelled by impulses that seem beyond his control, there is no available psychiatric treatment effective for his kind of problems; 2) it would help prevent Mr. U from being labeled sick and therefore someone who could not be held responsible for past, present, and future criminal acts; and 3) in a subtle way it would enhance Mr. U's respect for the consultant, as he realizes that despite his charm, she is someone he cannot manipulate.

On the other hand, the recommendation of no treatment has certain disadvantages in this instance, and the consultant must beware that the recommendation is not the result of a moralistic countertransferential response to feeling exploited. Mr. U's multiple substance abuse is a potentially treatable disorder that is no doubt contributing to his irresponsible behavior. The recommendation of no treatment carries the risk of denying Mr. U an opportunity to get help for his substance abuse. He may be more receptive to such treatment now that he has gotten himself into such a jam.

Whatever the recommendation, an important aspect of the consultation will be a no-nonsense approach in which all the cards are put face up on the table. Considering Mr. U's antisocial personality disorder, he will be able to determine quickly if the consultant is being knowledgeable and straightforward. If she is not, he will respond with a mixture of wariness and contempt that probably will prevent his accepting any suggestions.

CHOICE AND OUTCOME

In an open and nonapologetic way, the consultant explained her dilemma. She saw Mr. U's current crisis as not simply a predicament, but rather an opportunity for him at last to get help for his substance abuse problems. She in no way wanted to impede his receiving this help for a potentially treatable disease. But she also did not want Mr. U once again to use psychiatry as a way of escaping criminal responsibility. This manipulation might only encourage his being more irresponsible in the future and cause him to get into the kind of trouble that not even psychiatric testimony would enable him to escape. As a compromise, the consultant recommended a second session to reassess the problem after the trial—or after imprisonment, if that proved to be the sentence. This second session would enable the consultant and Mr. U to work out a treatment program for his substance abuse without the distraction of the pending trial. Mr. U, although clearly dissatisfied with this arrangement, said he would call for another appointment.

A notable incident occurred at the conclusion of the first session. The consultant requested that Mr. U pay for the visit in cash before he left, explaining that Mr. U had a problem in this area. She knew that if she did not get paid, she would lose Mr. U's respect and might also be angry at him. Mr. U nonchalantly pulled a roll of large bills out of his pocket and paid the consultant her fee.

Not surprisingly, Mr. U never phoned for a second session. Nothing was heard about the trial or about Mr. U until two years later when a 40-year-old businessman called for a consultation. This new patient, seeking help for serious cocaine abuse and moderate alcoholism, had been given the consultant's name by Mr. U, who apparently had not gone to jail and was now a Caribbean realtor. Unlike Mr. U, this patient had no underlying personality disorder and responded to a brief inpatient detoxification followed by active participation in Cocaine Anonymous (CA).

SUGGESTED READING

1. Usdin, G. Psychiatric participation in court. *Psychiatric Annals,* 7:42–51, 1977. (Practical advice if and when patients like Mr. U come to trial.)
2. Woody, G. E., Luborsky, L., McLellan, A. T., et al. Psychotherapy for opiate addicts: Does it help? *Archives of General Psychiatry,* 40:639–645, 1983. (Clarifies why Mr. U was not as treatable as the friend he referred.)
3. Rounsaville, B. J., Weissman, M. M., Cilber, C. H., et al. The heterogeneity of psychiatric diagnosis in treated opiate addicts. *Archives of General Psychiatry,* 39:161–166, 1982. (Though focused on heroin and not cocaine addiction, this article describes how the treatment of Mr. U's substance abuse is complicated by his underlying personality disorder.)

■ BORDERLINE PERSONALITY DISORDER

45. The Case of the Stormy Treatment

(Guest Expert: Toksoz Byram Karasu, M.D.)

Authors' Note:
Dr. Karasu is Professor of Psychiatry at Albert Einstein College of Medicine. He is Chairman of the American Psychiatric Association's Commission on Psychiatric Therapies and has been deeply involved in studying how best to determine which treatments are most effective for which psychiatric disorders in which patients and circumstances. Here, he discusses a therapeutic dilemma that commonly occurs with borderline patients who are most attracted to a treatment situation that reproduces the very difficulties they are experiencing in their lives. As Dr.

Karasu points out, borderline patients may choose a treatment that is likely to be harmful.

Ms. S is a 28-year-old single operating room nurse who was seen in the emergency room after ingesting 15 tablets of meprobamate. Shortly after swallowing the pills, she induced vomiting; now, after gastric lavage, she feels "terrific" and wants to go home.

Since age 12, Ms. S has been preoccupied intermittently with suicidal thoughts, but this is her first actual suicide attempt. Her state of mind preceding the attempt was characterized by intense anger and despair, precipitated by her boyfriend's storming out of their apartment because he was fed up with her constant demands. Ms. S then called her psychiatrist and spoke to him for 10 minutes, but found him perfunctory and not concerned enough about the extent of her suffering. As she took the pills, her thought was "those bastards will be sorry when they realize what they made me do."

Ms. S had begun psychodynamically oriented, twice-a-week psychotherapy nine months ago, following the breakup of one of her many stormy love affairs. For the first few months, her therapy seemed the solution to all her problems. She and the therapist discussed the meaning of her intensely pleasurable but ultimately disappointing relationships with men, and were able to trace a clear line back to a similarly labile relationship with her father.

Ms. S was psychologically skilled and made rapid discoveries that clarified the roots of her feelings, thoughts, and behaviors. She was delighted that her therapist seemed so pleased with her progress and assumed that he regarded her with fondness as his best patient. It seemed like a promising treatment induction.

Then the roof fell in. Ms. S discovered, through a mutual friend, that her therapist was married, apparently happily, and had two children. She became increasingly jealous of his wife and preoccupied with wondering who the therapist would really prefer as a mate if he were given the choice. She discussed with him her many fantasies that they might marry, or at least have an affair.

The patient's associations, dreams, and behavior were clear and focused enough to allow the therapist to make frequent pithy interpretations and Ms. S to gain seemingly useful and affectively charged insights. Unfortunately, however, her desire to marry the therapist grew progressively stronger and was accompanied by a growing sense that he didn't really like or prefer her after all. She accused him of treating her only for the money or for the chance to play "mind games" with her. The treatment had been stuck in this bitter stalemate in the months preceding her suicide attempt.

Ms. S is now taking her suicide attempt lightly and treats the emergency room psychiatrist (a male) with a combination of contempt and seduction. She refuses to speak to anyone but "my own psychiatrist," and insists that he come to the emergency room to see her or that she be allowed to go home immediately.

DSM-III-R DIAGNOSIS

Axis I: Adjustment disorder with depressed mood
Axis II: Borderline personality disorder
Axis III: None
Axis IV: Stress—moderate (fights with boyfriend)
Axis V: Highest level of functioning past year—fair

DISCUSSION OF TREATMENT SELECTION

A thorough discussion of differential therapeutics in the treatment of this patient obviously requires additional data to describe the family history of psychiatric disorders, developmental history, sexual and work history, level of various ego functions, interests, social activities, and so on. Nevertheless, within the given limitations, I'll attempt to design a treatment plan.

The treatment of Ms. S may be conceptualized in stages: an immediate plan for treatment while she is in the emergency room; an intermediate plan for the postsuicidal period; a long-term therapy, and an intermittent intervention, if needed, for crises similar to the present situation.

The seriousness of her suicidal attempt has to be carefully evaluated. One needs to know whether there were more than 15 meprobamates in the bottle, how many she swallowed, and who brought her to the emergency room. If she herself decided to go to the ER, that and the fact that she induced vomiting immediately after ingestion of drugs suggest that she may have enough psychological distance from self-destruction not to require hospitalization. To hospitalize such a patient against her wishes may prompt further regression and undermine self-esteem without preventing future suicidal behavior.

Her refusal to speak to anyone in the emergency room appears to be motivated by her desire to involve her private psychiatrist. The ER psychiatrist may explore with her the messages that she conveys—that her seduction and contempt express the wish and fear to be close, and that her rejections of others may stem from the fear that she will be rejected.

The ER psychiatrist should inform the private psychiatrist about the situation and ask him to speak briefly to the patient on the phone and to make an appointment to see her as soon as possible.

Were the private psychiatrist to come to the hospital, his succumbing to her manipulation may also reinforce a pattern of self-destructive behavior whenever he frustrates her needs. A brief telephone conversation confirming an appointment would convey the message that the relationship will be continued, that it has limitations, and that suicidal behavior as a communication will not be rewarded or indulged.

The planning of long-term psychotherapy for Ms. S requires that the intensity and frequency of the sessions be carefully considered and the goals be clearly identified. Long-term psychoanalytic psychotherapy, emphasizing transference relationships with accompanying regression, may generate vivid material but also encourage acting-out. Since Ms. S's tolerance for frustration is limited, the therapist must modulate his activities to prevent acting-out.

A more supportive psychotherapy, with emphasis on the therapeutic alliance, may dilute such an intensive transference. This approach would generate less emotional upheaval between patient and therapist but may shortchange the patient's potential. Nevertheless, within such a supportive and accepting environment, the patient might eventually evolve towards better interpersonal relations and more adaptive defense mechanisms. Support would be especially needed when her intensive transferential feelings began to flood or she repetitively acted out in spite of the interpretations.

Management of the therapeutic relationship and transference would be the most difficult and also the most important aspect of the treatment of Ms. S, who would be fluctuating between anger and despair, and dependency and demandingness. Unsuccessful management is generally contingent on the therapist's capacity to allow the transference to develop but to modulate it in such a way that the patient's contempt and seduction will not be reciprocated in reality or in her perceptions. The patient should certainly not be allowed to experience a transference neurosis because she is currently incapable of tolerating the intensity of such feelings and the frustration that comes with such regression.

With a male therapist, an erotic transference is quickly established. The relationship goes through an early honeymoon period until the therapist disappoints the patient when he makes transference interpretations or frustrates her sexual and other demands. A female therapist, although less exciting and acceptable to the patient, might provoke a less intense heterosexual erotic phase of the transference. But sooner or later either therapist would end up in transference conflict with the patient—not an erotic conflict, but one based on dependency, deprivation, and individuation.

A male therapist must be especially sensitive to his countertransference to this young woman. There is a thin line between liking a patient and vicariously enjoying the situation and unconsciously encouraging her sexual feelings. Ms. S accuses the therapist of playing "mind games," a gentle term for "mind-fucking," which is of course always a poor substitution for the real thing. When the treatment has been stuck in a "bitter stalemate" for months, it is time for the therapist to request a consultation, regardless of the seeming acceptance of failure and sense of injured narcissism this involves. Therapist and patient both are well rewarded by a properly conducted consultation.

Were this patient to be on any medication, meprobamate is certainly not the appropriate one. Ms. S's learning to tolerate some anxiety might be useful unless, of course, the anxiety is high enough to interfere with her work and social life. In such a situation, a small amount of benzodiazepine (no more than a week's supply) may be indicated temporarily, especially when Ms. S is under stress. The nature of her anxiety and depression should be evaluated. A trial of MAO inhibitors may be worth attempting because it may stabilize the patient's mood and improve her subjective well-being. This would lay the groundwork for improvement in her relationships with people, including the therapist, as well as in her work. One must, of course, evaluate the likelihood of Ms. S's adhering to the diet required while taking MAO inhibitors and, again, not give her a large amount of pills because of her potentially suicidal behavior.

It may be desirable for Ms. S to engage in coed peer group therapy as well, to receive feedback on her fluctuating behavior and manipulativeness and to work on her interpersonal conflicts. Through her peers she may learn that people don't "make" her do things but that she is ultimately responsible for herself. Group therapy may also help her to identify her secondary gains and her "suffering," and learn that demands by others to grow up (as her boyfriend wanted her to) are not personal attacks, but age-specific expectations. The therapist may also explore the possibility of seeing her and the present boyfriend jointly for a limited number of sessions. If nothing else, the therapist would have the chance to observe their interactions and get his sense of the relationship. Conjoint therapy would also dilute the transference and give a needed reality perspective to her relationship with the therapist.

In addition, Ms. S still has to work individually, via the therapeutic relationship, on her intrapsychic conflicts, difficulties in relating to men, longstanding deprivations, potentially self-destructive behavior, and earlier relationship with her father. Also, she will have to learn to establish an intimacy with the therapist through which she will be able to moderate her demands and, one hopes, transfer such a prototype relationship to someone outside therapy. Through subtle forms of behavior modification, the patient may be encouraged to join organizations and to take classes reflecting (or developing) her interests. She should be encouraged to socialize. She certainly should not be allowed to consider therapy a convenient solution to all her problems, especially to her stormy affairs with men. Relationships are not found but developed; they require ongoing exposure, experience, and persistence while psychotherapy simultaneously removes the blocks and paves the way.

Differential diagnostics and differential therapeutics go hand in hand for every patient. The therapist must consistently consider therapeutic alternatives, realizing that the course and nature of treatment may change, not only as more objective information becomes available but as the therapeutic relationship evolves.

SUGGESTED READING

1. Gunderson, J. G., & Singer, M. T. Defining borderline patients: An overview. *American Journal of Psychiatry,* 132:1–10, 1975. (Reviews the literature in search of a consensual definition of borderline personality disorders.)
2. Buie, D. H., & Adler, G. The uses of confrontation with borderline patients. *International Journal of Psychoanalytic Psychotherapy,* 1:90–108, 1972. (After describing the subjective experiences of borderline patients, the authors support the value of confrontation in the treatment of this disorder.)
3. Masterson, J. F. *Psychotherapy of the Borderline Adult: A Developmental Approach.* New York: Brunner/Mazel, 1976. (Complements the works of Kohut, Kernberg, Bernstein, and Modell, all of whom have suggested specific psychoanalytically oriented approaches to treat these difficult patients.)

■ AVOIDANT PERSONALITY DISORDER

46. The Case of the Timid Librarian

Mr. X is a 43-year-old bachelor who lives alone and seeks psychiatric help because he fears the second half of his life will be no different from the first—boring and unrewarding. This chief complaint now is no different from the one he had three years ago when he called for a consultation but then failed to keep the appointment.

Mr. X's view of his life makes sense. It is indeed very dull, uneventful, and unchanging. Timid and easily daunted, he avoids new experiences in order to avoid feeling inadequate, embarrassed, or even slightly uncomfortable. He would like to date. Through his work with the Library Association he has contact with many single women (perhaps with similar problems) who would probably be most delighted by an invitation, but he lacks the courage to ask someone out. He would be terrified if the woman said yes, and humiliated if she said no. Mr. X has been in love all his life with a childhood sweetheart who, after years of a compatible but asexual relationship, refused to marry him because he lacked "backbone."

Mr. X's professional life is also in a rut. He would advance to a more stimulating and responsible position at a university library if he were more productive, but for 10 years he has worked and reworked his master's thesis for eventual publication in book form. Each time he has written a "final draft" the fears about exposing his work prevent his moving the project forward, and he decides to make one more revision. Even if the thesis were published, he realizes that he might be once again passed over for a promotion because his supervisors have openly stated that he lacks the air of authority to supervise others. Mr. X does not deny their assessment. He realizes that unless some dramatic changes are made, he will probably be doing the same work for the next 20 years until retirement, feeling frustrated by the repetitive routine but frightened by anything new.

Mr. X's life away from the library is as regimented as his life among the stacks. Because any new experience feels risky, he is a creature of habit. He has the same breakfast in the same coffee shop at the same time every morning (including days off) and is somewhat annoyed if his customary booth is occupied. When feeling adventuresome, he will occasionally depart from his weekly dinner menu in his apartment and go out for a Chinese or Italian meal—but he always orders the same dish in the same familiar restaurant.

The boring quality of Mr. X's life is all the more distressing because he himself realizes that he has the capacity to be and do and feel so much more. A bright and attractive man, he has a wide variety of interests, everything from ballet to engravings. He is also on close terms with many professional colleagues who admire his quiet intelligence and integrity. Because of Mr. X's shyness, these relationships are never pursued outside of work hours.

Mr. X is interested and well read in psychodynamic theory and has attempted his own self-analysis to determine if a traumatic event during childhood might have somehow contributed to his timidity. To Mr. X's dismay, this pursuit, including conversations with his parents and two older sisters, has only uncovered that he was considered a timid, easily startled baby from birth and, unlike his siblings, was upset by any minor changes in the nursery or dietary routine. He had difficulty adjusting to babysitters, playgroups, and kindergarten. Whereas many of the first graders were more excited than frightened about entering school, Mr. X cried piteously each morning his mother left him with the teacher, who in turn became frustrated when Mr. X was so difficult to console and showed little interest in getting to know his peers.

Later in grade school, Mr. X was regarded as an outsider and was teased by the other boys for being a "scaredycat." To relieve the loneliness, Mr. X would usually be able to find a close friend—sometimes a boy, sometimes a girl—who was also outside the "in groups" and who also felt frightened. Along with this capacity to always find at least one close friend, Mr. X's other saving grace has been his ability to perform research by doggedly pursuing every small reference until a given subject has been thoroughly mastered. Because of this ability, he was an exceptionally fine graduate student and was encouraged to go on for a doctorate degree. He declined on the grounds that doctoral candidates were too competitive (i.e., intimidating) and that he would be comfortable living at a level that was more relaxed. He now realizes that in seeking comfort he has found boredom and loneliness.

DSM-III-R DIAGNOSIS

> Axis I: None
> Axis II: Avoidant personality disorder
> Axis III: Essential hypertension, well controlled on medication
> Axis IV: Stress—none
> Axis V: Highest level of functioning past year—good (able to support himself, but feels frustrated both at work and in his personal life)

TREATMENT PROBLEM

An affable and intelligent man who avoids any situation in his personal or professional life that might be unfamiliar, uncertain, and therefore uncomfortable. The result is boredom and loneliness.

DISCUSSION OF TREATMENT SELECTION

Setting. Outpatient therapy is the only reasonable choice.

Format. At this point, Mr. X is probably too frightened to participate in group therapy. This anticipated refusal is unfortunate because a heterogeneous group would be the most effective format for confronting his social fears and diminishing the embarrassment and anxiety that can occur when interacting with others. A homogeneous, task-oriented assertiveness training group would also be highly desirable. Although an individual treatment would no doubt be more acceptable to Mr. X, reliance on this format alone runs the risk of constructing a therapeutic situation which, by its design, prevents the very kind of anxiety and spontaneous interactions Mr. X wishes to avoid. For this reason, an individual treatment may be viewed as a tolerable prelude for group therapy.

Duration and Frequency. Sessions must be long enough and frequent enough—at least 45 minutes once or twice a week—to arouse some anxiety in Mr. X. If too short or too infrequent, the discomfort Mr. X avoids in his professional and personal life will also be avoided in treatment. Mr. X's anxiety will thereby become only an abstract concept rather than something that is being experienced within or between sessions. Because Mr. X's symptoms are so chronic, the temptation is to recommend an open-ended treatment, but any prolonged therapy might prevent rather than enable Mr. X to change. This kind of avoiding patient often uses treatment as a reason for *not* taking risks and altering behavior; the patient rationalizes that treatment itself is enough of a risk and that he will take chances outside of treatment only once treatment is over (a day that is therefore put off). A treatment with a fixed termination date would be more likely to convince Mr. X that the time is ripe and that unlike his master's thesis, therapy is not something that will be continually revised and perfected so that it will never need to be completed.

Approach. Of the various approaches, directive techniques will probably be the most effective but, here again, what Mr. X wants and what he needs are not the same. He himself would probably be more inclined to favor an exploratory approach that would meticulously research and uncover the emotional conflicts that have led to his anxiety and avoidance. In an exploratory treatment Mr. X might learn that he refuses supervisory responsibilities because he feels that promotion is a form of defeating others and of subjecting himself to their jealousy and retaliation; he might also learn that he avoids women because sexual desires are reminiscent of oedipal longings and expectations of punishment or humiliation at the hands of a mocking father; but all the while that these insights are being obtained, Mr. X might very well continue to avoid those anxious situations he is now coming to "understand" better. Psychodynamic exploration of fantasies and irrational fears is usually most vivid and useful when the avoidant patient begins actually to perform some of the activities that previously had been avoided.

Mr. X might also favor an experiential approach in which the therapist, like Mr. X's other isolated close friends, remains comfortably situated on the outside of everyday risk-taking. There the two of them can avoid life while discussing from afar those situations they find intimidating. However, the therapist may initially need to establish a nonthreatening, accepting relationship with the patient before beginning to make demands for increased performance.

Behavioral techniques that have been developed for the treatment of social phobias are also often useful in treating avoidant personality disorders: The major target symptom would be Mr. X's avoidant behavior. The goal would be for him to learn to expose himself to and tolerate the inevitable anxiety that accompanies many professional and social situations. To accomplish this goal, Mr. X would need to undertake the very activities he has dreaded. These activities could be organized from the start in a hierarchy, with graded tasks that produce only minimal anxiety as first steps and tasks that produce much greater anxiety as concluding steps. For example, a step that would produce only minimal anxiety might be having Mr. X eat breakfast at a different table, then at a different coffee shop, then try a different food order—a danish instead of a doughnut.

By learning to tolerate the anxiety that inevitably accompanies his breaking of routines, Mr. X would proceed through a hierarchy of tasks until eventually he was instructed to ask a woman out on a date. The therapist would make it absolutely clear that the major therapeutic task was not that Mr. X succeed in getting the woman to accept but rather that he confront and deal with the anxiety that surrounds asking. In addition, support and encouragement would positively reinforce whatever attempts the patient dared to make.

The technique of graded exposure could be complemented with paradoxical injunctions. For instance, the therapist might tell Mr. X that a requirement for treatment would be for Mr. X to find five women during the next month who would reject an invitation for a dinner date. Paradoxically, Mr. X would need to be rejected in order to succeed. Such an injunction not only reduces Mr. X's performance anxiety (he must only ask, not be successful), but also reduces the humiliation accompanying the woman's rejection. Mr. X can honestly state that the rejection is part of the treatment plan.

Somatic Treatment. At present Mr. X does not have panic attacks for which imipramine is often helpful. Psychotropics may possibly become indicated once Mr. X stops avoiding because he may then develop symptoms that require treatment. It is generally advisable to begin with a behavioral approach and add drugs only when patients are very symptomatic or have difficulty complying with the tasks. This approach to medication reduces the tendency of patients to attribute the benefits of therapy to the medication alone rather than to the changes they have made in their behavior.

CHOICE AND OUTCOME

The consultant spent most of the second session outlining for Mr. X the nature of his avoidant personality disorder and the recommendations for treatment: once-weekly individual sessions with graded exposure techniques followed in three months by a weekly heterogeneous group. Not surprisingly, Mr. X felt that these recommendations were more than he could handle, stating with a hint of wit, "It's like I have to get all better before I can accept treatment." The consultant admitted that the recommended treatment would produce anxiety, but that the anxiety was tolerable; without it, therapy would only perpetuate rather than change the course of Mr. X's life. The remainder of the session was spent with the consultant answering questions about the available outcome research regarding the treatment of social phobia and avoidant personality disorders. The consultant cautioned Mr. X that he might be using these detailed questions to avoid getting started, but Mr. X was determined to gather all the known facts. Indeed, when he returned for the third visit, he had reviewed the cited literature on phobic behavior, had concluded the consultant was probably right, and was now ready to start.

Mr. X began in a program of graded exposure and eventually was able to enter a heterogeneous group. The therapist also added an additional technique—modeling. Rather than have Mr. X attempt the anxiety-laden tasks on his own, the therapist accompanied Mr. X to restaurants and, on one occasion, to a large Library Association meeting to teach Mr.

X "on the spot" how to avoid avoidance and to extinguish anxiety or at least to tolerate the anxiety associated with a given social task.

Mr. X made remarkable progress. Although far from a social butterfly, he is now actively participating in group therapy, has submitted his thesis for publication, and has had a few dates. In addition, now that his presenting problems have improved, he is considering entering a more psychodynamically oriented treatment to understand and work through his characterologically ingrained fear of success.

SUGGESTED READING

1. Goldstein, A., & Foa, E. B. *Handbook of Behavioral Interventions: A Clinical Guide.* New York: Wiley, 1980.
2. Kazdin, A. E. Covert modeling and the reduction of avoidance behavior. *Journal of Abnormal Psychology,* 81:87–95, 1978.
3. Kazdin, A. E. Covert modeling, imagery assessment, and assertive behavior. *Journal of Consulting and Clinical Psychology,* 43:716–724, 1975.
4. Lange, A. S., & Jakubowski, P. *Responsible Assertive Behavior.* Champaign, IL: Research Press, 1976. (The above readings provide the rationale and specific steps for improving social skills through asssertiveness training, modeling, graded exposure, and other behavioral techniques.)

47. The Case of the Painfully Shy Cashier

(Guest Expert: John C. Nemiah, M. D.)

Authors' Note:
Dr. Nemiah is Professor of Psychiatry at Dartmouth Medical School and Professor of Psychiatry Emeritus at Havard Medical School. He is also editor of the *American Journal of Psychiatry.* Here, he discusses the process of selecting a dynamic therapy (brief focal therapy, more extended analytically oriented psychotherapy or full psychoanalysis.)

Mr. D is a 32-year-old single graduate student who presents for consultation because he feels that he is getting nowhere in advancing his work or love life. For several years now, he has been unable to complete his dissertation. Although he has amassed thousands of index cards and hundreds of references, Mr. D finds himself unable to bring the project any nearer to completion. He works as an assistant cashier in a bookstore and is becoming increasingly convinced that he will be behind a cash register for the rest of his life.

Mr. D is also painfully shy. Every now and again he becomes involved with a woman, generally someone introduced by a mutual friend, but things usually end badly. Women are surprised by his lack of sexual forwardness and find that they have to take the initiative. Mr. D then becomes painfully self-conscious and fearful of performing badly, and is often plagued by premature ejaculation.

Mr. D grew up as the eldest of three children of a lower-middle-class family. He was very much the apple of his mother's eye, and he felt that she had very high, perhaps unattainable, expectations for him. His father, on the other hand, was a very pious, humble, and unambitious man whose favorite expressions were "Nobody has anything to be proud of" and "Self-praise stinks."

The patient was apparently a fairly aggressive, free-spirited, lusty five-year-old until his father caught him in the process of stripping the neighbor's little daughter and playing with her vagina. Mr. D had the stuffings beaten out of him and was also subjected to a round of mortification of the soul delivered by the local priest. After months of rigorous training in religion and self-discipline, Mr. D lost his spunk and defiance, became increasingly timid, and was proclaimed forgiven for his sins. He has been avoidant and an underachiever ever since.

The patient is intelligent and psychologically-minded. He volunteers that his self-consciousness and fears of criticism stem from the vigilance with which he felt both parents tracked his behavior. When the consultant asks how this affects his sexual performance, the patient laughs and says, "It's like always having my father watching." He then recalls a dream in which he is making love to a woman in the back seat of a taxi, then the taxi driver interrupts and takes the woman over. The patient is forced to move to the front seat and watch the sexual proceedings in the rearview mirror. He mentions in passing that the woman is much older and not really very pretty.

During the second session, the patient becomes silent and self-conscious in relation to the therapist and consciously withholds a sexual memory. When pressed to investigate what is happening, the patient notices with surprise that he is already expecting the therapist to be demanding and critical.

The patient is interested in understanding his behavior and changing it, but he is not sure he can stand the embarrassment of having to reveal all of his thoughts to someone who he is sure must judge what is said to him. This self-consciousness is why he has never appeared previously for treatment, and he is not sure now how long he will stick to therapy. He is also concerned that time and energy spent in treatment will distract him from his Ph.D., and that he may be opening a Pandora's box. His financial situation is tenuous.

DSM-III-R DIAGNOSIS

Axis I: None
Axis II: Avoidant personality disorder, compulsive personality features
Axis III: None
Axis IV: Stress—mild (dissertation, dating new women)
Axis V: Highest level of functioning past year—fair

DISCUSSION OF TREATMENT SELECTION

Brief psychodynamic focal therapy, more extended analytically oriented psychotherapy, or full psychoanalysis—which form of treatment should we prescribe? It is not a question that can be answered with dogmatic certainty, for although from the material presented we may judge that the patient appears in general to be a good candidate for exploratory insight psychotherapy, we have fewer data on which to decide which of the three modalities would be the most appropriate.

Perhaps, with the accountant's vision that the current greenbacking of American medicine increasingly forces upon us, we might start from the given fact that the patient's "financial situation is tenuous" and attempt to determine whether focal therapy, the briefest and least expensive form of treatment, would be suitable.

What are the clinical features that augur well for a successful outcome of brief focal therapy? First and foremost, the patient must be motivated for psychological change. Second, he must be psychologically-minded with a capacity for introspective self-exploration and self-observation. Third, his affects and fantasies should be readily available to him, and he should be able to tolerate the emergence of painful affects without undue disruption of his daily life and relationships. Fourth, he should give evidence of at least one good, loving relationship during his childhood.

Fifth, the patient should be able to select a circumscribed chief complaint as the focus of therapeutic work. Sixth, as a corollary to the criterion just noted, he should be at least partly aware of the nature and origin of the psychological conflict related to his chief complaint. Although the conflict may derive from a variety of levels of early growth and development, the prominence of oedipal issues is the best prognostic indicator of its successful resolution.

Measured against these prerequisites, Mr. D has many positive assets to bring to therapy. That he is motivated for treatment is evident from the specific statement that he is "interested in understanding his behavior and changing it." One could, therefore, embark on therapy with the patient with a reasonable degree of confidence that his goal is to resolve his conflicts through self-observation rather than merely to seek a nurturing, supportive relationship with an authoritative therapist.

The patient's alleged psychological-mindedness is amply documented, not only by the nature of his motivation but by his ability to bring forth in his associations a rich network of memories, feelings, fantasies, and dreams. It appears, as well, that he had a close, loving relationship with his mother during the early years of his childhood, although its exact quality is not fully elaborated in the case history. Further exploration is needed to determine whether it gave the patient a solid basis for developing potentially mature personal relationships.

So far, so good. The patient clearly fulfills three of the six criteria for brief psychodynamic focal therapy. The evidence for evaluating the remainder is somewhat more equivocal. The patient initially presents several complaints: his inability to complete his dissertation, his lack of advancement at work, his painful shyness, his repetitive pattern of abortive relationships with women, and his specific difficulties in performing sexually. We are not informed whether the patient himself singles out one of these problems as the focus for therapy.

Given a choice, one would select the patient's relationship with women as the primary target. Not only does it appear to be the central difficulty (to which the other symptoms and complaints are secondary), but using it as a point of departure gives both patient and therapist the widest opportunity to explore the central conflict as it is manifested in the triad of current adult relationships, the transference, and the early life relationships that constitute the template and source of his later relational disturbances.

As the patient presents his life history, we note that he describes a traumatic experience during his childhood with an apparent recognition that it is related to his adult problems. He volunteers that his self-consciousness and fears of criticism stem from the vigilance with which he felt both parents tracked his behavior. Furthermore, he connects this with his sexual difficulties and laughingly adds that "it's like always having my father watching."

The oedipal tone of this last statement is strongly reinforced by the patient's account of his sexual explorations at age five and their disastrous aftermath, which appears to have crushed his adventuresome spirit and induced a lifelong timidity. Oedipal issues, it would seem, play a central role in the patient's adult conflict, and their presence lends further support to the judgment that focal therapy is indicated.

We must, however, be careful not to be swept off our clinical feet by the wondrously oedipal quality of the patient's productions. There is no doubt that he has oedipal problems, but there are hints that they may not represent the primary source of his adult psychopathology and that he may have earlier, preoedipal conflicts that will prove less easily resolvable by briefer psychotherapeutic techniques. For in evaluating the patient's ability to tolerate painful affects, we note not only that his chronic anxiety (his "painful shyness and self-consciousness") has unduly troubled him throughout most of his life, but that he experiences enough anxiety in his second hour with the psychiatrist to silence his associations and to raise doubts in his mind about whether he will be able to continue with therapy. These observations suggest that the patient's anxiety not only stems from the oedipal phase but may have significant roots in earlier problems related to separation, placing him at risk for developing potentially disruptive separation anxiety as his relationships deepen.

At this early point in the evaluation of the patient, one cannot give a definitive answer to the question raised here; only further observation will clarify the situation. We may note, however, the reassuring fact that the patient has sufficient distance from his anxiety to realize, with the surprise of insight, that he expects his therapist to have the same critical, demanding attitude that he has always felt from others. Perhaps, with interpretive reinforcement from the therapist, the patient will be able to see that he is in danger of repeating in the transference his habitual pattern of anxiety-induced termination of relationships. Fortified with this insight, he may be able to avoid his threatened premature termination of therapy.

With these caveats, we may conclude that the patient is a suitable candidate for focal therapy. If, as the treatment progresses, the patient's anxiety proves after all to be unmanageable within this therapeutic approach, one may be forced to switch to a more extended form of treatment. Although one might at that point consider classical psychoanalysis, psychoanalytic psychotherapy, apart from being more within the patient's financial means, would have certain advantages. Like analysis, analytic therapy would enable the patient to utilize his capacity for self-exploration and insight to achieve internal psychological change. At the same time, it would allow the therapist to be more supportive and directive, especially during periods of mounting anxiety.

Finally, it should be noted that among the patient's presenting symptoms, premature ejaculation is a prominent concern. If this dysfunction did not improve despite significant resolution of the patient's psychological conflicts, one might wish to add the specific techniques available in a program of sexual therapy aimed at symptom removal. Such a modality would, of course, be complementary to the psychotherapeutic endeavors; and with the greater maneuverability permitted to the psychiatrist engaged in psychoanalytic therapy (in contrast to psychoanalysis proper), it could be effectively incorporated into the overall treatment program.

Successful treatment for Mr. D, as for every patient, requires a therapist flexible enough to change course as indicated and to include necessary adjunctive measures. With such a therapist, and with Mr. D's motivation and psychological capabilities, the prognosis would be highly favorable.

SUGGESTED READING

1. Kazdin, A. E., & Wilson, G. T. *Evaluation of Behavior Therapy: Issues, Evidence and Research Strategies.* Cambridge, MA: Bellinger, 1978. (Accumulated evidence from outcome studies supporting the efficacy of behavior therapy.)
2. Kelly, J. A. *Social-skills Training: A Practical Guide for Interventions.* New York: Springer, 1982. (A basic "how to" text, especially for those lacking experience or training in this area.)
3. Meichenbaum, D. *Cognitive-behavior Modification: An Integrated Approach.* New York: Plenum, 1977. (A step-by-step guide for altering maladaptive thinking as well as maladaptive behavior.)
4. White, H. S., Burke, J. D. Jr., & Havens, L. I. Choosing a method of short-term therapy: A developmental approach. In S. H. Budman (Ed.), *Forms of Brief Therapy.* New York: Guilford Press, 1981, pp. 243–267. (Hypothesizes that the approach used in brief treatment should be influenced by the developmental stage in which the problem originated.)

■ DEPENDENT PERSONALITY DISORDER

48. The Case of the Anxious Artist

Mr. G is a 33-year-old self-described "starving artist" who has come to a mental health clinic for "a crash course in growing up."

His most pressing problem began two months ago when he learned that his wife had "accidentally" become pregnant for the first time, allegedly because of a misfitted diaphragm. Although she was delighted and could not imagine having an abortion or giving up the child, Mr. G saw the situation as a disaster. The thought of a crying baby in his already cramped apartment, along with the demands on his time, his strained finances, and his struggling career, were intolerable to him. He had tentatively presented a watered-down version of these feelings to his wife, but when she erupted into tears, he decided to keep his doubts to himself and resolved to make the best of it. His anxiety, however, would not go away. Unable to relax, to concentrate on his work, to sleep, or to get the burden of being a father out of his mind, he decided the only way to feel less trapped was to have a counselor make him more mature.

When asked about these feelings of being immature, Mr. G stated that he still saw himself as "a pimple-faced kid." He traced this self-image to his youth. A shy, frail, but artistically-gifted child, he grew up in a strict Catholic home. He is still plagued by the painful memories of how frightened he was by his father's alcoholic rages and how he was unable to console his chronically depressed and rather timid mother, whom he tried to comfort daily at her bedside. During adolescence he hid from these difficulties by burying himself in his drawings; but when his father died in an accident at work, he was prematurely forced to become the man of the house. He quit high school, took a menial job at the same factory where his father had worked, and spent most of his free time arranging for his depressed mother's psychiatric hospitalizations and trying to protect her from life's inevitable stresses and disappointments. In his view, he was a failure both at work and at home: He never was promoted at the factory and, despite his major efforts at trying to comfort his mother, she committed suicide when he was 25.

Following the loss of his mother, Mr. G came to the city to become an artist. He worked as a school janitor during the day and, remaining socially isolated, painted into the night. Those who saw his work praised it highly, but Mr. G kept the paintings piled up in a closet in his apartment, too frightened to put his work on display.

By the age of 30, Mr. G saw himself as a lonely failure, a boy who had inherited his father's ineptness and his mother's despair. He sought psychiatric treatment from a Jungian analyst, but after seven months found the twice-weekly sessions too superficial and unhelpful. The analysis of dreams seemed unrelated to his problems and he felt the therapist was not sufficiently encouraging.

Shortly after stopping this treatment, he met a young waitress, who was also an aspiring artist. After only a few dates, they had intercourse. For Mr. G, this was the first time. As the relationship developed over the ensuing weeks, it was characterized more by compatibility and respect rather than by passion and spontaneity. They lived together for a few months in his small apartment and financially scraped by. Emotionally, however, Mr. G still felt dissatisfied. He was hoping that this girlfriend would be stronger, more dynamic, and colorful and thereby make up for his own deficits. Instead, she seemed to him oppressed, drab, and at heart a "simple country girl." Sex also became "just something to do." After a few months, they got married because Mr. G was "afraid to hurt her feelings." As they drifted along with their marriage and struggling careers over the next two years, Mr. G grew more dissatisfied with his wife, but he avoided any confrontation or even a candid discussion of these doubts.

Now with her pregnancy, Mr. G felt trapped. In a reflective moment during the initial interview, he recalled that he felt incapable of protecting his mother in solving her problems and even incapable of protecting the girls in school from getting their pigtails pulled by bullies. Now once again he was in the role of protecting a woman—this time his wife—from the distress of giving up a child she wanted and he didn't; and once again he felt inept and helpless in dealing with the task at hand. Could the therapist help him become more of a man so that he could accept the idea of managing a family? He waited anxiously for the consultant's recommendations.

DSM-III-R DIAGNOSIS

Axis I: Adjustment disorder with anxious mood
Axis II: Dependent personality disorder
Axis III: Asthma, in remission
Axis IV: Stress—severe (prospect of unwanted child in unwanted marriage)
Axis V: Highest level of functioning past year—fair (limited social relations, marginal functioning at work, inhibited about exhibiting his paintings)

TREATMENT PROBLEM

A 33-year-old artist presents with anxiety about assuming the role of father and provider as now demanded by his wife's unplanned pregnancy. He has been afraid to share with his wife his concerns about the pregnancy and about their unfulfilling marriage. Although apparently quite talented, he has also been afraid to exhibit his paintings and instead has stuck to a menial job beneath his capabilities.

DISCUSSION OF TREATMENT SELECTION

Setting. Outpatient treatment is the only reasonable setting for this patient.

Format. The patient presents the current crisis as a marital problem, specifically, that he wanted out of the marriage soon after he entered it and is now fearing that with his wife's "accidental" pregnancy he will forever be trapped and burdened by a woman he does not love. This presentation would strongly suggest that a marital format is indicated to help the couple either to establish a commitment and closeness with one another or to determine that their unexpressed dissatisfactions with one another are irreconcilable. The crucial decision about an abortion can clearly not be made by Mr. G alone; bringing the couple together in conjoint therapy might be the best, and perhaps the only, way of dealing with this dilemma while abortion is still a tenable option. In addition, a marital format will convey to Mr. G in the most concrete manner that he must—and can—deal with the responsibilities of marriage, whereas an individual format runs the risk both of allowing Mr. G to sidestep those responsibilities and of encouraging a dependency on the therapist in a way that recapitulates rather than solves his problems.

Despite the strong indications for a marital format, it does have some disadvantages. First, it may not even be possible at this time. Mr. G has always had trouble being open with his wife and, in his typical manner, has not told her that he is seeking psychiatric help. He may therefore adamantly refuse to involve his wife in the treatment, rationalizing that she would become too upset. Second, even if Mr. G does convince his wife to participate in a conjoint therapy, her presence may shift the focus from intrapsychic to interpersonal problems. Although Mr. G has sought treatment at this time because of his wife's accidental pregnancy, he himself admits that his primary problem is difficulty "growing up."

Duration and Frequency. Mr. G has requested "a crash course," indicating he believes that by necessity treatment must be brief. But there are advantages to prescribing a treatment that is not limited in duration. A crisis approach might suggest to Mr. G that the real problem is the decision about the abortion and once that decision is made, his need for treatment is over. By negotiating for an open-ended therapy that will continue "until the work is done," the therapist will indicate that the central problem is not so much what to do about the pregnancy but rather what to do about Mr. G's inability to assume a more assertive and mature role with his wife and in his profession as an artist. Although the duration may be kept open-ended, the frequency should be sufficiently intense to deal with the current crisis. Spacing the sessions too far apart may preclude an opportunity for Mr. G (and perhaps Mrs. G) to understand and resolve the current problem in a way that is best for them. Although distressing, the pressure they feel may be the very requirement to mobilize change of longstanding problems. Furthermore, Mr. G might interpret infrequently scheduled sessions as a sign of indifference on the part of the therapist.

Approach. Under the circumstances, the therapist is likely to feel pressured into assuming a directive and advisory role and permitting the patient to avoid responsibility both for what has occurred and for what should be done. This temptation must be overcome. If Mr. G is told simply what to do, directly or implicitly, he will lose this chance to (in his words) "grow up." On the other hand, the therapist cannot simply maintain a strictly neutral, passive attitude. While Mr. G is feeling so anxious, he might perceive this kind of therapeutic stance and recommendation as demanding too much autonomy.

The therapist must therefore walk a fine line between offering sufficient support and encouragement and yet not infantilizing Mr. G by permitting him to defer responsibility to the therapist. A focal dynamic therapy might be a wise compromise in that the therapist would assume the responsibility only for maintaining the focus of the treatment and expect Mr. G to assume the responsibility for providing the material and insight in the sessions and for autonomously directing his life.

Somatic Treatment. In the short run, a benzodiazepine may be necessary to reduce Mr. G's anxiety, help him sleep, enable him to concentrate at work, and participate more effectively in psychotherapy; but because a primary goal of treatment will be to increase Mr. G's confidence and sense of mastery "on his own," medications should be withheld unless Mr. G is so overwhelmed that he cannot participate effectively in treatment or cannot handle the demands at home and at work. If anxiolytics are necessary, the expressed plan would be to stop the medication within a few days after Mr. G is more in control of his life and more supported by the psychotherapeutic process.

CHOICE AND OUTCOME

During the negotiation phase of the consultation, Mr. G was informed about the possible advantages of conjoint therapy to understand and resolve the current crisis. Mr. G said that he would consider the possibility, but when he returned for the second session, he stated that he could not imagine including his wife in the treatment. He would never be able to talk openly in her presence, and the last thing he wanted to do was upset her during this critical trimester of pregnancy. Even the idea of informing her that he was seeking psychiatric help was unimaginable. In response, a twice-weekly focal dynamic therapy was arranged with the specified goal of understanding and resolving his need to be dependent upon and overprotective of his wife. Mr. G agreed that until this problem was overcome, he would be unable to deal effectively with the current crisis. The patient was referred to a male social worker at the mental health clinic.

During the first four sessions, as the patient focused on his painful experiences of caring for his depressed mother, Mr. G recognized that he was needlessly assuming the same overprotective role with his wife who, by his description, was socially withdrawn and somewhat naive but not the mental cripple he feared. However, this insight did not change his behavior. On the contrary, he became even more solicitous towards his wife; for example, he started bringing her breakfast in bed, arranged her obstetrical appointments, and did all of the housework even though she felt perfectly able to help out.

But his behavior within the therapeutic situation was just the opposite. In a passive and depressed manner, he would elaborate in detail the chronic dissatisfactions with his wife and expect the therapist magically to make everything all right. In the fifth session, the patient reported a dream that shifted the focus of the brief dynamic therapy. He dreamt that both he and the therapist had been drafted into a foreign war; one of the two was killed (he was not sure which one) and the other returned with jewelry to console the widow. Mr. G's first association was to the "jewelry" which reminded him of his mother's wedding ring and other valuables that had been stolen during one of her hospitalizations. He then recognized that at one level the dream expressed his wish to "leave the scene" (like the father) and have the therapist (like the patient) remarry his wife-mother and take on the responsibility. He also realized that his passive behavior in treatment stemmed in part from an identification with his depressed mother in hopes of being rescued by the therapist.

The therapist inquired about the other elements in the dream, specifically, about the death in a foreign war and the fact that valuables had been stolen. The patient had no immediate associations but in the following session, the sixth, he began by stating that on the way to the mental health clinic he had worried that the appointed hour might have been unexpectedly changed and the therapist would not be there. He then became quite tearful. Further exploration of this fantasy and of the dream brought into view a heretofore unexplored dynamic, namely, a deep yearning for his deceased father ("stolen" and "valued").

Additional transference material confirmed that Mr. G's overinvolvement with his mother during his formative years only partially explained the current difficulties in dealing with his wife. At a deeper level, he was also struggling with the infantile oedipal wish to be the man of the house. On the one hand, he was afraid of the retaliation (castration) by his violent alcoholic father that would result if that wish were put into action; and on the other hand, he was also struggling with the unconscious guilt that derived from having that wish come true when his father died. (As in the dream, it was not clear who was killing whom.)

As a result of this understanding, the therapist redirected the focus of the treatment. Instead of concentrating on the wife-mother paradigm, the therapist focused on Mr. G's yearning to have and to become a father and his fear and guilt of again acting on that infantile wish. After a period of delayed mourning for the lost father, who was no longer devalued, Mr. G felt far more capable of being a husband and father himself and actually looked forward to having the child, though he was appropriately worried about his financial situation. He began to share his concerns with his wife who responded by being more supportive, nurturing, and capable than he had ever imagined she could be.

In addition, Mr. G realized that by settling for a menial job, he was assuming the same inept passive role that he had taken in the transference. The same was true of his artistic pursuits; he had been afraid to display his works and instead had been waiting in the wings, dreaming of one day being "adopted" by a senior artist. By the time treatment terminated after three months, Mr. G had enrolled for evening classes at a city college and was arranging with a gallery a long-delayed exhibition of his work.

SUGGESTED READING

1. Frances, A., & Perry, S. Transference interpretations in focal therapy. *American Journal of Psychiatry*, 140:405–409, 1983. (Suggests when transference interpretations are indicated and necessary and when they are not.)
2. Clare, A. W. Brief psychotherapy: New approaches. *Psychiatric Clinics of North America*, 2:93–109, 1979. (In contrast to the approach used for Mr. G, discusses alternative and less conventional treatments, such as Gestalt therapy, bioenergetics, psychodrama, Erhard seminar training, and primal therapy.)
3. Perry, S., & Michels, R. Countertransference in the selection of brief therapy. In: H. Meyers (Ed.), *Countertransference and Transference*. Hillsdale, NJ: Analytic Press, 1985. (Illustrates with case examples how countertransference prob-

lems can influence the decision to choose or not choose a brief treatment; in addition, the transference-countertransference paradigm with Mr. G is presented in more detail.)

■ HISTRIONIC PERSONALITY DISORDER (WIFE) AND OBSESSIVE COMPULSIVE PERSONALITY DISORDER (HUSBAND)

49. & 50. The Case of the Odd Couple

Mr. and Mrs. C have been married for seven years and have two children of their own (a five-year-old daughter and a three-year-old son), plus a 14-year-old daughter from Mr. C's first marriage. Since daily disagreements have peppered their courtship and marriage, the consultant is unclear why they are seeking marital help at this time. Within moments into the first session each is insisting that the other must change.

Mr. C, a 38-year-old research scientist, is a perfectionist at work, on the golf course, and in the home. He insists that others—colleagues, golf partners, and especially his family—be equally rigorous in their performance. For instance, he regards himself as something of a domestic efficiency expert and, as though plotting an experiment, has developed elaborate schedules intended to guide the family's round of activities. When someone leaves the faucet dripping or leaves a bike on the yard overnight or is tardy for breakfast, Mr. C explains with a tightly clenched jaw the necessity for punctuality, obedience, and team play. These recurrent reprimands are embellished with aphorisms that the recipients find puzzling and annoying but also amusing, such as "responsibility is a privilege; privilege is a responsibility." In response to his demands, the children (especially the teenage daughter) have become increasingly rebellious, a fact which both bewilders and infuriates Mr. C since he has only asked for "just a little cooperation and consideration, nothing more." As for Mrs. C, she is tired of her husband's quiet bullying, his sanctimonious superiority, and his fastidious attention to her (in Mr. A's words) "well-documented failures to conduct her household tasks."

In his early adult years, Mr. C's attention to detail had been an asset in his professional life. Now it is becoming a problem. When he was a junior scientist and working for someone else, his rigor and reliability were highly praised. Because of his conscientiousness, Mr. C eventually earned his own laboratory, but he is now expected to spend more time generating ideas and grant money and less time ensuring that every procedure is done correctly. He has failed to meet this expectation for reasons that would not be mysterious to his family. Mr. C is handicapped by his inability to delegate responsibility or to reduce his demands for absolute perfection, including how the pipettes are washed and how the storage cabinets are arranged. He typically sets up elaborate schedules for his technicians and junior scientists, then is frustrated and bewildered when they rebel against these guidelines in a fashion that resembles the lack of compliance displayed by his family. His response to the oversights and mistakes made by the staff is to become even more caught up in the disciplining of his co-workers and in the specifics of even minor projects. He therefore has no time for publishing the work already done or for writing new grants, even though he is under considerable pressure by the department to do so. He ends up feeling at work just as he does at home—burdened, frustrated, and unappreciated.

Mr. C's attempt to escape these pressures is equally unsuccessful. On the golf course he is the butt of many jokes because his insistence that he tee off precisely at the designated hour (7 a.m.), that course etiquette be followed to the letter, and that absolute silence be maintained as he proceeds through the ritual of lining up his putts. Even when "relaxing" alone, he is similarly demanding; his collection of stamps and of antique bottles are so neatly catalogued and stored that they cannot be enjoyed by him or others. And on vacations, he prearranges every second so that no time should be left unscheduled. Once the trip is underway, he is fretful that the experiments in the lab are being done sloppily in his absence and he worries inordinately about the expenses involved. He economizes in a penny-wise, pound-foolish manner that ruins the trip for the entire family.

As for Mrs. C, she cannot understand how she ever came to marry "a computer." She does acknowledge that during their courtship she initially admired Mr. C's ability to take control, for at the time she herself was without much direction. In that regard, Mrs. C has not changed much. She continues to be a woman of mercurial interests and temperament, using her many talents to make a good start at several different careers—home decorator, professional photographer, home realtor, tennis instructor—but then never following through with any of these endeavors. She typically gets bored, neglects important details, is late and erratic in meeting deadlines and schedules, or quits in a huff when she is not sufficiently admired and appreciated, especially by a male boss.

Mrs. C is also very competitive with other women. Unusually attractive and young-looking, she dresses very much like her teenage step-daughter and is proud when the two of them are mistaken for sisters. Her stepdaughter is much less delighted by this and wishes her stepmother would act her age and stop being so friendly with her boyfriends when they come by the house. Mrs. C resents the implications of her stepdaughter's remarks and believes that she is only trying to be friendly and not turn out to be "an old fogy" like so many mothers of her stepdaughter's friends. Mrs. C has always felt that women are catty and prefers men for companionship. Whenever any of these men have eventually suggested a sexual liaison, Mrs. C has become shocked and outraged with an ingenué's innocence that her flirtatious and flattering behavior could in any way have provoked their invitations.

Even during the consultation when the couple was asked directly about their sex life, Mrs. C blushes and tries to dismiss the issue by saying that she has her "occasional orgasm," finds sex in general more of a chore than a pleasure, but would just as soon not talk about the matter. The couple would clearly prefer to discuss other points of disagreement. They fight constantly over money (she's a spendthrift, he's a tightwad), time (he's always punctual and busy, she's always late and often idle), the children (he's strict, she's relaxed), activities (he wants to do the same things over and over, she craves constant variety), and friends (his are "dull," hers are "flaky").

Despite these many points of disagreement, there is a glue that holds the relationship together. Mr. C finds his wife exciting and invigorating, a breath of fresh air; although she is shallow, vain, immature, and irresponsible, Mr. C vicariously enjoys her lust for life, aesthetic interests, and wild emotions. In the same way, although Mrs. C resents her husband's need to maintain such tight control, she admires his integrity. Whereas she bubbles over with feelings that often seem superficial and are reactive to other people's attitudes about her, she realizes that Mr. C's emotions run deep. She has seen him cry in a hidden but subdued fashion (at movies and at concerts) and is not at all surprised to see him cloud up with tears during the consultation as he discusses the distance he feels from his children. In fact, the consultant senses that perhaps the couple's reactions to the older daughter's budding adolescence may have been the catalyst for their seeking help at this time.

DSM-III-R DIAGNOSIS

Axis I: None
Axis II: Obsessive compulsive personality disorder (Mr. C)
          Histrionic personality disorder (Mrs. C)

AXIS III: Essential hypertension (Mr. C)
          Endometriosis (Mrs. C)
AXIS IV: Stress—mild (pubescent teenager)
AXIS V: Highest level of functioning past year—good (although neither Mr. nor Mrs. C is completely fulfilled in the marriage and although neither has accomplished the level of their capacities, they are still able to function at an above-average level)

TREATMENT PROBLEM

The problems are threefold: a 38-year-old man who has such a rigid need to control others and himself that it is interfering with his professional and personal fulfillment; his 28-year-old wife who has considerable warmth and energy but has difficulty becoming deeply involved in any relationships or activities; and a stormy marriage between them in which the personality of each spouse complements yet also aggravates and brings out the worst in the other.

DISCUSSION OF TREATMENT SELECTION

Setting. Outpatient treatment is the only reasonable option.

Format. There are many advantages of a marital format for Mr. and Mrs. C, not the least of which is that this format is what the couple wants and expects. Since Mr. C has come for help at this time only at his wife's insistence, he may be more motivated if the treatment is conducted with both of them together because: 1) He would not be designated as the one solely responsible for the difficulties; and 2) he would be more inclined to see treatment as something potentially helpful rather than just a punishment for being stubborn. In addition, given Mr. C's capacity to be inordinately reasonable and controlled, an individual treatment might proceed for an extended period of time before Mr. C revealed his tendencies to act like an infuriating and frustrated tyrant, whereas these feelings most likely would quickly emerge during conjoint sessions with his wife.

A marital format also has many advantages for Mrs. C, but for different reasons. In individual sessions, she is likely to flood the therapist with all sorts of feelings while maintaining the view that her main problem is her husband: If he were warmer and less demanding, they would be much happier. She would thereby be able to avoid for an extended period of time acknowledging that her behavior contributes to his reactions and elicits from him the very things she finds least attractive. The give-and-take of a conjoint therapy would be more effective in helping her see, for example, that Mr. C might be less rigid in his scheduling if she were not always late, and he might be less strict about the budget if she did not constantly overspend. Family sessions would also make some points of disagreement more immediate and palpable, but the inclusion of the children on a regular basis might distract from a working-through of the more subtle interactions that occur between Mr. and Mrs. C (e.g., how he always introduces the issues of time or money as an annoying preface to their lovemaking).

The one possible disadvantage of a marital or family format is that Mr. and Mrs. C might focus only on problems within the home, not appreciate fully how these problems extend to areas outside the marriage, and not examine and resolve their individual intrapsychic causes. An individual format might therefore be used subsequently to treat remaining problems not directly related to the marriage.

Approach. No matter what techniques are eventually used, the first approach for each partner is to make their own problems more ego-dystonic and to remove the other as scapegoat. Mr. C must realize that his problem is not simply that his wife does not like his ways of managing the family, but that his very need to control is now itself out of control and that his preoccupation with detail is limiting his success both at work and at home. Similarly, Mrs. C must realize that although many of her perceptions regarding Mr. C are accurate, her tendency to be irresponsible and easily bored is interfering with her achieving satisfaction both within and outside the marriage. Because Mrs. C is likely to take offense or feel misunderstood whenever the therapist displays anything less than open admiration and a complete endorsement, clarifying her own contribution to the difficulties in the marriage will require considerable tact.

After both partners are more aware of their own individual difficulties, either an exploratory or behavioral approach could be implemented in either a marital or individual format. For Mr. C, psychodynamic techniques would fit his reflective style and wish to understand. The danger is that Mr. C would come to realize that his controlling attitude comes from a need to repress unacceptable impulses and feelings, but that he would not be able to use this understanding as a way of changing his behavior. If he were to start using psychological rationalizations for his annoying behavior, Mrs. C would doubtlessly become all the more enraged.

The course of an exploratory therapy for Mrs. C would largely depend on the therapist's sex, age, and physical characteristics. With a younger male therapist, for example, she might be seductive and charming whereas with an older female she might be competitive and disparaging. Either course could eventually enhance her understanding of why she feels so competitive towards women and why she craves admiration from men; although the work with a female therapist might be more difficult at the start, it ultimately might be more rewarding in that Mrs. C would be less inclined to sexualize her other difficulties.

A behavioral approach might be rejected at the start by both Mr. and Mrs. C. He would resent being arbitrarily controlled and she would find the procedures tedious and boring. Nevertheless, if some compliance could be assured during the negotiation phase, behavioral techniques could be quite helpful for both partners. For Mr. C, a hierarchy could be established which would expose him in graded fashion to those situations eliciting his anxiety. For instance, he might be instructed to be five minutes late to work three days a week, spend a morning each week with no scheduled activity, forgo checking procedural details of his technicians' work, and finally spend a day with the family doing activities he has not planned. Mrs. C's hierarchy would be just the opposite. In a step-by-step fashion, she would be instructed to assume increasing responsibility so that she would no longer be in the defenseless position of being dominated and parented by her husband. An assertiveness training program would also teach her how to respond self-assuredly to her husband's criticisms rather than to retreat into the helpless posture of a pouting little girl (a position that only fuels her husband's fury).

In addition, specific behavioral interventions could be applied to alter the couple's ingrained pattern of interacting; for example, Mr. C could be instructed to enjoy the newspaper at breakfast instead of going through his morning ritual of unleashing a litany of complaints, and Mrs. C could be instructed to awaken 15 minutes earlier to prevent the frenetic inefficient scurry that starts the day with both partners scratching at each other. When these instructions are given from a neutral outsider and designated expert, they might be more acceptable. In addition, role-modeling or even a modified psychodrama could be used to teach alternative ways of interacting and to intercept the patterns each has learned to provoke the other.

Also, the value of experiential techniques for both Mr. and Mrs. C should not be underestimated. In different ways, both partners are unconsciously striving to be the most loved child. The positive regard extended from the therapist can meet this need and diminish the marital conflict while each partner acquires a capacity to function at a more mature level. Though Mr. C would be inclined to conceal his attachment to the therapist, he would appreciate gaining respect and care without needing to perform. Mrs. C, who felt loved by her parents only for beauty or talent, would profit from experiencing herself in a therapeutic situation as a competent and likable person who did not need to rely solely on stereotypic feminine charm. Using the caring relationship with the therapist as both a corrective and a supportive experience, each partner might then be able to seek and express affection towards the other in ways that would break the current vicious cycle and reinforce the best rather than the worst aspects of each spouse.

Duration and Frequency. After Mr. and Mrs. C stop using the time during sessions merely to express dissatisfactions with each other and after homework assignments between sessions have assumed an increasingly important role, sessions can be shortened and spaced at greater intervals. Although a fixed termination date might be too difficult to determine until a therapeutic process has begun, some indication should be given from the start that the marital therapy will not be extended beyond a few months. A completely open-ended treatment is likely to give the message that the couple can maintain the status quo just as they have for the first seven years of their marriage. Most marital therapies tend to be relatively brief, that is, fewer than 20 sessions.

Somatic Treatment. Psychotropic medications are not indicated.

CHOICE AND OUTCOME

The consultant recommended marital therapy for Mr. and Mrs. C. He explained that a weekly conjoint format of 90-minute sessions over the next three months could be used to clarify how each partner brought out the worst in the other and to establish new ways of interacting. This understanding and modification of behavior might in turn not only reduce tension within the marriage, but also help each partner understand and improve individual personality problems. Mr. and Mrs. C accepted this treatment plan, although each probably maintained the secret wish that the primary goal of the marital therapy would be to force the other partner to realize the error of his or her ways and to change.

For scheduling and financial reasons, the couple was referred to a reduced-fee clinic and assigned to a female social worker. The disdain for this new therapist was thinly disguised in the first session and obviously apparent in the second: Mr. C wondered aloud if the therapist had adequate "training" (i.e., status and power) and Mrs. C questioned if any woman could ever influence her husband. The therapist pointed out that these concerns reflected Mr. C's own doubts about the respect and authority he commanded at home and at work and Mrs. C's own doubts about her capacity as a woman to take more control of her life instead of being dependent on men for support and direction. Both Mr. and Mrs. C were impressed by the incisive (and undefensive) manner in which these interpretations were presented, and the ensuing sessions became more productive, though at times quite stormy.

Typically, Mr. C would begin the session by reprimanding his wife for failing to "remember" what had transpired the previous session and what the therapist had recommended; Mrs. C would respond by accusing her husband of not being more understanding and forgiving; and as each supported his or her position with additional facts from the recent and distant past, the tension between the two would escalate until they were both yelling at each other at the same time. The therapist would intervene by clarifying how each had provoked the other and would then suggest alternative ways of responding. The couple would "rehearse" these alternatives in the sessions and be advised to practice them at home. For example, Mr. C was instructed how to ask what his wife was feeling (rather than telling her what she should or should not be doing), and Mrs. C was instructed how to list specifically her three main complaints towards her husband on a given day (rather than responding to his criticism with an outburst of tears and declaring that he was "just impossible").

These and other interventions were met with the expected kinds of resistances. Mr. C complained that he was being asked "to wag the dog's tail to keep it happy" (the "dog" being his wife); he wanted her to change from within. Mrs. C complained that the therapist's instructions were too rigid and tedious and were not designed to make Mr. C "have a change of heart."

But despite these reservations, the couple responded to the therapist's clarifications, behavioral suggestions, encouragement, and gentle prodding. The intensity of the arguments in sessions and at home notably diminished; and one partner was no longer inclined to blame all problems on the other. Yet, after three months, the therapist and Mr. and Mrs. C took stock of the treatment and all agreed that it had been only a partial success. Mr. and Mrs. C related to each other more like roommates who had learned to get along with one another. They were mutually respectful, but the affectionate and nourishing aspects of the relationship were still sparse. For two sessions the therapist included the three children, hoping that their presence would generate the feelings of fondness and affiliation as the family recounted their shared experiences over the years. The inclusion of the children did provide more information; for example, the stepdaughter documented that her stepmother was little different from her own mother, but Mr. C responded to this allegation by rather snidely agreeing that he "made the same mistake twice." In short, the presence of the children was neither mutative nor healing; it only seemed to poke at old wounds.

With the recognition by all parties that the conjoint sessions had been helpful in improving the marriage but that neither Mr. nor Mrs. C had made substantial gains in resolving other problems, the therapist suggested that treatment be discontinued with the recommendation that they all convene again after several weeks to ensure that the gains were being consolidated and to explore what steps might then be taken regarding the treatment of problems that were independent of the marriage. Mrs. C accepted the recommendation to stop but saw no reason to meet again, implying (though not stating openly) that the therapist was too intellectual and mechanical and had never appreciated Mrs. C's assets nor her burden (i.e., Mr. C). Mr. C was less accepting of the plan to discontinue treatment and to the surprise of everyone, including Mr. C himself, he spontaneously asked for a few more sessions to discuss problems he was having at work. The therapist was unsure whether to accept this request or to refer Mr. C elsewhere for treatment of nonmarital problems. She was concerned that seeing Mr. C individually might be divisive as he became intimately involved with the "good" therapist to the exclusion of his "bad" wife. The therapist was also concerned that Mrs. C, feeling rejected, would be even more reluctant to resume conjoint sessions if she felt the therapist was no longer neutral but instead more tightly allied with Mr. C.

These concerns proved to be well-founded. Because of countertransference problems that were not recognized until much later, the therapist agreed to meet individually with Mr. C to examine other problems in his life. These individual sessions gradually developed into an exploratory twice-weekly psychotherapy which technically contrasted with the marital sessions. Instead of a directive and experiential approach, treatment began to explore Mr. C's early life and current dreams and fantasies. In the process, he learned that his difficulties stemmed primarily from a poorly resolved conflict between obedience and defiance. On the one hand, he wanted to be "the good little boy" who would be admired by his doting mother and who would be respected by his ambitious father. On the other hand, he was enraged that (in his view) he needed to be perfect to gain the admiration and respect of his parents and of those onto whom he transferred these feelings. Responding to this resentment, he unconsciously was defying the authority of others (e.g., the departmental chairman) by using passive-aggressive mechanisms, such as procrastination. This defiant behavior then made him all the more frightened of losing love and respect, which in turn only increased his need to be perfect and to demand the same of others. His wife's impulsivity and irresponsibility represented both his strongest desires and his worst fears.

After a year of this exploratory treatment, acting out an eroticized transference, Mr. C went through what his wife termed a mid-life crisis but which Mr. C labeled his delayed adolescence. He traded in his station wagon for a sports car, started wearing turtlenecks instead of white shirts and ties to work, and took more trips alone to research meetings, leaving his wife to contend with the domestic problems as best she could. Though he had no extramarital affairs, he yearned continuously for illicit relationships. The therapist, alarmed by this development in treatment, entered supervision. The supervisor was helpful both in pointing out the therapist's subtle seductive countertransference responses and in providing support for the otherwise superb manner in which the therapist had conducted the treatment.

During the second year of treatment, with correction of the countertransference problems, Mr. C was able to work through rather than act out oedipal themes, especially his wish to break free of ("kill") his controlling father and have an illicit ("incestuous") relationship with the therapist or her transferential surrogates. With authority figures at work, he no longer vacillated between superciliously complying with their demands and then, out of resentment, using procrastination and other passive-aggressive maneuvers to get back at them—ultimately, of course, sabotaging his own professional advancement. In addition, more aware of and comfortable with his sexual and aggressive fantasies, Mr. C was able to be far more spontaneous with his friends and family.

Mrs. C responded initially to her husband's "frivolousness" with teasing and disparaging remarks, but soon became worried, especially when he wanted their lovemaking to be more varied and less mechanical. These demands led Mrs. C to seek psychotherapy. Feeling disenfranchised by the first consultant and therapist, this second time around she saw a different consultant. He recommended a homogeneous group for assertiveness training because, in his judgment, Mrs. C's primary problem was a fear of acting on her own aggressive and sexual impulses. As a result of this unconscious fear, she assumed a coquettish "little girl" stance and expected the man in her life (surrogate father) to take all the responsibility; then when the man (husband or boss) did not behave like the ideal father, Mrs. C would become enraged and demeaning. The consultant suspected that if Mrs. C were referred to a woman in any individual treatment, regardless of the technique, she would engage in a nontherapeutic competitive struggle; and if Mrs. C were referred to a man, she would become engaged in a dependent, infantilizing relationship that would be refractory to interpretation.

Mrs. C was at first hesitant to accept the recommendation of a homogeneous group for assertiveness training. She believed that she would be receiving less than her husband, and she also felt rejected by the male consultant for not immediately wishing to see her frequently in an intensive psychotherapy. When the consultant explained his reasons for not recommending an individual treatment, Mrs. C agreed to try the group.

The 12-week assertiveness training course turned out to be the right thing at the right time. Mrs. C rapidly identified with the female group leader whom she saw as powerful yet feminine, a paradox for Mrs. C. She returned to her real estate business with a different boss, a woman, and after three years was matching her husband's income. By this time the stepdaughter had left for college; Mr. C had left academic life and switched to a less rigid research position for a pharmaceutical firm; and both Mr. and Mrs. C were pursuing interests in nonsexual friendships outside the home. By being more independent, each was now less involved in the limitations of the other. Both were now happier, with themselves and with their partner, but neither was exactly sure how psychotherapy had achieved these goals.

SUGGESTED READING

1. Paolino, T. J., & McGrady, B. J. (Eds.), *Marriage and Marital Therapy*. New York: Brunner/Mazel. (Offers a psychoanalytic, behavioral and systems-theory perspective.)
2. Dicks, H. V. *Marital Tensions*. London: Routledge & Kegan Paul, 1967. (How childhood relationships [real and imagined] shape a marriage.)
3. Kinston, W., & Bentovim, A. Creating a focus for brief marital or family therapy. In S. H. Budman (Ed.), *Forms of Brief Therapy*. New York: Guilford Press, 1981, pp. 361–386. (Along with a helpful bibliography, describes how a therapist would determine the focus for treating Mr. and Mrs. C in a conjoint brief therapy.)

■ MIXED PERSONALITY DISORDER

51. The Case of the Uncaring Nurse

Miss B is a 30-year-old nurse who arranges for psychiatric consultation because "I'm holding myself together with bits of glue." In contrast to this chief complaint, when she arrives for her first appointment she looks more aloof than fragile. Although an attractive woman, she has made no effort to appear appealing and wears a drab blouse, no make-up, and cropped short hair. In a somewhat wooden manner, she takes a seat, stares into space, and recites her life story as though it had been experienced by someone else.

She was considered by her mother to be a "bubbling bundle of joy" from the moment she was born and maintained a special relationship with the mother by being an angelic, precocious little girl. This allowed her to avoid the severe punishment given to her four siblings; whenever they were disagreeable, her mother literally would not talk to the "bad" child for a week or more. As a result of being so "good," Miss B was held in higher esteem than her siblings, and feared their envious retaliation. Her father, a factory worker who maintained two additional jobs, was rarely available to support his burdened wife, and when he was home, would spend the time doting on Miss B, his "little princess."

When Miss B began school, she dealt with this separation from her mother by maintaining a characteristically calm façade, concealing her terror and secretly vomiting in the bathroom morning after morning before going off to catch the bus. This fear and associated emesis lasted several months. Throughout her grade school years Miss B repeated this same pattern with her teachers: Terrified of displeasing them, she concealed her fears and acted like the perfect student, once again collecting the resentment of her peers. Consequently, by Miss B's early adolescence, her girlfriends had completely rejected her. Privately hurt and depressed, she acted indifferently and even contemptuously towards her former friends and turned to boys for nonsexualized companionship. This made her feel even more alienated.

In high school and then nursing school, Miss B continued to lead this double life; while appearing to be self-sufficient and confident, inwardly she felt empty, different, alone, and at times wondered if she'd be better off dead. For many years she had secretly thought of joining the International Red Cross as a way of escaping her inner turmoil, but she was afraid that her mother, because of increasing depression and alcoholism, would never survive this separation from her "little angel." Miss

B's fears were almost confirmed. When Miss B informed her mother about the plans to spend two years in the Far East, the mother wailed, accused the daughter of taking away her lifeline, hinted about suicide, and still unconsolable at the airport, clutched her daughter desperately till the final minutes before departure.

While abroad, Miss B for the first time in her life felt free. She completely forgot about her family, did not write home for many months, and threw herself into her work with dedication. Although Miss B remained somewhat distant from her female co-workers, she developed her first sexually intimate relationship with a man.

When she returned home two years later, Miss B tried to maintain this same geographical and emotional distance from her family by living in her own remote apartment with a man of a different race and by assuming very liberal political and moral beliefs that were in direct opposition to her strict conservative background. Insidiously, however, these personal declarations of independence began to take their toll in ways Miss B did not expect or understand.

With her boyfriend, she began to have the same kind of conflicts she had experienced with her mother: She was afraid to let him know whenever she was the least bit annoyed for fear that he would respond by totally rejecting her and, conversely, she was afraid to show how much she needed him for fear that he would become too close and would control her. She wrestled with this problem for several months, self-consciously asking herself, "Am I being too needy? Am I being too nice? Is he getting too close? Can I really trust him?" Unable to find any satisfying answers, she resolved her dilemma one night, after catching him in a rather insignificant lie, by coldly informing him that the relationship was over and that he must leave the following day. Just as she had said good-bye to her mother when traveling abroad four years before, she had nothing more to do with her boyfriend after she insisted that he leave.

Following the breakup of this relationship, Miss B buried herself in isolation. She changed job assignments at the hospital to avoid working with nurses with whom she had socialized in the past. She refused all invitations to go out, preferring to stay within the confines of her apartment. She elected to take evening and night shifts so that she could spend her days sleeping or staring into space in what was described as a derealized and depersonalized state. She avoided her patients as well, feeling like a robot as she mechanically distributed drugs and gave bedside care. Although most of the time she simply felt numb and adrift, every few days intolerable waves of despair would come over her during which she could barely go through the motions of life. She would call in sick to work and stay in bed until the terror passed, or if she did go to work, she would feel as though others could tell that she was gradually losing her mind. She tried using alcohol, diazepam, marijuana, amphetamines, and cocaine to relieve these symptoms, but without effect. If anything, medications had made her more suspicious of others and more hopeless about her own fate. The one thing she found which did provide some comfort was an early memory, real or imagined, of being held by her father reassuringly when she was three years old: The two of them, on vacation at the beach, were being submerged under a wave while the father kept his treasured daughter from being drowned.

The consultant, after hearing Miss B's story, was still unsure about why the patient was seeking treatment at this particular time since her symptoms of depersonalization and withdrawal had apparently been severe for at least two or three years. The only possible reason he could uncover was that Miss B reached her 30th birthday a week before she scheduled the initial appointment.

DSM-III-R DIAGNOSIS

AXIS I: Possible mood disorder (recurrent major depression or dysthymia); substance abuse

AXIS II: Mixed personality disorder with borderline, schizoid, avoidant, compulsive, and dependent features

AXIS III: None

AXIS IV: Stress—mild (30th birthday)

AXIS V: Highest level of functioning past year—fair (social withdrawal, absenteeism at work)

TREATMENT PROBLEM

Thirty-year-old woman who, unable to maintain trusting relationships within her family or with others, has retreated into a chronic depersonalized state to protect a very fragile sense of herself.

DISCUSSION OF TREATMENT SELECTION

Setting. Although Miss B believes her situation is quite precarious and although she has little in her environment to offer support, she does manage her own affairs and is not an immediate suicide risk. Hospitalization is therefore not necessary and might provoke further regression. Outpatient treatment is the preferred choice.

Format. A family treatment could directly examine Miss B's problems with separation and basic trust. The family process would reveal how Miss B fears the mother's disapproval, control, and separation and how the father intervenes to separate the two women from destroying or merging with each other. However, Miss B is probably unwilling to accept a family format at this time since she has adamantly decided to place the past behind her; and this format might compromise her hardwon, but fragile, autonomy. A heterogeneous group could help Miss B understand that she relates to others in the present in much the same way she related to her family in the past. For example, Miss B would most likely assume the role of group "co-leader" and try to gain the group leader's favor in a way that would elicit resentment from the other group members. Her participation in the group process could in time help Miss B to realize that her need to be the "angel" is based on a fear of total rejection if she does not meet the presumed needs of those from whom she wants support and admiration. The group could also help her find the right distance in her interpersonal relationships so that she is neither too far removed (to protect herself against being controlled by others and the inevitable pain of separation) or too close (to seek her unrequited dependency yearnings). At the present time, however, given Miss B's sense of fragility and her resolve to exclude others, she probably would not accept a group format. Role induction and education would be necessary in an individual treatment before she would be prepared for group psychotherapy.

Duration and Frequency. Prolonged open-ended treatment might not adequately provoke Miss B's difficulty with separation until termination seems likely. In fact, Miss B might consciously or unconsciously present "new" problems to forestall dealing with her inability to tolerate separation. A time-oriented treatment with a termination date set long in advance could help make this difficulty of Miss B more palpable and available for discussion. The danger of time-limited treatment is that if Miss B were aware that a separation was pending, even in the distant future, she might understandably protect herself against separation anxiety by remaining detached from the therapist and disavowing any emotional involvement. She is already practiced in this defensive reaction. Similarly, if the duration is too short and if the sessions are too infrequent, Miss B may not develop within the transference the significant interpersonal difficulties that are such an important aspect of her psychopathology. For example, the history indicates that Miss B tends to become very attached to another, loses her self-boundaries, then fears she is being controlled by the very person she thinks she needs. This crucial psychopathological pattern may not develop if the treatment is neither intense nor sustained. The problem would therefore be kept from view and not resolved.

On the other hand, a danger of a prolonged or an intense involvement is that the patient will indeed manifest her needs and fears, but will not be able to work them out within the context of treatment. Should this occur, therapy would be no more than a repeat performance of what she has already experienced with both her mother and her boyfriend. A possible way of resolving this dilemma about duration and frequency is to inform Miss B from the start that she will be inclined at times to become overinvolved with the therapist and, in reaction, frightened of the power she has given to another. This kind of predictive interpretation will probably not prevent the problem from occurring, but it might help strengthen Miss B's observing ego so that the problem can be noted, discussed, and worked through before it becomes severe within the transference.

Approach. Directive, exploratory, and experiential techniques all have distinct advantages and disadvantages for Miss B. In regard to directive methods, Miss B is currently isolated and paralyzed by her avoidant behavior, which might respond to graded exposure or another behavioral approach; and the negative view of herself, of the world, and of the future—the cognitive triad—might respond to cognitive therapy as described by Beck. On the other hand, Miss B has shown a capacity to put on a good façade with her parents, teachers, colleagues, and even lovers. She might comply with directive treatments in order to gain the therapist's approval, but her undisclosed resentment about being the perfect patient might ultimately backfire before or after treatment terminates. For example, she might initially follow the therapist's suggestions to socialize more, to reconcile differences with her family, and to complete homework assignments for cognitive reappraisal, but then sabotage these gains and become even more symptomatic because of an unconscious rage towards a therapist-mother who demands that the patient be good in order to be cared for.

Exploratory techniques also have potential risks and gains for Miss B. She is already very detached from the world and enmeshed in a fantasy life that has almost reached autistic proportions. An introspective approach to treatment might only make her more ruminative, self-absorbed, and ultimately despairing as she attempts to analyze her impulses, fantasies, and memories. In addition, if the therapist overuses anonymity, abstinence, or neutrality to facilitate this exploration, there is a risk that Miss B will respond to a relative lack of structure and guidance by becoming even more regressed with boundary diffusion. Certainly the use of the couch appears to be contraindicated and might well produce a psychotic transference. On the other hand, Miss B has used her intellect academically and professionally to gain some mastery over her emotional problems and to increase her self-worth. Within limits, some exploration might therefore be helpful for her to acquire an understanding about the nature and unconscious derivatives of her difficulties.

An experiential approach that empathically conveyed a non-judgmental regard for Miss B might initially be effective in relieving her sense of alienation and her social withdrawal; but exclusive reliance on this approach might preclude a working-through of the "bad" self-object representations and might run the same risk of actualizing the transference relationship if Miss B became overinvolved with the therapist. Considering the above, it would appear that if not used exclusively, directive and exploratory and experiential techniques all offer potential benefits. An admixture of the three might therefore be the wisest choice.

Somatic Treatment. The evaluation so far has provided no definite evidence that psychotropic medication is indicated, but there is some suggestion that Miss B has a major affective disorder. She has become socially and professionally withdrawn, has severe depersonalization, fears that she is losing her mind, feels helpless and hopeless about her situation, and experiences some sleep disturbance. Another diagnostic possibility is a schizophrenic-spectrum disorder as suggested by the chronicity of her depersonalization and the marked retreat into a fantasy life. In addition to a more thorough clinical assessment with standardized ratings, psychological testing may be helpful in making the diagnosis and in deciding whether antidepressant and/or neuroleptic medications are indicated. In the absence of more clear indications for psychotropic medications, prescribing these drugs at the present time does not seem advisable. If Miss B does not respond to an adequate trial of psychotherapy, the possibility of introducing these drugs to her therapeutic regimen could be reconsidered in the future. Regarding other kinds of medication, Miss B has already tried benzodiazepines (as well as illicit drugs) for her symptoms but has not found them effective. This failure to respond in the past and the absence of any clear indications in the present make the prescription for anxiolytics or hypnotics inadvisable for her chronic problems.

CHOICE AND OUTCOME

After two additional sessions with Miss B, the consultant was still not sure of the diagnosis or the best treatment plan. He was reassured that more systematic and extensive questioning had not disclosed any definite evidence of a major affective or schizophreniform disorder, but he was concerned that the patient's need to be "a bubbling bundle of joy" (her mother's phrase) might unconsciously be causing Miss B to minimize the severity of her problems. There was already some indication that she was trying to impress the consultant and was becoming overattached to him. In just two weeks she had changed dramatically; her manner was less wooden, her dress was more stylish, and her ability to engage, even charm, the consultant was more prominent. Because the consultant was still unclear about the wisest course of action and because he feared that further clinical evaluation by him would encourage Miss B's premature attachment to him before her actual therapist was arranged, he recommended a battery of psychological tests. Despite Miss B's fear that the tests would expose a severe mental problem, she agreed.

The psychological tests were quite helpful in deciding a treatment plan. The WAIS indicated an IQ in the superior range with no subtest scatter; the Rorschach did not uncover an underlying psychotic process but rather a histrionic and colorful way of elaborating conflict; and the Thematic Apperception Test repeatedly pointed to conflicts around the issue of separation.

After the consultant reviewed the psychological tests, the standardized rating instruments (Beck Depression Scale and Brief Symptom Inventory), the personal and psychiatric history, and Miss B's engaging and insightful interaction with the consultant during the evaluation process, he concluded that a focal therapy would be the best recommendation. As conceived, this kind of treatment would focus on one specific conflict, namely, Miss B's difficulty in establishing an adaptive distance in her interpersonal relationships.

Using primarily exploratory techniques, the aim of the treatment would be to point out that Miss B's fears of separation from a loved one (either actual separation or symbolic separation by disapproval) cause her to become overly invested in pleasing the other, even to the point of trying to figure out what the other person is thinking so that she can anticipate and respond in advance to the other person's wishes and needs. These attempts always fail because, despite her best efforts, some separation (physical and emotional) is unavoidable. Furthermore, by becoming so attached to another, Miss B loses her own autonomy and boundaries; and by trying to read the other person's mind, she soon fears that the other is becoming intrusively too close to her. She then reacts to this fear by extreme withdrawal. The consultant believed that a focal therapy focusing on this dynamic conflict held the possibility of symptomatic improvement and even character change without the risk of regression in a more prolonged treatment. It would also bring the issue of separation immediately to the forefront. Miss B seemed sufficiently psychologically-minded and motivated to change herself to participate in this form of treatment.

When Miss B arrived for her next consultation visit, she actively and intelligently engaged in the negotiation process. As suspected, her one reservation about a focal therapy was the relative brief period of time (an estimated 50 sessions over the next 12 months). In a tactful and understandable way, she argued that her chronic problems would probably require a more prolonged treatment, though she acknowledged that however long the treatment may be, termination would no doubt be difficult for her. Nevertheless, she was willing to give the consultant's recommendation a try. A referral was made to a male therapist specializing in focal therapy and treatment began the following week. (A female therapist might have been a better and more provocative choice, but none was available at the reduced fee clinic to which she was referred.)

Because the therapist presented the case of Miss B at a teaching conference on focal therapy, more extensive followup data are available than might otherwise be the case. During the first three weeks of treatment, the patient typically would arrive at the exact moment of her appointment, give a furtive greeting in the waiting room, then embark on a vague recount of the chronic difficulties in her life without elaboration, fantasy, or dream material. As if talking to herself, she would use words instead of silence to build a wall between herself and the therapist. During the first three weeks of treatment, the therapist avoided asking too many questions because he believed that the patient would experience his interest as intrusive.

At the end of the first month of once-a-week treatment, the patient reported a transference dream which opened the door for an exploration of a crucial, though complex, dynamic: "I was in an empty auditorium talking into a tape recorder. It was a weekend so you weren't there. I didn't feel anything. I was fogged out and getting shaky, then I started to fall and, out of nowhere, you caught me." In working with the associations to this dream, the patient recognized that she had been trying not to get "sucked in" by the therapist for fear that he would then be able to control her. She preferred that their sessions be like talking into a tape recorder in an empty room so that she could disavow ("erase") her feelings before the therapist ever had a chance to use them to his own advantage. On the other hand, she realized that this lifelong adaptation had resulted in numbness, isolation, and loneliness. These feelings then reinforced a wish to be saved ("caught") by the therapist and never to separate from him.

The ensuing weeks of Miss B's focal dynamic therapy uncovered the oedipal and preoedipal derivatives of her difficulty with separation. Dreams and transference material were the main vehicles used on this road towards self-discovery. Another dream, reported during the third month of treatment, helps illustrate this therapeutic process: In the dream, Miss B is having sex with an older brother until she is discovered by her parents; at the end of the dream, she and her father conduct a detached intellectual conversation, while her mother flees in a rage into the kitchen. An immediate association to this dream was the recovered memory of sharing the same bedroom with an older brother throughout her youth and of fearing that she might act on her incestuous desires and "lose herself" in the process. As similar illicit wishes were now develop-ing in the transference, Miss B hoped that the therapist-father would remain intellectually detached and neither act on these wishes nor con-demn her for having them. This wish to be protected by the father-therapist was similar to the memory of how her father had allegedly rescued his "treasured princess" when she was drowning in the ocean.

Several sessions were devoted to unraveling the many dimensions of this dream and its associations. Miss B came to understand that on the one hand, she wanted a man (the therapist-father) to rescue her from being immersed ("fused") with others; but, on the other hand, having this kind of special relationship with a man elicited the unconscious guilt and rejection associated with an oedipal triumph (sending the mother off in a rage).

As a result of these conflicts, Miss B had trouble establishing a com-fortable distance from the therapist, the same problem that had plagued her life. She vacillated in sessions between becoming frightfully close to the therapist and, in reaction, coldly detached. Accordingly, the focus of the treatment was to help Miss B establish a feeling of intimacy within the therapeutic relationship without feeling fused, controlled, illicit, or extraordinarily special. For example, during one session Miss B noticed that the therapist seemed preoccupied with another thought when he greeted her in the waiting room. By exploring this concern and eventually appreciating that she in fact may not be the cause of the therapist's presumed preoccupation, she was painfully forced to admit to herself that the therapist had a life separate from her own and she was not the center. These kinds of transferential explorations characterized the 15 months of her focal treatment.

Towards the end of therapy, Miss B was far less wary of extending herself professionally and personally. She was making plans to apply to graduate school as a first step towards becoming an instructor in psychi-atric nursing. In addition, she had begun to date and was successfully avoiding her previous pattern of either prematurely throwing herself into the relationship or remaining too distant.

During the last three weeks of treatment, the patient again became socially and professionally withdrawn and in sessions was often sullen and silent for extended periods of time. The therapist interpreted the return of Miss B's symptoms as a reaction to the inevitable separation and an attempt to prevent it. Using the material that had been uncovered during the treatment and the understanding attached thereto, the therapist explained to Miss B why she was doing what she was doing and why treatment must stop regardless. In the next-to-last session, Miss B's symptomatic deterioration improved dramatically as she recognized (and felt relieved) that both the therapist and the patient would survive the planned separation. During the last session, Miss B tearfully and nostalgically reflected on the therapeutic experience; her sullenness was gone. She remarked on the difference between separating from the therapist and the past separations from her mother and her first few boyfriends.

Neither the consultant nor the therapist heard from the patient until four years after the termination of treatment when Miss B (now Mrs. T) invited both to a workshop she was running on how administrative and personal problems affect nursing care. A personal note accompanied the brochure for the workshop thanking the therapist for "helping me find myself without getting in the way."

SUGGESTED READING

1. Davanloo, H. *Basic Principles and Techniques in Short-term Dynamic Psychotherapy.* New York: Spectrum Books, 1978.
2. Malan, D. H. *The Frontier of Brief Psychotherapy.* New York: Plenum, 1976.
3. Balint, M., Ornstein, P. H., & Balint, E. *Focal Psychotherapy: An Example of Applied Psychoanalysis.* London: Tavistock Publications, 1972.
4. Mann, J. *Time-limited Psychotherapy.* Cambridge, MA: Harvard University Press, 1973.
5. Sifneos, P. E. Short-term anxiety-provoking psychotherapy: Its history, techniques, outcome and instructions. In S. H. Budman (Ed.), *Forms of Brief Therapy.* New York: Guilford Press, 1981, pp. 45–81. (The first five readings are representative publications by five leaders in individual dynamic brief psychotherapy.)
6. Holt, R. R. *Methods in Clinical Psychology, Vols. I & II.* New York: Plenum, 1978. (These two volumes offer a valuable reference for the clinician, specifically how psychological testing can be used to determine diagnosis and thereby guide treatment selection, as was true in the case presented.)

XV

Conditions Not Attributable to a Mental Disorder That Are a Focus of Attention or Treatment

■ MALINGERING

52. The Case of the Homeless Murderer

Mr. E is a 42-year-old man who is brought to the hospital outpatient clinic by his alcoholism counselor who then manages to disappear immediately. When the consultant meets Mr. E, she understands (though does not excuse) the irresponsible behavior of the counselor: Mr. E is a filthy, foul-smelling man with a horrible past and a grim future. His problems are hard to assess and harder to solve. It is not surprising that the counselor wants no part of it.

The story, as told disjointedly by Mr. E, began three years ago. At that time he was withdrawing from alcohol as an outpatient when he suddenly heard voices that his wife was having an affair with his younger brother. Responding to these accusatory hallucinations, Mr. E grabbed his deer rifle and began shooting wildly throughout the house. In the process, he wounded his wife and killed his mother. He was taken by the police to the forensic psychiatric ward. Three days later, his sensorium finally cleared and he was no longer psychotic. Mr. E could not remember what he called "the incident" but was now competent to participate in his own defense. After many months of being ushered by court-appointed guardians and lawyers through a labyrinth of hearings and testimonies, he was judged as not legally responsible for his actions and thereby acquitted. In addition, the psychiatrist at the state mental hospital where he had been kept during all these proceedings stated that Mr. E was no longer dangerous and could be discharged, to be followed as an outpatient. The court accepted this recommendation.

There was a slight problem with the court's discharge plan: Mr. E had no place to stay. His wife and children, refusing to have any contact with him, had sold the home and moved, presumably to another state. Whereas Mr. E had before been a steady worker and (despite his drinking) a family man, he now had no relatives who would speak to him, no friends, and as both "a convict and a nut," no hopes for employment. Since his discharge from the psychiatric hospital, Mr. E has spent the last two years drifting from one cheap hotel to another, convinced that he must serve this penance for his past sins. During most of this time, he was supported by a small disability payment, but a few months ago when a cost-conscious federal government terminated these monthly checks, he was forced to live either in a municipal shelter or on the streets.

After leading the consultant through this convoluted tale, Mr. E finally states more directly why he asked his alcoholism counselor to bring him to the psychiatric clinic. He claims that he is hearing voices—the same ones he heard before "the incident"—yet he denies that he has had any alcohol for several months. To support this claim, he points out that he has no alcohol on his breath and that his mild cirrhosis is a result of his drinking in the past. Without evidence of alcohol withdrawal, the nature and cause of the hallucinations are all the more mysterious because Mr. E's description of them does not ring true. Rather than describing a particular person's voice and a particular phrase, Mr. E gives a vague, paragraph-long narration of what the "voices" are saying. In addition, his sensorium is clear and he has no signs of impaired mood or thinking other than the claimed hallucinations.

By the end of the evaluation, the consultant strongly suspects that Mr. E is making up his symptoms or at the very least embellishing them. She further suspects that Mr. E is malingering because he would prefer to spend some time in the hospital rather than be condemned to the men's shelter or to the street—and yet Mr. E's past history of violence weighs heavily on her mind. To help her decide what to do, the consultant calls the counselor for additional information (and to register an objection to the unprofessional way in which Mr. E had been "dumped" in the hospital clinic). The counselor, abrupt and unapologetic, replies that he saw no reason to stay because once the consultant learned from Mr. E about the fire, the disposition would be obvious. When the consultant explains she knows nothing about any fire, the counselor reports that Mr. E had been evicted from the men's shelter in the middle of the previous night because he had endangered others by setting a fire in a wastepaper basket "to stay warm." When the consultant asks Mr. E about this incident, he shrugs and says that he considers the fire "no big deal."

DSM-III-R DIAGNOSIS

Axis I: Probable malingering; possible atypical psychosis or dementia associated with alcoholism.
Axis II: None confirmed
Axis III: Cirrhosis, mild
Axis IV: Stress—severe (no family, funds, friends, shelter, or support)
Axis V: Highest level of functioning past year—very poor

TREATMENT PROBLEM

Disposition of a potentially violent man feigning hallucinations to obtain psychiatric hospitalization.

DISCUSSION OF TREATMENT SELECTION

Mr. E presents with an awesome combination of psychiatric and social problems that appear all the more oppressive under the shadow of possible violence. Of the many decisions regarding his treatment, the most immediate is the choice of setting. If it were not for the past history of an accidental murder and the current episode of fire-setting, Mr. E would probably not require hospitalization. His psychiatric symptoms, even if they were completely genuine (which seems doubtful), are mild and not associated with specific command hallucinations; if they exist at all, they probably would respond to neuroleptics in an outpatient setting. There is another point in favor of outpatient treatment: Hospitalizing Mr. E might set a destructive precedent by reinforcing his suspected malingering. In times of crisis, he would be back at the clinic again and again with yet another fire and story. On the other hand, given Mr. E's track record of impulsive violent behavior, he may in desperation up the ante and become even more dangerous in order to convince others that he must be hospitalized and cannot stay in a men's shelter.

Instead of either outpatient or inpatient care, a third alternative would be a partial hospital. A night hospital would offer a place to stay without fostering further regression and complete dependency. In this structured setting Mr. E could begin to get his life back together. Prevocational counseling could provide the guidance necessary to return Mr. E to his premorbid level of reliable job functioning; groups and social networks could help counteract his sense of being an isolated outcast; individual experiential therapy could help Mr. E mourn and expiate "the incident"; and neuroleptics could be monitored if they were considered advisable.

CHOICE AND OUTCOME

Since Mr. E had no medical coverage and was not in the catchment area of the psychiatric clinic, an attempt was made to transfer him to the appropriate municipal hospital. For reasons that are probably all too familiar to many readers, Mr. E's catchment hospital would not or could not accept the transfer. As the evening wore on and all other possibilities diminished, Mr. E, still "hallucinating" and still shrugging off the incident about the fire, was admitted to the inpatient service associated with the psychiatric clinic to which he had come.

Not surprisingly, the patient's "psychosis" was miraculously cured by the elevator ride to his desired destination—the hospital ward. The inpatient staff was alerted to the joint necessities of keeping the hospitalization brief while at the same time improving Mr. E's outside prospects. This improvement would make him more willing to leave the hospital and less desperate to return. A concerted social service effort resulted in the rapid acquisition of emergency welfare funds, the reinstatement of disability payments and other administrative requirements that would enable Mr. E to be discharged to a halfway house sponsored by the local state psychiatric facility. After three days on the inpatient service, he left encouraged and grateful. Three months later, because of a further cutback in federal and state funds, the halfway house was closed. How Mr. E fared with this next crisis in his life is not known. He has not returned to the psychiatric clinic.

SUGGESTED READING

(As the titles indicate, the first five readings describe institutional or community-based treatments for patients like Mr. E. The last three articles describe the management of those compelled to make themselves ill.)

1. Stein, L. I., & Test, M. A. (Eds.). *Alternatives to Mental Hospital Treatment*. New York: Plenum, 1978.
2. Bachrach, L. I. Overview: Model programs for chronic mental patients. *American Journal of Psychiatry*, 137:1023–1031, 1980.

3. Budson, R. D. *The Psychiatric Halfway House: A Handbook of Theory and Practice.* Pittsburgh: University of Pittsburgh Press, 1978.
4. Carpenter, W. Residual placement for the chronic psychiatric patient: A review and evaluation of the literature. *Schizophrenia Bulletin,* 4:384–398, 1978.
5. Davis, J. M. Overview: Maintenance therapy in psychiatry: I. Schizophrenia. *American Journal of Psychiatry,* 132:1237–1245, 1975.
6. Spiro, H. R. Chronic factitious illness: Munchausen's syndrome. *Archives of General Psychiatry,* 18:569–579, 1978.
7. Hyler, S. E., & Sussman, N. Chronic factitious disorders with physical symptoms. *Psychiatric Clinics of North America,* 4:365–377, 1981.
8. Asher, R. Munchausen's syndrome. *Lancet,* 1:339–341, 1951.

■ UNCOMPLICATED BEREAVEMENT

53. The Case of the Dying Nurse

Miss N, a 24-year-old former nursing student, was referred for psychiatric consultation because her internist was concerned that the patient had become depressed now that her lymphoma was no longer responding to treatment and was more clearly terminal. During the consultation, Miss N appeared obviously ill with the many side effects of her chemotherapy—thin hair, pale skin, cushingnoid features—yet despite her physical frailty, she presented her story in an animated and quite moving way.

Her symptoms began three years ago during her final semester in nursing school when she noticed a tightness in the chest. She tried to explain away this nagging symptom by attributing it to a preoccupation with illness, a "nursing school neurosis." After a couple of months the tightness gradually became so pronounced that it could no longer simply be explained away. Rather than going to the personnel clinic, she casually dropped by the emergency room one evening and had a harried and relatively inexperienced intern examine her. The intern found nothing note-worthy during her exam, said it was probably the flu, and suggested rest, fluids, and aspirin.

Two weeks later, still unrelieved, she made an appointment to see a psychiatrist for the first time because she now believed (and hoped) that her symptoms were due either to the pressure of nursing school or to her relationship with a medical student whom she had met earlier that year. The psychiatrist, aware that the patient was all too eager to attribute her physical problems to a psychological origin, suggested the patient first have a more adequate medical evaluation. The patient followed this recommendation and the lymphoma was disclosed.

Miss N then described in a poignant manner how the story evolved: her shock over the diagnosis; the steroid therapy; the radiation therapy; the chemotherapy; the attempt to continue nursing school but the necessity of eventually taking leave; the physical changes (loss of hair, gain of weight, acne); the relief with remissions; the anguish with recurrences; the breakup with the medical student; and, of course, the financial difficulties of her parents to pay for the expensive treatment. Miss N recounted these difficult situations over the past three years without berating herself or others.

On the contrary, she displayed an admirable, stoic quality. She admitted that she tried not to dwell too much on the future, yet she had confidence that she could face whatever lay ahead. Aware that her tumor had become refractory to standard approaches of radiotherapy and chemotherapy, she hoped for a remission with one of the new experimental drugs which were now being tried. Meanwhile, she lived one day at a time, spending most of her day writing long thank you notes to the many relatives and friends who had comforted her. She said that she liked her doctor, had confidence in his abilities, and knew that he was trying hard; but she also realized by the way that he "popped in and out of the room" that he was upset by the way her treatment was going. She wondered aloud if he might be more depressed than she was.

The psychiatrist then asked with whom the patient could talk more openly. Miss N replied that her mother was "an angel"; she would sit with the patient, often in silence, but at times the two of them would sadly reminisce about times gone by, what had been shared in the past, and what might be lost in the future. During this last phase of the interview, Miss N looked down at her body and commented that all through her childhood she had hoped to grow up and care for others, but now she was the one who was sick and possibly dying.

DSM-III-R DIAGNOSIS

Axis I: None
Axis II: None
Axis III: Lymphoma
Axis IV: Stress—severe (terminal illness, multiple medical procedures)
Axis V: Highest level of functioning past year—good (complying with treatment; maintaining self-esteem, hope, and supportive relationships with others)

TREATMENT PROBLEM

Facilitating appropriate grief response in dying patient while preventing the primary physician from becoming too discouraged.

DISCUSSION OF TREATMENT SELECTION

This patient is coping remarkably well with her severe illness and its treatment. Although the primary physician believes she is "depressed," her psychiatric evaluation does not disclose any symptoms or signs of a pathological depression. True, she is understandably sad about the losses in her life (her education, her caregiving capacity, her boyfriend, her physical appearance and functioning, etc.), but her sadness is not associated with a loss of self-esteem or unreasonable guilt. Her control of intolerable affects, her maintenance of interpersonal relationships, her confidence to deal with the future, and her capacity to elicit empathy from others without appearing whiny, clinging, or exasperating are all signs of a good adaptation to her disease. Furthermore, she is able to share her most desperate feelings with relatives. Offering antidepressants or even psychiatric treatment at this time might erroneously lead her to believe that she is not coping well and that her feelings are pathological rather than normal and expected. The preferred treatment for her, therefore, would be no treatment at this time. This choice may in itself have a therapeutic valence by reassuring her that she can take pride in how well she has dealt with her circumstances up until now and that she need not hesitate to request psychiatric help in the future.

The situation with the primary physician is not so easily resolved. The psychiatrist has a collegial but not a therapeutic relationship with the referring doctor, so the therapeutic boundaries and contract are more ambiguous if they exist at all. If the psychiatrist makes no intervention, the internist may continue to avoid the patient and feel depressed himself about the patient's fate and his inability to alter its course. On the other hand, if the psychiatrist intervenes too directly, the treating physician may take offense and inwardly feel all the more hopeless and inadequate.

CHOICE AND OUTCOME

The patient was told that she was handling "the work of mourning" over her many losses admirably, but that she should not hesitate to call the psychiatrist if and when he could be of help or if she just wanted someone else to talk to. Regarding the internist, the psychiatrist phoned to say that he appreciated the opportunity of meeting such a courageous patient, that he had learned a great deal about the dying process from her, and wondered if this might not be a good time for a staff conference on the issue. The internist agreed and arranged for a grand rounds on the topic of death and dying. In a direct way, the psychiatrist outlined the differences between pathological depression and normal grief and, in a more oblique way, commented on the depression that can occur in the treating staff when they come to terms with their own limitations.

The patient added the psychiatrist to her list of thank you notes, writing that she found the consultation very helpful and encouraging. She never requested another session. The internist complimented the psychiatrist on "one of the best grand rounds ever" and appeared, at least around the doctor's lunch table at the hospital, to be far less depressed—even when, two months later, the patient died at home.

SUGGESTED READING

1. Peretz, D., Carr, A. C., Schoenberg, B., & Kutscher, A. H. A survey of physicians' attitudes toward death and bereavement: Comparison of psychiatrists and non-psychiatrists. *Journal of Thanatology,* 1:91–100, 1971. (A reminder of inherent biases among mental health professionals towards loss and grief.)
2. Norton, J. Treatment of a dying patient. *Psychoanalytic Study of the Child,* 18:541–560, 1963. (In contrast to the case presented, the author describes her assumption of a "real" surrogate relationship with a dying young woman.)
3. Eissler, K. R. *The Psychiatrist and the Dying Patient.* New York: International Universities Press, 1955. (By presenting three case histories, this book helps place in perspective the psychodynamic and sociocultural factors that influence the therapist and the dying patient.)

XVI

The Last Chapter: Some Generalizations Based on Our Case Method

It is sad but true that it will be a long time before treatment selection in psychiatry will have a solid scientific foundation. During the last 25 years, we have benefited from the proliferation of hundreds of promising treatments and the naming of hundreds of psychiatric diagnoses, but with these benefits has come a burden. The permutations of possible diagnostic-treatment interactions could keep researchers busy for eternity. The student of differential treatment planning is overwhelmed with data. Comprehensive studies clearly documenting which patient should get what treatment will take years to accomplish for even the most common diagnoses.

Given this situation, clinicians—confronted with the complexities and uniqueness of a particular patient and asked to recommend the best treatment—must continue to rely upon an informed consumption of the available literature and upon the case method. Our jobs have required that we participate in literally hundreds of treatment planning decisions each year. These experiences have forced us to examine the assumptions and patterns that have guided our intuition. While the discussions presented in this book have neither the precision nor the statistical power of large and comparative studies, we believe that this aggregation of cases, both our own and our colleagues', provides a basis for generalizations to treatment planning that extends beyond the experience of any one clinician.

One of the numerous problems with the case method is that it is very subject to biases, the biases that arise from one's training, temperament, style, locale, and all the other systematic and unsystematic experiences that influence the clinician. This strong potential for bias in treatment selection can be counteracted at least in part by a careful review of the relevant scientific literature (our first book, *Differential Therapeutics in Psychiatry*) and by a similarly careful review of actual cases (this current book). As enunciated in both of these books, the six components of treatment planning that every clinician must address include: treatment setting, format, duration and frequency, technique, somatic treatments, and combination of treatments. Here, then, are some concluding generalizations regarding each of these components, plus some additional suggestions based on the cases we have presented.

Treatment Setting

a) Inpatient psychiatric hospitalization is used too often and too soon; more patients should be treated in day hospitals, halfway houses, and crisis intervention settings.

b) Deinstitutionalization has its limits; inpatient settings, for both acute and custodial care, will always be necessary for some patients.

c) Because many crucial decisions must be made in the emergency room, more systematic studies are needed to investigate this setting.

d) As the general hospital has become an increasingly important setting for psychiatric care, the range of effective interventions, for both patients and staff, has been expanded.

Format

a) Therapists have appreciated the efficacy of marital, family, and group formats for psychiatric problems that traditionally were assigned to an individual treatment; they have also appreciated the value of using different formats for a single case, either concurrently or sequentially.

b) Families have a lot to tell us, often things that individual patients cannot or will not reveal.

c) Marital or family therapy is the treatment of choice when the presenting complaint is a marital or family problem.

d) The homogeneous group is often the treatment of choice for specific target problems.

e) The heterogeneous group is particularly useful for treating interpersonal problems and for establishing social networks, but role induction is often necessary to reduce dropouts.

f) Individual treatment is best for individual intrapsychic problems of longstanding duration.

g) For the patient in crisis, a combination of individual and family treatment is usually best.

Duration and Frequency

a) Briefer therapies have increasingly become the treatment of choice for even longstanding problems; they can also serve as a trial of treatment to guide longer term recommendations.

b) Longer treatments should most often be reserved for character change or for supportive treatments with chronic conditions.

c) Treatment does not need to be continuous; patients can enter an active treatment phase and leave "with the door open" to return months or sometimes years later for another active treatment phase as stresses and conditions change.

Approach

a) Although we are not yet able to match with scientific certainty specific emotional problems to specific therapeutic approaches, the state of the art suggests that certain marriages work particularly well:

Psychodynamic techniques—character change

Behavioral techniques—targeted symptoms (e.g., eating disorders, phobic disorders)

Strategic and paradoxical techniques—oppositional behaviors (i.e., those who have difficulty accepting direct advice)

Cognitive techniques—anxiety disorders and mild-to-moderate depressions

b) Psychoeducation is useful across all conditions and at times may be the treatment of choice.

c) Supportive techniques are the most common and most versatile in reversing demoralization, buttressing defenses and teaching coping skills.

Somatic Treatment

a) To increase compliance and to enhance the placebo effect, somatic treatments should always be provided within the context of a therapeutic relationship.

b) For patients with serious psychiatric disorders that have not previously responded to medication, it is important to ensure that their medications' trials are adequate in both dosage and duration and that the different families of psychotropic drugs for the disorder are prescribed sequentially until an effective one is found. The patient's informed participation in this thorough and serial trial of all possible medications will also reduce the patient's demoralization.

c) Within a given family of psychotropic medication, the particular choice of drug is usually based on the different profile of side effects rather than on the differential effectiveness.

Combination of Treatments

a) Although some schools of therapy (e.g., psychoanalytic or behavioral) have at times emphasized an almost religious adherence to one approach, many patients require a treatment that interweaves strategies and techniques from different philosophical orientations.

b) If a specific setting, or format, or time frame, or approach, or psychotropic medication does not work, the therapist should feel comfortable in trying something else; therapeutic dogmatism must give way to flexibility.

c) The suggestion that combinations are useful is not an endorsement for "shotgun" prescriptions; combined treatments require a rationale.

d) The same therapist may be competent to provide the different treatments, but in many instances more than one therapist will be necessary either concurrently or in sequence; therefore, therapists must know not only what they do well but also what they don't do well, what else needs to be done, and how such a referral to another can be done effectively.

Additional Suggestions

a) In most instances, patients should have the opportunity to interview several therapists before choosing the one with whom to work.

b) Although the sex of the therapist is very likely to influence transference manifestations and treatment outcome, this important issue is difficult to classify and is therefore insufficiently discussed. Treatment aimed at character change should probably be conducted by a therapist whose sex presents the most difficulties for the patient, whereas treatments designed to alleviate symptoms should most often be conducted by a therapist whose sex poses the least problems for the patient.

c) Consultation during a psychiatric treatment is generally used too little or too late. If a treatment seems stalemated, consultation should be arranged. Even if the stalemate is secondary to a particular transference paradigm that is amenable to working through with the present therapist, a consultation more often catalyzes rather than disrupts this process. In other kinds of stalemates, transfer to another therapist is indicated if the consultant cannot provide specific and mutually acceptable advice that will improve the therapeutic situation.

A Final Word

Like the cases themselves, these concluding generalizations are presented to provoke discussion and stimulate further research of treatment selection in psychiatry. Charles Darwin said, "I have steadily endeavoured to keep my mind free so as to give up any hypothesis, however much beloved (and I cannot resist forming one on every subject), as soon as facts are shown to be opposed to it." It is in this spirit and with this intent that this casebook has been written.

Appendix:
Reference Tables

TABLE 1
Treatment Planning Axis I: Setting

Setting	Case Illustration #
Intensive Care Psychiatric Hospital	10, 11, 15, 17, 18, 23
Chronic Institutionalization	5, 13
Partial (Day/Night) Hospital	10–14
Drug Maintenance Clinic	9, 17, 21
General Hospital	1, 5, 6, 8, 9, 23, 29, 31, 32
Crisis Intervention	16, 24
Outpatient Office	2, 4, 7, 12, 15, 17, 19, 20, 22, 23, 25–35, 38–42, 44–51

TABLE 2
Treatment Planning Axis II: Time

Duration	Case Illustration #
Crisis Therapy	1, 9, 16, 31
Planned Brief Therapy	26, 29, 31, 46, 47–49
Long-term Open-ended	4, 15, 23, 27, 28, 32, 35, 39, 42, 49–51
Maintenance	2, 6, 7, 9, 12, 13, 20, 40

Treatment Planning Axis III (Technique/Strategy) by Axis IV (Format)

Technique/Strategy	Case Illustration #		
	Individual	Family/Marital	Group
Establishing Therapeutic Relationship	2, 8, 9, 15, 17, 22, 23, 29, 31, 32, 38–40, 42, 45, 46, 51	6, 20, 24, 30, 33, 34, 49, 50	7, 29
Providing Support	1, 2, 6, 10–12, 14–18, 29, 31, 32, 40, 45, 46, 51, 52	2, 6, 16, 20, 24, 32, 34, 49, 50	7, 17, 22, 29, 46
Educating	1, 7, 12, 17, 20, 23, 29, 37	2, 3, 12, 20, 30	7
Reducing Painful Affects	11, 16, 17, 23, 29, 39, 40, 51	16, 24, 49	29
Modifying Behaviors	4, 5, 12, 25, 26, 28, 31, 32, 35, 36, 38, 39, 45, 46, 48	24, 30, 33–35, 49, 50	4, 7, 11, 30, 46, 49
Modifying Misperceptions	1, 2, 11, 12, 14–18, 23, 40, 42, 46	16, 33, 34	
Conveying Psychodynamic Explanations	8, 12, 15, 17, 19, 20, 23, 27, 28, 35, 39, 42, 46–49, 51	34, 49, 50	22
Expanding Emotional Awareness	4, 15, 39, 46, 51		
Enhancing Interpersonal Behavior	12, 36, 37, 39, 42, 45, 46, 48, 51	2, 24, 30, 33, 34, 48–50	4, 7, 11, 30, 46, 49

TABLE 4
Treatment Planning Axis V: Somatic Therapies

Choice	Case Illustration #
Neuroleptic	1, 3, 10–15, 17
Tricyclic Antidepressant	11, 17, 20, 23, 40
Monoamine Oxidase Inhibitor (MAOI)	21, 26, 45
Benzodiazepines	7, 9, 29
Lithium	11, 18, 20, 40
Electroconvulsive Therapy (ECT)	17, 23, 40
Disulfuran (Antabuse)	6, 7
Methadone	9
Anticonvulsant	4
Propanolol	37
Biofeedback	31

TABLE 5
No Treatment as Prescription of Choice

Rationale	Case Illustration #
Likely Negative Effect	17, 44, 52
No Efficacious Treatment Available	43, 44
No Treatment Needed	53
No Treatment as Therapeutic Challenge	36

TABLE 6
Psychiatric Diagnoses of Presented Cases
(Including Secondary Diagnoses)

Disorders	Case Illustration #
Organic Mental	1, 2, 3, 4, 5, 52
Psychoactive Substance Use	5, 6, 7, 8, 9, 40, 44, 51, 52
Schizophrenia	10, 11, 12, 13, 14
Psychotic Not Elsewhere Classified	15, 16, 17, 52
Mood	2, 5, 6, 7, 17, 18, 19, 20, 21, 22, 23, 24, 32, 40, 41, 51
Anxiety	17, 25, 26, 27, 28, 29
Somatoform	17, 30, 31, 32
Sexual	33, 34, 35
Factitious	36
Impulse Control	37, 38
Adjustment	38, 39, 42, 45, 48
Psychological Factors Affecting Physical Condition	40
Personality	5, 6, 7, 9, 10, 15, 17, 20, 21, 22, 23, 25, 27, 28, 30, 31, 32, 35, 36, 41, 42, 43, 44, 45, 46, 47, 48, 49, 50, 51
Malingering	52
Normal Bereavement	53

Index